MARGARET
OF YORK
DUCHESS OF BURGUNDY 1446–1503

MARGARET OF YORK

DUCHESS OF BURGUNDY 1446–1503

Christine Weightman

ALAN SUTTON · Stroud

ST. MARTIN'S PRESS · New York

First published in the United States of America in 1989
Paperback edition, with corrections, first published in 1993

All rights reserved. For information, write:
Scholarly and Reference Division,
St. Martin's Press Inc. · 175 Fifth Avenue · New York · NY 10010

ISBN 0-312-03104-1 (hbk)
ISBN 0-312-10323-9 (pbk)

Library of Congress Cataloging in Publication Data

Weightman, Christine B.
　　Margaret of York, Duchess of Burgundy, 1446–1503 / Christine
　Weightman.
　　　p.　cm.
　　Bibliography: p.
　　Includes index.
　　ISBN 0-312-03104-1 (hbk)
　　ISBN 0-312-10323-9 (pbk)
　　1. Charles, Duke of Burgundy, 1433–1477.　2. Burgundy (France)—
　Kings and rulers—Biography.　3. Margaret, of York, Duchess,
　Consort of Charles the Bold, Duke of Burgundy, 1446–1503.　4. Wives—
　France—Burgundy—Biography.　5. Burgundy (France)—History—House
　of Valois, 1363–1477.　6. Great Britain—History—House of York,
　1461–1485.　7. Netherlands—History—House of Burgundy, 1384–1477.
　I. Title
　DC611.B781W4　1989
　944'.4026'0924–dc20
　　[B]　　　　　　　　　　　　　　　　　　　　　　　　　89–32024
　　　　　　　　　　　　　　　　　　　　　　　　　　　　　CIP

First published in the United Kingdom in 1989 by
Alan Sutton Publishing Limited
Phoenix Mill · Far Thrupp · Stroud · Gloucestershire

Paperback edition, with corrections, first published in 1993

British Library Cataloguing in Publication Data

　Weightman, Christine
　Margaret of York
　1. France. Burgundy. Margaret, Duchess of Burgundy, 1446–1503
　I. Title
　944'.027'0924

　　ISBN 0–86299–555–8 (hbk)
　　ISBN 0–7509–0378–3 (pbk)

Typeset in 11/12 Ehrhardt.
Typesetting and origination by
Alan Sutton Publishing Limited.
Printed and bound in Great Britain by
WBC, Bridgend, Mid Glam.

CONTENTS

LIST OF ILLUSTRATIONS

Cover:

A detail from a miniature depicting Margaret perfoming acts of charity from *Benois seront les Miséricordieux*, studio Jean Dreux; ms. 9296, f. i. Royal Library, Brussels

PREFACE AND ACKNOWLEDGEMENTS

The story of Margaret has attracted much more attention in Belgium than it has in England. Her private interests in both religious matters and as a collector of fine books placed her at the forefront of educated lay opinion and printing technology. Indeed, she has long been recognised as a major bibliophile and as such has received considerable attention from specialists in this field. In English history books, however, Margaret has been confined to a few brief appearances concerning her marriage and the conspiracies against Henry VII. Yet her life and the events in which she took part had a wide-reaching influence on England. Apart from her direct participation in the reigns of Edward IV and Henry VII, her action in bringing the Habsburgs into the Netherlands was to have a long lasting impact on English relations with the continent.

This book attempts to provide a whole picture of Margaret, to examine her political activity, motivation and lifestyle. It is essentially a study of how a woman of the second half of the fifteenth century could ensure her personal survival and prosperity, in the face of a series of disasters which removed all her most powerful relations in both England and Burgundy and which left her as the relict of a failed alliance. Indeed it is the story of a survivor, of a woman who took a keen interest in all that her status and society had to offer and was eager to use her considerable talents to the advantage of others as well as for her own advancement.

The final completion of this book is my tribute to the very happy years I spent in Belgium and also to all the scholars, both Belgian and British, who have given me such pleasure, many of whom are cited in the Notes and Bibliography. Throughout my research I have received kindness and assistance in all the various archives, libraries and public record offices which I have used. I owe a particular debt to the British Public Libraries Lending Service and to the librarians of many small branch libraries who still make it possible for books from the British Library or from the university libraries to be made available to individuals who are working at some distance from a major library.

No historian works in isolation and I am well aware of my debt to all those who have written on these themes before me, especially to Richard Vaughan whose three books on the Valois dukes first attracted me to the fascinating world of Burgundian history, to C. A. J. Armstrong whose many studies on this period are both penetrating and entertaining, and to Patricia Robins whose comprehensive thesis on Margaret's dower is available in the university library at Brussels and in the archives at Mechelen. My thanks for advice and encouragement are also due to R. A. Griffiths, P. W. Hammond, M. A. Hicks, Rosemary Horrox, and to David Morgan of the University of London who kindly read through the almost completed work and made many helpful comments and suggestions. I am deeply thankful for the most generous help which came from Roger Tavernier of Leuven University Library who has been a reliable source of information during all the time that I have been working on this subject. Above all I am grateful to my husband John whose encouragement and patience has sustained this study over ten years and three house moves and who has read and reread the emerging text and to my daughter Elizabeth who was such a useful contact in Brussels during my search for the illustrations.

In the last resort, however, I remain solely responsible for any remaining errors and I hope this study will at least provide a springboard for future work on the subject.

Christine Weightman
1989

Prologue

Cheapside was *en fête*, banners, tapestries and garlands of flowers hung from the high windows and the city guard had taken up their positions along the well swept streets. The Mayor and Aldermen, uncomfortably hot in their fur-trimmed robes of office, stood at the Cross, awaiting the arrival of the king's sister coming to say her farewells to all the city merchants who had stood surety for her dowry.

As the cheers greeted Margaret's cavalcade there was delight and a sense of relief. It was not merely the Londoners' pleasure at the sight of an elegantly dressed bride, but much more significantly the fact that she came riding pillion behind her cousin, the Earl of Warwick. The rumours that the powerful and popular earl had fallen out with the king over her marriage had alarmed the city. Nobody wanted a return to the anarchy and civil war which had crippled the country for more than a decade until the young Edward had come fresh from the battlefield to be crowned at the bidding of Warwick.

Reared in a dangerous and unpredictable world, where her father, brother and uncle had all perished in a single skirmish at Wakefield, Margaret too was relieved to have the approval of her mighty cousin. Listening to the speeches and receiving the gift of rich plate which the Mayor offered on behalf of the city, she was well aware of her new importance as the bride of Charles the Bold, the richest duke in Europe. She rode off through the cheering throng towards London Bridge, her serious demeanour reflecting her responsibilities both towards her own family whom she was leaving behind and to the new country which awaited her.

A mature and intelligent young woman, a strong sense of duty was to be the hallmark of her whole life and, in spite of the most appalling catastrophes, Margaret, unlike her brothers, would always show a consistent and courageous loyalty both to the House of York and to the House of Burgundy.

1 Daughter of York

'she seldom smiled and was rather reserved'

Margaret was the third daughter and the sixth of the twelve children born to Cecily Neville, Duchess of York. Hers was a dynamic inheritance, three parts Plantagenet and one part Neville and her birth on 3 May 1446 came at a critical watershed of her father's career.

If noble lineage merited high office then Richard, Duke of York, could claim a very prominent place indeed. In the absence of a royal heir, York with his descent from the second and fourth sons of King Edward III was widely regarded as heir-apparent.[1] He had inherited all his titles and lands from his two uncles, Edward, Duke of York, who was his father's brother, and Edmund Mortimer, Earl of March, his mother's brother. His father Richard, Earl of Cambridge, had been executed at Southampton on the eve of King Henry V's expedition to France in 1415. He had been accused of conspiring to place his brother-in-law, Edmund Mortimer, on the throne, a plot which was betrayed to the king by Mortimer himself. After his father's execution, Richard had been made a ward of the crown, but before the year was out the death of Edward, Duke of York, at Agincourt, made the four-year-old boy the heir to the Duchy of York.

Since Edmund Mortimer had no issue, all the Mortimer and Clare lands together with the Mortimer claim to the throne came to Richard through his mother, Anne Mortimer. This was a very important inheritance since the Mortimers were directly descended from Edward III's second surviving son Lionel, Duke of Clarence, through the marriage of his heiress Philippa to the Mortimer Earl of March. The son of this marriage, Roger Mortimer, had been named by Richard II as his heir, but he had been killed in Ireland in 1398 and the rights of his infant son, Edmund, were set aside when Henry IV seized the throne in 1399. Although Richard of York's Mortimer claim to the throne had passed through two female lines, there was nothing in English law to prevent female inheritance. Richard certainly emphasised his Mortimer lineage. He named his eldest daughter Anne after her Mortimer grandmother and his second son Edmund after his Mortimer uncle; he also persuaded the young King Henry VI to allow Edward, the duke's eldest son, to assume the title of the Earl of March.

Aristocratic children were well schooled on the subject of their genealogy and Margaret and her brothers and sisters would have been made fully aware of their

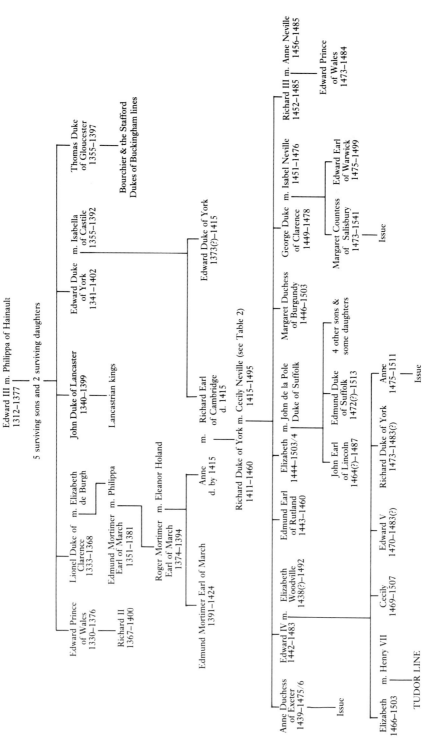

Table 1 Selected Genealogy of the Houses of York and Mortimer

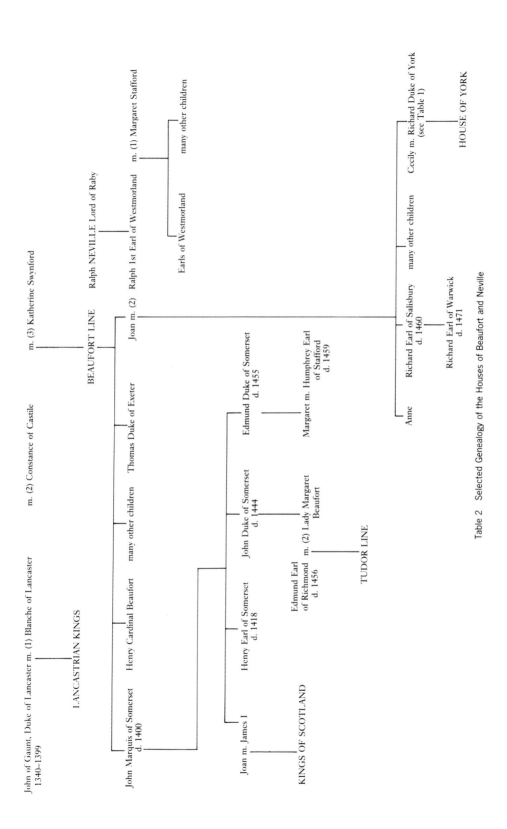

Table 2   Selected Genealogy of the Houses of Beaufort and Neville

family history and their royal rights. They learned their lessons well. Among the first acts of Edward IV's reign was the revival of the Duchy of Clarence for his brother George and the annulment of the sentence of treason passed against his grandfather, Richard, Earl of Cambridge. Moreover, Margaret's mother Cecily entitled herself 'the widow of the late Richard Duke of York, rightful King of England'. Throughout her life Margaret displayed the arms of a princess of England and she did not fail to remind Queen Isabella of Spain of their close relationship when she wrote to her for help against Henry VII.[2] In this case Margaret was referring to her third line of Plantagenet descent, through John of Gaunt, Duke of Lancaster, which came from her mother Cecily Neville.[3]

The union of Richard of York and Cecily Neville would ultimately destroy the House of Lancaster, although it was intended to submerge all the dangerous Mortimer pretensions within one loyal Lancastrian framework. After the death of Henry V, the wardship of twelve-year-old Richard was granted to Ralph Neville, Earl of Westmorland, the brother-in-law of the chancellor, Cardinal Beaufort. Within a year the boy was betrothed to the earl's youngest daughter, nine-year-old Cecily. The dowerless Cecily came from a stock which married and bred well. Her mother was the youngest daughter of John of Gaunt, by his third wife and former mistress, Katherine Swynford. Her father, Earl Ralph, was always on the lookout for suitable husbands and wives for his brood of twenty-two children, who had been born to him by his two wives, Margaret Stafford and Joan Beaufort. Whereas the York and Mortimer lines were notable for their lack of offspring, Margaret was connected to a vast affinity through her mother. The family network included the King of Scotland, the Dukes of Exeter and Norfolk, the Earls of Northumberland, Westmorland, Salisbury, Warwick, Kent, Worcester and Buckingham and the Lords Latimer, Despenser and Howard. There was also a wider European connection, through John of Gaunt's daughter Philippa, who married into the Portuguese royal family. Margaret was thus related to the royal Houses of Aragon, Castile and Portugal, to the imperial House of Habsburg and to the ducal House of Burgundy.

Signatures of: (left) Richard, Duke of York and (right) his wife Cecily

This network of relationships was not necessarily an advantage either to Richard or to his children. The very extent of these connections made him seem dangerous to the crown. Newer and less well-connected men like the Duke of Suffolk were more dependent on court favour and therefore more trustworthy. Moreover any extension of this affinity through the marriages of the York children would be closely scrutinised and blocked if it enhanced their claims to the throne. Nor were these large numbers of relatives necessarily a reserve of powerful friends. There were many disagreements over property and interests. The Neville connection brought with it its own internal feud between the children of Earl Ralph's two marriages. The widowed Countess Joan had succeeded in depriving the second Earl of Westmorland (who was Earl Ralph's grandson) of some of his inheritance, which she held for her own eldest son Richard, Earl of Salisbury. Lengthy litigation ensued between the two parties and since it was never settled to the full satisfaction of the Earls of Westmorland, they allied with the Percys against their half-brothers. This family feud led to ever increasing violence in the north which was ultimately to erupt into widespread civil war.

However, in 1446 the battles were a decade away. Richard of York was still expecting to receive honourable treatment from the king and he looked forward to an appointment which reflected his noble lineage. He had no reason to fear the ill will of Henry VI. Both of the previous Dukes of York had proved themselves loyal servants of the crown and Richard had had a good relationship with the young king who had always shown him favour and friendship. Up to 1445 fortune smiled upon Richard, Duke of York.[4] When Henry VI had been crowned King of France at Notre Dame in 1431, Richard, ten years older than his royal cousin, was one of the most resplendent knights in his retinue. Four years later, after the death of the Regent Bedford, Richard was appointed Lieutenant in France with 'like and semblance power as my lord of Bedford had by commission.' The stage was set for him to follow in the footsteps of the great Regent as a pre-eminent and loyal servant of the Lancastrian crown. But this was not to be and the consequences were grave both for England and the House of York.

As the royal representative at Rouen, Duke Richard held great honour. He was regarded as the near equal of England's two most powerful neighbours, the King of France and the Duke of Burgundy. Through the good relations he established with the nobility and the church in both Normandy and Burgundy he had won support and popularity among his Norman subjects. Although the English armies were attacked with increasing success by a revitalised France, inspired by Joan of Arc, his period of office could not be viewed as a complete failure. He showed considerable administrative skill and a sensible, cautious approach to military matters. Indeed he could claim with some justification that he was more successful than the Dukes of Somerset who succeeded him. After his experience in France, he might reasonably have expected to be consulted over the Anglo-French negotiations which sought an end to the long conflict between the two nations. Yet on his return to England he found himself disregarded by the men who had gathered around King Henry VI's new queen, Margaret of Anjou. Chief among these was William de la Pole, Earl of Suffolk. It was he who negotiated Margaret's marriage to King Henry in 1445 and he was the most ardent proponent of a policy of reconciliation with France.

Richard's appointment in France came to an end in the year before his daughter Margaret was born. His promising career had come to a peremptory stop. During the next decade, throughout the whole of Margaret's childhood, his frustration grew. As less and less royal patronage came his way, Richard, his family and his clients found themselves in an increasingly dangerous situation, confronting a series of crises which culminated in their open rebellion against the crown and, ultimately, in the deaths of Richard and his second son Edmund, Earl of Rutland. The birth of a third daughter was of little significance compared with the serious loss of political power resulting from the termination of the duke's appointment. Since his return from France Richard had tried to re-establish himself at court, but in common with many young men before and since, he found that his overseas posting held mixed blessings. Although it had given him heavy responsibilities and prestige, in his absence he had lost touch with the more powerful members of the court and had few allies among the most trusted courtiers. The new queen having found herself married to a gentle and inactive king could not fail to regard Richard, with all his Plantagenet inheritance and his family of five living children, as a threat to the smooth succession of her own future offspring. Her fears were not allayed when the Duke and Duchess of York paid the young queen the compliment of naming their first child born after her accession in her honour. It was not the first time that they had sought royal favour in this manner. Five years earlier, they had called their first born son Henry and the king had been well pleased, but the child had died in infancy. Now they hoped to charm the queen, but their gesture of naming their new daughter Margaret appears to have made little impression on her.

The doubts surrounding the family's future are reflected by the uncertainty over the location of Margaret's birthplace. Fotheringhay Castle and Waltham

Falcon and fetterlock, heraldic badge of Richard, Duke of York

Abbey were both named by contemporary chroniclers and either of them could offer an appropriate birthplace for the future powerful and pious duchess.[5] Of the two, Fotheringhay Castle is the most immediately appealing as it was the chief seat of the House of York.[6] The family badge of the falcon and fetterlock had stood guard over the castle's grey keep since the days of Edmund Langley, the first Duke of York (1341–1402). Lying close to the great north road, about 80 miles from London, the castle was particularly well situated, looking south across the River Nene over the gentle Northamptonshire countryside and surrounded by the large hunting forest of Rockingham. It was conveniently central to all Richard's lands, which were scattered across England and Wales from Yorkshire to Sussex and from East Anglia to the Welsh Marches.

At the time of Margaret's birth, Fotheringhay was still a strong, defendable castle protected by a double moat. The main entrance lay through an impressive gatehouse on the north-west side. Once inside the final drawbridge, there was a whole range of buildings including the ancient keep, a newer and more comfortable manor house, two chapels and all the usual workshops, stables, kitchens, brewhouses, bakeries, butteries and barns making up the castle complex. At least two other York children were born at Fotheringhay: Anne, the eldest and Richard, the youngest. It was certainly a pleasant and well favoured place and it must have had considerable appeal to the Duchess Cecily brought up in the bleaker and colder environs of Raby Castle.

Today only a few ruined walls mark the site of what was, for two hundred years, one of the finest castles in England. There is, however, one substantial survivor from the time of Margaret's birth and that is the unusually large and magnificent parish church dwarfing the small village of Fotheringhay. Yet this is only a fragment of the collegiate church which stood there in the fifteenth century. The older, smaller church standing on the site since pre-Norman times was completely rebuilt with a new lantern tower over 100 feet high, which has survived to the present day, and a very beautiful choir which has totally disappeared. Lying to the west of the castle the great church had been established and endowed by the first and second Dukes of York, Edmund Langley and his son Edward, who made it the religious centre and mausoleum of the House of York. It was a chantry for the deceased members of the royal and ducal family where five Masses were sung on every weekday and six on Saturdays and Sundays. Margaret's father, the third duke, continued the building and by 1446 the college establishment had twelve chaplains or fellows, eight clerks and thirteen choristers under a master. It was becoming a centre of learning and religion for the whole area, its buildings covering a site of more than 2½ acres. They were on a lavish scale with rows of stained glass windows in the cloisters and the library.

As the mausoleum for the House of York the church of Fotheringhay still contains two major tombs. The first duke to be buried there was Edward who met a gallant, if slightly risible, death at the battle of Agincourt. He was struck from his horse and, as it was a hot day and he was a very fat man, he had been suffocated by the weight of his armour. Margaret's parents and her brother Edmund were also buried there. The Duchess Cecily's will showed her deep attachment to Fotheringhay,[7] as she left the college a whole series of bequests

Fotheringhay church, Northamptonshire

including graduals, processionals, mass books, a quantity of ecclesiastical vestments, three blue velvet copes and a great canopy of state made of crimson cloth of gold. Today, although the falcon and fetterlock badge has vanished from the castle, it survives on the York tombs which lie near the main altar of the church. The original gothic monuments were destroyed during the Reformation but new Renaissance tombs were built at the command of Queen Elizabeth I who was very mindful of her York inheritance. The coffins of the ducal family were transferred from the ruined choir into the chancel. The bodies were inspected and a papal pardon was found hanging on a silver ribbon, 'fair and fresh', around the neck of the pious Duchess Cecily.[8] Margaret's own remains, although buried with similar devotion, would not find so peaceful a resting place.

Whether she was actually born at Fotheringhay or not, Margaret certainly passed some part of her childhood there. It may have been in the collegiate library that she acquired her first knowledge of the beautiful manuscripts which she was later to collect with such enthusiasm and discrimination. With all its fine new buildings and high standard of comfort, Fotheringhay also prepared Margaret for the luxury and elegance with which she was to be surrounded for the rest of her life.

Considering Margaret's reputation for piety, the abbey of the Holy Cross at Waltham would perhaps make the most appropriate birthplace.[9] It lay on the Essex side of the River Lea, close to Epping Forest and only about 25 miles from London, on the direct route to Fotheringhay. The duchess must surely have broken her journey there on many occasions since it had a famous and comfortable hostel well used by noble visitors as well as a famous history. It was claimed that Waltham Abbey was founded by a Danish thane called Tovi, who had endowed it with the Holy Cross discovered on his manor of Montacute. The abbey church was rebuilt by Earl Harold and reconsecrated on Holy Cross Day in the presence of King Edward the Confessor. Tradition has it that Harold stayed at the abbey on his way south to Hastings, that his war-cry had been 'the Holy Cross', and that after his defeat and death his body had been brought back to the abbey and secretly buried there. Due to its associations with Harold it was ignored during the Norman period, but it recovered much of its prestige by the thirteenth century when it became a popular centre for pilgrimage and one of the richest Augustinian foundations. When Margaret had the opportunity to found and reform religious orders in the Low Countries, she was to show a definite partiality for the Augustinian order.[10]

In 1446, the Abbot of Waltham was William of Hertford. He was a courtly abbot who had entertained many important visitors including Queen Catherine de Valois and John, Duke of Bedford. The latter was so devoted to the abbey that he asked to be buried there if he should die in England.[11] Since she had only recently returned from Rouen, with all its associations with the Duke of Bedford, Duchess Cecily would have known all about the attractions of the abbey, and she would have been especially interested in its well known hospital which had flourished since the early thirteenth century. However the so-called Annals of Waltham Abbey, which are extant for the years 1445–7, have references to the winter storms and to the parliament of January 1447, but there is no mention of a visit by the duchess or of the birth of her child. There remains a further twist to the puzzle: 3 May was the feast of the Holy Cross and it is possible that the chronicler may simply have confused the feast day with the abbey of the same name.

In the year of Margaret's birth, the Duke of York was particularly busy in the area around Waltham. In March he obtained a licence to retain twelve masons and bricklayers on his manors in Essex, Hertfordshire and Middlesex, and in the following October he was granted the royal income from Waltham to cover his expenses when on royal business to London.[12] During July Richard visited Hunsdon, a manor lying only 9 miles north of Waltham Abbey. By 1448 Hunsdon belonged to Sir William Oldhall, one of the duke's most loyal supporters, who seems to have acquired a group of York's manors in Hertfordshire when Richard was in need of cash. Certainly money had been lavished on Hunsdon which was described as a 'fine house after the mode of a castle.'[13] It was reputed to have cost £4,667, a huge sum for a knight to spend but understandable if it was the duke to whom it belonged. This seems most likely since, in the year after Margaret's birth, Richard was granted a licence allowing him to build and crenellate the tower there. It was more than 100 feet high, and was known as one of the finest constructions of its age. It was built in the 'new' Flemish style with an elegant overstorey, called an oriel, and decorated with gilded vanes. Hunsdon was not merely a very opulent house, it was also a convenient residence close to London. Between 1445 and 1447, Duke Richard's affairs involved him in close attendance on the court and the council. Thus it would have been very convenient for him and his family to use Hunsdon as a base, near to London but free from the pestilence which so often affected the city during the summer months. There is, moreover, some evidence that Margaret had a special interest in the manor of Hunsdon. Nearly half a century later, as the Dowager Duchess of Burgundy, she signed a series of contracts with *Richard of York*, better known as Perkin Warbeck.[14] In these contracts she was promised two pieces of property in England: Hunsdon and Scarborough, which she would receive when *Richard* became King of England. Is it possible that Hunsdon rather than Waltham Abbey or Fotheringhay Castle was in fact Margaret's birthplace? Fotheringhay, Waltham or Hunsdon? Fortunately the puzzle of Margaret's birthplace is not typical of the task facing her biographer. All the major events of her later life are documented with much greater accuracy and, in certain matters such as her marriage and the administration of her dower lands, the chief problem lies in selecting from the great mass of evidence which has survived. It is however difficult to discover anything about her early life except in as much as she was an integral part of her family. This is to be expected. Margaret's importance can only be appreciated when she is seen within her family context. There was little place in the world of the late fifteenth century for the individual and little interest in their origins except for genealogical purposes.

Hunsdon house in 1547, detail from portrait of Edward VI as Prince of Wales

Money was one of the many causes of friction that existed between Richard and the Crown. The duke claimed that he was owed more than £30,000 in arrears for his salary and expenses in France. Although he was the richest noble landowner in England, Wales and Ireland, he seems to have had a regular shortfall of income.[15] Due to his lengthy absences abroad his estates were probably not well managed. Unlike his daughter Margaret, Richard did not attend closely to the management of his estates and neither did the Duchess Cecily. His officials had a relatively free hand and this seems to have resulted in a considerable leakage of funds. In the year of Margaret's birth, he was in particularly urgent need of large sums of money. Not only was he committed to paying out a costly dowry for his eldest daughter, Anne, he was also in the process of establishing an independent household for his two eldest sons, Edward, Earl of March and Edmund, Earl of Rutland. He met these needs by selling off or mortgaging some of his manors, by raising loans on his plate and jewels and also pressing the crown for payment of its debt to him. This caused considerable irritation in the royal council which was already facing problems in finding the money required for the defence of Normandy, Maine and Anjou. There were stormy scenes between the duke's supporters and Adam Moleyns, Bishop of Chichester, Keeper of the Privy Seal and a supporter of the Duke of Suffolk. Moleyns retaliated by accusing the duke and his supporters of misappropriating funds intended for the army in France. Although the duke successfully sued Moleyns for slander, the confrontation increased his alienation from the court and especially from the Duke of Suffolk and the queen.

This lack of royal favour had serious implications for Margaret and her sisters. Richard needed court influence to achieve suitable marriages for his two sons and three daughters.[16] Procuring worthy and honourable marriages for their children was one of the major duties and preoccupations of all noble families. Indeed the success of Cecily's own parents contrasts sharply with the failure of Richard of York; Earl Ralph had pursued his dynastic ambitions and fulfilled his responsibilities as a father with a great deal of determination. Richard, however, did not enjoy the same success. By 1446 only the eldest child, Anne, had secured a suitable marriage, to Henry Holland, the heir to the Duke of Exeter and one of Richard's wards. This was exactly the sort of marriage alliance which Cecily Neville must have wanted for all her children. Henry Holland was a direct descendant of Edward III and the marriage would enhance Anne's own royal inheritance. Richard had had even more ambitious marriage plans for his eldest son. During the diplomatic exchanges which accompanied the marriage of Henry VI to Margaret of Anjou, the duke entered into negotiations for the marriage of his eldest son Edward to Madeleine, the younger daughter of King Charles VII. The Duke of Suffolk had apparently given York's proposals his full support, but as soon as the Anglo-French treaties were completed and Margaret of Anjou had become Queen of England, Edward's French marriage receded from view. No doubt Richard had suspicions that he had merely been encouraged to expect a royal marriage for his own son in order to buy his support for the king's marriage and the peace treaty. After this Richard was unable to find suitable betrothals for his children. It is significant that Anne's marriage took place before the new Queen Margaret was fully established and the betrothal of Elizabeth, the second daughter, was only secured when the queen's influence was curtailed and Richard of York was acting as Protector of England for the second time.

The correct lineage was very important to the Duke and Duchess of York in the selection of marriage partners for their children. It was not to be a paramount issue for their eldest son Edward, but it was a matter which concerned their youngest son Richard when he set aside his 'less royal' nephews in 1483. Margaret too was well aware of the dangers of disparagement by marriage. In 1477, Anthony Woodville was rejected for her step-daughter Mary on the grounds that he was a mere earl[17] and although Margaret herself was widowed at a relatively early age, she was not one of those dowagers, so common in the fifteenth century, who remarried a man of lower rank. Duke Richard's failure in the important field of matrimonial alliances lay at the heart of all his problems and was to have serious consequences for the House of York. To secure marriages with high-born English nobles or foreign royalty he needed royal favour and this was exactly what he failed to secure.

Thus at the time of Margaret's birth, Richard found his political ambitions, his personal fortunes and his marriage plans for his children all blocked by the lack of royal patronage. In addition to these personal problems there was a major political storm brewing between the court party, who supported a policy of peace with France, and their opponents who resented any surrender of English territory. The hawks had gathered around Humphrey, Duke of Gloucester, the king's only surviving paternal uncle.[18] The popular old Duke Humphrey had emerged from the semi-retirement into which he had been forced by the disgrace of his wife, Eleanor Cobham, to lead the opposition to the surrender of Maine and Anjou. It was common knowledge by December 1446 that the king had agreed to the surrender of these territories and that the Duke of Suffolk was ready and willing to confront the Duke of Gloucester over this policy. Suffolk prepared for this clash of wills by summoning parliament to meet at Bury St Edmunds, a city well within his own area of influence. When Humphrey arrived he was met with a long indictment against him and placed under arrest. Within the week he was dead officially, and probably truly, as the result of a stroke. This event was to have wide repercussions within Margaret's family, although Richard of York's immediate role in the conflict between Gloucester and Suffolk is not at all clear. He was certainly not an open supporter of Duke Humphrey. Perhaps he was still hoping for a royal appointment and did not wish to antagonise the crown. Moreover he had not opposed the king's marriage to Margaret of Anjou, and he may well have supported the general drift of Suffolk's policies. In the months which followed York was rewarded for his silence over Gloucester's death. He was given Gloucester's old office as the Steward and Justice-in-Eyre of all the royal forests and he also acquired some of his property, including Baynard's Castle, Gloucester's London house. Finally, late in 1447, the Duke of York was given a new royal appointment. He was made the Lieutenant of Ireland.

At first sight this would appear to have been a poor alternative to the Lieutenancy of France which was granted to Edmund Beaufort, Duke of Somerset. Contemporaries saw the Irish appointment as a sign of ill favour, 'ande in that same yere the Duke of York Richard Plantagenet was exsyled to Ireland.'[19] The duke showed himself in no hurry to take up the appointment. He did not leave from Beaumaris until July 1449, and he was to remain in Ireland for little more than a year. There were uncomfortable precedents with the last two Mortimer Earls of March both of whom had died in Ireland. Perhaps Suffolk and the queen were hoping that the latest Mortimer heir might perish in the same way. Nevertheless Richard may not have been entirely dissatisfied. He was at least fortunate to be out of France at a time when so much of the English territories were being surrendered, even Rouen was lost. Financially too the crown tried to satisfy the duke, settling a large part of its debt to him and offering generous terms for his service in Ireland. Moreover, he had private interests in Ireland, his estates of Meath, Connaught and Ulster, lands which had been a part of his Mortimer and Clare inheritance.

There is no evidence that Margaret accompanied her parents to Ireland. She may well have been left behind at Fotheringhay. The two eldest sons remained at Ludlow and both Anne and Elizabeth seem to have been boarded out in suitable noble households, as was the English custom. Two more male infants, William and John, were born to the Duchess Cecily in the two years after Margaret's birth but both had died. Margaret remained the only child in the York nursery probably under the care of Anne of Caux, who had joined the family at Rouen as a nurse to Edward and stayed with them for the rest of her life. Her pension was paid by both Edward IV and Richard III.[20]

In Ireland the Duke and Duchess of York again enjoyed the autonomy of their own court, the duke rapidly becoming known as a popular and competent governor. His success must have given little satisfaction to Margaret of Anjou and the news that Cecily had given birth to yet another healthy son would have added to her anxieties, especially as there was still no royal heir.[21] The choice of a name for their fourth son was also likely to alarm the court since he was called George, after the patron saint of England, whose cult was very fashionable among the aristocracy of England, France and Burgundy. The two leading families of Ireland, the Butlers and the Fitzgeralds, provided godparents for the infant at his well-nigh regal baptism in the church of St Saviour, Dublin. This Irish connection was to be exploited by Margaret when she promoted the claims of George's son against Henry VII.

Enjoying his success in Ireland and with the losses in France in mind, Duke Richard wrote confidently to the king vowing that: 'it shall never be chronicled . . . by the grace of God that Ireland was lost by my negligence.'[22] From Ireland he watched as the growing crisis in England paralysed the government. The widespread anger over the losses in France led inexorably to the overthrow of the Duke of Suffolk, who was blamed for the English surrenders. Adam Moleyns, York's old adversary, was assassinated and Suffolk himself was brought to trial, exiled and murdered. Throughout these troubles a stream of messengers was kept on the road between England and Ireland. Sir William Oldhall was one of the duke's most important contacts and he left for England in January 1450, returning in the summer to report personally.

Duke Richard's part in the rebellion of 1450 is difficult to assess.[23] Contemporaries were also confused. The court was suspicious of his involvement especially since Jack Cade, the rebel leader who marched on London from Kent in June, claimed that he was a Mortimer and a cousin of York, and the falcon and fetterlock badge was displayed and paraded around London during the disturbances. However, York's own property was attacked by the rebels and he later claimed that jewels had been looted from his houses. During this serious emergency he seems to have expected to be recalled to lend assistance to the crown and fill the place left vacant by the fall of the Duke of Suffolk. He was therefore alarmed and angered to hear that his rival the Duke of Somerset had been created Constable of England and was taking over Suffolk's powers and offices. This not only excluded York from political power, it also threatened his claims to the throne. Edmund, Duke of Somerset, was the nearest male relation to the king on the Beaufort side and, like the Duchess Cecily, a descendant of the marriage of John of Gaunt to Katherine Swynford.[24] Although the Beauforts had been specifically excluded from the royal inheritance, the presence of Somerset at court and the favour with which he was regarded by the childless queen was a clear threat to the prospects of the Duke of York and his children.

Early in September 1450, Richard left Ireland and returned to England at the head of about 4,000 armed men. In advance of his arrival he prepared a series of petitions to put his case to the king and to justify his return.[25] He claimed that 'many promises had been to me made not performed' and that he was owed large sums of money. He declared that he had three main reasons for his return: he was coming to defend his reputation against rumours of his involvement in the rebellion, to take his rightful place as a royal adviser and, above all, to uphold his lineage, 'the issue that it pleased God to send me of the royal blood' from all who intended 'to have undo me myn issue and corrupt my blode.'

The duke's petition drew attention to his six living children, a clear sign of God's blessing, and a slur on the queen who was still childless after five years of marriage. His sudden return without royal invitation, at the head of a body of troops and at a time when violence was prevalent and unrest still widespread, was seen as an open challenge to the crown. From the time of his arrival back in England until early 1452, an uneasy impasse existed between the supporters of York and Somerset both at court and in the country at large. However, in 1452, Duke Richard was tricked, isolated from his troops at Greenwich and forced to accept the pre-eminence of Somerset and arbitration by a royal committee of all his financial demands. He was also obliged to renew his act of allegiance to the king in a public ceremony at St Paul's.[26]

Cecily followed her husband back to England and during the next five years three more children were born to her, Thomas who died young, Richard, the future King Richard III, born at Fotheringhay in October 1452, and another daughter Ursula, who also died young. With the birth of Ursula in 1455, Cecily's childbearing years seem to have come to an end, she was then forty years old. Her lengthy and regular childbearing since the age of twenty-four had left no apparent toll on her health. She was to outlive her husband, all her brothers and sisters and all but two of her own children, living on until she was nearly eighty. None of her children would live as long, and only two matched her fecundity, Edward IV and Elizabeth, Duchess of Suffolk.

These years were a difficult time for York, his family and followers. Sir

William Oldhall was forced to take sanctuary at St Martin-le-Grand, and York's tenants were harassed by Somerset and his allies. Open warfare broke out in the north, triggered off by feuds between the Percys and the Nevilles.[27] The Earl of Warwick's arguments with the Duke of Somerset over the Beauchamp inheritance and his clashes with the king's Tudor half-brothers over lands in Wales drove both Warwick and his father, the Earl of Salisbury who was Cecily's eldest brother, into a closer alliance with Duke Richard.[28]

In October 1453 any hopes that Richard still harboured of being declared heir to the throne finally collapsed when the queen at last gave birth to a son, Edward, Prince of Wales, 'of whoos birth the peple speke strangley.' 'The Quene was defamed and descaundered that he that was called Prince was nat hir son but a bastard goten in avoutry.'[29] This royal birth came at a momentous time in the struggle between England and France. In the autumn of 1452 John Talbot, Earl of Shrewsbury, had recovered control over Bordeaux and Gascony, but early in the spring the French king, Charles VII, began a major campaign. This reached a peak in July with the defeat of the English at Castillon and the death of the great Talbot himself. English Gascony collapsed, leaving England with barely a vestige of her former possessions in France. In the midst of this crisis the health of Henry VI suddenly gave way and by the late summer he apparently became insane. The queen and her friends tried to conceal the king's incapacity and to exclude the Duke of York from the Great Council summoned to meet on 24 October. Pressure from other nobles and a well-timed letter from the Duchess Cecily congratulating the queen on the birth of her son finally secured a summons for Duke Richard.[30]

By March 1454, York had enough backing among the Lords and the Commons to ensure that he was made Head of the Council for the duration of the king's illness. The Duke of Somerset and young Henry Holland, Richard's rebellious son-in-law, were both imprisoned.[31] The Earl of Salisbury became Chancellor and, for a few months, York was firmly in the saddle. But the king regained his sanity, Somerset and Exeter were released, and York then found himself in a very perilous position. With Salisbury and Warwick, York began to muster a large army explaining in a series of manifestos that they were coming in force because otherwise they dared not attend the council which had been summoned to meet at Leicester. York found his attempts to communicate with the king blocked by the queen and Somerset. The result of this political stalemate was the first major military engagement in the Wars of the Roses, the battle of St Albans fought on the 22 May 1455. King Henry was wounded and Somerset and the Percy Earl of Northumberland were among the dead.[32]

The Duke of York and his Neville allies were once more in control and they were able to consolidate their power and reward their followers. Warwick obtained the Captaincy of Calais and Viscount Bourgchier, York's brother-in-law, became Lord Treasurer. Although the Duke of York was only in power for a short time he secured some substantial financial advantages for his family. He obtained the wardship of Suffolk's heir, John de la Pole, and was thus able to provide his second daughter Elizabeth with a suitable marriage. He also ensured the settlement of all the outstanding crown debts to himself and was granted the licence to exploit the gold and silver mines of the south-west. By the late-1450s, the family fortunes were so much improved that the Duchess Cecily was interested in purchasing the fine castle at Caistor which had belonged to Sir John Fastolf.

In reality, however, the position of Duke Richard and his family was more perilous than ever. There was now no room for a reconciliation between York and the queen who feared his intentions towards Edward, Prince of Wales. Nor could all the deaths from the battle of St Albans be easily forgotten, even though the duke paid for a chantry chapel on the site of the battle. King Henry tried to promote peace between the protagonists by encouraging a great public act of reconciliation, the so-called 'love day' at St Paul's, when the Duke of York led in Queen Margaret, 'with great familiarity in all men's sight.'[33] But this familiarity came to nothing and by the summer of 1459 both sides were once again preparing to fight.

The royal forces were gathering in the Midlands, Cheshire and Shropshire and the queen made a serious effort to prevent the Earl of Salisbury's forces from meeting up with York. They were attacked at Blore Heath as they marched south on 23 September, but Salisbury fought off the royal troops and reached York at Ludlow with the bulk of his men. By 12 October the royalist forces had grown considerably while the Yorkist army had been weakened by the desertion of Andrew Trollop and the men of the Calais garrison who refused to fight against their king.[34] The Yorkists were therefore forced to retreat. The duke, with Edmund, made his way to Ireland, and Salisbury, with Warwick and March, left from the Devonshire coast to seek refuge in Calais. There followed what is known as the rout of Ludford Bridge when 'the toune of Ludlow longyng thaan to the Duk of York was robbed to the bare walles and the noble Duches of York unmanly and cruelly was entreted and spoyled.'[35]

Much historical and fictional imagination has gone to work on this episode at Ludlow. Ludlow was the principal residence of York's two eldest sons, Edward and Edmund, but the rest of the family also stayed there from time to time. Large domestic buildings had been added, full of the comforts which had so improved the quality of life for the fifteenth century aristocracy.[36] There were chimneys in most of the rooms, great windows full of the new window-glass and plenty of private rooms, a far cry from the dark, communal accommodation which the old keep had offered. Contemporaries might well assume that the whole family was often in residence at this most comfortable castle. Both the writer of *Hearne's Fragment* and John Wheathampsted recorded that the duchess and her two young sons were taken prisoner at Ludlow, but we have no other evidence that the duchess was there at the time. Both the *English Chronicle* and Fabyan recorded only that the duchess submitted to the king at the parliament called to Coventry in November. The lands of York, March, Rutland, Salisbury and Warwick were attaindered and the king made provision for 'the relief and sustentation of her [Cecily] and her young children what have not offended against us.' This included Margaret. The duchess was allowed an income of 1,000 marks per annum to be drawn from the York estates and she was put into the care of her older sister Anne, Duchess of Buckingham, where according to Fabyan, 'she was kept full straight and with many a rebuke.'[37]

Yet by January 1460 Cecily was travelling freely in Kent and by July she was with Margaret, George and Richard in London 'staying till Michaelmas at Fastolf's place in Southwark.'[38] Fastolf had also owned Crosby House, one of the most modern properties in London with Purbeck marble floors and fine airy windows. Cecily was there for only two days, for as soon as she heard that the Duke of York had returned from Ireland she rushed off to meet him 'in a chair covered in blue velvet and four pair coursers therein.'[39] Margaret, then aged fourteen, and her two brothers remained in London. John Paston, who reported their residence there, was anxious to show that he was discharging his responsibilities as Fastolf's executor with true care. He recorded that 'my lord of March cometh every day to see them.'[40] Edward, Earl of March, was then aged eighteen and at over six feet tall he was a powerful and attractive young man as well as a proven soldier. This is the first documentary reference to Margaret herself. It implies that, unlike her older sisters, she had remained within the family household, a situation reflecting the political problems of the 1450s. The seven surviving children of the House of York may be divided into two groups, the older four, all placed in suitable establishments from an early age, and the younger three who remained at home. Of these three younger children, all of whom were reared in the stormy years of Duke Richard's rebellion, only Margaret would survive to live out a full and successful life.

Events moved quickly and dramatically after the rout of Ludford. The ferocity and extent of the attainders decreed at the Coventry parliament resulted in a reaction in favour of York and his fellow rebels. They had already established strong power bases. York was so strong in Ireland that the new governor's emissary, the Earl of Wiltshire, was hanged as a traitor when he tried to proclaim his master's appointment, and no royal force could dislodge Warwick and Salisbury from Calais. Efforts to do so resulted in Warwick's daring retaliatory raid on Sandwich when he seized both the royal ships and their royal commanders including Lord Rivers and his son Sir Anthony Woodville, Edward's future father- and brother-in-law. They were abducted to Calais and rebuked for their interference in the earls' affairs by Warwick and Edward himself.[41] Meantime the efforts of the crown to crush Yorkist support within England had only stirred up more agitation and Yorkist propaganda was being widely circulated. Warwick sought and obtained support from abroad, both from the papal legate Coppini and from the Dauphin Louis, who was in exile at the Burgundian court. By June, the Calais earls considered themselves sufficiently strong to invade England and by 2 July they were in control of London, albeit with a strong Lancastrian garrison still holding out in the Tower. Warwick and March left to meet the royalist forces at the Battle of Northampton. This was Edward's first personal military success, the royal army was totally defeated and there were many casualties including Cecily's brother-in-law, the Duke of Buckingham. The king was taken prisoner by the rebels though the queen and the Prince of Wales remained at liberty. With the king back in London, the Tower was assaulted and seized and by the end of July the Yorkists were in full control of both London and the king.

Their triumph determined the Duke of York to make an outright bid for the throne. Reviving all the old Mortimer claims he arrived from Ireland, was met by the duchess, glorious in her blue litter, and marched south through Ludlow and

Hereford to Abingdon. On his banners he displayed the arms of England and his claim to the throne was justified in yet another series of manifestos. His arrival in London in September 1460 was both triumphal and royal. Falcons and fetterlocks were embroidered on his livery beside the white roses of the Mortimers, but above everything floated the royal arms. As he entered Westminster Hall for the session of parliament, the sword of state was borne unsheathed before him. Everything was designed to emphasise his right to the throne which, 'though right for a time rest and be put to silence yet it rotteth not nor shall it perish.'[42]

His entrance was met with an embarrassed silence from the nobility, while the Archbishop of Canterbury asked the duke if he wished to see the king. It was at once apparent that his royal pretensions had very little support. Contemporaries reported that the Calais earls, including his eldest son, the Earl of March, opposed the duke's attempted usurpation. There must have been some angry sessions at Baynard's Castle. Although he persisted in his claim for several days, issuing lengthy genealogical proofs to support his right, he was reminded of his repeated oaths of allegiance to King Henry and was eventually forced to accept a compromise in the form of the Act of Accord. In this he was acknowledged as the heir-apparent, the Prince of Wales was set aside and the income from the principality was to be paid to the duke. The Coventry attainders were annulled and large annuities were to be paid to the Earls of March and Rutland. Finally the Duke of York was declared Protector of England and granted all the powers of a regent.

This disinheritance of the Prince of Wales, while leaving King Henry on the throne, was clearly not going to last. Throughout the last months of 1460 both sides gathered troops. The queen, accompanied by her son, recruited in the north with the full support of Westmorland and the Percys; Edward, Earl of March, went west to recruit along the Marches, and York rode north with Salisbury to bring in their own forces from Yorkshire. Warwick remained in control of London and the king. The duchess together with Margaret, Richard and George also appears to have remained in London, probably at Baynard's Castle.

York's arrival at his castle of Sandal was intended to support his loyal tenantry in the West Riding from the raids of the Percys and their royal allies. But the Lancastrian force at the nearby castle of Pontefract seems to have been larger and by the end of the year the duke found that he was virtually besieged at Sandal. On 30 December a brief skirmish between a Yorkist foraging party and a Lancastrian ambush resulted in a catastrophic clash of arms and the deaths of Richard, his son Edmund, Salisbury, his son Thomas and the duke's nephew, Sir Edward Bourchier.[43]

The news of this 'evil day of Wakefield' reached London in the first days of January striking horror into the party that had been keeping the Christmas feast at Baynard's Castle. The reports must have seemed incredible. The duke was forty-nine years old and not given to rash military ventures. Only a breach of the Christmas truce by the Lancastrian forces could make any sense of what had occurred. Rumours that Edmund had been killed while fleeing from the field and that Salisbury had been executed without trial at Pontefract added to the sense of terror. News too that Richard's head wearing a paper crown had been mounted on the walls of York added a final macabre note. Cecily acted swiftly exhibiting a calmness in the face of serious crisis which Margaret would later emulate. She sent her two youngest sons off to safety in Burgundy, 'unto a towne in Flaundyrs namyd uteryk.'[44]

Duke Philip of Burgundy greeted the news of their arrival in his dominions with some embarrassment. The boys were sent to Utrecht to be cared for by Bishop David, one of the ducal bastards who could be relied upon to carry out his father's orders. The two boys settled down to their studies under the bishop's enlightened eye. The Yorkist disaster of Wakefield had attracted much attention in Burgundy where there were virtually three courts at that time, the duke's own court which was centred on Brabant and Flanders, the court of his heir Charles the Bold, the Count of Charolais, who was either at The Hague or with the ducal armies in the field, and the court of the Dauphin Louis of France, who lived in exile at Jemappes. The latter was enthusiastic in his support for the Yorkist cause chiefly because he opposed all the policies of his father, Charles VII, from whom he had fled. Louis' response to the news of Wakefield was to send his own personal messenger with a small force to support the Yorkists. They eventually fought beside Edward at the battle of Towton under the dauphin's standard.[45] Due to the dauphin's Yorkist leanings, Charles the Bold,

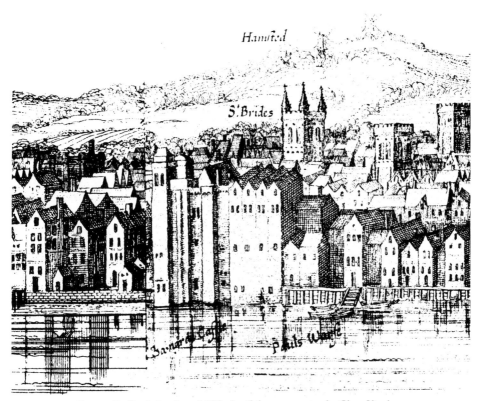

Baynard's Castle in about 1625, detail from engraving by Claes Visscher

who was hostile to Louis' influence on Burgundian policy, inclined towards Lancaster. The old Duke Philip steered a middle course preserving an austere neutrality to the anarchical wranglings of the English nobility. George and Richard were left at Utrecht and it was not until the Yorkist victory at Towton that they were invited to the court at Bruges where they were shown 'great reverence' and entertained to a ducal banquet.[46] When they returned to London in June, they would have been able to provide Margaret with first-hand descriptions of the splendour of the Burgundian court which was then at its apogee under the third 'Great Duke of the West', Philip the Good.

In the five months between the disaster at Wakefield and the coronation of her brother Edward in June, Margaret remained with her mother in London which was still in Yorkist hands. While the rest of the country offered unknown dangers, Baynard's Castle became the safe house for the family. It was a large house, capable of accommodating the 400 armed men which Richard of York had brought with him in 1458.[47] The great hall was over 40 feet long and 24 feet wide, there were large undercrofts and several courtyards. It lay between Thames Street and the river and its pleasant gardens ran beside the Thames. The elegant gardens of the London houses were a well known feature of the medieval city and they were planted with a wide variety of trees and flowers. The views from the terraces were spectacular and exciting; the Thames was full of vessels, with foreign galleys and the local craft which were manned by the formidable boatmen who had to be strong and tough to enable them to get their small boats through the nineteen narrow arches of London Bridge in the face of the rushing currents and tides. Further downstream towards the Tower was the quay where the Venetian galleys loaded and unloaded under the watchful eye of the Tower garrison.

It is likely that both Cecily and Margaret stayed at Baynard's Castle until after the coronation of Edward IV. From January to March, they faced some very uneasy times, especially after Warwick was defeated at the second battle of St Albans and the way to London lay open to the queen's northern army. The city was only spared by her hesitation and reluctance to launch an attack. A delegation of ladies who were known for their loyalty to the royal cause, including Anne, dowager Duchess of Buckingham and Jacquetta, Lady Rivers, went to plead with the queen not to bring her northern rabble into the city. Fortunately for London she listened to their appeals.[48]

The queen's hesitation gave time for Edward, Earl of March, to act. As soon as he heard of his father's death, he attacked the royal forces to the west, defeating them at Mortimer's Cross. With the new ruthlessness which followed Wakefield, Owen Tudor, the king's step-father, was executed at the market cross in Hereford. The battle of Mortimer's Cross became a very important part of the Yorkist iconography. According to tradition there appeared just before the battle 'three suns in the firmament shining full clear.'[49] With true piety these were interpreted as signs of the Trinity and therefore of God's blessing for their cause. Edward adopted the three suns as his emblem and together with the Mortimer roses they gradually replaced the falcon and fetterlock as the main badges of the House of York. When he became king they were adopted as royal symbols. Fresh from his triumph, Edward marched directly to London and conferred with Warwick as to their next move. With the deaths of both their fathers at Wakefield, a new generation was in the saddle and the young men did not hesitate. Edward was proclaimed king on 4 March, basing his right to the throne on his father's claim of 1460 and on the fact that royal forces had broken the Act of Accord at Wakefield. It was less than a year since Richard of York had made his abortive bid for the throne but the whole political situation had been transformed. Warwick had lost his possession of King Henry at the second battle of St Albans and the rebels needed a king of their own. Coppini, the papal delegate, who like many foreigners, was misled by Warwick's authority in Calais declared that 'in the end my Lord of Warwick has come off best and made a new King of the son of the Duke of York.'[50] But in England it was more a question of the old Mortimer magic at work, perhaps also something to do with the fact that Edward was a handsome young giant and a proven general in marked contrast both to his father and to the old King Henry. As one of the chroniclers wrote, 'let us walk in a new vineyard and let us make a gay garden in the month of March with this fair white rose and herb the Earl of March.'[51]

Following the declaration of his royal title and the celebration of a Te Deum at St Paul's, the new King Edward IV left London to put his claim to the decisive ordeal of battle. The hard fought battle of Saxton Field at Towton in the West Riding was the largest and bloodiest conflict of the civil wars.[52] Edward claimed, in a letter to his mother, that 28,000 men had died, while modern estimates of the numbers involved in the fighting vary from 50,000 to 75,000. At least three-quarters of the aristocratic families had members on the field, and after the battle 113 attainders were issued. The hapless King Henry, who was not at the battle, escaped with the resolute queen and her son. Sheltered by loyalists, Queen Margaret, a woman of great courage, fled first to Scotland and later to Burgundy and France where she sought in vain for help.

In London, the House of York celebrated the coronation of King Edward. Prominent at the new court was the widowed Duchess Cecily. The most important ladies of the new court were the king's three sisters: Anne, Duchess of Exeter, still accepted although her husband was an irreconcilable Lancastrian; Elizabeth, Duchess of Suffolk whose husband proved to be as reliable as a Yorkist courtier as he would later be as a Tudor courtier; and Margaret, who was now wholly dependent upon her brother the king for her maintenance and a marriage settlement. On their return from Burgundy George, newly made Duke of Clarence, was given particular honours as the heir-apparent and the younger brother Richard was made Duke of Gloucester. Both boys became Knights of the Garter and were heaped with lands and offices. Margaret and her two younger brothers were, for a short time at least, all established under one roof at the pleasant country palace of Greenwich.[53]

It was now Edward's duty to arrange marriages both for himself and for his siblings. Unfortunately, like his father before him, he would fail lamentably and fatally to provide suitable brides for his brothers and Margaret had to wait long and patiently until an appropriate bridegroom was found for her. The new Yorkist princess was fifteen years old when her brother was proclaimed king. By fifteenth century standards she was already a young woman whose education and training was complete. By her age, her mother, sisters and most of her other

King Edward IV

female relations had been betrothed and left the family household, but Margaret was to remain at court and unmarried for another seven years. In appearance she was fair-haired like her mother although she was much taller like her brother Edward, but she certainly inherited her mother's energy and her keen interest in political and dynastic affairs.

The Duchess Cecily was no cypher. In spite of her long years of childbearing she had remained constantly at her husband's side and, after his death, she continued to play an active role in the family and to take part in political and administrative affairs. After the battle of Towton, the papal legate Coppini was advised to 'write to the Duchess of York who has a good regard for you and can rule the King as she pleases.'[54] In the first decade of Edward's reign, we find her energetically supporting the promotion of one of her chaplains, Thomas Bann, to a preferment at Folkestone despite the combined opposition of the Archbishop of Canterbury and Lord Clinton. In the later years of her life, when most of her day was devoted to religious matters, she still set time aside to deal with her petitioners and business matters. This diligent pursuit of the long term interests of the family both in heaven and on earth was very typical of the great ladies of the fifteenth century. Margaret's own success in securing for herself a respected and honoured position at the Burgundian court was due to her constant vigilance and care in matters of administration and politics. She learned much of this from her mother's example.

However, the Duchess Cecily's greatest legacy to her youngest daughter was in the field of religion. The central place of religion in the history of the fifteenth century was especially important in the lives of the aristocratic women who had both the time and opportunity to lead a full religious life. Like the Lady Margaret Beaufort, the mother of the future Henry VII, Margaret and Cecily found no conflict between their piety and a ruthless determination to promote the fortunes of their families. These ladies were typical of their age and of their country. Their religious practice was full of indulgences and relics. Schatzel, who travelled to England with Count Leo of Rozmittal early in Edward's reign, wrote that he had never seen so many relics as in England.[55] Without a strong faith and a belief that this world was merely a temporary vale of tears, it is difficult to see how either the Duchess Cecily or her daughter Margaret could have survived the many disasters and disappointments which they had to endure. The Duchess of York was certainly no patient Griselda and her survival through all the crises shows a strong and remarkably positive character. Her capacity to endure was passed in good measure to Margaret and it was based on a deep religious faith which is well documented in the description of her household during her last years.[56] Cecily taught Margaret to set aside regular hours for prayer, contemplation and reading. Essential reading included the lives of the saints, Cecily being particularly interested in the lives of St Catherine of Siena and St Brigid of Sweden.[57] St Catherine's life recorded a very emotional religious experience in which the practitioner tried to imagine the sufferings of Christ and the martyrs. The saint had even signed her letters 'yours in the blood of Christ'. Both Cecily and her daughter Margaret shunned this level of spiritual excess but they were both personally and publicly devout. The proper duty of a Christian noblewoman was to provide lavish vestments, books, plate and reliquaries for the church, to support good clergymen and to observe all the feasts and liturgies of the Christian year. Both Cecily and Margaret fulfilled their duties in this respect with conscientious attention, munificence and splendour.

While Margaret owed her training to her mother, her inheritance from her father was not insubstantial. Richard of York showed considerable skill in maintaining the loyalty of his servants and followers, including those he had inherited from his uncle Edward, Duke of York, and from his predecessor in Rouen, the Regent Bedford, men such as John Russel, Sir John Popham and Sir William Oldhall.[58] Margaret too was able to keep the allegiance of her staff such as Olivier de La Marche, who served as chamberlain to her husband, to her and later to Philip the Fair. Duke Richard was significantly less successful in attracting support from among his peers in spite of the large affinity he had acquired through his marriage. Did the emphasis which he placed on his royal blood alienate him from the less royal nobility or was he personally a cold and reserved man unlike his amiable and charismatic son King Edward? If so, then perhaps Margaret was more like her father, for she was described as reserved and seldom smiling.[59] She also inherited his deep sense of dynasty which showed throughout her life in her steadfast loyalty to the Houses of Burgundy and York.

Margaret was born at a time when written communication had become an important part of estate management and social life. Great nobles normally used secretaries for their correspondence and business affairs. It was still considered clerkish to write a good hand but Margaret was sufficiently learned to be able to supervise her officials and subject their work to a close personal scrutiny. She was probably schooled with her younger brothers. Her autograph was very confident and untidy, showing a reasonable degree of literacy and a strong character.[60] Classical learning and humanism had not yet affected the education of the English aristocracy and neither Margaret nor her brothers were given the sort of grounding in Latin which was to become commonplace in the next generation. Her extensive use of French translations of Latin authors shows that, like the rest of her family, she was no classicist. However she was probably familiar with both church Latin and basic legal Latin. Her knowledge of spoken French began in the nursery with Anne of Caux, but although fluent in speech, even after years of living in Burgundy, her written French was still far from accurate. Nevertheless her ability to read French was such that she was later able to correct Caxton's translation.[61] She also appears to have had no difficulty in learning some Dutch. In Edward IV's instructions for the education of his son, the Prince of Wales, 'grammar, music and other exercises of humanity' were recommended. No doubt Margaret was also taught music, dancing and embroidery, the standard skills for a woman of her class. She would have become a competent rider, though it was the custom for ladies to ride pillion behind a man, or to travel long distances in a 'chair' or litter. Travel was never viewed as a problem and Margaret, like her mother Cecily, was to set off on long and laborious journeys at all seasons of the year.

Very little is known about the personal tastes and interests of Richard of York or of his wife. Both he and the duchess kept a great retinue and made full use of finery and splendour in their costume, jewels and plate, a great contrast in style to the modesty and simplicity of Henry VI. On the miniatures and paintings that have survived, Margaret is always portrayed dressed with elegance and opulence in the fashion of her day but she was not, like her brother Edward, noted for finery or sense of display. Her most lavish personal spending was apparently on her purchases of fine manuscripts. She may have acquired her original interest in such matters from her parents but neither of them displayed the discrimination which was to distinguish Margaret's collection. Duchess Cecily's books appear to have been confined to religious subjects and Richard of York's only known instance of literary patronage was an English translation of the book by Consul Stilicho. Since Stilicho was a much wronged Roman noble who was finally made consul due to the great favour of the populace, the selection of this subject by the duke was probably not merely a question of literary taste.[62] Her father's uncle, Edward, Duke of York, had shown some interest in books. He translated and amended a French treatise on hunting and the training of hunting dogs, a work based on much practical experience.[63] Margaret's own interest was to go far beyond that of her parents or her great-uncle for she was to have the benefit of access to the famous Burgundian library.

This educated young woman with decided religious and bookish interests found herself in 1461 the only unmarried sister of the King of England. For the next seven years she divided her time between the various royal lodgings which were provided for her and the court itself. Three main routes ran across the city and Baynard's Castle was on the most southerly route in Thames Street. The Royal Wardrobe, where rooms were prepared for Margaret when she stayed in the city, lay on the central route to the east of the Blackfriars monastery where Puddle Dock met the end of Carter Lane. This old royal property had been refurbished to provide lodgings for royal guests and members of the family. It was conveniently close to Baynard's Castle and a short ride from the Palace of Westminster.[64]

London, in spite of the hazards of the plague, was a very attractive city. It was relatively small with a population of about 40,000, four times smaller than Paris, but about the same size as Florence or Rome, and larger than any city in Burgundy. It covered an area of about one square mile, from the Tower to Blackfriars and from the river to the north wall. With its many gardens, kites wheeling overhead and salmon and pike in the Thames, London was a very rural place by our standards but it enjoyed all the advantages of a great medieval city. The most skilful craftsmen worked there and it was famous for its goldsmiths, silversmiths and jewellers. It was the only place in England where foreign luxuries were readily available. Only in London could one purchase fine cloth, tapestries, wall-hangings, furs, spices, sugars and exotic fruit like lemons, oranges and pomegranates. Great sums of money were spent on these luxuries, especially on such fabrics as silks and damasks which were used for clothing and wall-hangings. In spite of many contemporary improvements in the collection of sewage and the provision of fresh water, London was still an unhealthy place. In 1464, two hundred people died of the plague in one month alone and 1467 was another bad year. The prevalence of plague led to the gradual closing down of the public bath houses though two or three which were well known for their respectable clientele had survived. Noble ladies were also in the habit of dining out at some of the city's inns, a fact noted with amazement by Schatzel.[65]

It was perhaps to escape the worst of the plague that the king also accommodated his sister and younger brothers out of the city at the 'playsaunce' of Greenwich.[66] Like Baynard's Castle, the Greenwich manor had belonged to Humphrey, Duke of Gloucester, who had rebuilt it to a very high standard of luxury. After Gloucester's death, Margaret of Anjou made Greenwich her favourite country residence. She had the pillars decorated with marguerites, which would have pleased Margaret too, and a new pier was built. Greenwich was also used by Edward's queen and their first child, Elizabeth of York, was born there. The king had numerous chambers added for the convenience of his family so that it was possible for George, Duke of Clarence, to stay there with his large household of almost three hundred servants and officials. The households for Margaret and Richard were much more modest and sometime in 1465 Richard left Greenwich to join of the Earl of Warwick's household.

In the seven years that Margaret was maintained by her brother she was provided with an income paid out of the Exchequer.[67] In 1462 she was to receive 40 livres a year and from 1465, when she was over eighteen, this was raised to 400 marks, a generous but still modest allowance. Like most royal annuities these payments were frequently in arrears. In addition to her annuity the officials at the Treasury were expected to meet her expenses, both for the household at Greenwich and for her clothing and personal furnishings. When she stayed at court her expenses would be met directly through the royal household. From 1461 to 1464 her life was conducted within the compass of Greenwich, the Royal Wardrobe and the court, but this modest existence changed dramatically with the marriage of the king to Elizabeth Woodville. From 1464 onwards there are more frequent references to Lady Margaret, the king's sister.

Bearing in mind both Richard of York's efforts to secure a French princess as a bride for his eldest son, and all the diplomatic activity aimed at procuring a suitable bride for King Edward from the courts of Scotland, France, Italy, Spain or Burgundy, it came as a great surprise to everyone when the king did not marry 'some noble progeny out of his realm,' but 'a mere widow of England.'[68] Cecily seems to have been appalled that her son had been 'led by blind affection and not by the rule of reason.' Yet in spite of the lack of international benefit, Edward's marriage was not the sheer folly that some contemporaries considered it. Through his marriage to Elizabeth Woodville, the king greatly increased his own personal following, attracting a numerous family who had previously been loyal to the House of Lancaster. Nor was Elizabeth Woodville the lowly creature that some commentators suggest. Her mother, Jacquetta de St Pol, was the daughter of one of the most noble and powerful families in Luxembourg and northern France and could claim a descent from Charlemagne.[69] Jacquetta's first marriage, to the Duke of Bedford, had been a great affair of state, but her second marriage shortly after Bedford's death to Sir Richard Woodville was a love match. It was regarded as a shocking disparagement by her own family and by the English crown, though she was eventually able to obtain a pardon from the king. Sir Richard Woodville was indeed a mere knight but he had been knighted at the same ceremony as Richard, Duke of York, and he had served

ELIZABETH · VXOR
EDWARDVS · IIII ·

Queen Elizabeth Woodville

under Bedford in France. In 1448 he was elevated to the peerage as Lord Rivers and he, with his whole family, had remained a loyal supporter of Henry VI. His son-in-law, Lord Grey of Groby, was killed fighting for the royal cause at the second battle of St Albans leaving an attractive widow, Elizabeth. With her marriage to Edward the whole family transferred its loyalty to the Yorkist king.

By the time of Elizabeth's coronation in May 1465 most of the court had come to terms with the new queen apart, perhaps, from Cecily, who is distinguished by her absence from the lists of those attending the ceremonies.[70] The Duke of Clarence, as High Steward of the realm, led the queen's procession and her train bearer was Anne, the dowager Duchess of Buckingham, and an old friend of Jacquetta's. Following the queen came Elizabeth, Duchess of Suffolk, and Margaret. It was the first time that her presence was recorded at a great occasion of this sort. At the coronation banquet Margaret sat on the queen's left hand and from this time on she became one of the circle of ladies who attended upon the queen.

Tetzel, who visited England a year later, described Margaret's attendance at the elaborate ceremonial which followed the queen's churching after the birth of Elizabeth of York.[71] There were, he claimed, eight duchesses and thirty countesses present and they stood in silence as the queen was seated in her 'costly golden chair.' The queen was attended by her mother and by the 'king's sister,' presumably Margaret, since both Anne and Elizabeth would have been accorded their titles. Margaret and the Lady Jacquetta stood some distance away from the queen and when she addressed them, they knelt before her and were only seated when the queen had been served with her first dish. Then all three ladies dined in state attended by other noble ladies who knelt in silence as long as the queen was eating. The meal lasted for three hours. Silence was an important part of the strict court etiquette and protocol. After the banquet came the entertainment with music from the king's choristers followed by dancing. Margaret danced a stately measure with two dukes, probably her brothers, during which she made constant 'courtly reverences' towards the queen. Deep curtsies were a part of the fashionable promenading dances and they were usually addressed to the highest ranking person present. From this description it is clear that Margaret was very visibly under the direct patronage of the queen and completing her courtly education. She was also for the first time open to foreign influences. Edward laid considerable emphasis on his wife's continental connections. Her uncle Jacques de St Pol, Count of Richebourg, had attended the queen's coronation with a retinue of 100 knights. Jacquetta had maintained her French and Burgundian contacts and among her books were several manuscripts of continental provenance including Christine de Pisan's spirited defence of women, *Book of the City of Ladies*.[72]

After the modest lodgings in the Royal Wardrobe and the quiet Palace of Greenwich Margaret, now a young woman of twenty-one, must have found life at court interesting and exciting. She surely learned much from the new queen who set the highest standards both in courtly etiquette and in the management of her household. Queen Elizabeth's household was administered with much greater efficiency and economy than that of her predecessor, Margaret of Anjou.[73] Margaret probably found Queen Elizabeth a good model. Later, when she became the Duchess of Burgundy, she was to show a keen interest in household management and retained as her own chamberlain Europe's foremost expert on noble households and etiquette, Olivier de La Marche.

It was, however, above all in the question of her marriage that Elizabeth played a crucial role in her sister-in-law's life. The new queen was a much more able and energetic exponent of the marriage game than her husband. She was extremely successful in promoting marriages within her own family, and seems to have taken a similar interest in the marriage of the king's sister. There had indeed been a few proposals for Margaret's hand before 1465.[74] In 1462 the French reported that a marriage alliance was being negotiated between Margaret and King James III of Scotland but nothing more was heard of this. Two years later, when Edward was considering his own marriage to Isabella of Spain, the sister and heiress of the King of Castile, there was a suggestion that Margaret might marry a Spanish or Burgundian prince but once more nothing came of it. After 1465, however, some more substantial proposals appeared.

The first real candidate for Margaret's hand was Don Pedro of Aragon and the match was urged forward by the Duchess Isabelle of Burgundy who was Don Pedro's aunt.[75] Isabelle encouraged her nephew, a contender for the throne of Aragon and a claimant of Catalonia, to propose marriage to Margaret and so obtain the support of England against his enemies the Kings of Aragon and of France. Negotiations between Don Pedro and Edward IV were underway by late 1465 and there was a very positive response from the English court to this proposal. In the following January, Edward despatched his own envoys to Don Pedro's court at Barcelona and two months later Don Pedro sent his secretary a detailed description of the betrothal ring which was to be presented to Margaret on his behalf. It was to be a very fine diamond set in gold costing £200, a high price indeed.[76] It seemed that at last Margaret's marriage was to become a reality although Don Pedro's prospects were not very promising. The betrothal came to an abrupt end with his sudden death in June 1466. Don Pedro's demise was, for Margaret at least, well timed, since late in 1465 another and much more interesting candidate appeared on the scene. Instead of becoming the wife of a pretender in Spain, Margaret was to become the greatest duchess in western Europe, the Duchess of Burgundy.

2 The Marriage of the Century

'at King Arthur's Court'

Measured by the sheer bulk of surviving contemporary accounts, the marriage of Margaret to Charles was without doubt the most important wedding of the century.[1] Princes, nobles, clerics and merchants all crowded into Bruges to attend in person and, when they returned home, they reported at length to their colleagues. Those unable to be present commissioned and collected detailed descriptions of those who had been, of what had been worn in the wedding processions, eaten at the banquets and achieved in the jousts. Princes and nobles wanted blow-by-blow accounts of the nine day tournament of the Golden Tree. Merchants and bankers were more practical; they wanted full details concerning all the fashions and fabrics worn by the magnificent retinues and the furnishings and food supplied for the banquets. One such report was despatched to the headquarters of the Hansa at Lübeck and another, sent to Strasbourg, included precise figures for the daily consumption of food and drink. Proud and patriotic Burgundian chroniclers and writers embellished page after page with such elaborate and elevated prose that even Edward Hall, the Tudor chronicler, normally only too willing to embroider a good story, commented that he thought 'they saye not true in a grete dele.'[2] Ambitious young men like Simon Mulart turned the whole occasion into a Latin epic and hoped thus to secure lifelong patronage from the great duke. Among the English sources, the thirteen pages in the *Excerpta Historica* provided the fullest account, but the Paston letter of 8 July is the most succinct. For once John Paston was lost for words concluding his letter; 'And by my troth I have no wit nor remembrance to write to you, half the worship that is here.'[3] No doubt the Paston family was furnished with much greater detail when he returned home.

Olivier de La Marche, the ducal chamberlain, who was in charge of all the arrangements for the procession, banquets and tournaments, wrote what is probably the most detailed account of the whole proceedings. However, it was to be almost forty years after the event before he found time in his busy life to sit down and compose his memoirs. Moreover like most of the writers of the period he was totally indifferent to chronology, even dating the wedding after the siege of Neuss in 1475. He was also vague and confused concerning the events which took place in the weeks immediately before the wedding. Presumably he was so preoccupied with all the last minute preparations that he had to rely on others to tell him what was happening at Sluis and Damme. Perhaps too he thought that all this had already been well reported and his own special interests lay elsewhere. Thus he devoted only one paragraph to the actual wedding ceremony, seven pages to the procession, five pages to the banquets and no less than seventy-two pages to the tournament.

The survival of so many accounts of the wedding is also a consequence of the fact that within a decade the marriage of Margaret to Charles would be regarded as the last great scene of Burgundian glory. Indeed the marriage had a sound literary appeal. After the debacle of Nancy and the loss of the duchy to the French, there was a widespread and morbid interest in the ill-fated life of Charles the Bold. Legends gathered around the memory of this fierce, energetic man and the description of his magnificent marriage to a princess from the equally ill-fated House of York provided fascinating material for chroniclers and moralists alike.

In every respect the marriage lived up to what was expected from a great dramatic event. The negotiations had been dogged with interruptions and arguments, there had been cliff-hanging delays over the provision of the papal dispensation and the bride's dowry. Margaret's journey across the Channel was suitably hazardous. Her reception was well prepared and beautifully staged and the ten day celebrations were both magnificent and exciting. Neither the English king nor the Burgundian duke omitted anything that could promote and emphasise their own honour and the importance of their new alliance.

Edward IV was, in every way, a contrast to his predecessor and he never missed an occasion to enhance his own glory. As a usurper he was anxious that the new Yorkist court should be recognised throughout Europe as truly regal. He would have been well satisfied to know that Gabriel Tetzel had already judged his court to be 'the most splendid Court that could be found in all Christendom,'[4] and that Tetzel had come to this conclusion immediately after his visit to the Burgundian court, reputed to be the wealthiest and most magnificent in Europe. For her marriage Edward provided his sister with a luxurious trousseau and a noble entourage which would uphold his own reputation and satisfy her honour. Charles was equally ambitious. He had succeeded his father in June 1467 and his marriage to Margaret was the first great event of his reign. He was thus resolved that it should be a celebration without equal in all the annals of Burgundy, outshining the famous feasts of his father's reign.[5] Nothing was spared that was necessary to make the occasion an ostentatious display of the opulence and might of the Burgundian court.

There was also an element of triumph and relief in the final preparations for the wedding. The whole extravaganza came at the end of two years of long and serious negotiations. In May 1467 the diplomatic arguments had reached such an indeterminate point that Sir John Paston thought it worth his while to have a bet on the result.[6] He agreed to pay 80 shillings for a horse if the marriage took place within two years but only half as much if it did not. Paston lost his wager but at least he had the satisfaction of attending the wedding. There were many others who had also thought or even hoped that the wedding would never take place.

King Louis XI, by J. Fouquet

The origin of the many difficulties which dogged the negotiations for this marriage lay in the tricky diplomatic situation existing between France and Burgundy. The Valois Dukes of Burgundy were in a very special position in relation to France. Although their title derived from a French duchy founded by John II for his son Philip the Bold, the Dukes of Burgundy had, during a century of war and marriage, acquired many territories lying beyond the jurisdiction of France.[7] Duke Charles had inherited a vast agglomeration of lordships and counties, including the duchy of Burgundy and the counties of Charolais, Artois and Flanders which lay within French suzerainty, and the duchies of Hainault, Holland, Zeeland and Brabant and the county of Burgundy or Franche Comté which were all fiefdoms of the Empire. These extensive possessions in the richest trading and manufacturing area of northern Europe made the Dukes of Burgundy powerful rivals to the Kings of France and England. Throughout the Hundred Years' War the friendship of Burgundy had been essential to the success of both England and France. Indeed the withdrawal of Duke Philip the Good from his earlier alliance with England enabled Charles VII to drive the English out of France in the mid-fifteenth century. As heir-apparent, Charles the Bold had opposed his father's rapprochement with France and he had been especially angered by the return of the Somme towns to Louis XI in 1463. He feared an Anglo-French alliance which would leave Louis free to oppose the consolidation and expansion of Burgundy. It was for this reason that Charles became interested in a marriage with Margaret of York.

Louis XI was equally anxious to prevent an Anglo-Burgundian alliance and during the first years of Edward's reign it seemed that he might succeed. As the Dauphin of Jemappes, Louis had supported Warwick and Edward against the Lancastrians, even sending a small body of men to fight for the Yorkists at the battle of Towton. It was in Edward IV's interest to keep this friendship and so deter Louis from giving any real assistance to Queen Margaret of Anjou. Thus early in his reign negotiations began for an Anglo-French marriage. At first the proposals had concentrated on the person of the eligible Edward. He was offered the hand of Louis' sister-in-law, Bona of Savoy, but Edward's marriage to Elizabeth Woodville brought this and any other proposals to an abrupt halt. In spite of this set-back Louis and the Earl of Warwick continued to press for an Anglo-French marriage alliance with the proposals now centred upon Margaret and her brother George, Duke of Clarence.

Burgundian interest in an English marriage began immediately after the death of Charles' wife, Isabelle of Bourbon, in September 1465.[8] Her death left the Count of Charolais, as he then was, an eligible widower and the inheritance of the duchy was dependent upon the lives of Charles himself and his only child, the eight-year-old Mary. Louis lost no time in offering Charles the hand of his eldest daughter Anne. But since the princess was only four years old, not even the tempting offer of a dowry which included the counties of Ponthieu and Champagne could compensate for the fact that it would be many years before the infant princess could provide Burgundy with an heir. Moreover by this date relations between France and Burgundy had deteriorated. The old Duke Philip the Good was forced to abandon his policy of friendship towards France. He fled from his own castle of Hesdin because he feared an assassination attempt inspired by Louis XI. There was, after all, a precedent for such a murder. Duke Philip's father had been butchered in 1419 by servants of the Dauphin Charles on the bridge of Montereau. Following the incident at Hesdin, Charles' influence grew more dominant and his policy to ally Burgundy with Brittany and Bourbon in the War of the Public Weal against France was given free rein. At the treaty of Conflans, which finally brought the Franco-Burgundian conflict to an end, Louis was forced to return the Somme towns. Charles was well satisfied with the outcome, and in order to maintain his position he considered an English marriage.

It was not the first time that a marriage between the Burgundian heir and a Yorkist princess had been contemplated.[9] When Charles' first fiancée, Catherine of France, had died in 1446, the Duchess Isabelle had suggested a marriage between her son and Anne of York. However, her husband had opposed the idea and Charles remained unmarried until October 1454 when Duke Philip decided on Isabelle of Bourbon. Charles' marriage to Isabelle of Bourbon had lasted eleven years and was considered to have been a particularly happy match although it had produced only one healthy child, the Lady Mary. Both Wrelant and Commynes claimed that a Yorkist alliance was fundamentally abhorrent to Charles because of his mother's Lancastrian blood and his own sympathies for the deposed Henry. Wrelant had a story that Charles disliked Margaret so much that he was drunk on his wedding night and was never a good husband to her. However, there is really no evidence of any strong feelings either for or against the House of York on the part of Philip or his son Charles. Moreover in spite of her descent from John of Gaunt, the Duchess Isabelle had favoured a Yorkist marriage. She was well aware that the Duchess Cecily was, like herself, a grand-daughter of Lancaster.[10] Burgundy had given shelter to both Yorkist and Lancastrian exiles, maintaining the youngest sons of Richard of York in 1461 and the Lancastrian Dukes of Exeter and Somerset after the accession of Edward IV.

There were other important considerations which affected the relations between England and Burgundy. Although the rulers may have been primarily interested in their own territorial and dynastic standing, they could not ignore the economic links which were so vital to the prosperity of both countries.[11] Both Edward and the Dukes of Burgundy were dependent on the merchant community for loans and on trade for a substantial part of their income. Economic recessions were liable to make themselves felt in civic riots and rebellions. Throughout the fifteenth century the Dukes of Burgundy used Anglo-Burgundian trade as a weapon against England, imposing restrictions and boycotts to force the English into negotiations either with them or France. English kings retaliated by moving the wool staple from Antwerp to Calais and by imposing reciprocal restrictions on Burgundian manufactures. This type of economic warfare reached a peak between 1462 and 1465 when Philip was trying to force Edward into a tripartite treaty with Burgundy and France. Burgundian restrictions on the export of bullion hit English exports of wool and raw cloth and the trade in these commodities reached its lowest level for the century. English merchants and producers were badly affected but so were the merchants, weavers and cloth-finishers of Holland, Zeeland and Flanders.

Edward enacted reciprocal boycotts and a wholesale economic war ensued with restrictions on credit, fighting at the fishing grounds and increased piracy in the channel. It was a situation which could not be allowed to continue too long without serious internal difficulties in both England and Burgundy.

Commercial interests were closely involved in the marriage negotiations, especially on the Burgundian side. The international commercial community, centred on Bruges, eagerly supported any moves which would improve the situation. Tommaso Portinari, the Medici agent in Bruges and the chief economic adviser to Count Charles, was a prominent member of the diplomatic team. Lord Louis of Gruuthuyse and Lord Jehan of Hallewijn, who were the ducal governors in Holland, Zeeland and Flanders, were also among the Burgundian negotiators and they represented the noble and economic interests of their provinces. As soon as the negotiations for the marriage were underway, both sides relaxed some of their boycotts and restrictions. Although a final settlement on the rates of exchange was not reached until the 1470s, the export of raw cloth from England increased sharply after the marriage and within ten years it was running at double the rate of 1462 to 1465. The enthusiasm for the marriage which was felt in the merchant community was expressed in the close cooperation among English, Flemish and Italian merchants over the arrangements for the payment of the dowry and in the large merchant delegations which took part with pride in the bridal procession.

When Isabelle of Bourbon died, Margaret was still betrothed to Don Pedro, but even before he too died the following June an embassy had been sent to England to discuss a marriage.[12] Late in 1465 or early in 1466 Guillaume de Clugny, one of Charles closest advisers, arrived in London to propose the marriage. In reply to this proposal Edward set up a special negotiating team which he commissioned in March 1466. It was a very high powered team with Warwick, Hastings and Wenlock in charge. They were instructed to discuss two possible marriages; Margaret with Charles and Clarence with Mary of Burgundy, Charles' daughter. To the disappointment of Clarence this second marriage soon vanished from the negotiations.[13]

In April the English embassy met Charles' negotiators at St Omer, to discuss not only the marriage but also the economic situation and to plan a general treaty of friendship. But Edward was at that time by no means committed to the Burgundian alliance and Warwick, one of the chief negotiators at St Omer, was actively promoting the alternative alliance with France. Nevertheless the conference bore some fruit and Edward and Charles signed a secret treaty of friendship. However Warwick left St Omer to negotiate with the French and to renew the Anglo-French truce.[14] Louis put forward various counter-proposals for Margaret's hand. He could not find a candidate equal in status to Charles but he had assembled no less than four possible candidates: his brother-in-law Philip, Count of Bresse; René, Count of Alençon whose sister had been suggested as a bride for Edward IV in 1455; Philibert of Savoy, the young Prince of Piedmont, who was his nephew and had been brought up at the French court and Galeazzo Sforza, the new Duke of Milan and, at that time, still Louis' ally. Edward was really in a very comfortable position. Both France and Burgundy sought his alliance and both were offering full treaties encompassing favourable

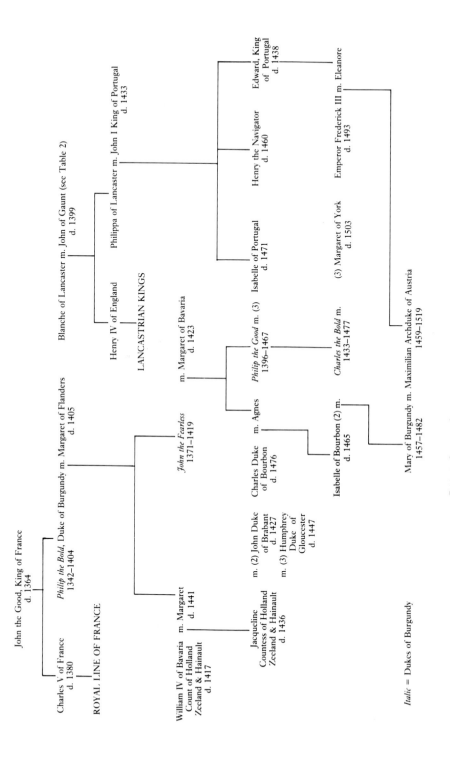

Table 3   Selected Genealogy of the Valois Dukes of Burgundy

John the Good, King of France
d. 1364

Charles V of France
d. 1380

Philip the Bold, Duke of Burgundy m. Margaret of Flanders
1342–1404   d. 1405

ROYAL LINE OF FRANCE

Blanche of Lancaster m. John of Gaunt (see Table 2)
d. 1399

Philippa of Lancaster m. John I King of Portugal
d. 1433

Henry IV of England

LANCASTRIAN KINGS

John the Fearless
1371–1419

William IV of Bavaria   m. Margaret
Count of Holland   d. 1441
Zeeland & Hainault
d. 1417

m. Margaret of Bavaria
d. 1423

Edward, King
of Portugal
d. 1438

Henry the Navigator
d. 1460

m. Agnes

Charles Duke
of Bourbon
d. 1476

Isabelle of Portugal   *Philip the Good* m. (3)
d. 1471   1396–1467

Emperor Frederick III m. Eleanore
d. 1493

Jacqueline
Countess of Holland
Zeeland & Hainault
d. 1436

m. (2) John Duke
of Brabant
d. 1427
m. (3) Humphrey
Duke of
Gloucester
d. 1447

Isabelle of Bourbon (2) m.
d. 1465

Charles the Bold m.
1433–1477

(3) Margaret of York
d. 1503

Mary of Burgundy m. Maximilian Archduke of Austria
1457–1482   1459–1519

Italic = Dukes of Burgundy

economic and marriage settlements. He should have been able to benefit from the situation yet, ultimately, not only did he have to pay a high price for the Burgundian marriage, but it almost cost him his throne.

By the end of 1466 Margaret's marriage had become a focus for domestic rivalries between the Woodvilles and Warwick. A new English team was appointed to deal with Burgundy and this time it was headed by the queen's eldest brother Anthony, Lord Scales. In the meantime Warwick continued to deal with the French match. Throughout 1467 the rival embassies were at work. In spring a French embassy was in London and an English embassy was in Bruges. In June Edward sent Warwick to France at the head of a large delegation of three hundred men to discuss Louis' proposals and draw up a treaty. The Anglo-French conference at La Bouille near Rouen was a very elaborate affair, Louis providing splendid entertainments and showering the English lords with gifts. Warwick received a gold cup encrusted with gems and he was presented with the keys of Honfleur which he was to use to his advantage in 1470. A wide-ranging treaty covering dynastic, political and economic matters was discussed and two marriage alliances were proposed: the first between Margaret and Philip of Bresse and the second between Richard of Gloucester and Jeanne, Louis' younger daughter. With Jeanne went a secret promise that France would help Richard to obtain Holland, Zeeland and Brabant from the defeated and dismembered Burgundy. This proposal would have reminded the English of the war fought by Humphrey, Duke of Gloucester a generation earlier.[15] Louis also undertook to bear all the costs of Margaret's wedding, even including the provision of the bride's dowry, and he offered Edward a substantial French pension. Moreover, recognising the urgency of the economic problems which troubled the relations between England and Burgundy, Louis made attractive trading concessions for English merchants in France.

Warwick was well satisfied with these generous terms and Louis was confident in the outcome of the conference of La Bouille. He had great faith in Warwick's power in England and in his influence over Edward, an influence persistently exaggerated by French commentators like Commynes who wrote that 'Warwick was like a father to Edward.'[16] Yet even while Warwick was negotiating in France his influence was waning in England. His brother and ally, George Neville, Archbishop of York, was abruptly dismissed from his post as Chancellor and at the same time the Anglo-Burgundian negotiators were pressing ahead with their treaty both in England and in the Low Countries. Early in June the Burgundian presence in England was increased on a grand scale by the arrival of Anthony, Count of La Roche. Known as the 'Grand Bastard of Burgundy', he was one of the many half-brothers of Count Charles. He came to London as the protagonist in a magnificent tournament which had been arranged at Smithfield. It seemed almost as if Warwick's delegation to La Bouille had been engineered to ensure his absence from England at a time of great honour for the Woodvilles.

The role played by the tournament in the context of the Anglo-Burgundian marriage negotiations is difficult to assess but it can be seen as a Woodville enterprise.[17] Their support for the tournament indicated their strong support for the marriage as well. It was reported that the whole tournament was inspired by the queen and her ladies (who included Margaret, perhaps taking measures to hasten her marriage settlement). It seems that following a rather wet weekend at Sheen, the royal ladies had composed a chivalrous petition to Anthony, Lord Scales, beseeching him to defend their honour against an unknown knight. In a preface, which he wrote later, Anthony Woodville gave his own reasons for taking part in tournaments:

> Tournaments were for the augmentacion of Knyghthode & recommendacion of nobley; also for the gloriouse scool & study of Armes & for the vailliance thereof . . . and for to voide slewthfulnes of tyme loste and to obeye & please my feire lady.[18]

The 'feire ladyes' were an integral part of the tournament which was only truly chivalrous when it was fought in their name and in their presence. There is, alas, no evidence that Margaret was at Smithfield nor that she was particularly interested in jousts and tournaments, but it may not be entirely coincidental that the two greatest tournaments of the age, the Smithfield tournament and the Bruges tournament, were both associated with her marriage. The tournament was, officially at least, quite separate from the marriage negotiations, though the Bishop of Salisbury, one of Edward's chief diplomats, provided his London house in Fleet Street and his country house in Chelsea as hotels for the Count of La Roche and his retinue. Popular opinion certainly saw a connection between the marriage and the tournament. Edward Hall, writing almost a century later, claimed that the count openly contracted with the Lady Margaret and presented her with a rich and costly jewel in the name of his half-brother Charles.[19]

The tournament was regarded by the court as an opportunity for display. It would impress the City of London and the nobility with the authority and splendour of the new Yorkist monarchy. Edward appreciated lavish ceremonial and glorified in military prowess, although unlike Charles, he did not take much part in the jousts himself. Indeed the Yorkist propaganda of 1467 was so successful that the Smithfield Tournament became a model for future tournaments. Its procedures were carefully copied not only in 1477 at the jousts honouring the marriage of Richard, Duke of York, Edward's second son, to the Mowbray heiress but also at the great Tudor tournaments in the reigns of Henry VII and Henry VIII.[20]

Both the leading protagonists of the tournament were regarded as paragons of their age. Anthony, Count of La Roche, was accorded a great position at the Burgundian court and led the ducal armies into battle. Anthony Woodville's father, Lord Rivers, had a lasting reputation as a jouster. He had taken part in the 1440 tournament at Smithfield where he had conducted himself with honour against a knight from Spain. Both the Count of La Roche and Lord Scales were typical of the late fifteenth century aristocracy, a peculiar blend of the medieval knight and the renaissance prince. These men saw themselves in the context of medieval chivalry, loyal to their lords, serving them in peace and war, faithful and obedient sons of the church, zealous to set forth on crusades, and above all as the honourable knights of fair ladies, prepared to defend their honour against all-comers. But they were also men of the quattrocento, learned and well educated patrons of the arts, shrewd and aggressive politicians maintaining large estates and followed by a powerful coterie of tenants, officials and annuitants. Equally the noblewomen were both the remote and idealised ladies of the ballads and the practical administrators and managers who ran their estates in the absence of their lords. The late medieval tournament was the perfect theatre for the demonstration of chivalry and political power.

The king attended the tournament in person and he gave a ceremonial banquet at the Mercers' Guildhall on the second day of the joust. George of Clarence was present bearing one of Anthony Woodville's great helms in the opening processions. It was not all pomp and show however, the fighting was very fierce with courage and honour being put to the test. Count Anthony's horse was killed under him and the fighting on foot in the mêlée was so ferocious that the king had to terminate the struggle shouting 'whoa'.[21] Though precisely how splendid and magnificent the whole affair really was is thrown into doubt by Edward Hall's comment that the 'Lord Bastard was somewhat dim of sight.'[22] On the whole the English commentators judged that Lord Scales had the advantage over the Count of La Roche.

All this excitement was dramatically cut short when the news arrived in England that the old Duke Philip had expired at Bruges. With considerable haste all the Burgundian nobles returned home for the funeral. By this time it was becoming clear that Edward had decided to marry his sister to Charles, now the Duke of Burgundy and thus an even more eligible match. The French embassy which arrived in London at the end of June was shown only the barest essentials of royal courtesy. After receiving them on their arrival, the king withdrew to Windsor leaving Warwick to entertain them and he only met them again, very briefly, on their departure. The royal gifts to the ambassadors were considered paltry in comparison with those which were given by Louis at La Bouille and, when the French embassy had departed, Warwick, feeling that his own honour had been slighted, retired to his estates.[23]

During the late summer of 1467 the commitment towards Burgundy became more and more obvious. Another delegation was sent to Brussels in September under the leadership of Lord Rivers, Lord Scales and the Bishop of Salisbury. The working members of the English team included the king's private secretary, William Hatcliffe, Thomas Vaughan, Treasurer of the Chamber and three other key officials; Thomas Kent, Henry Sharp and John Russel.[24] They were instructed to deal with three treaties, the marriage treaty, a trade treaty and an alliance of friendship. As a gesture of goodwill the economic statutes of 1464 and 1465 which prohibited the import of Burgundian manufactures into England were annulled, even though most of the Burgundian protectionist legislation against England remained in force. This situation brought protests from merchants in both London and Burgundy and riots in the Low Countries were exacerbated by political agitation over the accession of Duke Charles. On 1 July the new duke had to flee from rebels in Ghent, barely escaping with his daughter and his treasure.[25]

These troubles distracted Charles from the English marriage but he too assembled a powerful team to negotiate on his behalf. Now that he had become the Duke of Burgundy his demands were more exacting and Edward found

Anthony Woodville, Earl Rivers, presenting his translation of Christine de Pisan's 'Dictes and Sayings of the Philosophers', printed by William Caxton, to King Edward IV, who is attended by Edward, Prince of Wales and Queen Elizabeth

himself paying dearly for Margaret's marriage. It is difficult to understand why he was prepared to pay such a high price and why he discarded all considerations of a French marriage. Ultimately Edward's preference for the Burgundian marriage seems to have been grounded in the traditional English hostility towards France. In spite of all the seductions of Louis XI, the young Edward still preferred the old anti-French policies. All the English alliances of 1467–8, with Castile, with Brittany and earlier with Don Pedro, were part of a diplomatic offensive against France. This hostile policy had long been favoured by the Yorkists and it was apparently also backed by the Woodvilles.[26] It found a wide degree of popular support both in London and in the country at large. Moreover as long as Louis gave any support to the Lancastrian queen and her son, no Yorkist usurper was likely to agree to an alliance with France.

In October 1467 Edward at last made his decision public and Margaret appeared before the great council at Kingston-upon-Thames to give her formal consent to her marriage with Charles.[27] Her personal appearance at the council meeting indicates the active interest that she was taking in her own marriage. Following her declaration of consent, negotiations moved on to the highest level and Charles invited his mother, the Dowager Duchess Isabelle, to take responsibility for the final marriage treaty which would be based on the treaty drawn up for Isabelle's own marriage to Philip in 1429.

Yet even after this there was to be a further delay of eight months. This was partly due to the complicated nature of the negotiations. The new Anglo-Burgundian alliance covered mutual defence, trade, currency exchange, fishing problems, the movement of pilgrims and travellers as well as the marriage itself. Questions concerning the trade in arms and the export of English cloth were left unsolved, to be dealt with at another conference due to meet at Bruges in January 1469. Problems over the exchange rates were also found to be too difficult to be settled quickly and they too were set aside for the time being. Also most of the negotiations took place in Brussels necessitating several adjournments to allow the English envoys time to consult the king. The marriage treaty and the Anglo-Burgundian alliance were finally signed and ratified in Brussels in February 1468 and in London a month later.[28]

Although the treaty had followed the 1429 precedents closely, it was, in several respects, much more favourable to the Burgundians than the earlier treaty between Burgundy and Portugal had been. Margaret's rights of collateral inheritance in England were preserved. The Yorkists with their own claim to the throne based on two Mortimer heiresses could hardly deny Margaret's rights of inheritance. There were further advantages to Burgundy in the dowry arrangements. If Isabelle had died within a year of her marriage, her whole dowry and all her jewels would have been returned to Portugal. In Margaret's case only the jewels would be returned, the dowry would be kept by the Burgundian duke.

The dowry settlement was the most important element in any marriage treaty. It was a question of honour both for the bride and groom. The provision of dowries had first claim on a father's pocket and, since Margaret was his only unmarried sister, she had the same claim on her brother Edward. The dower which the bridegroom settled upon his wife was dependent upon the payment of the dowry, and a dowry payable over several years created a link between the two families which would guarantee financial and economic cooperation. Edward pledged himself to provide a large dowry of 200,000 crowns, a quarter of this was to be paid before the wedding, a quarter by the first anniversary and the rest by the second anniversary. The bridal dower which matched this included the cities of Malines, Oudenaarde and Dendermonde. The rents and aides from the dower property were estimated to reach 16,000 crowns a year and if they should fall below that level the duke would make up the difference. The new duchess was promised an allowance of 22,000 livres a year for her normal expenses and an extra 4,000 livres for abnormal expenses. The order for the payment of the first part of the dowry was made by the king at Greenwich on 11 April 1468 and at about the same time a ring valued at £20 was bought and sent from Margaret to the duke.[29] This might offer some substance to Hall's story that Anthony, Count of La Roche, had presented Margaret with a ring from Count Charles during the tournament in June 1467, since it was customary for the groom to send the first ring.

Another delay was caused by the length of time it took to obtain a papal dispensation, necessary because Margaret and Charles were cousins of the fourth degree. Charles was responsible for obtaining the papal dispensation and Guillaume de Clugny, the papal notary in Flanders, travelled to Rome in October but he did not succeed in obtaining the dispensation until May of the following year. Louis made strong diplomatic efforts to block the dispensation and de Clugny only achieved the desired result after lengthy argument and costly bribery.[30] As soon as the dispensation arrived at Westminster, Edward announced in parliament that his sister Margaret was to marry 'oon of myghtyest Princes of the world that bereth no crown.'[31] At the same time he reminded parliament of his claims in France and declared his intention of enforcing these claims. He demanded and obtained aides from parliament for the marriage of his sister and his projected invasion of France.

Charles announced his forthcoming marriage to the estates general of all the provinces of the Low Countries and to the chapter of the Order of the Golden Fleece, both of which met at Bruges in May. He had obviously noted Earl Ralph's twenty-two children as well as the seven healthy children born to the Duchess Cecily, for he promoted the marriage as being in the best interests of the duchy and likely to produce more princes for the realm.[32] He ignored the infertility in the York and Mortimer lines but it was surely these genes, rather than any rumours of bad relations between Margaret and Charles the Bold, which would lead to Margaret's subsequent childlessness.

By May 1468 preparations were well underway to supply the princess with a suitable trousseau and entourage. Invitations went out to those fortunate enough to have been chosen to accompany the bride to Bruges and John Paston had received his summons from the king as early as 18 April.[33] All now seemed ready for the wedding to take place but there was a final delay while Edward raised the 50,000 crowns to cover the first dowry payment and the money needed to pay for the trousseau and the travelling expenses. The wedding was postponed twice, first to the 24 June and again to the 3 July. Edward had not found it easy to raise the dowry. The parliamentary aides were not immediately available so he had had to raise loans wherever he could. Rumour had it that some of the great nobles including Warwick refused to help. The parliamentary fifteenths and tenths were assigned to the merchants of the staple and to prominent citizens of London who furnished a bond of £13,000 and in addition the king was obliged to pledge some of the crown jewels to Hugh Brice, a London goldsmith.[34]

One of those who guaranteed the bond was Sir Thomas Cook, but before Margaret could leave the country his arrest had put his own financial position and the bond in jeopardy.[35] In June Edward's agents had arrested John Cornelius, servant of a well known Lancastrian, Sir Robert Whittingham, and he was found to be carrying a packet of incriminating letters from Lancastrian exiles to their friends in England. When he was tortured, he named many Lancastrian supporters including John Hawkins, one of Lord Wenlock's servants. He, in his turn, accused Sir Thomas Cook, a prominent citizen of London who had twice served as lord mayor. He was also well known at court where he was a royal supplier of tapestries and fine fabrics. In his own house he had valuable tapestries, one set depicting the 'Last Judgement' and the 'Passion of Our Lord' and another on the 'Life of Alexander'. These were valued at nearly £1,000 and were apparently coveted by the queen's mother, the formidable Lady Jacquetta.

The arrest of one so closely associated with the marriage bond provoked a scandal in the city and promised to cause yet another delay in the marriage arrangements. Margaret intervened personally and appealed to her brother, this time, it would seem, against the interests of the Woodvilles. Cook was released from prison, but his freedom was only temporary for 'as long as she [Margaret] was within the land'[36] and he was eventually to suffer both re-imprisonment and the pillaging of his property by Lord Rivers' men who carried off the coveted tapestries. Since several others involved in the affair including Cornelius and Hawkins were hung, perhaps Cook came off well after all. This sort of crisis hardly smoothed Margaret's path to her wedding.

The tithe from convocation had furnished the costs of Margaret's own apparel and her travelling expenses which were very generous.[37] Her trousseau included £1,000 worth of silks, £160 worth of gold, silver and gilt dishes and £100 worth of bedding, cushions and carpets. She received £900 in cash and a further £200 was paid directly to her steward Sir John Scott for 'her diet from London to Bruges.' Sir John, Comptroller of the royal household, was one of those who had been closely involved in the marriage negotiations. There is no mention at all in the English records of the golden coronet which is today in the treasury of the cathedral at Aachen.[38] The coronet is quite small, only about 12 cm in diameter and equally high; it seems to have been intended as a votive crown. It is trimmed with pearls and decorated with precious stones set into very finely wrought enamelled white roses. Alternating with the jewelled roses are red, green and white enamelled letters which spelt out 'Margaret of York', but some of the letters are

The votive coronet of Margaret

now missing. At the centre front there is a diamond cross with a great pearl above it set into a large white rose. Above the coronet rises a diadem of seven jewelled roses with smaller roses in between them. Along the lower edge are golden 'Cs' and 'Ms' entwined with lovers' knots. The coronet is a beautiful example of the jeweller's crafts and it was surely the most important part of all her regalia. It was carried in a fine leather case made specially for the occasion with the arms of Burgundy and England embossed on the lid. The presentation of a crown asserted the royal status claimed by the House of York. It may have been made earlier for the coronation of Edward IV and certainly the prominence of the white roses would indicate an English provenance. If so the initials and knots must have been added for this occasion. It is, however, equally possible that Charles presented the coronet to enhance the majesty of his bride. At the wedding Margaret is reported as wearing a coronet above her loosely flowing blonde hair. This votive coronet is a unique survivor and a significant witness to this important marriage alliance between England and Burgundy.

Not everyone though was pleased with the marriage alliance. Jehan de Waurin recorded that the wedding took place 'in spite of Louis XI, Warwick and nearly all the people of England.'[39] He was certainly right about Louis XI who had done all in his power to prevent the marriage. When he failed to secure his preferred Anglo-French marriage, he tried to prevent the issue of the papal dispensation and then to obstruct the loans being raised to pay for the dowry. He used his financial contacts in Milan to bring pressure on the Florentine bankers and he spread the word that Edward was a poor man who could not be expected to raise the money in time. He also increased his support for the deposed King Henry, and encouraged Jasper Tudor to invade Wales. When this too failed he spread slanderous stories about Margaret herself, which were willingly retold by Panicharola, the Milanese ambassador to the French Court. These rumours have been enthusiastically repeated by many more recent historians too.[40] Panicharola reported to the Duke of Milan that Duke Charles had himself been told 'of what more and more people now know' that Margaret was 'somewhat attached to love affairs and even, in the opinion of many, has had a son.' He also described Charles' reaction to the story, which sounds, if anything, rather mild for such a brutal man. Anyone repeating the story within the duchy was to be thrown at once into the nearest river. Aliprando, Panicharola's successor, repeated the tale in 1472 when he wrote to his master that 'all was not well between the King of England and the Duke of Burgundy . . . on account of the duchess who did not go to her husband a virgin.'

These stories seem to have originated in the court of France and they were perhaps the origin of a lengthy personal antagonism between Margaret and Louis XI. There is no evidence that the slanders had any substance. Indeed Margaret would appear to have been the very model of female propriety. Even Edward Hall, who stretched himself to the limit in hunting for unpleasant epithets for the wicked 'old Lady of Burgundy' who so plagued the first Tudor king, did not repeat these stories. Indeed in his account of her marriage Hall described the young Margaret as 'a fayre virgin of excellent beautie and yet more of womanhode than beautie and more of vertue than womanhode . . . not to be unworthy to match in matrimony with the greatest prince in the world.'[41]

On the other hand it was well known on the continent that Edward IV was notorious for his amorous adventures and also that Margaret's sister Anne, had taken a lover, Thomas St Leger, while her husband the Duke of Exeter, was living in exile. Anne's marriage was later annulled and she married St Leger. Louis could profitably equate Margaret with her sister and brother. Moreover, at the age of twenty-two, Margaret was considered to be rather old to be marrying for the first time and therefore unlikely to be still a virgin. The French king's efforts to prevent the marriage did not end with the purveyance of gossip. He may also have ordered French ships to waylay the fleet conveying the princess from England to Flanders. According to Jean de Haynin, the English crew told him that there was a skirmish at sea and they showed him a blue and red silk standard seized from the French.[42]

Apart from Louis' displeasure, there was some dissatisfaction in England too. The Earl of Warwick did not attend the council at Kingston when Margaret gave her consent and according to Calmette he refused to assist with the dowry. Margaret's marriage was regarded by contemporaries as a serious cause of friction between Edward and his 'kingmaker'. The king certainly made some efforts to conciliate his mighty cousin. At the end of 1467 Warwick was granted the wardship of Francis, Viscount Lovel and at the great council of January 1468, the two men appeared together in public, having apparently settled their differences.[43] Clarence also had good reasons to be displeased by his sister's marriage. Nothing had come of the earlier proposals for himself and within the year the aggrieved Clarence began to conspire with Warwick to marry his elder daughter and heiress.

As to 'the people of England' they too were not entirely pleased with the new Anglo-Burgundian treaty. Duke Charles continued to restrict English cloth imports and when the new exchange rate was finally fixed at Bruges in 1469 it was very unpopular. There were substantial numbers of Flemish immigrants in England who had arrived from Holland and Flanders during the 1440s and many of these had settled in Southwark. There were attacks upon them in the late summer of 1468 and again in 1469. The first riots involved John Poynings and William Ashford who had attended Margaret's wedding in the train of the Duchess of Norfolk, and they were accused of making contact with the Lancastrian exiles in Burgundy and of plotting on their return to attack the Flemings. The riots were in part due to English xenophobia but they also seem to have been provoked by the high prices charged in Bruges during the marriage ceremonies which may have inflamed the English guests who regarded the Flemish as profiteers. 'The Burgoners showed no more favour unto the Englishmen than they would to a Jew.'[44] How far these feelings were stirred up either by the French king or by Warwick, who was always very popular in the city of London, is a matter for conjecture.

In spite of the opposition at home and abroad and after all the delays, Margaret, at last, set out on her future life, leaving from the Royal Wardrobe on Saturday 18 June.[45] Warwick's approval was made public when Margaret rode behind him on a pillion through the streets of London. At St Paul's she made an offering 'with great devotion' and then progressed along Cheapside where she was greeted by the Lord Mayor and Aldermen, who presented her with a pair of

Margaret of York, c. 1468, portrait from the Louvre Museum

rich silver-gilt bowls, worth £100 in gold. Her procession crossed London Bridge where she spent the night with the court in residence at the abbey of Stratford on the south side of the Thames. After attending service on the Sunday, Margaret made her final farewells and then left, accompanied by her two younger brothers and a large retinue, to make a pilgrimage to the shrine of St Thomas à Becket. Edward impetuously decided to accompany Margaret and the whole royal party spent three days on the journey stopping at Dartford, Rochester and Sittingbourne *en route*. On the Thursday morning, accompanied by all her brothers, Warwick and the Earls of Shrewsbury and Northumberland, Margaret made her pilgrimage at Canterbury. The next day she embarked on the *New Ellen* at Margate and as soon as the wind and tide were favourable the fleet of about sixteen ships set sail. They included some of the largest English ships, the *St John* of Newcastle and the *Mary* of Salisbury. These large ships were needed not merely to carry over the vast entourage and all their horses and equipment, but were also essential to protect the wealthy passengers and their luxurious cargo from the threat of both the French and the pirates who infested the Channel.

Margaret's chief presenter was Anthony, Lord Scales.[46] With his own deep piety and interest in books and manuscripts he may well have been a pleasing personal choice for Margaret, but his presence there together with his youngest brother, Sir Edward Woodville, affirmed the queen's strong commitment to this marriage. Lord Scales was also travelling to Bruges to answer Count Anthony's challenge and he would play a leading role in the wedding tournament of the Golden Tree. Margaret's chamberlain was Lord Dacre, a close friend of Edward IV, who together with William Hatcliffe, another member of the wedding party, would visit Margaret on several future occasions as emissaries between the English king and his important sister.

Lord Wenlock was another leading member of the wedding party. No official notice had been taken of his servant's accusations that he was in touch with the Lancastrian exiles, and his presence on board was an indication of Warwick's approval since Wenlock was one of the earl's closest allies. The bridal retinue was augmented by many diplomats including Sir John Howard, John Russel, Sir Thomas Montgomery and Henry Sharp, all of whom had been involved in the negotiations and were now present to see the fulfilment of the contracts. The bride's ladies were headed by the beautiful Elizabeth Talbot, Duchess of Norfolk, who took with her her own large retinue.[47] Among the other ladies was Lady Willoughby, 'a lovely widow', whose husband had died fighting against Edward at the battle of Towton and whose son and grandson, Sir Richard and Sir Robert Welles, were to be executed for treason in 1470. There were more reliable Yorkists including the Lady Scrope, wife of Lord Scrope of Bolton, and a Neville relative, the Lady Clifford. A welcome addition to this highly political party were two of the royal jesters, John Lesaige and Richard l'Amoureux.[48]

The sea crossing took one and a half days and although it may not be true that they were attacked by the French, it is still most likely that Margaret and her ladies knelt on the deck in relief when they saw the church towers of Aardenburg and Sluis and knew that their journey was nearly over. The Channel had a fearful reputation for storms, shipwrecks, delays and piracy. The English fleet made port at Sluis at 6 o'clock on the evening of Saturday, 25 June. A most auspicious day for the arrival of an English princess since it was the anniversary of an English victory over the French fleet there in 1340.[49]

Simon de Lalaing, one of the ducal chamberlains, and the Bailiff of Sluis went out on a barge to greet Margaret,[50] with them went musicians playing trumpets and clarions. The whole of her reception had been very carefully prepared and from the moment of her arrival everything was done to honour and please the new duchess. While Margaret had been making her farewells in England, Duke Charles personally checked all the arrangements at Bruges, Sluis and Damme. He was in the area from 16 June and actually at Sluis on the day of her arrival. He then remained either at Sluis or Bruges for a further two weeks, an unusually static period in the life of such an active ruler who seldom remained in any one place, except with his armies, for more than a few days. Although he was in the vicinity the duke did not meet Margaret on her arrival, since this would have broken all the rules of court etiquette. He had deputed the Bishop of Utrecht and the Countess of Charney to meet Margaret on his behalf. The countess and the bishop were Charles' half-sister and half-brother, more of the old duke's many bastards. They were both politically important at the Burgundian court. David, the Bishop of Utrecht, had previously made contact with the House of York when he entertained Richard and George after Wakefield. He was also one of the most important bishops in the Burgundian church and a key figure in the Burgundian control of the northern Netherlands.

The whole of the small port of Sluis was *en fête* to welcome the English princess. By the time Margaret came ashore it was already dark and all the householders had been ordered to stand at their doors bearing flaming torches to light her way through the town. She was met at the Watergate by the chief burghers who presented her with a purse containing 12 gold marks. Wearing a crimson dress with a long train trimmed in black, a compliment to her new country since these were the Burgundian colours, she made her way through carpeted streets to the Market Place where the town house of the wealthy merchant Guy van Baenst had been appointed for her residence. Opposite the house a platform had been built and throughout the week she stayed at Sluis pageants were performed daily for her entertainment. There were more pageants at Damme and during her procession into Bruges. Every theme and detail of these displays had been carefully chosen for its symbolism and significance. For the most part they portrayed scenes of appropriate marriages selected from biblical, classical and historical sources such as the weddings of Ahasuerus, Paris and Clovis.

The symbolism of the subjects chosen for the pageants would not have been lost on Margaret or any of her contemporaries. The Jewish Esther had married King Ahasuerus and because of her influence over the king she was able to save the chosen people from destruction.[51] She was regarded as one of the most noble women in the Old Testament and in Margaret's case there was a further analogy in that Margaret, like Esther, was a foreign bride. Since the story of Esther stressed the bride's responsibilities both to her husband and to her own people, scenes from her history were often performed at great state weddings. They would be seen again in Burgundy when Joanna of Castile married Philip the Fair, Duke Charles' grandson, and in England when her sister Catherine of Aragon married Prince Arthur half a century later.[52] Margaret certainly never forgot her dual loyalties to her family and her husband. She would have justified her actions against Henry VII in terms of her moral obligation to her own people.

The same medieval mixture of religion, myth and politics was recognised in references to the legend of Troy, and regarded as particularly relevant to the marriage of Margaret of York. According to medieval historians Brutus, the grandson of Aeneas, had finally reached Albion which had been renamed Britain after him. He had founded a new city of Troy on the banks of the Thames but the name of this city was changed later during the rule of a chieftain called Lud who fought against Julius Caesar.[53] Thus Margaret came from the 'New Troy' or London, crossing the Channel on the *New Ellen*, arriving with her fleet at Sluis. The duke's great set of Brutus or Troy tapestries included the beautiful 'Ships' tapestry showing the Greek fleet in the waters outside Troy looking not unlike the English wedding fleet waiting in the harbours of Sluis.[54] Both Margaret and Charles exhibited a lasting interest in the story of Troy. In 1472 the magistracy of Bruges gave the duke another set of Troy tapestries commissioned from Pasquier Grenier, a gift intended both to delight their ruler and as a reminder of his marriage celebrations in their city. At about the same time, the first book ever to be printed in English was made at Bruges by the command of Margaret. It was a collection of the tales of Troy diplomatically chosen by William Caxton to catch the eye of the duchess.[55]

The legend of Jason was another example of the medieval talent for synthesising religious and classical stories and it too was particularly appropriate to the Burgundian court. Jason, the hero of the Argosy, had become merged with Gideon the shepherd hero of the Book of Judges.[56] Since the foundation of the Order of the Golden Fleece in 1430 the legend of the argonauts had been specially important in Burgundy. The Order of the Golden Fleece rivalled the English Order of the Garter and enhanced the prestige and status of the dukes themselves. Other rulers were offered membership of the order as signs of friendship and alliance. In 1467 Charles had invited Edward to join the order. The chain of the order decorated by a pendant in the form of a golden fleece hung around the necks of all the greatest men in the ducal domain and these knights in their brilliant robes escorted the bride into Bruges on her wedding day.

Some of the wedding pageants may have been chosen to echo the themes of the magnificent ducal tapestries which were on display in the palace at Bruges throughout the wedding.[57] Three themes, the story of Esther, the legend of Jason and the Golden Fleece, and the legend of Troy, were particularly prominent in the marriage celebrations and there were tapestries on each of these subjects in the ducal collection. The wedding pageants mirrored the tapestries and the tapestries in their turn mirrored the wedding. On the Esther tapestries, there was a scene of a wedding feast which was a replica of that being so busily prepared at Bruges while Margaret was entertained at Sluis.[58]

The day after her arrival Margaret received the two most important ladies of Burgundy, the Dowager Duchess Isabelle and the Lady Mary, Charles' eleven-

Isabelle of Portugal in middle age, by Rogier van der Wyden

year-old heiress. The old dowager must have been reminded of her own arrival at Sluis nearly forty years earlier when she had come from Portugal to marry Duke Philip. Isabelle had endured a much worse journey than Margaret. On the long voyage the fleet had been scattered by storms and some of the ships had taken refuge in English ports. Two of them had reached Sluis a full month before the ship bearing Isabelle herself had at last arrived, on Christmas Day 1429. As the sister of Henry the Navigator, Isabelle was, no doubt, well informed as to the hazards of sea travel, but she still needed to rest for two weeks before her triumphal entry into Bruges. Throughout her forty years as duchess, Isabelle played a significant role in Burgundian politics, although in the last years of Philip's reign she had been in semi-retirement. This was hardly surprising since, by 1468, Isabelle was almost seventy-years-old, but she remained very active, well able to take charge of the marriage negotiations and to receive important diplomatic embassies on behalf of her son. She was clearly pleased that her frequent suggestions for Charles to marry one of the daughters of Richard, Duke of York, had at last been fulfilled.

The first meeting of the dowager and Margaret had been carefully planned.[59] Isabelle and Mary arrived with Lord Ravenstein, Charles' cousin, and Jacques, Count of St Pol, one of the English queen's uncles. Margaret met Isabelle at the door of the house and they both knelt to each other for a long time, observing the full solemnity of the court etiquette in which Margaret had been so well drilled by the Queen of England. They embraced and 'stood still in communication for a tract of time.' The dowager then took Margaret 'very moderly with grett revrance' and led her into the house. The ladies dined in private and the dowager was well pleased with 'the sight of this lovely lady and pleased with her manners and virtues.'

With the dowager came the Lady Mary, Charles' only child and the greatest heiress in western Europe. Her baptism in 1457 had been a splendid affair, 'the greatest magnificence ever seen for a girl.'[60] The Dauphin Louis had been god-father to the child. Most of Mary's childhood was spent at the ducal castle of Ten Waele in Ghent under the care of the Lady Hallewijn, a cousin of the chronicler Commynes. Anne of Burgundy, later to become the wife of Lord Ravenstein, had been responsible for her education and the little girl was entertained by a private menagerie of monkeys and parrots which were sent to her by her grandmother, the Duchess Isabelle. At Brussels she enjoyed the Warende, a great deer park which surrounded the ducal palace, and she had grown up with a keen interest in animals, hunting and outdoor sports. Mary's meeting with her step-mother and her reactions to Margaret passed unrecorded, but judging by their lasting affection for each other, Mary was probably just as delighted with her new step-mother as was the dowager with her new daughter-in-law.

Although she is never described as a beauty, Margaret was a good looking and intelligent young woman. Only Jean de Haynin included a description of the bride in his account of the wedding.[61] He noted especially that she was tall 'like her brother Edward,' and since he was 6 foot 3 inches, Margaret may well have been very tall for a woman. Charles on the contrary was below average in height, even shorter than his father. Margaret was also slim with a very straight carriage, her face was oval with dark grey eyes and, added de Haynin, she had 'an air of intelligence and will.' Charles, thirteen years older than his bride, was 'stout, well grown and well knit with a clear dark complexion and a dark beard and hair.'[62] His contemporary sobriquet was 'le travaillant' for 'no other ruler worked as hard as he did'. Margaret met her future husband for the first time two days after her arrival. There are no reports of any secret earlier meetings usually so popular among fifteenth century chroniclers. Such tales would have been quite out of character for there was nothing frivolous or informal about the duke.

On the Monday after her arrival Duke Charles visited Margaret 'with twenty persons secretly.'[63] They exchanged 'reverent obeissance' and the duke then took her in his arms 'and he kissed her in open sight of all the people of both nations.' Foreigners frequently commented that the English ladies kissed freely and often, but on this occasion Duke Charles impressed even the English commentators. Each time he visited her while she was in Sluis he repeated the process and he also kissed all the other noble ladies and gentlewomen present. Their formal betrothal took place in the garden of the house of van Baenst. There was presumably no room in the house large enough to have contained all the company who had to witness this important event. The duke stated his intention to marry 'this noble lady' and Margaret declared that she 'had come for this cause and for no other.' Their hands were joined by the Bishop of Salisbury attended by the Bishops of Tournai and Utrecht and Margaret was then acclaimed as the Duchess of Burgundy.[64]

The new duchess remained in Sluis until the following Saturday and throughout her stay there were firework displays, 'castles of fire', pageants and music. Isabelle, Mary and Charles made several more visits and Lord Scales and the Bishop of Salisbury made at least one visit to the castle at Bruges to meet the ducal staff there. Time was needed for the transfer of the dowry and the final wedding preparations. The first instalment of the dowry was handed over to Charles' four receivers at Bruges on the morning of the marriage day. Chief of the receivers was Tommaso Portinari, who had also raised 41,000 crowns to cover the duke's own expenses for the wedding.[65] The delay also gave time for the Lancastrian exiles, the Dukes of Exeter and Somerset and their followers, who were ducal pensioners, to leave Bruges. They finally moved out on the day before Margaret's own entry into the city.[66]

A week after her arrival at Sluis the duchess was taken by barge up the river to Damme, the outport of Bruges.[67] Damme, like Bruges, had passed its peak as a trading port; the river was gradually silting up and already the larger ships had to unload their cargoes at Sluis. But the quays were still busy with luxury goods for Bruges, and the town had some very large merchant houses including the house of Eustace Weyts, the ducal steward, which had been prepared for Margaret's visit and where the dowager was waiting to welcome her. At Damme there were more gifts and presentations and the citizens, well informed of her interests, gave her a rich cope for her chapel. Once more she processed through carpeted streets and was entertained by tableaux vivants and the evening was passed with more fireworks and pageants.

The next morning, between 5 and 6 o'clock, Charles arrived at Damme and they were married in a private ceremony in a room in the house of Weyts, though tradition has it that they were married in the church of Our Lady where they attended High Mass afterwards. Immediately after Mass, the duke left for Bruges leaving for his new duchess the full honours of a Joyeuse Entrée into the city. This was the ceremonial entry accorded by all the cities and provinces of the Low Countries to their new rulers and there was a considerable rivalry among the cities to entertain and impress. On this occasion the corporation of Bruges and the ducal household had excelled themselves in preparing a stupendous reception for the English princess, and Margaret and her entourage were equally magnificently arrayed.[68]

The bride arrived at the gates of Bruges in a gilded litter draped with crimson cloth of gold and drawn by richly caparisoned, matching white horses. She wore a gown of white cloth of gold trimmed with white ermine and a cloak of crimson. Her hair was worn loose but 'honnourablement' wrote de La Marche since it was normally considered very improper for a lady to show her hair in public. On her head was a golden coronet. She was escorted by all the English lords, the great lords of Burgundy including the Knights of the Golden Fleece, and the heralds and kings of arms. Trumpeters, clarion and tambourine players and minstrels walked beside the bridal litter and alongside those carrying the other English ladies such as the Duchess of Norfolk. Archers and armed knights escorted the whole procession.

The new duchess was met at the gate of the Holy Cross by four more processions which welcomed her into the city and led her through the streets to the ducal palace. First came the procession of the city of Bruges itself, the mayor, the city magistrates and burghers all in sober black damask and followed by more musicians, minstrels and pages. They presented Margaret with a gold vase filled with gold pieces and with an enamelled statue of St Margaret in addition to the traditional gifts of candles and wine. The second procession represented the Burgundian church and included 'eight score Bishops and Abbots.' Six fine processional crosses soared over this entourage and the procession probably included the papal legate, Onofric, who had been invited to the Low Countries earlier that year by Charles to help him to settle his long standing dispute with the city of Liège.

The third and most magnificent procession was that of the merchants. There were so many of them and they were so colourful that the commentators became confused. An English writer identified seven groups apart from the English: Florentines, Venetians, Genoese, Luccans, Esterlings (Hansards), Spanish and Scots, adding that 'all were on horseback saving the Scots which were all on foot.' Waurin, however, found only four groups: the Florentines, Lombards (who may have included the Genoese and the Luccans), Hansards and Spanish. De Haynin thought there were Genoese present but admitted that he was not sure and thought that they might have been English. La Marche, writing much later, seems to have simply collected all the earlier lists together and made a synthesis of them all. The Florentines were certainly present, at least a hundred of them, dressed in the Florentine colours of red and green and led by the Medici agent, Tommaso Portinari. They gave Margaret four white coursers harnessed and saddled in blue and white which were also the colours of Burgundy. There were at least two other groups of Italian merchants demonstrating their continuing dominance of the trade of northern Europe. All the merchants were magnificent advertisements for their fine draperies, clad in silks, brocades, damasks and velvets, plain, figured and embroidered. Hansard merchants were also present and of course the well mounted English merchants were there in great numbers wearing violet livery. William Caxton, the dean of the Merchant Adventurers at Bruges, and soon to become a financial adviser, translator and printer for Margaret, probably headed the English contingent. The Spanish and Portuguese were also on horseback wearing liveries of crimson, violet and black. There were at least 500 merchants present and they were accompanied by their own retinues of pages, musicians and singers.

The last procession to join in was the delegation from the ducal household. Olivier de La Marche had his place here along with all the chamberlains, councillors, gentlemen of the court and ducal servants, all dressed in the Burgundian court liveries of purple and crimson and black. The whole cortège, now numbering about 1,500, wound its way through the streets of Bruges, which were decked with carpets and hung with banners and tapestries. The windows were garlanded with flowers and crammed with spectators who had paid up to a crown for a seat to watch the processional entry into the city. All the way from the city gate to the palace there was a series of pageants, 'the best I ever saw' wrote John Paston, and 'marvellously well done' added another. And so they should have been since more than seventy-five talented artists from all over the Low Countries were employed to prepare these and all the other decorations and displays for the ducal palace, for the banquets and for the tournament.

The themes of the ten pageants were mostly biblical: as well as Esther and Ahasuerus there were Adam and Eve, the Song of Solomon, the Psalms, Tobias and the Angel, the marriage of Moses and Thorbis and the marriage at Cana. Classical confusions included the marriage of Alexander and Cleopatra and feats of Hercules. Everywhere were the arms of England and Burgundy: the lion, the lily and the leopard and the devices of the duke and duchess. 'Je l'ay emprins', ('I have undertaken it') for the duke and 'bien en aviengne' ('may good ensue') which had been chosen for the duchess.

The whole affair was arranged by a committee headed by Olivier de La Marche and Jacques de Villiers, the ducal cup-bearer. La Marche had a considerable reputation for this type of work. He had first attracted attention by his spirited performance as a young girl at the great feast of the Pheasant at Lille in 1454. By 1468 he was considered to be an expert impresario for great court occasions. Under him he had a huge team of artists and officials. Craftsmen were brought in from all over the duchy. The Bruges team was headed by Jacques Daret, who had also worked on the Pheasant banquet and who had years of experience preparing displays for the meetings of the Order of the Golden Fleece. The highest paid artist at the marriage was Daniel de Rijke who, with the most famous painter present, Hugo van der Goes, had arrived with the team from Ghent. There were other groups from Antwerp, Ypres, Brussels and Tournai including painters, sculptors, carvers in wax, fine leather workers and jewelsmiths. Mechanical devices were displayed at the palace and during the banquets and they were masterpieces of ingenuity. They included a 41 foot tower inhabited by monkeys, wolves and bears which danced. Huizinga loftily condemned these entertainments as 'incredibly bad taste'[69] but they certainly provided ducal patronage for a wide range of craftsmen and artists.

Margaret's arrival in Bruges was so splendid that it has passed into folklore

Tommaso Portinari by Hans Memlinc. The Metropolitan Museum of Art

and is still re-enacted for tourists today, but in none of its re-enactments does it achieve anything approaching its original ostentatious pomp. However the original procession was marred by one factor upon which all the commentators were agreed. It poured with rain all day, storm clouds and heavy showers blew into Bruges from the North Sea. An English chronicler, more honest than some and doubtless with some patriotic satisfaction that such things happened abroad, wrote 'than the storme of the rayne came soo faste, I might nott wryght the certayne of the p'sentacions.'[70] However regardless of the weather the procession wound its way solemnly through the streets.

In spite of the rain Bruges provided one of the most elegant settings possible for such a royal reception. There were: 'many canals in the town and some 525 bridges over them. At least it is so reported, but I did not count all of them. It is also the custom in Flanders for noblemen and well born persons to live in the towns where there are many diversions and delights.'

It was 'a large and beautiful city rich in merchandise' where the great merchants resided in 'princely houses in which are many vaulted rooms.'[71] In 1468 Bruges was still the greatest cloth market, commercial exchange and banking centre north of the Alps. The proud splendour of the merchant delegations which greeted Margaret on that wet July day showed the pre-eminence of business and trade in the city which was also a centre for all sorts of manufactories: armourers, leatherworkers, goldsmiths, jewellers and book-makers all had their workshops in Bruges. Hans Memlinc and Petrus Christus were among the many famous artists working in the city and the studios continued the vigorous tradition of great Flemish art which had reached a peak with Jan and Hubert van Eyck in the 1440s. Since it was one of the principal ducal residences, the surrounding countryside was full of the castles and hunting grounds of the wealthy Flemish and Burgundian nobility. As a main centre of the court it was famous throughout Europe for its high standard of living, elegant style and fine taste.

Escorted by this great procession and led by Lord Scales and Lord Ravenstein, Margaret reached the ducal palace entering through a decorated gateway, where red and white wine flowed freely from the bows of sculpted archers.[72] In the courtyard, sweet ippocras, a mixture of honey and mead, spurted from the breast of a golden pelican perched on an artificial tree. Inside the castle Margaret attended a private Mass and rested until dinner. Her rooms had been specially painted with marguerites and hung with tapestries showing the life of 'the good Lucresia', a popular model of wifely chastity.

The Bruges palace had been built and rebuilt many times during the four hundred years that it had been in use, first by the Counts of Flanders and later by the Dukes of Burgundy. For the chapter of the Order of the Golden Fleece which had assembled there in May, a large wooden hall had been erected in the courtyard and this was refurbished for the wedding. Parts of it were made in Brussels and brought by water to Bruges. It was a large construction, 140 feet long and 70 feet wide and it included two upper galleries, turrets and glass windows with gilded shutters. This was the golden age of gothic tapestries and for the wedding ceremonies the magnificent gold and silver Gideon and Clovis tapestries glowed on the walls. Above the dais hung dazzling verdure tapestries displaying the arms of Burgundy and within the palace thirty-two rooms had also been hung with more sets of tapestries. Made chiefly in Tournai, these great hangings were among the most treasured possessions of the Burgundian dukes. They were woven of silk and wool with gold and silver threads and were incredibly costly. One set alone might cost the equivalent of the total annual income of a noble landowner,[73] so that apart from kings and great dukes, few noblemen owned more than two or three pieces. The Burgundian collection was the richest in Europe as can be seen from the fragments which still survive scattered in art galleries and museums all over the world. In July 1468 the entire collection was concentrated at Bruges, a symbol of almost fabulous wealth and a magical experience for those fortunate enough to walk through the candlelit rooms of the palace.

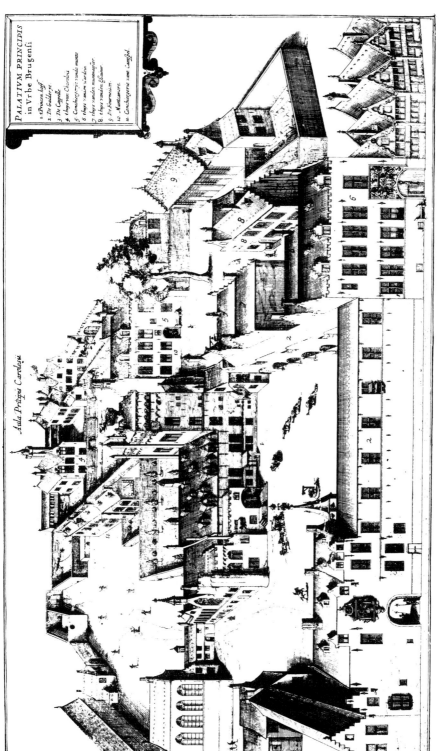

PALATIVM PRINCIPIS
in Vrbe Brugenſi
1 *Princen hof*
2 *De Galderye*
3 *De Capelle*
4 *thof van Chirsdes*
5 *Conchiergerye vande munte*
6 *thof van de munte*
7 *thof vande muntmeester*
8 *thof vande ghiſeur*
9 *De boomeester*
10 *Muntcamer*
11 *Conchiergerye vande Canſph.*

Aula Prĩcipis Caroliₐ

The ducal palace at Bruges in the mid-seventeenth century

For the banquets, the roof of the wooden hall had been draped in blue and white and the high table was splendid in purple, black and gold. Illumination was by an elaborate system of candelabra and mirrors arranged by the lighting expert Jean Scalkin. The ducal plate of gold, silver and copper dishes shone on elevated cupboards made specially for this occasion and decorated with pinnacles, each of them crowned with a 'unicorn's horn'. No wonder Edward Hall doubted the veracity of these reports. The duchess dined in state with the dowager and Mary, attended by all the most important members of the English entourage and of the Burgundian court. The remaining ladies were served in one of the galleries and musicians played in the other.

The arrival of the duchess at the first banquet was the signal for the beginning of nine days of continuous festivities. On every day there was a great feast at the palace.[74] Gilded and silvered swans, peacocks, unicorns bearing baskets of comfits, harts carrying panniers of oranges and roasts laid out on thirty vessels, each one representing one of the Duke's lordships; these were the sort of elaborate dishes set before the ducal guests. The entremets included mechanical surprises, plays and more pageants. The Lady Mary's dwarf, Madame de Beaugrand, rode in on a gilded lion, a pedlar pretended to sleep while monkeys stole his wares and gave out purses, brooches, laces and beads to the company, and a dromedary in Saracen style was ridden in by a wild man who threw coloured balls among the guests. As well as unicorns which were, it seems, readily available in Burgundy, there were giants and ogres, dragons and griffons to delight and astound the court. There were classical mimes of the deeds of Hercules and historical ones of the marriage of Clovis and, after each of the banquets, there was dancing and more music.

No wonder a tone of exhaustion crept into John Paston's letter home:

> As for the Duke's Court as of ladies and gentlewomen, knights, squires and gentlemen I heard never of none like to it save King Arthur's court . . . for of such gear and gold and pearl and stones they of the Duke's Court, neither gentlemen or gentlewomen they want none; for without that they have it by wishes, by my troth, I heard never of so great plenty as there is.

After dinner the duke made his first appearance in public on his wedding day, joining his new wife to attend the opening ceremonies for the tournament of the Golden Tree, held in the Market Place beneath the famous tower of the Bruges' Halle or market hall.[75] For this occasion the duke wore robes which were more the work of a goldsmith than a tailor. His golden gown was encrusted with diamonds, pearls and great jewels, 'and on his hede a blake hate one that hat a ballas called the ballas of Flanders, a marvellous riche jewell.' The English writer had never seen 'so great richez in soo littel a space.' His horse too was richly caparisoned and hung with golden bells. For this celebration the sober duke was transformed into a veritable knight of medieval tapestry and legend.[76]

The tournament of the Golden Tree arranged by Anthony, Count of La Roche, as a rejoinder to the Smithfield tournament, provided that mingling of chivalry and honour, courage and brutality which satisfied the desires of the court for entertainment, display and sport.[77] The presence of a 'Great Lady' made it an even more important occasion and it was Margaret who was now the centre of all attention as the first lady of the Burgundian court. As with all tournaments the action was woven around a fantasy composed specially for the occasion. The legend centred on the standard figures of medieval romance and included enslaved knights, evil dwarfs, ogres and mysterious strangers who inhabited gloomy forests. The tournament was at the bidding of the 'lady of the Hidden Ile', who had asked the Count of La Roche to undertake three great tasks on her behalf: to break one hundred and one spears or to have them broken, to make or to suffer one hundred and one sword-cuts and to decorate a Golden Tree with the arms of illustrious champions. The Golden Tree had been erected at the entry to the lists and as each knight entered his coat of arms was mounted on the tree. The costumes of all the participants were colourful and elaborate and the horses were covered in cloth of gold, with gold and silver harnesses and feathered plumes. Some of the noblemen entered the lists disguised as legendary heroes, as Black Knights or as Ancient Knights. Some arrived concealed within decorated pavilions, such as Anthony of Luxembourg who entered chained within a black castle from which he could only be released with a golden key when the ladies gave their approval. The pages wore harlequin costumes and carried shields of green and gold, crimson and silver. It was a great theatrical entertainment and the market place of Bruges was a kaleidoscope of colour and drama.

In spite of all the pageantry when the fighting began it was truly fierce and dangerous and Duke Charles did not hesitate to participate himself. The unfortunate Count of La Roche broke a leg, and was still receiving treatment from the doctor six months later. There were many great 'buffets' and the cries of wounded knights filled the air. Margaret was apparently greatly alarmed and she waved her handkerchief to persuade Charles, who was in the thick of the fighting, to unhelm and stop the fray.

The jousts, banquets and entertainments continued unabated for nine days. Each day there were more fantasies and all the events were attended by the duke and duchess personally. Sir Edward Woodville was declared the prince of the Tournay and the Lord d'Argueil, a brother of the Prince of Orange, was judged to be the prince of the Joust, a diplomatic selection which would have pleased the English queen and satisfied the honour of both Burgundy and England. The festivities finally came to an end on 13 July when Charles left for Zeeland and Holland. The English guests took their leave and the Burgundian nobles and clerics returned home. Among the latter was Jean de Haynin who hurried back to his castle at Bavay and five days later sat down to write his account of the wedding, which is certainly the liveliest and freshest of all the reports which have survived.[78]

Margaret was now duchess of the mightiest and richest duchy in Europe. Her marriage celebrations had shown the opulence of the court and the imagination of the artists. It was a situation to please even the most ambitious child of Richard, Duke of York. With her intelligence and the court experience she had acquired during the past eight years she was well fitted to play an effective role in Burgundian affairs. As Duchess of Burgundy, Margaret would find ample scope to develop her political and administrative talents. When the duke left Bruges, she set forth on a series of journeys around the Low Countries to enable her to get to know her new homeland.

However Charles had not married Margaret because he sought a partner in government, far from it. The main significance of the wedding for him was the procurement of an English alliance against France. Louis XI had not been able to prevent the marriage but he was to be more successful in neutralising its threat to France. During the next nine years Margaret received an education in European politics which went far beyond the insular feuds of the English court.

3 The Duchess of Burgundy

'One of the greatest ladies in the world'

Duchess of Burgundy and of Lotharingia, of Brabant, Limbourg, Luxembourg and Guelders, Countess of Flanders and of Artois, of Burgundy, of Hainault, Holland, Zeeland, Namur and Zutphen, Marchioness of the Holy Roman Empire, Lady of Friesland and of Salins and Malines etc., the list of Margaret's new titles was a long one.[1] These honours represented one of the most extensive and valuable collections of territory in medieval Europe. Not as large as the Empire, nor as consolidated as the kingdoms of England and France, yet the Valois Duchy of Burgundy rivalled and frequently outshone the power and influence of its European neighbours. Philip the Good had died one of the greatest princes of his era and certainly the richest. His personal treasure amounted to 400,000 crowns.[2] In size the Burgundian lands were equivalent to Portugal or England and Wales, but they accommodated a much more diverse collection of peoples, resources and industries. The languages of the duchies ranged from French to German and the ducal government was conducted in French, Dutch and German. The population was not large when compared with France or England, there were only about two and a half million people in the northern lands between Friesland and Picardy, but the density of population in Flanders and Brabant was the greatest in northern Europe.[3]

Although Burgundy was the creation of a series of historical chances and was really only secure when its neighbours were disunited and weak, there were some strong elements of cohesion within the Valois duchy. The duke's possessions snaked across the most important trade routes of Europe from the Zuider Zee to Lake Geneva, a distance of 500 miles. Although the whole of the Rhine–Maas routes were never completely controlled by the dukes, Burgundian merchants and their associates dominated all its trade from the wines, spices and olives of the south to the wool, fish and furs of the north. The waterways connecting Basle and Strasbourg with Bruges and Antwerp spawned a collection of vigorous and enterprising cities, and it was the same along the overland route from Bruges through Ghent and Brussels to Cologne and from Dijon and Nancy through Luxembourg to Liège. The cities which transmitted the trade were also famous for their fine craftsmanship and manufactures. The large and beautiful town halls of Bruges, Brussels, Ghent and Louvain, all built within the Burgundian period, still bear witness to the wealth and vigour of these cities under Valois rule.

With almost a third of their population in the towns, the Burgundian dukes ruled over the largest urban population in Europe. The urbanisation of the Low Countries was only surpassed by some of the Italian cities, but none of these were united within such a large and powerful state. The great cities often found themselves at odds with their dukes and they defended their independent rights jealously and fiercely. The citizens of Ghent and Bruges complained that they were expected to provide an unlimited resource of men and money to foster ducal ambitions abroad. The dukes retorted that these cities existed primarily to satisfy the needs of their lord and that all the ducal policies were designed to preserve the prosperity of the whole of their estates. Of all the ducal cities, Bruges was unique as the commercial and financial centre of northern Europe. Coming from London to Bruges in the summer of 1468 Margaret must have been immediately struck by the international nature of the ducal city. The lavish and ostentatious merchant participation in her marriage procession brought the new duchess face to face with the importance of trade and commerce in Burgundy. It was a lesson that would be not lost on the daughter of Richard of York and the sister of Edward IV, who both appreciated the value of a thriving merchant community. Her disembarkation at Sluis must have also made her aware of the great difference between London and Bruges as far as shipping was concerned. From her mother's house at Baynard's Castle, Margaret would have been able to see the largest galleys coming and going from their quays. London was directly accessible to trading ships of all sizes. It was only the delays caused by tides and currents and a wish to reduce the time spent on board that induced passengers like Margaret to embark at Margate rather than London Bridge. On the other hand, Bruges was totally inaccessible to the larger seagoing ships and even Damme, the foreport of Bruges, had failed to keep a deep enough channel open. As a result, Sluis, Veer, Vlissingen, Middelburg and Antwerp were becoming the main ports in the busy Walcheren roads where shipping arrived from all over the known world, from the Baltic, the British Isles, Spain, Portugal and the Mediterranean. The great rivers, the Rhine, Scheldt, Maas and Lys brought in cargoes from the vast hinterlands of northern Europe to be unloaded and reshipped. Bruges was no longer the centre of this shipping but it remained the headquarters of all the merchant traders and the centre of financial exchange. Because of this sovereign position in European trade, all kinds of foreign delicacies were readily available in Bruges, so that the banquets of the Burgundian court were famous for their lavish and various provisions. Margaret and Charles were both personally abstemious and, unlike her brother Edward, Margaret was never noted for any excesses in food and drink. But she must have been interested by the variety of exotic foods which were now regularly available to her; pomegranates, oranges, dates, figs, raisins, olives, sugar and spices would have become familiar items at the duchess' table. Moreover there were other desirable luxuries on offer in Bruges: silks, velvets, damasks and embroideries, gilded retables, reliquaries of the finest crystal, silver and gold vessels and crosses for her chapel and the most magnificent tapestries and wall-hangings for her chambers. Above all other luxuries, the duchess found a lasting delight in the magnificent books which were available from the master craftsmen of Bruges, Ghent and Brussels and she became an ardent and discerning collector.[4]

Bruges was not, however, the capital of the court and government in the same way that London was; indeed the ducal palace was almost dwarfed by the great civic buildings such as the town hall and the market hall. Margaret would have soon learned that the government was much more widely dispersed across the duchy than was the case in England. As a female member of the English court, Margaret had passed most of her time in a small area between Greenwich, London, Westminster, Windsor and Sheen. As Duchess of Burgundy she would be expected to travel much greater distances, to make regular progresses through Flanders, Brabant, Hainault and Artois, and even to venture north over the great rivers into Holland and Zeeland. The ducal palaces at Brussels, Ghent and Hesdin were all larger than that at Bruges while in size and opulence they rivalled the royal residences of the Kings of England.

The duchess was to play an active role in the Burgundian court and government, not merely as the focus of the ducal household but also as an administrator and as the duke's representative. Traditionally Burgundian duchesses had complemented and assisted the work of their husbands.[5] All Margaret's predecessors had cooperated in the growth and development of the duchy. The county of Flanders with its various appanages had come to the first Valois duke, Philip the Bold, through his marriage to the heiress Margaret of Flanders. The first duchess had continued to govern and administer her provinces, frequently staying in the north while her husband was at Dijon or Paris. The second duchess, Margaret of Bavaria, maintained the duchy in the crisis caused by the murder of her husband, John the Fearless, and Charles' own mother the third duchess, Isabelle of Portugal, had worked closely with Chancellor Rolin in the administration of the duchy. Isabelle acted as regent and also played an important diplomatic role heading the Burgundian delegation at the conference of Gravelines in 1438 and at Utrecht in 1453.[6] She had never hesitated in putting forward her own policies, urging a Yorkist marriage for her son in spite of her husband's opposition, and encouraging the duke to undertake a crusade against the Moors, a proposition dear to her Portuguese heart.

Since no ruler was more industrious than Duke Charles, Margaret was also expected to be incessantly active and there are no signs of the temporary bursts of indolence which were such a characteristic of her brother Edward. Her function in the government of Burgundy was not as clear as Isabelle's had been, due probably to the fact that Charles, unlike his father, avoided the company of women and had little appreciation of their usefulness.[7] During the first three years of her married life, Margaret's role in the government of Burgundy appears to have been negligible, but by 1472 she was actively concerned with affairs of state. In the early years she had to familiarise herself with the Burgundian system of government as well as win the trust of the duke and his officials. Also perhaps she was expected to concentrate on her first duty and on her primary function, in which she was to be totally unsuccessful.

Charles had recommended Margaret to his subjects as 'bien taillée pour avoir

Charles the Bold, by Rogier van der Weyden

generation de prince du pays,' (well built for the production of an heir).[8] During the first few years of her marriage, Margaret doubtless expected to become pregnant. No contemporary comments, not even from the gossipy Milanese ambassadors, have survived on the question of Margaret's sterility, though it must have been a source of speculation. Perhaps the tales about her earlier unchastity and the rumours of Charles' homosexuality are remnants of the gossip which must have circulated around the courts of Europe as Margaret continued to be childless.[9] There were certainly no signs of infertility on the duke's side. Apart from his sole legitimate daughter he had at least two illegitimate children, John and Pierson of Burgundy.[10] It seems Margaret was anxious about her infertility as she made several pilgrimages to shrines known to help in such cases, visiting the miraculous Black Virgin of Halle and the shrine at the Val Notre Dame Abbey near Huy.[11] From February to March 1473, Margaret stayed at the well-known country hospice of St Josse ten Noode in the forest of Soignes. This delightful lodge close to Brussels, near the source of the River Maelbeek had been specially built by Duke Philip as a health resort and spa. The waters were considered to have curative properties and the wines made in the valley were reserved for the exclusive consumption of the sick since their medicinal properties were famous.[12] But in spite of all her retreats and pilgrimages, Margaret remained childless.

Both the duke and his duchess presumably accepted the situation as the will of God. There were no public signs of their anxiety. They seem to have considered that there was plenty of time to secure the dynasty and Charles could use his lack of a male heir as a factor in his negotiations with the emperor. The duke was certainly not any more cautious due to his lack of a male heir and he was to throw his life away at Nancy with all the abandon of a man whose dynastic future was totally secure. Nor are there any signs that Margaret's failure to produce the expected heir had any detrimental effect on the relationship between her and her husband.[13]

Margaret's status at the Burgundian court depended primarily on her relationship with her husband. While the relationships between rulers and their mighty subjects may be quantified in terms of land grants and annuities which arose out of economic and political necessities, simple human preferences and affections also played a large part. Richard, Duke of York's inability to build up a loyal noble following and Warwick's failure to remain on good terms with his cousin Edward were as much due to aspects of their personalities as to any policy differences. In Burgundian politics much rested on the character of the duke, and Charles' personality was vitally important to the nature of his court and government and to the position of Margaret, first as his wife and later as his widow.

The era of the Valois Dukes of Burgundy coincided with a great development in portraiture, and detailed descriptions of the appearance and character of Charles have come down to us from the brushes of great masters like Rogier van der Weyden and from the pens of the court chroniclers such as Chastellain, Molinet, Commynes and La Marche.[14] The superb portrait attributed to van der Weyden, which today hangs in Berlin, was painted when Charles was in his mid-twenties. It shows an introspective and serious young man of strong and even obdurate temperament. Charles' sensitively modelled face indicates vigour

Reliquary portraying Charles the Bold kneeling under the protection of St George, made by Gerard Loyet and given by the duke to the Cathedral of Liège

and vitality but it lacks the humour and vivacity which is so apparent in the same artist's portrait of Philip the Good. The plainness of his costume adorned only with the emblem of the Golden Fleece belies the descriptions of the duke as a gaudily bejewelled figure. Privately the duke dressed as soberly as he lived and he kept his golden tunics and jewelled hats for occasions which demanded great public display.[15] There are several other paintings of Charles and all reveal a man who took life very seriously and who would govern with great determination. The famous Liège reliquary made by Gerard Loyet of Bruges also shows the same solemn, dour face.[16] On his great seal engraved in 1468, Charles is depicted sporting a moustache, but on the effigy on his tomb at Bruges and on the nearly lifesize effigy erected by his son-in-law at Innsbruck, Charles is clean shaven. All the portraits match closely with Chastellain's description of the duke as 'strong, well grown and well knit'.[17] In the pen-portrait, which Chastellain wrote in about 1467, Charles' eyes were described as 'laughing expressive and angelically bright and when he was thinking his father seemed to come alive in them' perhaps a discreet courtier's reference to the duke's fiery temper.[18] Olivier de La Marche who knew Charles throughout his life wrote that he was:

> hot blooded, active and irritable and as a child always wanted his own way and resented correction. Nevertheless he was so sensible and understanding that he resisted his natural tendencies and as a young man there was no one more polite and even tempered.[19]

In a violent age, a ferocious temper was rather admired in a ruler; indeed Edward IV was criticised for being too affable. Charles drove all his staff and servants hard, he spared no one when he was angry, but neither did he spare himself and he worked hard at his duties. This is shown by the vast amount of material initialled by him or even written in his own crabbed gothic handwriting.[20] He was criticised by his peers in the Order of the Golden Fleece for his undue severity towards his servants, for being over zealous and for failing to curb his impatience when dealing with other rulers. Commynes, who deserted the service of Charles for Louis XI, attributed all Charles' great endeavours to his lust for fame and glory and his ardent desire to be remembered as a hero. Throughout his life Charles was surrounded with tapestries and books recalling the great heroes of myth and history: Hercules, Jason, Alexander, Pompey, Caesar and Hannibal. In his emulation of these he never showed the slightest signs of fear, an attribute which Commynes laid at the feet of the duke's overwhelming egotism and arrogance.[21]

Charles was a talented linguist, a good orator and musician. He was competent in French, Dutch, Italian, Portuguese and German. He knew some Latin, though he preferred to read the classics in translation, and he spoke enough English to address his English mercenaries in their own language, and perhaps also his wife. His eloquence was well known; in 1468 he addressed the Ghent delegates for two hours and he appreciated the orations of others, such as those of his close friend, the chancellor Hugonet.[22] The ducal chapel included a large choir, orchestra and organist. This was the great age of Burgundian music, Mass was sung every day and Charles took his musicians with him even on his military campaigns. He enjoyed singing having had some excellent teachers, including an Englishman called Robert Morton, but although he had a lot of musical knowledge, his voice was not considered pleasant.[23]

The duke's sense of his own worth was reflected in his close attention to etiquette. This sometimes led to grotesque situations such as at Trier, when he and the emperor stood in the pouring rain for half an hour, each with his hat in his hand, rather than accept precedence over the other.[24] This exaggerated deference to the rules of etiquette was a prerequisite for the whole existence of medieval hierarchies. To uphold their authority over rebellious subjects and to maintain their place in the order of European rulers as second only to the kings and the emperor, the Dukes of Burgundy needed all the props which ritual, tradition, ceremony and honour could offer. Margaret, nurtured in the strict ceremonial of Elizabeth Woodville's court would have understood the significance of all this and she maintained the authority of both herself and her lord with keen enthusiasm.

The new duchess would also have appreciated the efficiency and thoroughness of the ducal government. The duke's ability to raise larger sums in taxation than any of his predecessors was due to both the efficiency and severity of his administration. His severity often amounted to brutality as at Dinant and Liège where the cities were sacked and looted and the citizens butchered. During the sack of Nesle, a town which had dared to stand out against the ducal army, Charles applauded the ferocity of his men, declaring 'here is a fine spectacle, truly I have good butchers with me'.[25] He used terror only as a means of demonstrating his power, his armies were strictly disciplined and were not allowed to loot and pillage at will. In this respect his armies were better restrained than the French or Swiss who massacred and looted after the battles of Grandson and Murten. Charles was, however, often accused by his contemporaries of especial cruelty because he punished nobles as if they were ordinary criminals and took such a hard line against the cities such as Liège.

vne bonne pieche de Remanant. Et si fu
sabit si grand et si large quil se conuient
dessaux / pour tant que pour sa trop gra
de largesse et longeur. Il estoit contre sainte
pourete. De chastete z virginite. ix.e chap

hastete est vne vrtus
aimable et joyeuse qui
fait lame prochaine
a dieu et samblable as
angeles. amie de sain
tete. z subside de charite

Miniature of Margaret and Charles kneeling behind St Colette and St Francis. Copyright ACL Bruxelles

This solemn, hard-working and proud man must have pleased Margaret with his piety and his punctilious regard for the religious festivals. 'He swore neither by God nor by the saints, he held God in great fear and reverence'[26] and he expected his subjects to show the same fear and reverence towards himself. Margaret would also have appreciated his interest in books. Indeed there was little in his character that his wife could not admire. His pride and self-esteem were considered the proper signs of a princely character and she was well endowed with these characteristics herself. After his death, Margaret maintained and upheld his reputation and by remaining unmarried she kept his memory fresh in the public eye. Twenty years after his death she donated a great window portraying the duke to the church of St Rombout's in Malines, and she was no doubt influential in ensuring that the duke's eldest grandson, the future Emperor Charles V, was named after him.

But was Charles equally well pleased with the person and character of his latest wife? None of the surviving portraits of Margaret have the same vigour and mastery as the van der Weyden portrait of Charles. The anonymous portrait which belongs to the Louvre was painted about the time of her marriage, perhaps by someone in the studio of Simon Marmion of Tournai.[27] The identity of the sitter is made clear by the large necklace of red and white roses which alternate with 'Cs' and 'XXs' (which seem to be interlocking 'Ms') in red and golden enamel. And there are more references to Margaret within the painting including the small golden marguerite on her dark dress and a pearl brooch with a golden 'B' which hangs from her sober black headcloth. Her dress is rich but discreet, she wears the hennin or steeple headdress covered with a light veil, her sleeves are trimmed with ermine, her dress with a few rows of braid and on her hands she wears two simple rings. Her oval face is painted with little character and shows merely the fashionable high brow, broad-set eyes which are cautious and circumspect, a well shaped nose and mouth and a small chin. Her whole manner is reserved and withdrawn but there is a suggestion of determination and resolve and an air of refined melancholy which matches the mood of the more revealing van der Weyden portrait of Charles. This portrait of Margaret may have been commissioned by the duke as one half of a travelling diptych. The small size, it is only about 20 by 12 centimetres, would certainly support this theory. Since she is painted looking towards the right and her hands are clasped in prayer, the other half of the diptych may well have portrayed the Virgin and Child.

Of the other possible portraits of Margaret one, today in the Robert Lehman Collection of the Metropolitan Museum of Art in New York, is the most lively and direct and the most interesting of all from the point of view of the portraiture.[28] This young woman with the cool introspective eyes certainly accords well with all the contemporary descriptions that indicate that Margaret was an intelligent and energetic woman well able to look after her own and her family's interests. She is portrayed within the arch of a window which cuts across the top of her brocade hennin and, as in the Louvre painting, she does not look directly out of the picture. Her headcloth of black velvet matches her dress which is trimmed with ermine and she wears little jewellery, only a simple gold chain and a fine black cord. This portrait has been attributed to Petrus Christus

Portrait of a woman, possibly Margaret of York. The Metropolitan Museum of Art

or to a French artist working at the Burgundian court. The woman so soberly portrayed in this picture shows a considerable likeness to the portrait belonging to the Society of Antiquaries in London, and also to the figure of St Barbara in the *Mystic Marriage of St Catherine* by Hans Memlinc which is reputed to be an idealised portrait of Margaret. This last painting still hangs in St Jan's Hospital in Bruges for which it was originally commissioned. In this great triptych

Margaret, as a charming and elegant St Barbara, is carefully and appropriately studying a finely decorated book. St Barbara was the patron saint of gunners, miners and builders and was a popular figure in the paintings of the Low Countries, very often portrayed together with St Margaret. Mary of Burgundy appears in the same triptych as St Catherine. The London portrait shows Margaret fuller faced, and older and may be a copy of one which was painted about the time of her visit to England in 1480. All these portrayals have features in common with a further possible representation of Margaret which can be found in an intriguing painting now in the J. Paul Getty museum, the *Deposition* painted *c.* 1500 by an unknown Flemish artist after the style of the great Rogier van der Weyden. Margaret may be portrayed among the group on the right of the picture. Apart from the white rose and the marguerites at her belt (the implications of these are discussed in Chapter 6), the face of this holy woman has the features in common with all the paintings of Margaret: the firm mouth, straight nose, rather full cheeks and recessive chin.

There is a similarity between the other supposed portraits of Margaret and the well accepted Louvre painting and this also matches the best known miniatures of the princess. It is perhaps no coincidence that Marmion was a famous miniaturist and the Louvre portrait is in this style rather than in the freer, more realistic, humanistic style of Memlinc and van der Weyden. Among the miniatures, the most colourful appear in the opulently painted *Benois seront les Misèricordieux* (Blessed are the Merciful) which came from the workshop of Jean Dreux. In one of these she is accompanied by her patron saint, St Margaret.[29] There are indeed many miniatures portraying the duchess, one of the most beautiful appears in the Douce manuscript in the Bodleian Library, Oxford, where she kneels at prayer accompanied by her ladies.[30] There is another in a life of St Colette given to the convent of the Poor Clares at Ghent by the duchess which has remained there ever since.[31] On the last page of this manuscript there is a dedication in Margaret's own hand and her bold open scrawl shows a great contrast to the narrow pinched letters of her husband.

All these portraits and miniatures reveal the sort of image that Margaret chose to project to the world. Her favourite saints, St Barbara and St Margaret, were both martyrs of the early Christian church and their lives were well known in the medieval world through their prominence in the best selling lives of the saints, the *Golden Legend*. St Margaret was one of Joan of Arc's special voices and St Barbara was popular as the patron of builders and the new artillery troops which were an important feature of fifteenth century armies.[32] In most of the miniatures Margaret is shown at prayer, reading or on errands of charity and her demeanour is always serious and dignified.

However, there are representations which belie this very sombre image. One, showing Charles and Margaret together, is a fragment of a larger tapestry, probably made at Lille in about 1470.[33] Here they are enjoying a day's hunting. Margaret is wearing a blue and white gown and is turning towards the duke who wears a red coat and a plumed hat. He walks boldly forward bearing a heart on his right hand and carrying a falcon on his left. This scrap of material shows the lighter side of Burgundian court life and is a rare sign that Margaret, like her step-daughter, enjoyed hunting and falconry. Another hunting scene, portraying

Margaret together with Mary and Mary's husband Maximilian, is a drawing by Frank van der Beecke entitled *The Bear Hunt*. Here Margaret is riding side-saddle, her horse led by a groom. All these representations supplement the brief descriptions of Margaret provided by her contemporaries such as Jean de Haynin and Olivier de La Marche. The duchess is consistently portrayed as an intelligent, thoughtful young woman who took her responsibilities very seriously indeed, an ideal match for Charles.

Her relationship with her husband cannot have been entirely easy. Wielant commented on a certain amount of misogyny in Charles' character, probably a reaction against his father's notorious womanizing. It was said the duke was resolved to keep his household free from silly female influences, he preferred the company of his councillors, financiers and soldiers and he made a practice of always lodging the ladies of the court at some distance from his own household.[34] However, there is no evidence that Charles deliberately avoided his wife or that he disliked her. Most writers were sure that he had been very fond of Isabelle of Bourbon, although he had spent long periods away from her and he had been too busy to visit her during her long, fatal illness. The separate residences of the duke and duchess were chiefly a matter of convenience; only the very largest castles could accommodate their combined households. Furthermore the duke was almost always on the move while the duchess made regular progresses around the Low Countries. Considering all these factors, together with the duke's very energetic and personal style of government, it is hardly surprising that they spent so little time in each other's company.

In fact in the first seven years of their marriage the duke and duchess spent a total of one year together and, after 23 July 1475, they never met again because Charles was continually with his army in the Rhinelands.[35] During the first four years they met fairly regularly. They were together for twenty-one days in 1468, ninety-six days in 1469, one hundred and forty-five days in 1470 and fifty-five days in 1471. They celebrated three consecutive Christmases together between 1469 and 1471 but after December 1471 they were together for only thirty-two days. His attention to the duchess up to 1471 may have been motivated by his wish for an heir, but after her failure to conceive, his attendance may no longer have seemed necessary and he had other more pressing matters with which to deal. In spite of long periods of absence the duke showed every normal consideration to his wife. He was quick to visit her in 1472, after a fire at Maele had frightened her and destroyed much of her property.[36] He also made generous provision for her in spite of the fact that her brother Edward failed to fulfil his dowry obligations.

During her first year as duchess, Margaret became known at court, in the cities and provinces of the Low Countries. A fifteenth century ruler had to be seen by great numbers of their people and Margaret, as an extension of the duke, represented his power and upheld his glory as she progressed throughout the land. The very nature of the Burgundian state made the mobility of the ducal household an essential feature of government. Unlike the Kings of England and France, the Burgundian dukes were still itinerant rulers. Margaret's procession passing through the countryside and cities of the duchy was an important sign of ducal presence and government.

Margaret of York.
Society of Antiquaries
of London

Immediately after her marriage Margaret, accompanied by Mary, left Bruges and went via Ursel, Ghent, Dendermonde and Asse to Brussels, where she was received on 23 July. The two ladies spent August in the city and its environs, probably enjoying some hunting in the forest of Soignes, and then set off again visiting Aalst, Oudenaarde and Courtrai *en route* for Aire where Margaret arrived on 7 September. There she was taken seriously ill but was over the worst and convalescing by the end of the month. Was her illness the result of a miscarriage or merely exhaustion caused by her strenuous and exacting new life? In any case she stayed on at Aire until Christmas. Throughout all this time Charles was fully occupied with affairs of state, first on his visit to the north, then negotiating the treaty of Péronne with Louis XI and finally subduing the rebellion at Liège with the reluctant Louis still in his entourage.[37]

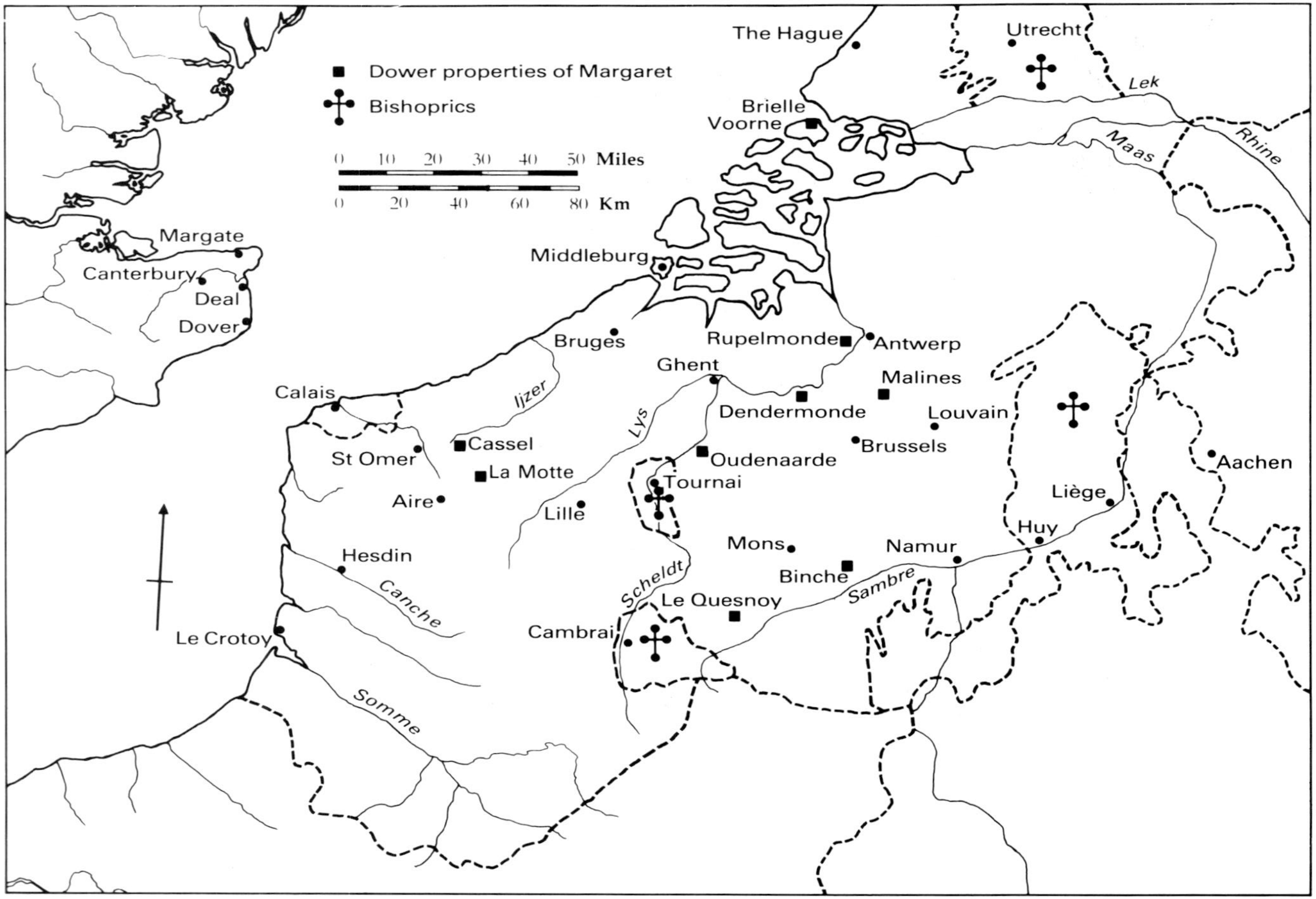
Dower properties of Margaret
Bishoprics
0 10 20 30 40 50 Miles
0 20 40 60 80 Km
The Hague
Utrecht
Lek
Rhine
Maas
Brielle
Voorne
Margate
Canterbury
Deal
Dover
Middleburg
Bruges
Rupelmonde
Antwerp
Ghent
Malines
Dendermonde
Louvain
Calais
Ijzer
Lys
Cassel
St Omer
La Motte
Brussels
Oudenaarde
Aachen
Tournai
Aire
Lille
Liège
Huy
Hesdin
Mons
Namur
Binche
Canche
Scheldt
Sambre
Le Quesnoy
Le Crotoy
Cambrai
Somme

The Burgundian Low Countries 1468–1503

Thus very soon after her marriage, Margaret became familiar with the life-style which was expected of the Duchess of Burgundy. During her eight and a half years as duchess, she was to undertake twenty-eight major journeys. She was always accompanied by a large retinue of soldiers, officials, servants and attendants and followed or preceded by cartloads of baggage. Each journey covered about 130 kilometres but was conducted at a gentle pace of 15 to 20 kilometres a day. She passed regularly through the heartlands of the Burgundian Netherlands. On a few occasions she ventured south to Boulogne and to Picardy as far as Le Crotoy at the mouth of the Somme.[38] Her visitations were planned with care each revolving around the great cities, the ducal palaces of Ghent, Brussels, Aire, Hesdin and Bruges and were timed to fit in with the major festivals of the church. Her dower towns were not particularly favoured. Oudenaarde hardly ever saw its duchess until after Charles died and Malines fared little better. Dendermonde, however, as a crossroads between Flanders and Brabant, was visited at least six times. The shorter stops *en route* between the larger palaces gave the duchess the opportunity to visit all the chief cities. At each of these she was welcomed with presentations of wine of honour and gifts, often bearing the city arms, and pageants, verses and orations by the literary guilds.

The journey of November 1470 was typical of many. Travelling at one of the worst times of year, when the heavy loam of Brabant was sodden due to the autumn rains, she left Brussels where she had spent most of the summer to join Charles at Hesdin for the Christmas celebration. Mary was with her and the two ladies rode out of Brussels on the 13th of the month. They probably went on horseback which, at a rate of only 15 kilometers a day, would be much more comfortable than the unsprung litters which were an alternative transport for ladies. Both Mary and Margaret were often presented with the hackneys or quiet horses, normally ridden by ladies. It took them sixteen days to reach Hesdin. On the way they visited the shrines at Alsemberg and Halle and the duchess made her first visit to Mons, the most important city in Hainault.[39] She was therefore accorded a grand reception and a Joyeuse Entrée. Mons was determined to rival the receptions already given for Margaret at Bruges, Ghent and Brussels and nothing was spared to make it a memorable occasion. Escorted by Lord Ravenstein, who often travelled with the duchess, the two ladies rode into Mons on a cold November evening. They wore warm black velvet gowns trimmed with fur and their white horses were caparisoned in cloth of gold. They were attended by a long procession of lords, ladies and soldiers.

The magistrates of Mons offered extravagant gifts of gold plate and enamels as well as the traditional wines of honour. A ducal visit was an expensive affair for the cities since they were expected to give suitable gifts to the whole entourage, as well as providing a lavish entertainment. But the magistrates hoped their expenditure would win a handsome return for their town in the form of ducal favours and perhaps even win them the greatest prize of all, the honour and profit of becoming a ducal residence, which would benefit all their citizens. Mons did not neglect to keep in contact with the duchess; they sent her 600 crowns after the fire at Maele and a further 800 livres during the civil wars. Their attentions bore fruit, Mary made the city her chief residence from 1471 to

1472 and Margaret continued to visit it regularly throughout her life, making several donations to religious foundations within the city. Certainly her first sight of Mons must have been both spectacular and memorable. The dark night was illuminated by torches and candelabra and all the houses on the route of the procession had been draped with green velvet and tapestries. Banners hung in the streets and all along the route there were the customary tableaux and pageants including the familiar tale of Esther and the Queen of Sheba. But Mons had added the story of Judith, the slayer of the tyrant Holofernes, a very popular theme in the art of the Netherlands, but a somewhat ambiguous choice to present to the wife of Charles the Bold. The duchess and her step-daughter stayed two nights in the city attending vespers at the church of the Friars Minor and Mass in the mighty church of St Waudrin, the patron of the city. Then they continued their journey to Hesdin visiting various ducal and noble castles on the way.

This type of journey was repeated at least three times a year. All her travelling was a means of upholding ducal authority, which was maintained not only by armies and officials but also by chroniclers, artists, musicians and ceremonial occasions. The supremacy and inviolability of the dukes were proclaimed for all to see as the duchess' richly caparisoned cavalcade with glittering knights and bejewelled horses trotted through the countryside and entered the villages and towns. These processions enhanced the reputation of the duke and Margaret who, with her regal solemnity, attracted respectful attention.

Margaret also travelled for more practical reasons. Some of her journeys were dictated by external events such as the serious outbreak of the plague in Flanders in 1471 to 1472 which kept the ducal ladies away from Bruges and Ghent. Sometimes she had to move because building alterations temporarily rendered one of the castles uninhabitable. The castle of Ten Waele at Ghent underwent major works in the early 1470s and towards the end of the renovations Margaret spent some time there apparently ensuring that the rooms were to her taste and comfort.[40] The duchess also attended the great functions of state, such as the chapter of the Order of the Golden Fleece which met at Valenciennes in May 1473 and the session of the great council at Malines a year later.[41] The needs of government obliged her to undertake several journeys and, during the last year of her marriage, most of her travels were concerned with her efforts to raise more money and men for the ducal wars in Lorraine and Alsace. Sometimes it was foreign policy which dictated her movements. In 1475 she had to hurry down to Calais to conciliate her brother Edward who, having finally arrived on the continent with a large army, found that his ally Charles was still far away at the siege of Neuss.

Apart from her active role as a ducal emissary Margaret also had other responsibilities. It was her duty to give guidance and support to the heiress Mary, a task Margaret entered into with loving enthusiasm. The close relationship which she built up with her step-daughter was to be of value to them both, especially in 1477. Mary had seen little of her mother who had been ill, probably with tuberculosis, for some time before she died at Antwerp in 1465.[42] The girl had a succession of governesses all under the supervision of Anne of Burgundy, her father's half-sister. Her childhood companions included her

The mystical marriage of St Catherine, by Hans Memlinc. St Catherine on the left and St Barbara with the book on the right are said to be idealised portraits of Mary and Margaret respectively. Copyright ACL Bruxelles

cousins, Ravenstein's son Philip, and John of Cleves. From 1463 to 1468 she had lived mainly at Ten Waele at Ghent where her chief female attendant was Jeanne de Clito, a cousin of the chronicler Commynes and the wife of the High Steward of Flanders, Jehan of Hallewijn, an eminent councillor and a ducal chamberlain. The Lady Hallewijn remained Mary's most constant companion throughout her short life. As befitted the greatest heiress of her age, Mary received a good education and was provided with every delight imaginable including many pet animals, including a giraffe, as well as the usual birds and dogs. She was a healthy energetic girl, especially fond of outdoor exercise such as hunting and falconry, but she also had a taste for music, chess and art.

From their first meeting at Sluis, Margaret and Mary enjoyed each other's company. There were only eleven years between them and while Margaret would find Mary a useful companion for improving her French and for learning some Dutch, Mary in her turn seems to have learned some English and to have enjoyed the attention of an older woman. They were together almost continually for the following nine years, apart from the five months of 1471 when Mary was based at Mons. From the middle of 1472, Mary was again with Margaret, chiefly at Ghent and Brussels, though she was often obliged to remain at Ghent as a virtual hostage for her father's extortionate loans. Like Margaret, Mary had received a pious upbringing and she took her religious duties very seriously. They went on several pilgrimages together with Mary showing a special devotion to the cult of St Colette whose life had been dedicated to the reform of convents in Burgundy and northern France. Margaret also supported the reformed orders and her donation of the beautifully illuminated *Life of St Colette* to the convent of the Poor Clares at Ghent was perhaps in honour of Mary.[43]

As his heiress, Mary was a valuable asset to Duke Charles and it was for this reason that she remained unmarried during his lifetime. From 1461 to 1477 she was offered to a bewildering succession of suitors, some whom she had probably never even heard of at all. The parade of candidates for the hand of the Burgundian heiress included Ferdinand of Aragon, who later married Isabella of Castile, Nicholas of Lorraine, George, Duke of Clarence, Duke Francis II of Brittany, the Dauphin Charles, Charles, Duke of Berry, the brother of Louis XI, Philibert of Savoy who had also been considered as a suitor for Margaret, Nicholas of Anjou and Maximilian, the Habsburg archduke and heir. From time to time the duchess and Mary were drawn into the negotiations, entertaining or writing to the suitor of the moment. In July 1472, Mary wrote to Nicholas of Lorraine expressing her delight at her father's decision that she should have no other husband but him. Her letter was merely another move in the duke's elaborate diplomacy and in any case Nicholas died in the following July.[44] Throughout all these long drawn out negotiations for Mary's marriage, the Duchess Margaret, with at least seven years of similar experience, would have been well able to counsel Mary and support her throughout all the diplomatic wrangles. The most frequently recurring candidate was Maximilian. A betrothal between them was first suggested as early as 1463, when Duke Philip was considering the advantages of acquiring an imperial crown. Maximilian's candidature was revived in 1467, in 1469 and again in 1473, but it was not until after the battle of Grandson in 1476 that the betrothal was firmly negotiated and a marriage was planned to take place at Cologne in the November of 1477.[45] Even this was not the final settlement, for after her father's death Mary's marriage was again the subject of great speculation and only firm action by Mary, Margaret and their closest advisers finally secured the momentous Burgundian–Habsburg marriage.

Mary was not the only woman at the Burgundian court with whom Margaret was expected to develop a valuable relationship. The dowager Duchess Isabelle of Portugal had, like Margaret, celebrated her marriage at Bruges with great splendour and the occasion of her wedding was marked by the creation of the Order of the Golden Fleece. Of her three sons, only Charles had survived and she had had to endure the perpetual infidelities of her husband. With some reason she became, according to her husband, the most jealous woman alive. Her closest supporter at the court was the able Chancellor Rolin and after his resignation she played a less visible role in politics. After 1468, the dowager withdrew once more to her finely situated castle at La Motte aux Bois in the forest of Nieppe, southern Flanders, where the duke and the duchess visited her on several occasions. We know that Margaret kept her mother-in-law well informed on matters of mutual interest especially over the dramatic events in England during 1470 to 1471.[46] Both Margaret and Charles were nearby at Arques when the dowager died at St Omer on 13 December 1471.

Margaret learned to work closely with both court nobles and important officials. The most important baron in the Low Countries was Adolph, Lord Ravenstein, Charles' cousin, and also after 1470 his brother-in-law.[47] Lord Ravenstein was a prominent member of Margaret's wedding party in July 1468 and he accompanied her on many of her journeys. Like his brother John, Duke of Cleves, he was a Knight of the Golden Fleece and belonged to the innermost circle at the court. In addition to his income from his large estates he received a ducal annuity of 6,000 francs, making him one of the richest noblemen in Burgundy. As Lieutenant-General of the Low Countries he worked with Margaret to raise troops and gather in money and support for the ducal armies in Lorraine.

Equally eminent at court was Anthony, Count of La Roche.[48] Margaret would have met him for the first time at the Smithfield tournament. He played a major role in her wedding ceremonies, especially at the tournament. His resultant injuries had been so long lasting that he was still allowed to sit in the ducal presence as late as January 1469, when the delegates came from Ghent to Brussels to make their formal submission to Duke Charles. Anthony was the first chamberlain of the court. He held the key to the ducal bedchamber and he had custody of the ducal seal. In battle he was in command of the ducal banner and was often deputed to act as regent for the duke. As a military commander he fought bravely for Charles on many occasions, losing his best jewels at Beauvais in 1472 and his personal seal at Grandson. He was sent on several diplomatic missions to Italy and England and in this capacity he may have been of some special service to Margaret, helping her to keep in touch with her relatives. However he showed no loyalty either to her personally or to his niece Mary. He was taken prisoner at Nancy and with the conquest of the Duchy of Burgundy, where most of his lands were situated, he transferred his allegiance to Louis XI.

Two other half brothers of Duke Charles were familiar and important members of the ducal court, David, Bishop of Utrecht and John, Bishop of Cambrai.[49] Both of these men were very worldly priests, David involved in the politics of the northern provinces and John embroiled with a succession of women. His funeral Mass in 1480 was attended by thirty-six of his illegitimate offspring. It was from John of Burgundy that Margaret eventually bought her house in Malines. Clergymen more likely to have been popular with Margaret were Ferry de Clugny, who became the Bishop of Tournai and his brother Guillaume, the papal pro-notary in the Low Countries.[50] Both men had been involved in the negotiations for her marriage and remained in her confidence after the death of the duke.

Margaret would also have had regular contact with Lord Louis of Gruu-thuyse, Phillippe of Croy, the Lord of Chimay, Anthoine Rolin, the son of the great Chancellor and the Lord of Aymeries and Guillaume Bische, the Lord of Clary.[51] During the last years of Duke Charles life these men all worked with Margaret. Louis de Gruuthuyse was also another useful contact with England since he became a close personal friend of Edward IV. The Lord of Chimay knew Charles very well indeed and his description of the duke at Neuss in late 1474 gives a good idea of this restless man. He described Charles as 'a flying duke who moves more than a swallow . . . always on his feet, never resting and managing to be everywhere at once.' Chimay was taken prisoner at Nancy, only returning to Ghent with Maximilian after he had been ransomed. He remained loyal and served both Mary and her heirs. Margaret honoured him by becoming the godmother to one of his sons. Anthoine Rolin was principally occupied in Hainault and in the crisis of 1477 he cooperated with Margaret in raising troops against the French invasion. Clary was another who stood by the dowager after the disaster of Nancy. The two most important officials who worked with Margaret were, however, both new men whose careers had been made in Charles' service: the Chancellor, Guillaume Hugonet, Lord of Saillant and Guy de Brimeu, Lord Humbercourt.[52] The latter came from a wealthy noble family in Picardy and he was both a military man and a clever administrator. Charles used him as a tough trouble-shooter sending him in succession to Liège, Luxembourg and Guelders to deal with powerful opposition parties and rebellions. As a result of his position, Humbercourt acquired large estates in the Meuse valley and around Maastricht. As one of the most zealous ducal servants he also attracted a great deal of hostility for which he was to pay in 1477. So too did Chancellor Hugonet, who had served Charles for many years before he inherited the duchy. Charles held Hugonet's erudition and eloquence in great respect; his two-hour-long speeches would be packed with classical and biblical quotations and allusions. They were not so well received by the Flemish estates and his hard line in dealing with his opponents inspired a deep hatred of him in Ghent and Bruges.

Tommaso Portinari was the duke's most important financial advisor and creditor. By 1477 Charles owed the Medici bank more than £57,000, a vast sum. Portinari lived the life of a great courtier accompanying Charles on the most important occasions of his life. He was at Trier for the famous meeting with the Emperor Frederick III. Another notable who must have cut a dashing figure on that occasion was Olivier de La Marche, in his crimson-violet satin and crimson pourpoints.[53] La Marche had a very close association with Margaret from the day of her marriage right up to her death.[54] His *Memoires* provide a valuable but tantalising source for the period. He was interminably long-winded on cere-monials and elusively brief on the subject of the duchess herself, but after all, the ceremonials were his very *raison d'être*. Coming from a minor family in Franche Comté he had risen rapidly in the service of Duke Philip to become an army captain and a useful diplomat. In 1477 his close association with the duke nearly cost him his life, but he received the protection of Margaret who took him with her when she left Ghent. At her dower town of Malines he became the master of her household and she later passed him on to the service of the Archduke Philip.

From his *L'estat de la maison du duc Charles de Bourgogne* we have a very comprehensive idea of the elaborate household within which Margaret had to function.

The ducal household aimed to reflect a perfect and heavenly order dedicated to the service of God in heaven and to his servant, the duke. All the ceremonial and the hierarchy reflected this divinity which gave meaning and importance to every act of court life and regulated the movement of everyone from the great lords to the least important kitchen boy. No one from the court of Louis XIV would have felt out of his depth in the finely organised liturgies of the Burgundian court. On his accession Charles had initiated a total reorganisation of his father's household bringing in many of his own men. He struck a much more severe note, gone were the 'dissolute frivolities'[55] of his father's time such as the 'Feast of Fools'. The emphasis was on a pious and business-like organisation with close attention to matters of precedence and etiquette. In this the duke was following the customs of his mother. It was one of her ladies, Alienor de Poitiers, who had written the manual on etiquette known as *Les Honneurs de la Cour*,[56] a book doubtless carefully studied by Margaret.

Each department of the ducal household was responsible for one of the functions of the court, and Margaret had a parallel household of her own mirroring the ducal structure on a smaller scale. Foremost among the court institutions was the ducal chapel supervised by the Bishop of Tournai and staffed by forty priests and chaplains and almoners who administered ducal charity. The chapel music came under the direction of some of the most distinguished musicians in Europe, such as the composer Anthoine Busnoys.[57] All the choristers and players were carefully selected and a wide range of instruments was used including harps, organs, bagpipes and German horns. The chapel was magnificently equipped with plate, reliquaries, breviaries, music books and vestments.

Within the ducal court were the great departments of state. The Council was most important and was headed by the Chancellor Hugonet who had a large staff of lawyers, officials, secretaries, *maîtres des requêtes*, wardens and constables. They covered all the legal business of the state. Charles was proud of his position as a law-giver and in peacetime he held public audience twice a week to deal with petitions. On these occasions the whole court was expected to attend. During the duke's absence the chancellor or the duchess herself might receive the petitions in his place. The Council for War was another department and a most active one.[58] His artillery and infantry were organised according to a series of ordinances issued by Charles personally. Margaret worked closely with this council in 1476 when she was raising men for the army and she made her own ordinances for the troops which she raised to support Mary after 1477.

The Treasury was under the supervision of the duke himself who kept a very close eye on the accounts, a practice followed by Margaret in her own dower affairs. The expenditure on the ducal household stood in the region of 400,000 livres a year with the military burden twice that sum.[59] This was a huge amount especially when we remember that a very wealthy baron such as Margaret's father, Richard, Duke of York, had a gross annual income of about £8,000 sterling.[60] A great part of the capital assets of the court was kept in the form of jewels, plate and other treasure. This was under the care of another department, the *Garde des Joyaux*. The Burgundian jewels were famous and the Swiss who captured the ducal baggage after Grandson, Murten and Nancy were astounded by the excess.[61] Apart from all the usual paraphernalia of a military campaign, tents, armour, cannons and banners, Charles had with him the regalia of the ducal chapel including a great reliquary of sculptured gold inlaid with gems adorned with statues and containing eighty separate relics and three- or four-hundredweight of silver, gold and silvergilt as well as chests of tapestries, cloths of gold, silks and satins. The finest pieces, so eagerly carried back to the Swiss towns, were the great sword of state encrusted with diamonds, pearls and rubies, and one of Charles' famous black velvet hats in which he had mounted one of the largest diamonds in the world.[62]

As well as these major offices of the court there was the household itself run by a first chamberlain and a master of the household with five controllers to supervise the vast staff.[63] There were forty *valets de chambres*, numerous servers, cup bearers, tasters and vintners, six doctors, two surgeons, two spicers and sixteen squires in constant personal attendance upon the duke. In addition were the kitchen staff who included twenty-five special cooks as well as all the scullery workers and the provisioners. Another chamberlain supervised the ducal stables where there were sixty squires and pages who served as messengers, as well as blacksmiths, farriers and stable hands. The master of the horse and the chief falconer were responsible for organising the hunting and were members of the great nobility such as Lord Ravenstein. They were also concerned with jousts and tournaments.

Great occasions of state required the cooperation of many departments and men who served at the head of one office often had a similar role in another, which must have ensured good joint operations. To complete the ducal household there was a bodyguard of a hundred and twenty-six squires and the same number of archers under a captain, the important and splendid office of the heralds headed by six kings of arms who wore crowns studded with sapphires, and a whole army of seamstresses, tailors, launderers and personal servants.

The household set up for Margaret in August 1468 was more modest. It had a full establishment of a hundred and forty persons though not all of them were expected to be in attendance at the same time. The duchess' servants worked in six or three monthly shifts and at any one time only about ninety would be on duty. Her ladies, who included twelve maids-of-honour and three ladies-of-the-bedchamber, were under the surveillance of Marie, Countess of Charny. Marie was one of Duke Philip's older illegitimate daughters. She married Pierre de Bauffremont, Count of Charny, a councillor for both Philip and his son Charles in 1447. The count himself was appointed as captain of Margaret's knights-of-honour. As a famous jouster, who had won reknown at the tournament of Arras in 1435, he was a figure of seniority at the ducal court. His connections went well back into the early days of Philip the Good's rule. In 1434 he stood as proxy for Duke Philip at the baptism of Jan van Eyck's eldest son and throughout his life he undertook many embassies on behalf of the ducal government. The rest of her staff were organised under three *maîtres d'hôtel*, two of whom were always

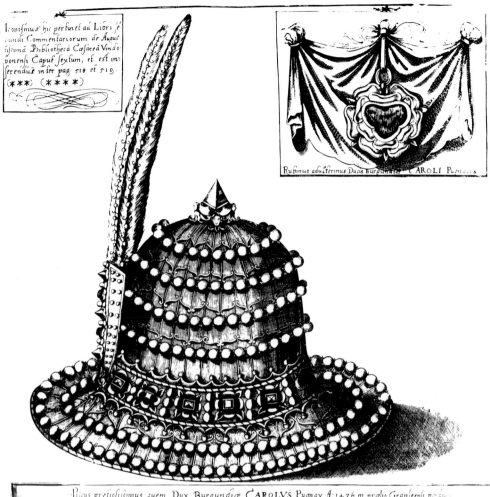

(Top) Jewelled hat of Duke Charles looted on the field of Grandson. (Bottom) The jewelled Order of the Garter probably given to the duke by Edward IV and also looted at the battle of Grandson

in attendance. They were to supervise the butlerage and kitchen staff which had a full complement of fifty with a further thirty responsible for provisioning and twenty-three in the stables. Although the personnel of Margaret's household would be changed many times during her time as duchess, the size of her household remained much the same and Margaret continued to require the services of about a hundred persons to supply all her personal needs although she could also draw on the large reservoir of court servants for any special missions.

Within this household and court Margaret's role was largely undefined. On the one hand she was a mere adornment and, with a partly paid-up dowry of 200,000 crowns, her monetary worth was about the same as the famous ducal mantle smothered with jewels worn at Trier to impress the Emperor.[64] On the other hand Margaret was a deputy for the duke himself. She received ambassadors and it was regarded as a great honour if she acted as a godparent or attended a noble wedding. In February 1470 both the duke and duchess were present at the celebrations accompanying a great double wedding between Jeanne, the daughter of Anthony, Count of La Roche, to the Lord of Culembourg, and Jeanne, the daughter of the Lord of Gruuthuyse to the Count of Hoorn.[65] These celebrations at Bruges were one of the last great ceremonials of Charles' reign and it was an important political event uniting as it did the nobility of Holland, Flanders, Burgundy and Brabant. During the long absences of the duke on his military campaigns it was left to Margaret to maintain social contact with the major noble families in the north.

In spite of the popular debate over the value and worth of women, which had been triggered off by the controversy surrounding the *Roman de la Rose* published in the previous century, the Burgundian court still pretended to regard women in the old chivalric terms. Although their realms may be seized, as in the case of Jacqueline, Countess of Holland, Zeeland and Hainault, who had lost all her territories to Duke Philip the Good, they were rarely imprisoned and seldom executed.[66] Since women had a wholly subservient role and were legally regarded as not responsible for their lord's actions, they were not made to suffer if their husbands were condemned as traitors and their dower lands were usually respected. Yet it is also clear from the behaviour of powerful women like Isabelle of Portugal and Margaret herself that women could and did act on their own authority and were expected to assume a wide range of responsibilities. Simply because they were survivors and outlived most of their husbands they accumulated a vast amount of experience enabling them to play an important, but often concealed, role within government.

During the first years of her marriage, Margaret's role was restricted by her inexperience and she passed her time travelling round the country and accompanying her step-daughter. Her life was led within the castles and palaces of the Low Countries. She never visited the Duchy of Burgundy or the county of Franche Comté. The castle within which she passed most of her short married life was Ten Waele at Ghent. If Bruges was the financial and commercial centre of Flanders, Ghent was its political capital and the 'town most to be reckoned with in Flanders.'[67] Ghent had, in spite of harsh ducal repression, continued to be the mainspring of most of the rebellions that broke out in the northern provinces. Together with Bruges and Ypres, it formed the alliance of the three members of a powerful force in the government of Flanders. The trading interests of Flanders made the county accessible to foreign influences and more than once English or French interference in the affairs of the duchy had been made possible by the actions of the citizens of Ghent. It was for this reason that the duke had to maintain a high presence in the city and why Margaret and Mary were obliged to remain there for long periods.

The grim exterior of the castle at Ghent reflected the toughness of the city, but inside many improvements had made it a most comfortable palace and, after 1472, the duchess spent every Christmas there.[68] The tapestries which had shone in the hall at Bruges adorned the walls whenever the duchess was in residence (they usually travelled with the duke or the duchess). During the first year of her marriage while work was started on her rooms at Ghent she stayed at Maele, one of the original castles of the Counts of Flanders. In the summer of 1472 she entertained the English ambassador there, an appropriate place for him to visit since the castle chapel was dedicated to St Thomas à Becket. It was shortly after this visit that a serious fire broke out in the duchess' rooms. It was considered sufficiently important for the duke to ride over from Bruges to reassure her and to assess the damage personally. Margaret claimed that the fire had destroyed her personal property to the value of 50,000 to 60,000 crowns and that she had lost rings, jewels, tapestries, robes and furs and had hardly anything left. The estates raised aides to replace her losses. Antwerp and Brabant sent an extra 4,000 ridders. This was in addition to their standard levy of 12,000 ridders payable every year for eight years for the maintenance of the duchess and her household. Similar arrangements were made with all the regions, Flanders paid 40,000 ridders over sixteen years and Hainault 28,000 livres over fourteen years. On the occasion of the fire contributions came directly from several cities with Lille, Douai and Orchies finding 2,000 francs and Malines sending 600 crowns.[69] The castle of Maele was so badly damaged that the duchess left it for the more southerly Bellemotte and there is no evidence that she ever returned there.

Only the castles of Ghent, Brussels and Hesdin were large enough to accommodate the households of both the duke and the duchess at the same time. At Brussels the palace of Coudenberg had been almost doubled in size during the reign of Philip the Good. The corporation of Brussels was eager to persuade their dukes to spend more time in their city and they paid for the building of the great hall, vast enough to hold assemblies of the whole ducal court.[70] Coudenberg was surrounded by an extensive park, known as the Warende, which was itself part of the enormous hunting forest of Soignes covering much of central Brabant. Compared to Bruges and Ghent, Brussels was a very loyal city and by 1470 it was one of the largest in the ducal territories. Its town hall had been doubled in size by the addition of the left wing for which Charles and his first fiancée, Catherine of France, had laid the foundation stone in 1440. The massive church of St Michael and St Gudule, whose twin towers featured in miniatures of the duchess, was used for ducal baptisms and marriages. The church of Our Lady on the Sablon, close to the ducal palace, was built by the guild of crossbowmen, an important element of the ducal

The ducal palace at Brussels

armies. Brussels' craftsmen were famous for the manufacture of arms, armour and leatherwork but it was also a city of art. Rogier van der Weyden was the chief civic artist and there were several famous book-making studios. However, although she made many visits to the city, Margaret never stayed at Brussels for long periods as she did at Ghent and Hesdin.

Hesdin had also been greatly extended by Philip the Good.[71] He held many fêtes there and the palace was certainly designed to appeal to his sense of humour. The River Cauche provided the source for the waterfalls and fountains which adorned the gardens and its waters were even brought inside the palace to cause amusement by drenching unsuspecting guests and wetting the ladies by spraying water up their skirts. There were statues which spurted paint, a book of poetry that squirted black ink, a staircase which tipped people into bags of feathers, corridors where rain and snow fell from the ceiling and a wooden hermit who spoke when addressed. More prosaic amusements included distorting mirrors, secret trap-doors and sacks which burst over the heads of guests. It is difficult to imagine these delights appealing to the sombre Duke Charles or his unsmiling duchess. Perhaps its fine park, the gardens and excellent hunting country around were sufficient attraction, also much of the ducal library was kept there. Margaret passed her first Christmas in Burgundy at Hesdin where she was joined by both Mary and the Dowager Isabelle. The duke was detained at Brussels receiving the submission of Ghent. The duchess returned for the

Christmas of 1470 when Charles joined her but after this, apart form a brief sojourn in 1471, Hesdin was deserted for Le Crotoy and Arques.

After 1471 Charles was away from the Low Countries more often and Margaret gradually assumed a more prominent role. By 1476 she was playing a very visible part in the ducal administration. The problems arising from the failures of Charles' foreign policy were the main cause of her increasing activity. The duke, following the aims and ambitions of his three predecessors, continued to strive to extend and consolidate the feudal territories which had been acquired by the first Valois duke. The Dukes of Burgundy held their lands from two sovereigns, from the Emperor and from the King of France. Since their various counties and duchies were physically separated by estates belonging to other lords, the dukes had to ensure that they could move their troops and goods easily from one territory to another. They were frequently involved in disputes over rights of passage and they therefore struggled to join their lands together. By 1468 the lands which Charles held from the emperor were very extensive and he was much involved in the politics of the empire. Some of the German nobles looked to him for support against the emperor and thought that the energetic Charles would make a better defender of the empire against the inroads of the Turks.[72] Charles was hopeful that he might achieve some sort of imperial crown as a Vicar of the Empire or even as the King of the Romans. He seems to have had hopes of inserting himself into the imperial succession between the Emperor Frederick III and his son Maximilian of Austria, whose marriage to Mary would eventually ensure the union of the Empire and Burgundy.[73] The Habsburg–Valois merger that Charles envisaged would indeed take place but only after his death and not on terms favourable to Burgundy which included the loss of some of the French lands.

In order to safeguard his French possessions while pursuing an expansionist policy within the empire Charles needed allies who would hold France in check; hence his alliance with England and his marriage to Margaret. Margaret's very presence in Burgundy acted as a warning to France. It was this fact which lay behind Louis XI's personal antagonism towards Margaret and also her own resolute opposition to France after 1477. By the treaty of Péronne in 1468, Charles achieved all that he wanted with regard to France and after this he was only concerned with maintaining the status quo. He was now at liberty to embark on his policy of expansion in the Rhinelands. By May 1469 he had negotiated the treaty of St Omer giving him control over Alsace, and in 1472 he secured power in Lorraine. The betrothal of Mary to Nicholas, Duke of Lorraine, was intended to consolidate his gains. But this was the peak of Charles' success and after 1472 he found himself forced onto the defensive. His failure to secure Alsace was the result of many factors, not least among them the tactless and belligerent attitude of Peter von Hagenbach the ducal bailiff there. In Lorraine too he found himself involved in a lengthy war of succession following the death of Nicholas.

Throughout the Rhinelands, Charles found himself facing an enemy whose power and significance he entirely failed to appreciate. The League of Constance was an alliance composed of Swiss and German cities and princes, who were encouraged by Louis XI in their efforts to extricate their territories from Burgundian influence.[74] But the mainspring of this determined opposition from the cities lay within the Low Countries themselves. The treatment of the cities of Dinant, Ghent and Liège by the Dukes of Burgundy had sent a shiver of horror through all the cities of the Rhine, none of whom wanted to find themselves subjected to the heavy taxation and ruthless punishments meted out to those disobedient cities. Dinant stood as a terrible warning, even before Charles inherited the duchy. Philip had watched while his son's army had sacked and plundered the city for several days, its leading citizens were tied back to back in pairs and hurled from the citadel. Refugees from Dinant, and later from Liège, had found shelter all along the Rhine and in other cities of the Low Countries. Wherever they went they carried with them accounts of the horrors which they had suffered. The assault and destruction of Liège, in 1468, added to the stories of Charles's cruelty. No wonder Ghent had submitted in January 1469 and Tournai paid to be left in peace.[75]

Margaret played her own small role in the control of the cities. Her visits were the gentler side of ducal influence and the means whereby city officials were kept under careful surveillance. This meant a close supervision of all local appointments. In 1472 she wrote to Dijon urging the appointment of a ducal nominee to the position of procureur, but on this occasion she did not succeed.[76] She was later to show a similar firm interest in the administration of her dower towns.

Margaret's role in foreign affairs was largely confined to the reception of embassies, heralds and foreign rulers. In 1472, throughout the negotiations for the treaty of St Omer, she entertained Duke Sigismund at Hesdin. The Duke of Guelders and his son were both guests, even enforced guests, of the duchess, and after Charles had seized Guelders for himself the dispossessed son became, for a short time, a permanent resident at Margaret's court.[77] However, Charles did not involve Margaret in his negotiations with the emperor. She was absent from the important meeting at Trier, though she travelled to Aachen two years later and perhaps it was then that she offered the beautiful votive coronet to the shrine of Our Lady in the cathedral.[78] The presentation of a Burgundian crown in Charlemagne's great basilica was a gesture not lost on her contemporaries who were well aware of Charles' ambitions.

Margaret's chief importance in Burgundy derived from the value of the Anglo-Burgundian alliance and it was in the relations between Burgundy and England that she was to play such an active role for thirty-five years. The fact that she remained so respected within Burgundy in spite of the problems in the alliance and her continued childlessness is evidence of her own intelligence and abilities. Charles' marriage to Margaret was intended to secure a lasting alliance with England, yet within a year the duke's confidence in the value of his wife must have been severely shaken. In the summer of 1468 Edward had seemed to be very securely established on the English throne, the deposed King Henry was held in the Tower and Queen Margaret and her son Edward were penniless petitioners at the court of Louis XI, who had shown little inclination to support the Lancastrian cause. But after the rejection of the Anglo-French alliance, Louis became much more sympathetic towards the Lancastrian queen. Warwick also had not been pleased by Margaret's marriage to Charles and it was his alliance with the King of France which was to prove so dangerous for both Edward and Burgundy.

Although Warwick had escorted his cousin on her farewell ride through London he was far from satisfied. In an effort to reconcile Warwick to the Burgundian alliance and to his role as the king's most important ambassador, Edward sent the earl to the Low Countries in March 1469. The main purpose of the mission was to offer the Order of the Garter to Charles in response to Charles' offer of the Golden Fleece to Edward. Warwick was received with great honour first by the Dowager Isabelle and later at Hesdin by the duke and duchess. There were no signs at these meetings of the 'deadly hatred' which was rumoured to exist between Charles and Warwick.[79] It is likely, however, that two proud and ruthless men would hardly find each other very sympathetic. Warwick may well have used his visit to Burgundy for his own ends, making contact with the Lancastrian exiles the Dukes of Exeter and Somerset who were still pensioners of the Burgundian court, and trying to discover whether Charles was likely to intervene to support his brother-in-law.

Warwick may also have warned Margaret of her brother Clarence's increasing dissatisfaction with his position at court. Clarence had been repeatedly disappointed over his marriage prospects, French and Scottish princesses and the Burgundian heiress had all slipped from his grasp. Nor had he succeeded in securing the hand of an English heiress, all of whom, it seemed, were being married off to the queen's numerous relatives. Warwick's proposal that Clarence should marry his own eldest daughter, the heiress Isabel Neville, had not found favour with the king and once again Clarence felt thwarted. His status as heir-apparent had been lost with the birth of the Princess Elizabeth and it was surely only a matter of time before a son was born to the prolific queen, so finally removing all his hopes of inheriting the throne. By the time of Warwick's visit to Burgundy, Clarence had decided to defy his brother and marry Isabel. Even as Warwick was being entertained by the mechanical contrivances at Hesdin, his envoys were busy in Rome obtaining the necessary dispensation for the marriage of such close cousins.[80]

Had Warwick attempted to ascertain Margaret's views on these matters, she would surely have counselled patience and loyalty to the king, both of which she always showed in good measure. But patience was not one of the nineteen-year-old Clarence's virtues and, by the end of June, Warwick's own supporters were informed of the impending marriage and rumours were widespread. Edward summoned them both to appear before him to establish that they were not 'of any such disposition towards us as rumour here runneth'.[81] Openly in defiance of the king, Warwick and Clarence left England for Calais and on 11 July, Isabel Neville and George, Duke of Clarence, were married there by the bride's uncle, George Neville, Archbishop of York. Immediately after the wedding the rebels issued a proclamation denouncing the bad government of England which they blamed on the evil advice of the queen's parents, Earl Rivers and Lady Jacquetta, and her eldest brother Anthony Lord Scales. This was a virtual declaration of war and was accompanied by well orchestrated rebellions in the north, the midlands and Kent. Throughout this period Margaret kept closely in touch with the events in England. Early in July she received another English embassy at Ghent and she was still there when the news of the rebellion reached her.[82]

During the summer of 1469 the crisis gathered momentum. Warwick and Clarence took control of London, Edward found himself a virtual prisoner at the hands of Warwick, and Earl Rivers, Sir John Woodville, William Herbert, Earl of Pembroke, and the Earl of Devon, along with many others, paid with their lives for Edward's strangely lethargic response to the rebellion. When the Bishop of Rochester arrived to report on Warwick's *coup d'état*, Charles was away in Holland.[83] The news was a personal embarrassment to the duchess. Far from being a diplomatic asset to Burgundy she was now the sister of an imprisoned English king. Moreover England now had two imprisoned kings, confirming popular continental opinion that it was a land of anarchy, violence and blasphemy, where consecrated monarchs could be set aside at the whim of the rebellious nobility. Would Warwick create yet another king out of the Duke of Clarence? The Burgundian court was very concerned and attempts were made to intervene. Sometime during that summer, Charles made contact with the corporation and merchants of London promising them his goodwill as long as they remained loyal to King Edward.[84] The city listened to his advice, especially since the new Anglo-Burgundian accord on exchange rates had just been reached and the merchant community wanted nothing to delay its operation. In September, the city issued a proclamation against all rioters, especially against anyone causing an affray against the new commercial accord. This pressure together with a Lancastrian rising in favour of Henry VI alarmed Warwick who was obliged to restore Edward and allow his return to London. A public reconciliation was staged between the king, Clarence and Warwick, but the queen was not likely to forgive the murder of her father and brother, and it was only a matter of time before the restored king would act to crush his former rebels. The proclamation of Princess Elizabeth as the heir-apparent was an open move against the pretensions of the Duke of Clarence. Duchess Cecily worked hard to achieve a real accord between her sons and as late as March 1470 she called Edward and Clarence together at Baynard's Castle to arrange a lasting settlement.

Margaret was also kept informed and Edward made an effort to strengthen his relations with Duke Charles. In January 1470 Edward sent another delegation to Ghent bearing a magnificently jewelled Garter which he had commissioned from John Brown of London at a cost of £8 6s. 8d.[85] This was presented to Charles in Margaret's presence. Among the duke's treasures looted by the Swiss at the battle of Grandson was a very fine garter, probably this one. Charles was proud to belong to an order dedicated to St George, to whom he was particularly devoted. He had always observed the saint's day and St George was portrayed as his patron on the reliquary he had presented to St Lambert's Cathedral at Liège.

Although Margaret may have hoped that this embassy marked the end of the troubles in England, by February rebellion broke out again. Typically the fighting began in Lincolnshire with a personal quarrel between the son of that 'lovely lady Willoughby', who had accompanied Margaret to her wedding, and Sir Thomas Burgh, the Master of the King's Horse. But the disturbances spread, inflamed by the activities of Warwick and Clarence.[86] Edward's victory over the Lincolnshire rebels at Empingham on 12 March served to isolate them and, fearing reprisals, they fled to Calais where Warwick's old ally, Lord Wenlock, refused them entry. Wenlock was later rewarded by Charles, so closely was Burgundy now involved with the troubles in England.[87]

Charles was soon to be even more deeply involved in the conflict because Warwick seized ships belonging to merchants from the Low Countries. The duke protested vigorously to Louis XI when Warwick was allowed to take his pirated ships into the shelter of the French ports in open contravention of the treaty of Péronne. On 15 July, Charles made a threatening statement in front of the whole court saying that:

> among us Portuguese [an unusual reference to his mother's native land] it is a custom that when those we had regarded as friends make peace with our enemies we consign them to hell.[88]

Louis was not yet ready for a war with Burgundy so he ordered the English lords to leave his lands, although he did offer hospitality to their ladies, sent a bale of silk to Clarence and offered to meet them privately. Charles, well aware of these machinations, retaliated by confiscating the goods of all the French merchants in Bruges, while he kept in close contact with Edward informing him of the movements of the rebel dukes.

Throughout the summer of 1470 the court in Burgundy appeared to be more concerned about the situation in England than was Edward himself. Repeatedly Charles warned Edward of the threats of invasion emanating from France and Margaret wrote to both of her brothers. According to Commynes, her letters reached Clarence even when he was in France, through a lady in his wife's entourage.[89] But nothing she wrote discouraged Clarence from entering into the unnatural alliance now arranged by Warwick and Louis XI. Margaret of Anjou was prevailed upon to make common cause with her old enemies and Louis even persuaded her to allow her son Edward to marry Warwick's second daughter Anne. Clarence was drawn into the alliance by being named as heir in the event of this marriage having no issue. The rebels promised to restore Henry VI and with the help of France they prepared to invade England. They landed in Devon early in September and rallied more support as they marched towards London. In spite of all Charles' warnings, Edward was totally unprepared to meet the invasion. Queen Elizabeth fled with her daughters into the sanctuary of Westminster Abbey and Edward IV, with a few hundred of his closest supporters, fled the country. He left King's Lynn on 29 September accompanied by his youngest brother Richard, Duke of Gloucester, his brother-in-law Anthony, now Earl Rivers, and his most loyal friend Lord Hastings. The readeption of Henry VI began on 15 October when the gentle king was brought out of the Tower to the acclaim of the fickle London crowd. In France, Queen Margaret and her son Edward, Prince of Wales, celebrated with a Te Deum and prepared to return to England.

Edward's small fleet was scattered as it was pursued across the Channel by hostile ships and storms and it eventually landed along a wide stretch of the coast of the Low Countries.[90] Gloucester and Rivers arrived at Weilingen in Zeeland

Louis, Lord Gruuthuyse. Copyright ACL Bruxelles

and the king with Hastings came ashore on the island of Texel much further to the north. Edward and his party were brought on to Alkmaar and by the middle of October the English party had been reassembled at The Hague, where they were received by the Lord of Gruuthuyse on behalf of Duke Charles. The English refugees were heavily dependent on their hosts, they had left England in such haste that they had very little money with them. Gloucester had to borrow from the town bailiff of Veer to pay for his minor expenses and Gruuthuyse sent his men out scouring the countryside to find rabbits to feed the unexpected guests.

Margaret must have heard of Edward's arrival when she was in Brussels and she sent the messengers on at once to inform Charles who was at Hesdin. The arrival of his brother-in-law as a penniless exile was an embarrassment to Charles. Far from proving himself a useful ally, Edward was clearly a liability likely to drag Burgundy into a war with both France and England. Charles had already been playing a devious game allowing the Dukes of Somerset and Exeter to leave his lands and travel to France in support of the Lancastrian cause.[91] Now he played for time and Edward was left in the competent hands of Gruuthuyse while Charles congratulated Henry VI on his readeption. Although money was sent to cover their expenses, the Yorkist exiles were kept in the north far from the court. Margaret made no public contact with her brother but throughout October and November messengers with secret letters moved between the exiles and the Burgundian court.[92] By 29 November the duchess had joined her husband at Hesdin where they remained throughout Christmas.

Charles' uncertainties over his English policies were soon resolved for him by the actions of Warwick and Louis XI. The latter, secure in a new English alliance and with the promised neutrality of Brittany, was at last confident enough to challenge the treaty of Péronne which he had always regarded as unfavourable to France. By December French intentions towards Burgundy were openly hostile and Louis was rumoured to be behind a plot to kill Charles while he was out hunting near Le Crotoy.[93] Charles was denounced for accepting the Order of the Garter since, as a vassal of the French king, he was not permitted to become a member of a foreign chivalric order and Louis enforced a boycott on Burgundian trade. Finally on 3 December Louis made an open declaration of war claiming that all Charles' possessions were forfeit to the crown of France because he had broken his oath of allegiance. As a result of this aggression, Charles was obliged to give his full backing to the restoration of Edward IV and at last Margaret was allowed to invite her brother to join them in the south.

During the Christmas period preparations were made to receive the English king and his companions at court. Edward came down to Ostcamp, near Bruges, the country castle of Louis of Gruuthuyse. Charles ordered £20,000 to be made available for an expedition to England and on 2 January the two men met for the first time at the dowager's castle of La Motte.[94] Three days later Edward rode on to Hesdin to visit his sister where during the next three weeks there were several meetings between Margaret and both of her brothers. Preparations were soon underway for another invasion of England and in addition to the ducal contribution which included three or four ships fitted out at Veer, the merchants and bankers in Flanders, Holland and Zeeland were encouraged to lend money for the venture and the local Hansa traders provided another fourteen ships. Margaret was now very active rallying support for her brother and urging the cities to raise money for the expedition. On 24 February five Dutch towns, including Leiden, agreed to make a loan of 6,000 florins to 'my gracious lady of Burgundy and the King Edward of England, her brother if my gracious lord [Charles] will approve.'[95] The duchess left Hesdin for Lille on 19 January and early in February Gloucester visited his sister and her step-daughter and stayed for a couple of nights. By this time, Charles was with his armies in Picardy and on the Somme. St Quentin was lost to the French and near Calais there were clashes between Burgundian troops and English soldiers loyal to Henry VI.

Accompanying the preparations for the invasion of England was a battery of propaganda. Jean Mielot, a poet in Charles' entourage, compared the Duke of Burgundy to Jason assisting the giant Anticles, a reference to Edward's great height, to regain his island where wolves were devouring his sheep.[96] Once more the Argosy provided a useful source for the analogies. There were many who thought that Edward's chances of regaining his throne were very fictional indeed. The ambassador of Milan commented that it was 'difficult to leave by the door and return by the window' and he thought Edward would 'leave his skin there.'[97] But in England the readeption government was facing serious difficulties. The redistribution of land had left many dissatisfied and Clarence was becoming increasingly doubtful about his attachment to a cause which meant that instead of being brother of the king he was merely the brother-in-law of the heir-apparent. Continual pressure on him from the Yorkist ladies was having its effect. The dowager Duchess Cecily and her two daughters in England, the Duchesses of Exeter and Suffolk, brought their arguments to bear on Edward's behalf, but their efforts were restrained by their residence in England. Margaret, however, was free to make the most open cause for Edward and in the eyes of her contemporaries it was her 'great and diligent effort' with her servants and messengers travelling at all seasons which won Clarence back to his old allegiance.[98] Even before Edward finally sailed for England, Clarence had probably made up his mind to change sides.

Edward's five months in the Low Countries were not entirely preoccupied with the preparations for his return. He was very impressed by the high standards of the Burgundian court and admired the jewels, plate, tapestries, paintings and especially the books and manuscripts which were displayed to him both by Lord Louis of Gruuthuyse and by Margaret at Hesdin. Gruuthuyse's collection was one of the finest libraries in Europe and after his death it was bought by Louis XII of France and became the core of the French royal library.[99] Many of his books were commissioned from the master bookmakers of Bruges, and he was a friend of Collard Mansion who ran a workshop in the city. William Caxton had joined the duchess' service as a business adviser soon after her marriage. He too was well acquainted with Collard Mansion and the first book ever to be printed in English was made by Caxton in Collard's studio. It was perhaps in 1471 that Caxton made his first contact with Earl Rivers, who was later to become his patron. As a result of his stay in the Low Countries and his discussions with two such knowledgeable bibliophiles as Margaret and Lord Louis, Edward became seriously interested in building up a royal library. After his restoration Edward began to buy in a large number of books and manuscripts, which were to become the core of the royal library of England, though his taste was never as discriminating as his sister's and he seemed to have preferred quantity to quality.

Edward was also influenced by other aspects of the 'Burgundian Renaissance' which was in full flower by the late fifteenth century. The Gruuthuyse Palace at Bruges was a fine example of Flemish architecture and the decorated brickwork for which Flanders was famous. It was built to a very high standard of comfort and elegance, while inside it was furnished with stained glass windows and tapestries. While Edward was at Bruges, Gruuthuyse was planning an extension which would give the house an oratory overlooking the sanctuary of the church of Our Lady.[100] This oratory was completed in 1474 and is a gem of Flemish Gothic architecture, light, elegant and charming. Several elements of its design were incorporated into the king's new chapel of St George at Windsor. Edward's palace at Sheen was also rebuilt in the Flemish style with patterned brickwork and large windows. Indeed many of the features popularly regarded as Tudor date from half a century earlier and have their origin in the architectural styles of the Low Countries. Edward's exile in Holland, Zeeland and Flanders and his close contact with Margaret served to increase the numbers of Flemish artisans working in England and to promote high standards of craftsmanship and design. Edward and his entourage were impressed by the whole conduct of the Burgundian court and after their return Lord Hastings consulted Olivier de La Marche on the establishment of the ducal household. Perhaps it was hoped that by copying the Burgundian model the Yorkist court could establish itself as an oasis of correct procedures in the uncertain and turbulent world of English politics.[101]

In spite of his natural anxieties over his future, Edward appears to have enjoyed his time in Bruges. He took his leave with a gesture that was typical of this good humoured man by walking from Bruges to Damme so that he could be seen by as many of the citizens as possible and thank them for all their support.[102] By 2 March he was on board the *Anthony*, a ship belonging to Henry of Borselem, Gruuthuyse's brother-in-law and one of the admirals of the duchy. After a delay caused by contrary winds, the fleet of about thirty-six ships set sail. The invading army was not very large and when Edward found his landing at Cromer opposed by the Earl of Oxford, he sailed north and landed at Ravenser on the north bank of the Humber. Assuring everyone that he had come (like Bolingbroke before him) only to claim his rightful duchy, he was permitted to enter the city of York though his army was obliged to remain outside the walls. From York he made contact with his friends and relatives in England, especially Clarence. Assured that support was widespread he began to march south and by the time he reached the midlands, Clarence was on his way to meet him.

Margaret, who kept herself closely in touch with all the developments in England, wrote to the Dowager Duchess Isabelle to describe the meeting of the two brothers:

> My lord the king and brother coming with all his people one morning and my brother Clarence coming also with great strength towards him they found themselves, by chance, close to each other near a town called Bancbry [Banbury]. Each of them put their people in readiness and Clarence with a small company left his people behind him and approached my lord and brother who saw him coming and Lord Clarence threw himself on his knees so that my lord and brother seeing his humility and hearing his words, lifted him up and embraced him several times and gave him his good cheer and then he [Clarence] cried 'Long live King Edward.'[103]

Once the brothers had settled their differences (for the time being at least), Clarence appears to have tried to win over the Earl of Warwick but he tried in vain. There was nothing that the Lancastrians could do to stop Edward entering London and taking possession of the city. Commynes commented sourly that Edward was welcomed so warmly into London because he owed so much both to the merchants and to their wives.[104] But in fact the various anti-Burgundian measures imposed by the readeption government had dislocated trade and the city burgesses were anxious to restore the Anglo-Burgundian trade treaties.

The two kings' armies met in the field at Barnet. It was a hard fought battle and marked a decisive victory for the Yorkists. Margaret wrote to Isabelle that her brother had had an army of 12,000 men and contemporaries put the casualties at between 1,000 and 4,000, one of whom was Warwick. It was widely rumoured that the earl had been taken alive and then killed on Edward's orders. In her letters to Isabelle, Margaret endeavoured to clear her brother of all blame for his cousin's death.[105] She claimed that Warwick had indeed been taken alive and that he was being led towards Edward when another group of soldiers arrived on the scene, recognised him and killed him. Edward hastening up had arrived too late to rescue his cousin and was full of sorrow. As well as absolving Edward from all responsibility for Warwick's death, Margaret also had to explain to Isabelle, who was very interested in her Neville cousins, why Edward had had the bodies of both Warwick and his younger brother Montague exposed to public gaze at St Paul's. It was, she wrote:

> because my lord the king and brother had heard that nobody in the city believed that Warwick and his brother were dead so he had their bodies brought to St Paul's where they were laid out and uncovered from the chest upwards in the sight of everybody.[106]

After the battle of Barnet, Edward once more regained possession of the unhappy King Henry. Margaret's description of the meeting between the two kings was also designed to show her brother in the best light possible and would throw doubt on the later rumours that Edward had ordered Henry's death in the Tower. She told Isabelle that Edward and Henry had come together in the presence of the Archbishop of York, and that:

> my lord and brother offered him his hand but King Henry came and embraced him saying: 'my cousin you are very welcome, I know that my life will be in no danger in your hands' and my lord and brother replied that he should have no worries and should be of good cheer.[107]

Margaret's propaganda on behalf of her brother may have served some useful purpose at the Burgundian court but there does seem to be a certain futility in her efforts to make the actions of her blood-stained brothers match her Christian principles.

Immediately after Barnet, Queen Margaret and Edward, Prince of Wales, arrived at Weymouth and made their landing totally unaware of the disaster that awaited them. Although the news of the Lancastrian defeat reached them a day later the queen must have been persuaded that there was still a good chance of victory or she would not have risked the life of her son, whom she had guarded for so long. She had not allowed him to come over to England with Warwick and Clarence and she had delayed their return until the readeption had seemed secure. However, this time she allowed her son's life to be fully committed to the cause and on 4 May the two armies met at Tewkesbury. The Lancastrian army proved to be no match for Edward, now one of the most experienced generals in Europe. His brother Gloucester was also gaining a reputation for his military abilities, he had fought bravely at Barnet and was rewarded with the leadership of the vanguard at Tewkesbury. All the Lancastrian leaders, including the Duke of Somerset, were killed and the queen was taken prisoner. Prince Edward was 'taken fleinge to the townewards and slayne in the fielde' and on the victor's return to London, Henry VI 'which was a gode, simple and innocent man' died 'of pure despleasure and meloncholy' in the Tower.[108] The unfortunate Queen Margaret remained in Edward's prisons until 1476, when she was finally ransomed by Louis XI and returned to her native land, where she passed the rest of her life in great penury relieved only by the loyalty of one of her French vassals. At her death her only possessions of any value were her hunting dogs and these were quickly appropriated by Louis XI. The Duke of Exeter survived

Tewkesbury and fled into sanctuary but his wife, Anne of York, was allowed to secure the annulment of her marriage to him and she married her lover Thomas St Leger, keeping the bulk of the Holland estates. Another Lancastrian who also evaded capture and found safety abroad was Jasper Tudor, the Earl of Pembroke, who escaped from Tenby a month after the defeat at Tewkesbury, taking with him his nephew and the new Lancastrian heir, Henry of Richmond.

The news of the Yorkist triumph brought great rejoicing to the Burgundian court. Bonfires were lit to pass the news swiftly across the land, and even before the battle of Tewkesbury a large English embassy, including such well known figures as William Hatcliffe and John Russel, arrived in Bruges. Margaret received them on 6 April and they visited her at Maele where they dined 'not at her owne table but in a chamber with her chamberleyn.'[109] They were also entertained by Count Anthony of La Roche at Bruges and by Gruuthuyse to whom they brought Edward's thanks and an invitation to become a Knight of the Garter. Margaret celebrated with a great banquet at Ghent on 16 June. She was not only pleased at the restoration of her brother, she was also personally relieved to find that she was still the honoured sister of the King of England. Edward rewarded his sister by granting her licences to export a large quantity of English cloth free of all custom dues either into Flanders or through the 'strait of Morrok' (Gibraltar) directly into the Mediterranean in the 'great ship of Burgundy' or in other ships.[110] This was the first of a series of licences that Edward was to grant to his sister, partly in gratitude and partly, perhaps, as an alternative to paying off the outstanding debt on her dowry which in spite of his many promises remained unpaid.

The consequences of the termination of the main Lancastrian line of English kings were not lost on Charles. He made the point of having the Dowager Duchess Isabelle's rights of inheritance transferred to himself and he registered his formal claim to the English throne with a notary.[111] As a great-grandson of John of Gaunt and Blanche of Lancaster, Charles was now one of the most eligible Lancastrian claimants. However he had no intention of pressing his claim at that time, occupied as he was with the war against France. He spent the summers of 1471 and 1472 with his armies in northern France while Margaret passed part of the summer close to the frontier at Le Crotoy. Edward despatched Earl Rivers to support the Anglo-Burgundian ally, Duke Francis II of Brittany, and Lord Hastings, newly appointed captain of Calais, was also ordered to give support to the Burgundian armies. But Charles had to wait three years before Edward fulfilled his main promise to bring the English armies across the Channel to invade France. As time went by and Edward's promises remained unfulfilled, it was observed that 'the English have cheated the duke promising to send him men everyday while he sent them money.'[112]

Throughout the campaigns of the seventies, Margaret and Hugonet were kept busy 'in Flanders and Brabant pressing the people to obtain money, they made a good collection of 140,000 leoni but the people are very discontented.'[113] Margaret was also disappointed with her brother for as late as May 1476 he was still promising to pay off the debt which he owed on her dowry. She became increasingly anxious about this because, in the event of Charles' death, her whole dower situation depended on the fulfilment of the original marriage contract. She wrote to Charles asking him to clarify the situation and he warned her that she would receive the full settlement only if Edward had paid the whole dowry. However due to 'his special love and delight' (la singulière amour et delection) for his 'very dear and well loved companion the duchess' (mon trèschere et tres amée compagne la duchesse), he promised that she would receive all which had been paid into the ducal coffers by Edward, even if the rest of the dowry remained unpaid and he further guaranteed her a dower income of 40,000 crowns per year.[114]

The year 1472/3 was the peak of Charles' achievements. He had restored his brother-in-law to the English throne and he had withstood the French invasion. Alsace, Guelders and Zutphen were in his hands and he was consolidating his position in Lorraine. Throughout the duchy there was peace and prosperity. The household and the army had been reorganised and his government was functioning well. He was regarded as one of the most successful and powerful princes in Europe. Yet it was this very triumph which eventually led to his fall. His reputation and power struck fear into the minds of other princes and especially into the magistrates of the cities. Gradually alliances were formed against him and from 1474 onwards he was drawn into ever more costly campaigns and forced to remain almost constantly in the field with his armies. With the duke's increased absence Margaret was obliged to spend more of her time at Ghent, where she could use her influence with the estates and keep in touch with the mood of the northern provinces. Her authority in Flanders may be judged by the determination with which the opposition sought to get her removed from Ghent after Charles' death.

Throughout 1474, Edward was urged to undertake his promised invasion of France and he slowly prepared to fulfil his promises. By the following spring he had mustered the largest English army ever assembled for an invasion of France. The king told the Milanese ambassador that he had 20,000 men and modern historians have estimated that it was at least 12,000.[115] With the king came all the greatest nobles of the realm including both the royal brothers. Their accoutrements and equipment were lavish, Edward would not return to the continent a beggar. By this date, however, Charles had transferred his military activity to the Rhinelands where he was occupied with the siege of Neuss. He showed no inclination to leave his armies to meet Edward and Margaret was kept hard at work encouraging Edward to invade. In the duke's absence she was also busy meeting ambassadors from Portugal and raising an army to withstand the French assaults on Artois and Hainault. Early in May she sent orders to Jehan, Lord of Dadizele, the ducal bailiff in Flanders, to come with all possible speed bringing his levies to fight the French in Artois and Hainault.[116] In the same month Earl Rivers arrived in Ghent only to be sent on to Neuss to urge Charles to leave the siege and come back to the Channel, but still Charles did not move and it was left to Margaret to oversee the arrangements for the Burgundian ships which were to bring over the English army.

On 7 June Margaret left Ghent and travelled down to St Omer, arriving there just two days before Edward landed at Calais with all his court. She immediately rode over to greet her three brothers, taking a gift of tapestries and fine Bruges cloth to placate the king. She spent two nights there and returned to St Omer close to the English lines, where the Dukes of Gloucester and Clarence rode over to visit her. Louis XI commented with satisfaction that so far the English had done nothing but dance at the duchess' court.[117] Charles finally abandoned the siege of Neuss and travelled across to Calais, arriving on 14 July, but he brought no army with him and his proposals that the English should engage the French alone while he drove into France from the east did not appeal to Edward. Nine days later the duke and duchess again entertained Edward and his entourage at Fauquemberges, a castle on the Aa not far from St Omer. Immediately after this, Margaret left for Ghent arriving on 1 August. This was the last time that Margaret was to see either Charles or her brother Clarence. Charles remained in the area for the next three weeks calling on the estates of Artois and Hainault to raise troops, but he failed to order his cities to open their gates to the English army. By this time, secret negotiations were well underway between Edward and Louis, both of whom preferred diplomatic agreements to military glory. Charles was kept informed and he had the terms of the Anglo-French deal explained to him. Although he was not best pleased, he left them to continue the talks, ordering the Count of Chimay and the Bishop of Tournai to keep an eye on the negotiations.

Louis made every effort to come to terms with Edward. He sent generous presents to the English courtiers and he ordered Amiens to open its gates and its taverns freely to the English soldiery. As a result of this and Edward's resolve to take his army safely back to England before the end of the summer, the two kings finally met on a bridge at Picquigny. There they agreed on a truce and a treaty. Although it was claimed that Charles was so furious that he could not say what he would do next, within the week the Burgundians were also negotiating with France and they too reached agreement.[118]

The treaty of Picquigny was very favourable to Edward. In return for withdrawing from France he was given a generous payment of 75,000 crowns, a pension of 55,000 crowns annually and the promise of the betrothal of the dauphin to the Princess Elizabeth. With the first installment of his 'danegeld' in his coffers Edward began to move his armies out of France. The nearest he came to glory was to spend two nights camping on the field of Agincourt. There were some like Gloucester who were reported to be very displeased with the whole arrangement but most of the protesters were bought off by Louis' generosity. The royal dukes were loaded with gifts of horses, plate and wine and Gloucester himself was given some fine pieces of artillery. Nevertheless Edward's return to England was marred by complaints that the resources of the kingdom had been needlessly consumed.[119]

By the treaty of Soleuvre agreed between Burgundy and France early in September, Charles achieved a full restoration of all his lands and a nine years' truce. The duke was once more able to concentrate on his affairs in the Rhinelands where he was further assisted by a contingent of 2,000 English archers who preferred to join the duke's armies rather than return empty-handed to England. Charles was not really dissatisfied with the outcome and once more Margaret too was rewarded with more licences permitting her to add wool, tin and lead to her duty-free exports from England.[120]

If the duchess had found 1475 a busy year with the French invasion in April followed by the arrival of the English in July, she was to find 1476 even more strenuous. Throughout the year Charles campaigned in Lorraine and Savoy. As the year progressed successive disasters hit the Burgundian armies and they were defeated ignominiously at Grandson in March and at Murten in June. Margaret, Hugonet, Humbercourt and Ravenstein were stretched to the limit trying to satisfy the ducal demands for troops and they summoned the estates to obtain their full support. It was not easy to persuade the Flemish estates to agree to pour more men and money into Lorraine. When the news of the defeat at Grandson arrived at Ghent, the estates were summoned to make good the losses. Margaret presided in person at the opening of the assembly and she informed them of the duke's demands for men and money and of his wish that Mary should be sent to join him in Lorraine.[121] The estates vigorously opposed both proposals and Margaret promised to try to persuade the duke to leave Mary in Ghent. By giving way on this she presumably hoped to carry the day on the issue of troops and money. But the delegates resisted all the demands especially the ducal order for a further levy of 7,000 troops to be drawn from all the cities of the Low Countries. The Chancellor Hugonet met their refusal with anger and he threatened the estates with the wrath of the duke if they did not immediately comply with his demands. The session ended in uproar but Margaret continued to work behind the scenes and she managed to ensure more troops were sent to Lorraine.

A contingent of about 8,000 foot soldiers were furnished with two months' pay and they were sent off in autumn under the Count de Chimay, all of them equipped with uniforms in the Burgundian colours.[122] The recruitment had been drawn from Brabant and Flanders and was well supported in the counties of Artois and Hainault where the threat of war with France was ever present, but the northern provinces opposed both further conscription and extra taxes. The duchess was forced to disband the estates and she undertook a series of personal visits trying to persuade the individual cities and nobles to support the duke. Throughout September and October Margaret travelled through Flanders, Brabant and Holland. It was her first trip to the northern province of Holland and she went by the overland route through Malines and Gertrudenberg to Dordrecht and Rotterdam, taking the many river ferries necessary, including the crossing over the wide Hollandse Diep.[123] She stayed in The Hague, Leiden, Delft and Gouda and seems to have had a modest success. In all about 4,000 more men were sent to Lorraine.

It was particularly difficult to extract contributions from the Low Countries at that time. Since June 1474, Charles had been trying to collect more money from the church and he had imposed a tax on all the lands and property granted to the church within the last sixty years.[124] This levy had been widely opposed and clerical lawyers had drawn up lengthy documents to expose the illegality of this innovative taxation. The persuasions of the ducal officials prevailed and by the autumn of 1476 much of this tax had been collected. However there was a widespread resentment and there were some in the monasteries and convents who no doubt saw Charles' defeats as acts of divine punishment for his blasphemous levy on the church. The news of the defeat at Murten was received with alarm in the castle of Ghent where, at first, there were fears for Charles' life, but they were reassured to hear that he was safely in Franche Comté and reports of his speech to the estates of Burgundy at Salins must have been even more encouraging. His self-confidence was unshaken and he reminded the delegates of the ancient Romans who had been so often defeated by Hannibal but were in the end totally victorious. He was so convincing that the Burgundians agreed to raise another 3,000 men and acquiesced to the ducal order that all the bells should be melted down to make new cannon to replace those seized by the Swiss.[125]

Margaret returned from Holland in November 1476 and was welcomed back to Ghent by her step-daughter. Within the month they had at least one piece of good news: Charles had at last decided to complete the arrangements for Mary's marriage to Maximilian. He asked the emperor to begin preparations for the celebrations which were to take place either at Aachen or Cologne. On 1 December the necessary papal dispensation was issued at Antwerp by the papal legate Cardinal Tolentis.[126] The news was greeted with delight throughout the Low Countries because it seemed to promise an end to all the wars in Germany. Bonfires were lit across the whole land to relay the good tidings and the magistrates of Ghent offered a banquet in honour of the Lady Mary. After all the hard negotiations and all her long journeys trying to raise men and money, Margaret must have been pleased to be able to plan something more pleasant. The Christmas celebrations at Ghent were particularly happy and they could hope that Charles too would soon be successful at the siege of Nancy so bringing an end the war in Lorraine.

4   1477

'Her hands on the reins'

The siege of Nancy began on 22 October and despite the most urgent arguments of his advisers Charles refused to withdraw for the winter. Throughout December, as the snow began to fall and ice gripped the countryside, the Burgundian army remained in position. The reinforcements sent from the Low Countries went little way to replacing those who deserted or died in the harsh winter weather of Lorraine. In his camp Charles continued to plan for his victory and to read about the heroes of ancient Rome. But his enemies were also making preparations and by late December they had collected together a huge army at least three times larger than the Burgundian force. During the last days of December this army of more than 20,000 men moved off over the frozen roads towards Nancy. As at Grandson and Murten before, Charles appears to have been totally oblivious to the advancing danger and he continued to expect the imminent surrender of the town.[1]

On 5 January it was snowing steadily and by midday, with hardly any warning, the besiegers found themselves surrounded by a large force of Swiss infantry supported by mounted knights led by René, Duke of Lorraine. In a devastating attack the Burgundian artillery was overrun, their infantry wiped out and many great lords were taken prisoner in the confusion. All the cannons, tents and baggage were seized and the last of the four great Valois Dukes of Burgundy vanished into the mêlée. It took two days to find his body and then only after a patient and macabre search over the battlefield. It appeared that his horse had fallen while trying to jump a frozen stream and the duke had been killed by a mighty blow to the head, which left him totally unrecognisable except to his Italian valet who knew him by his long fingernails, and to his Portuguese doctor who identified him by the old battle scars on the stripped and frozen corpse.[2]

The news of first the defeat and then the death of Duke Charles spread across Europe in a frisson of both horror and delight. Here was the most feared and redoubtable prince, the richest tyrant in Europe laid low by an army made up from the cities and small principalities, albeit with the covert support of the King of France. The imagination of writers ran riot: ballads, epitaphs and epics poured from their pens in German, Dutch, French, Spanish, Italian and Latin. The ambitious duke would have been well satisfied to find himself compared to all his old heroes, to Hercules, Hannibal, Caesar and Alexander, and to hear his military and political exploits exalted and extolled. Many could not believe the

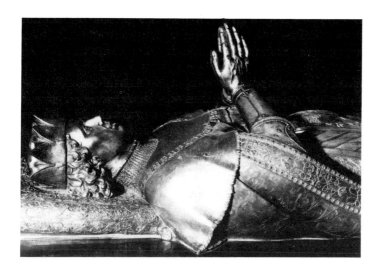

*Sixteenth-century tomb
of Charles the Bold.
Copyright ACL
Bruxelles*

news, the whole story seemed too incredible and for several decades rumours circulated that Charles was still alive and concealed either as a prisoner in some Rhenish castle or as a penitent hermit in some cave high up in the forests. He was absorbed into the world of sub-history and legend as another Arthur awaiting a resurrection.[3] The duke's death was one of the momentous events of the century. As the Venetian Senate concluded with their usual circumspection:

> The fate of the Duke of Burgundy cannot be otherwise than that of the greatest importance and seriousness because so much depended on him. It should surely provide food for thought for many a year in the minds of all intelligent men who are concerned with what the future will bring.[4]

For those who seek to parcel out our unwieldy past into neat packages, the duke's death might be regarded as the end of the Middle Ages. The period from Nancy to the accession of the duke's great-grandson as Emperor Charles V was to be half a century of dramatic transition. The maritime monarchies of England, France and Spain became increasingly powerful and there were fewer opportunities for the assembly or survival of those opportunistic collections of fiefs which had been so well exemplified by the Duchy of Burgundy. It is ironic that the victors of Nancy, the free cities of the Rhine valley, also suffered and their independence, security and prosperity also declined along with the vanquished Burgundy.

Nowhere were the shock waves felt more strongly than in the duke's own lands. With his death the whole process of Burgundian expansion was halted. Up to 1477 it had seemed likely that the Burgundian dukes would succeed in establishing themselves as new monarchs controlling the crucial wedge of strategically valuable territory between France and the Empire. With historical hindsight, the political unreality of the old middle kingdom of Lotharingia is in sharp contrast to its geographical, economic and cultural unity, but Duke Charles' efforts to centralise these lands had been taken very seriously by his contemporaries. Moreover the dream of a middle kingdom did not die with Charles. As late as 1903 the Kaiser Wilhelm II was reported to have told an astonished King of the Belgians that he would remake Lotharingia. In 1476 Lotharingia had been closer to reality than at any time since the tenth century. This had been the achievement of the four Valois Dukes of Burgundy who had patched together one of the greatest patrimonies in Europe. But with the sudden death of Charles and the accession of a young, unmarried and inexperienced heiress, the whole edifice cracked from top to toe.

In spite of the loss of the Duchy of Burgundy itself together with most of the southern French lands, enough was salvaged for the inheritance to be known as Burgundy for yet another half century. This was largely due to the valiant rearguard action fought by the duke's inheritors. No one fought for the inheritance with more stubborn determination than Margaret herself, who was resolved to thwart Louis XI's plans to dismember and destroy the duchy forever. Without Margaret's intervention, 1477 would have been an even more decisive date in European history and little of the administrative and political unity of the Low Countries would have survived.

All her life both as Duchess of Burgundy and, before 1468, as a daughter of the House of York, seemed to have been a preparation for the catastrophe which confronted Burgundy in January 1477. For Margaret at least there was a strong sense of déjà vu about the dreadful news which began to reach Ghent on the 8 or 9 January. It was sixteen years since she had waited with her mother for the confirmation of the deaths of her father and her brother at Wakefield. Nor was it the first time that Margaret and her step-daughter had received reports that Charles was dead. This had happened after the battle of Murten but they were relieved to hear that he was alive and safe in Franche Comté. No doubt this time too they continued to hope for better news before confronting the full extent of the disaster. The grim wheel of fortune had certainly taken a sharp downward turn, but Margaret was well steeled to face this downfall and she was also able to draw on her deep religious faith. Mary would have received strong and reassuring support from her step-mother during the dark days of January and February.

It is not known exactly when the first news reached the two women at the heart of the crisis. Louis XI heard the first reports of the battle late on 8 January. He announced the duke's defeat on the following day and gave orders for his armies to seize the Duchy of Burgundy, Mâcon, Picardy and the Somme towns. He was not, however, entirely confident in the accuracy of his messengers for he qualified his instructions to the Lord of Craon to move into Burgundy with the phrase 'if it is true that the Duke of Burgundy is dead.'[5] By the 12th however he was sure of the duke's death and he commanded the citizens of Poitiers, where he was staying, to stage a procession celebrating the deaths of his two greatest enemies, Charles and the Sforza Duke of Milan, who had been murdered on 26 December.

The palace of Ten Waele at Ghent is hardly any further from Nancy than is Poitiers. Like Louis, Margaret and Mary may have had the first bad news by the night of 8 January. But they continued to hope that the rumours were unfounded. On the 15th, Margaret was still writing to Malines that 'we are hoping that by the grace of God he is still alive and well and out of the hands of his enemies.'[6] In their first letter to Louis on 18 January the two women repeated their increasingly forlorn hope that Charles might still be alive. It was not until three days after this that the official memorial service was held at St Jan's Church in Ghent (now St Bavo's) and it was four days later before Margaret assumed full mourning for her husband.[7]

In this interim period Margaret and Mary acted jointly, Mary using the title of Duchess and Margaret styling herself 'Duchesse Mere de Bourgogne'. In spite of their hopes that Charles was still alive they had to act with speed and resolution for the situation was truly appalling. Not only was the French king invading all the French fiefs, but internal rebellions were beginning to erupt all over the Low Countries. There was an immense upsurge of anger and frustration. Since 1475 three ducal armies had been destroyed and there was general horror at this waste of men and money and at the oppression which had put these lost armies into the field. With few troops left to defend either their territories or themselves, Mary and Margaret faced assaults on ducal authority from every direction. David of Burgundy, Bishop of Utrecht, was driven out of his bishopric and revolt swept the ducal officials from Guelders. In Flanders the cities were united in their resolve to claw back the rights and privileges which they had been forced to abandon to the powerful and despotic duke. In their fury they even turned against the popular Mary, for as Commynes sagely commented, 'the men of Ghent always love the son of their prince but never the prince himself.'[8]

Margaret was well acquainted with the problems affecting the duchy and she knew that they must be resolved quickly if they were to present a united defence against France. Two days after the first news of Nancy, on 11 January, Margaret and Mary sent out a summons for the estates general to assemble at Ghent on 3 February. During the next two weeks, messengers were despatched to the cities and provinces urging them to support the new duchess against the French invaders and promising alleviation of the harsh taxation, better government and more gentleness from the ruler.[9] Margaret, then thirty-one years old and with considerable experience in government, was the most constant adviser and supporter of the twenty-year-old duchess. Their close and trusting relationship ensured that they could cooperate fully. Margaret appreciated the need to win the support of the estates and she was well aware of their complaints. She had had to listen to their protests regularly during the past two years and her approach had certainly been more conciliatory than that of other ducal councillors such as the Chancellor Hugonet.[10] By the time the estates began to assemble, late in January, Mary had been well prepared to meet their demands. In her opening speech she renounced the remainder of the 500,000 crowns levy which had been granted to Duke Charles for six years. Within a week the ducal councillors had accepted the draft of the Great Privilege, a charter designed to satisfy the many demands for the restoration of local rights and privileges.[11] The new duchess promised to rule with the advice of the great council, which would include delegates from the estates, and she assured them that all major decisions, such as her choice of husband and matters of war and peace, would be submitted to the estates for their approval. The estates would also be permitted

Olivier de La Marche

to assemble whenever they considered it necessary and the rights of the regional courts were upheld against the much hated central court at Malines. The extent of these concessions and the fact that the Great Privilege was available in both Dutch and French by 11 February suggests that it had been in preparation for some time. Margaret's advice together with that of Ravenstein and Gruuthuyse, who were also in close contact with the opinion in Flanders, Holland and Brabant, guided Mary to make this major move of conciliation as speedily as she did.

The Dowager Duchess Margaret's presence during the first months of 1477 was especially important because the young duchess had so few experienced advisers on whom she could depend. Louis' claims that, in the absence of a male heir, he had the right to repossess all the French fiefs of Burgundy, caused a clash of loyalties for many of the great lords of the duchy who owned lands in the south. There had already been a drift away towards France during Charles' lifetime. Commynes was not the only one who preferred the adroit and clever King Louis XI to the hard and stubborn duke. The calamity of Nancy turned this drift into a landslide. Amongst those who abandoned Mary were her step-uncle Anthony, Count of La Roche, Phillippe de Crèvecoeur, the ducal governor of Picardy and William Biche, Charles' first chamberlain.[12] As well as the defectors to France, many Burgundian nobles and officials had been taken prisoner at Nancy. It took time to arrange and pay all their ransoms and some of them were not freed until July when Maximilian rode north to his marriage. Among the prisoners were Josse of Lalaing, who had been appointed by Charles as the 'tuteur' for Margaret's dower lands, Olivier de La Marche and the Counts of Chimay and Nassau. La Marche was fortunate enough to be back in the Low Countries by Easter but Chimay did not return until July.[13]

Ravenstein and Gruuthuyse had both been members of the council established by Duke Charles to advise and guide Margaret in his absence. They had long experience, much local prestige and were loyal servants of the duchy. Three others who had also served Margaret and Charles well, but who were not so well trusted by the people of Flanders, were the Chancellor Hugonet, Lord Humbercourt and the Bishop of Tournai. They had all earned their unpopularity as the chief instruments of Charles' oppressive taxation and recruitment policies and were held responsible for the harsh and tyrannical administration. Mary was to find that although these men were both loyal and zealous she could neither profit from their counsel nor save them from the attacks of the people. In addition to her official counsellors, Mary had one other trusted companion, the Lady Hallewijn, who had been with her for many years. When the dowager had to leave Ghent, leaving Mary a virtual prisoner, it was through her services that the two women were able to keep in touch.[14]

Thus the Duchess Mary had a limited number of advisers available to help her in Ghent and she also could have little hope of any real assistance from abroad. Since 1475 the Anglo-Burgundian alliance had become a pale shadow of its former strength and although the emperor had assented to the marriage of Mary and Maximilian, he was in no position to send an army into the Low Countries quickly. Margaret did her best to stir Edward IV into action and she was also soon in touch with the emperor urging him to press ahead with the promised marriage. The death of Charles was known in England by mid-January but as late as the 24th of that month Richard Cely was unsure as to what was happening in Burgundy.[15] Margaret had certainly contacted her brother by early February and on the 14th the great council met at Westminster to discuss Charles' death and to decide upon their response to the events in Burgundy as well as to the French invasion of the duchy. Sir John Paston, in common with many others, thought that the Dukes of Clarence and Gloucester would soon be setting off for Flanders at the head of an army to assist both their sister and the new duchess.[16] But Edward was loathe to lose his French pension and the betrothal of his daughter Elizabeth to the dauphin, so he adopted a policy of neutrality. Lord Hastings was despatched to Calais with reinforcements in case the garrison there should be attacked by either side. No doubt he was also there to collect intelligence and to keep the king well informed concerning the course of the war.

Margaret must surely have hoped that Sir John Paston would be proved right. She may well have tried to encourage English intervention by reviving the old idea of a marriage between Mary and her brother Clarence, who was once more eligible for marriage after the death of his wife Isabel Neville in December 1476. English and French contemporaries certainly considered that Margaret:

> whose affections were fixed on her brother Clarence beyond any of the rest of her kindred exerted all her strengths and energies that Mary . . . might be united in marriage to that duke.[17]

But there are few signs of her 'strengths and energies' on the Burgundian side, and whether the idea for this marriage came from Margaret, from Clarence or from Louis XI, who was trying to undermine Margaret's influence both in England and in Flanders, it is hard to determine. An English embassy led by Sir John Donne and John Morton, which arrived in Ghent late in February, certainly proposed a bridegroom for Mary, but the king's candidate was the queen's brother, Anthony Woodville.[18] As a mere earl he was not considered as a possible contender either by Mary or Margaret, neither of whom ever seem to have seriously considered any bridegroom other than the long promised Archduke Maximilian. Maximilian wrote assuring Mary of his intention to marry her on 24 January, and throughout the next three months embassies went to and fro between Mary and Margaret on the one side and the emperor and Maximilian on the other. Margaret's close involvement is shown though the prominence in the negotiations of her *chevalier d'honneur* Guillaume de la Baume, the Lord of Irlain. Later it was he who covered the hotel expenses of the Germans accompanying Maximilian when they arrived penniless at Ghent.[19]

However, in January 1477, the arrival of Maximilian was still six months away and Burgundy had to withstand the invasion by France with no help from outside. While her forces were still inadequate to drive back the French, the duchess could only hope to buy time until the army had been rebuilt. In an effort to do this Mary and Margaret opened negotiations with Louis XI. They sent off a joint letter appealing to him to halt his invasion of their territories. The letter was dated 18 January and was probably an immediate response to the French assault on St Quentin. The letter appears to be a very naive attempt by two weak women.[20] They informed the king of their 'harsh fortune' but added that they still trusted that Duke Charles would return to them. Reminding Louis that he was Mary's god-father they appealed to his 'goodness and mercy', urged him to end his assaults on their territories and to extend to them the 'Christian and seignorial protection due to all widows and orphans'. They signed themselves as 'your very humble small relatives to you our protector'. At first glance the letter was an abject plea that could do their cause little good, but was it in fact a well judged piece of diplomacy? Only the events of the next few months would show. Their appeal was sent off in the care of two officials, Jacques de Tinteville and Thibault Barradot.[21] They tried to contact Louis at Péronne but missing him there they were sent on to Paris. As a result the letter was not delivered for some considerable time and, it seems, not before the first official ducal embassy had reached the king. This delegation included Humbercourt, Hallewijn, Gruuthuyse, Hugonet, the Bishops of Tournai and Arras and Guillaume de Clugny, the brother of the Bishop of Tournai.[22]

Louis brushed aside all their protests against the French invasion, maintaining that the Burgundian lands were, in default of a male heir, forfeit to the French crown. However his interest in Flanders and Hainault could not be based on this principle, since both these counties had come into the possession of the Dukes of Burgundy through the inheritance of the female line. Louis responded to the negotiations by proposing a betrothal between Mary and the seven-year-old dauphin (who was already betrothed to the English Princess Elizabeth), with the cession of Artois and Boulogne to France as sureties for the marriage. On these terms he would agree to renew the Franco-Burgundian treaties of 1475 and to accept Mary's homage. In spite of the negotiations he continued with his invasion and on 26 January, three days after Louis' meeting with the Burgundian delegation, the Hainault delegates arrived in Ghent complaining bitterly at the French attacks on their towns and villages.

While the Burgundian embassy was meeting Louis, preparations were in full swing at Ghent for the assembly of the estates.[23] Mary and Margaret both attended the opening session on 26 January and, after the announcement of the death of Duke Charles, Mary appealed for their loyalty and help against France. The Great Privilege and her other gestures of conciliation were largely successful and during the first week of the assembly a levy of 100,000 men was promised for the war against France, 34,000 of whom were to be recruited at once. The delegates from Hainault were particularly strong in their support of the duchess and in their resolution to drive back the French. On the other hand the Flemish delegates were more anxious to avoid the costs of yet another wasteful war and it was their arguments which persuaded the estates to send another delegation to Louis, including their own representatives, which was instructed to try to negotiate a peace. This embassy set off to meet Louis at the end of February. They reached him at Lens on 3 March but were obliged to follow him to Arras which was surrendered to the French the following day.[24] Some of the delegates from the estates seem to have believed that Hugonet and Humbercourt were responsible for surrendering the city and anger with these two officials was growing. Both Humbercourt and Hugonet owned lands under French suzerainty and they may well have taken the opportunity of their first meeting with Louis to do homage for their lands. This and the surrender of Arras led to accusations of treason being levelled against them.

By the time the delegation from the estates arrived at his court, Louis had received the first letter from Mary and Margaret and he had also conquered large areas of Burgundy. Confident now of the success of all his plans he determined to isolate the young duchess from all her most experienced advisers and so force her to accept a settlement agreeable to France. He therefore retracted his earlier marriage offer, preferring to maintain his original marriage treaty with England and he set to work to make things more difficult for Mary within the Low Countries. Olivier le Daim, Louis' barber-valet, who had risen to become the captain of Meulun and one of the king's most trusted agents, was sent to stir up trouble, first at Tournai and later at Ghent.[25] The king himself fostered the distrust which already existed between the delegates from the

puisses commaudier et a chief
mener ceste conqueste laquele
come il peult appauoir par ce lui
ne lune scauit impossible ne dif
ficile mais prouffitable honnou
ruble et mentouz adfin que St
autant que auez surmonte les
commencement dicestui alexan
dre dautant et plus puisses sur
passer le plushault comble de sa
gloire · A · M · C · n ·

Ce li fine le volume intitule qui
cause ruffe des faiz du grant
alexandre

for get not har that ys on of yor treu
wg ey t . . . . .
my vfarete yrok =

. . . mo . . . . . pour . . .
bonne anne . . . . . de . . .

'for get not har that ys on of yor treu frendes Margarete of York', dedication from Margaret and another from Mary flanking the Tudor arms from a copy of 'Des Faiz du Grant Alexandre' by Quintus Curtius

estates and the duchess' advisers by showing the delegates a letter, purporting to come from Mary, informing Louis that her chief advisers were Ravenstein, Humbercourt, Hugonet and the dowager and that he should deal only through these persons.[26] Thus the wily Louis identified Mary's most resolute supporters and set about reducing their influence. He was particularly keen to undermine Margaret's position and he warned the delegates that she was planning a marriage between Clarence and Mary. He even suggested that she was planning to kidnap her step-daughter and have her taken to England. He used the same story to undermine Margaret's credibility with her brother Edward.[27]

When the delegation from the estates arrived back in Ghent it seemed at first as if Louis' scheming would be wholly successful. The presence of the estates general had raised the political temperature within the city and the pressure for the arrest and punishment of hated ducal officials increased. There were daily parades and demonstrations by craftsmen denouncing bad government and corruption. In an attempt to rally support about her person, Mary was formally inaugurated as Countess of Flanders and Duchess of Burgundy.[28] However uproar broke out when the Pensioner of Ghent, the city's chief delegate to the estates, confronted Mary with the secret letter and denounced the advisers who were named in it. When Mary denied the existence of the letter, the pensioner produced the copy that had been obligingly provided by Louis. It looked as if the duchess had been trying to deal with the French king behind the backs of both the grand council and the estates and that she was acting through those very advisers who were held most responsible for all the bad government of the past. The popular demands for revenge and satisfaction could no longer be contained. The leaders of Ghent, who had submitted to Charles in 1468, were dragged out and executed and threats were made against many other ducal officials.

Of the four ducal advisers named in the secret letter, Ravenstein had too much power and influence in the Low Countries to be attacked openly. Margaret was in a more difficult position, she was now merely the dowager and she had been closely involved in the recruitment of the ducal armies. Moreover the accusation that she was plotting to marry the duchess to her brother Clarence amounted to a charge of treason. Realising that her presence would only inflame matters and make things more difficult for Mary, and also alarmed at the possibility of a direct attack upon herself, she was forced to leave Ghent. In her train she took with her some of the threatened officials such as Olivier de La Marche who later recorded his relief at being able to escape with Margaret. 'As for me I was advised not to fall into their hands and I went to Malines with Madame.'[29]

Margaret did not leave without making a public protest and she insisted on receiving a personal message from Mary who was, by this time, a virtual prisoner in her own castle. On the square outside the castle gates Margaret made a spirited defence of her own position declaring that although she was a foreigner by birth she was no foreigner in her heart nor in her courage.[30] Escorted by her personal bodyguard of 300 English archers and followed by a convoy of carts and carriages, she then rode off to her dower town of Oudenaarde. On her arrival she organised a solemn and impressive service in honour of the late duke. The long procession, which took place at night, wound its way through a city draped in black velvet and illuminated by torches and flambeaux. It included twenty paupers dressed in new black mourning clothes paid for by Margaret.[31] Oudenaarde was in southern Flanders and nearer to the French invaders. When the French reached Binche, another of Margaret's dower towns in Hainault, the dowager removed her court further north to Malines in Brabant which was to become her principal residence during the twenty-six years of her widowhood.

With the dowager out of Ghent the anger was turned against the remaining officials, especially against the hated 'foreigners' Hugonet and Humbercourt who were now without protection. They were arrested on 19 March together with Jan van Melle, the ducal treasurer for Ghent, and the papal pronotary, Guillaume de Clugny.[32] These four men were particularly unpopular. Humbercourt had been in charge of both Dinant and Liège after their suppression and was hated throughout the Low Countries. Hugonet, one of the late duke's most talented officials, was regarded as the chief enforcer of the harsh taxation through the unpopular central courts at Malines. He was also notorious for his interminable Latin speeches and he had harangued and threatened the estates general when they had resisted the ducal will. Jan van Melle was known as the most corrupt official in Ghent who had enriched himself as a tax collector. When his house was plundered, the contents were estimated to be worth the equivalent of twenty-three years' earnings for a skilled craftsman and one of his fur and velvet cloaks alone was valued at a year's wages.[33] Both Guillaume de Clugny and his brother Ferry, the Bishop of Tournai, were blamed for forcing through the unpopular levies on the church and also simply because they were well known ducal administrators. All these men were paying for Charles' unpopular policies and for his failures.

Humbercourt pleaded that he could only be tried by his peers in the Order of the Golden Fleece but his protests were ignored. Guillaume de Clugny was more successful in pleading benefit of clergy. They were all well aware of what lay in store for them for, in the days before and after their arrests, there had been daily executions of minor officials. All this was taking place during Easter week and the townspeople paraded every day with banners and arms. Mary did not lack courage and she went out into the square to plead in public for her officials. She also tried to get a proper commission established in an attempt to give them a fair trial but there was no time for this to operate.[34] Accused of surrendering Arras to the French, of trying to force Mary to marry the dauphin and of trying to kidnap her when she was out hunting, the three counsellors were found guilty of treason. In spite of Mary's tears, Humbercourt and Hugonet were tortured and condemned to death. The executions took place on 3 April. Van Melle died at 9 a.m. and Hugonet at 12 p.m. The Chancellor who had risen to power as a protégé of the old Chancellor Rolin met his fate with resignation. He wrote to his wife, 'I expect to die today and to leave this world as one could say, to satisfy the people.'[35] At 5 p.m. Humbercourt perished on the same scaffold. The cautious magistrates of Ghent ensured that they received pardons from the duchess for any offence they might have committed on that day.

Both Humbercourt and Hugonet had been associated with Margaret for the whole of her married life. They had taken part in the negotiations which had led to her marriage. Their execution could certainly be seen as a threat against the

Mary of Burgundy as a young girl. Copyright ACL Bruxelles

dowager herself. Both Margaret and the duchess did their best for the families of the dead officials. On 24 April Mary wrote to the magistrates of Malines asking them to give shelter and protection to the widow and children of 'our very dear and faithful cousin the lord of Humbercourt.' The widow was Antoinette de Rembures, and her family went to Malines under the protection of the dowager.[36] The deaths of these men, together with another sixteen of Charles' servants, finally satisfied the people and even provoked a certain reaction in favour of the duchess. Gruuthuyse used his influence to persuade Bruges to withdraw their support from the hard men of Ghent. On 2 April Mary was allowed to leave for her inauguration at Bruges and she stayed away from Ghent until 26 April.

Meanwhile both Mary and Margaret pressed ahead with the plans for the duchess' marriage to the Archduke of Austria. On 26 March, in the midst of all the troubles in Ghent, Mary had written to Maximilian urging him to hasten to her aid. On the day of her inauguration at Bruges she received a personal reply from the Imperial ambassador informing her that Frederick III had publicly invited the bishops and nobles of the empire to accompany his son to his wedding in the Low Countries.[37] But there were still rival candidates for the duchess' hand and Maximilian had not yet set off on his journey. Louis XI had withdrawn his proposal for a marriage with the dauphin but he offered other French princes such as the Count of Angouleme. Closer to home there were candidates whose names were put forward by the different factions within the Low Countries.

The Ghent council supported either a French marriage which would bring peace or a marriage to Adolphe of Egmond, the heir to the Duchy of Guelders. After the Burgundian seizure of Guelders, Adolphe and his brother had been kept under the eye of the Burgundian court. He was well known and popular in Ghent where he had been made an honorary citizen. His candidature was supported by the French agent Olivier le Daim whose intention was to thwart the imperial marriage while supporting the wishes of the Flemish. Moreover the English were hostile to the prospect of a Franco-Burgundian marriage so the promotion of Adolphe of Egmond would suit them also. Through French influence, Adolphe was made the leader of the Flemish militia, but his candidature came to an end when he was killed at the siege of Tournai on 27 June.[38] Another suitor from the Low Countries was Philip of Cleves, the son of Ravenstein and Mary's childhood companion and cousin. How much his candidature was merely a matter of gossip or even a calculated effort to hasten Maximilian's arrival it is hard to judge. Certainly Philip welcomed Maximilian when he came to the Low Countries. He was made Lieutenant General of all the Burgundian forces, fought valiantly for Maximilian at Guinegatte in 1478 and helped to restore order after the uprising in Liège. Indeed during the first decade of Maximilian's government, Philip cooperated very closely with him. Ravenstein certainly did not push his son's candidature with any real determination.[39]

While Europe speculated on the fate of both Mary and Burgundy, Mary and Margaret stuck to their decision that only an imperial marriage could save Burgundy from France and they resolved to follow the policy which had been laid down for them by Charles. They were supported in their determination to bring about the long planned marriage by Lord Gruuthuyse, who acted as one of the chief negotiators for the marriage treaty.[40] Margaret also took the matter firmly in hand and although away from court she pressed ahead with the negotiations and arrangements throughout March and April. She communicated with the emperor promising 'on the word of a princess' to support the match.[41] An imperial embassy visited her court at Malines on 15 April on their way to the duchess at Bruges. Margaret's *chevalier d'honneur* and chamberlain Guillaume de Baume was a signatory to the marriage treaty, and from the very beginning the dowager made her total commitment to Maximilian very clear. On his arrival she promised loyalty and fealty to the archduke and she helped Maximilian to alter the marriage treaty so as to give him more authority within the Low Countries. The original marriage treaty has not survived.[42] It was destroyed, perhaps by Mary and Maximilian themselves because it cut Maximilian out of the succession, leaving all the Burgundian lands to the children of the marriage and specifying that all Burgundian possessions must be under Burgundian rule. This was overruled by an act of 17 September cancelling the relevant articles and leaving all Mary's lands and goods to her husband. It was signed and sealed by Margaret, Mary and Maximilian. The only Burgundian official to sign this agreement was Guillaume de Baume.

A week after the arrival of the imperial embassy in Bruges, Mary married Maximilian by proxy. There was some agitation when the marriage was made public six days later because the duchess had not, as she had promised, consulted the estates or the grand council. However the bloodletting at Ghent seems to have exhausted the opposition and when the estates general reassembled on 7 May they accepted the statement by Jean de la Bouverie, the head of the grand council, that the marriage required no approval since it was merely the fulfilment of arrangements already made by the late duke.[43] Most of the delegates were by now much more sympathetic towards the duchess and the imperial marriage. The French destruction of farms and villages in Artois, Hainault and southern Flanders also served to rally support to the duchess. The estates therefore approved the marriage on the condition that Maximilian would confirm the Great Privilege and they voted more money to help the archduke to recover his wife's lands.

By the end of April Louis must have begun to realise that far from achieving the rapid disintegration of the Burgundian government, his policies had allowed the marriage of Mary and Maximilian to win wide support across the whole of the Low Countries and had increased the resolve to oppose the French invasion of Hainault and Flanders. Perhaps that first plaintive letter from Mary and Margaret had made him underestimate entirely the strength and resolve with which the two women intended to withstand a French takeover. Perhaps too that is exactly what the letter was intended to do. Realising that his plans were now going awry, Louis sent a succession of embassies to the duchess urging her not to marry a 'rude German', but the devastation of the harvest by the French army was not likely to increase the number of francophiles in the Low Countries.[44]

Maximilian's progress towards his beleaguered bride was far from speedy. Indeed he made one of the slowest journeys down the Rhine on record, scarcely in keeping with his armorial device of 'halt mass' ('keep pace'). He left Vienna on 31 May and did not reach Maastricht until 5 August. In his own account of the journey which was written many years later in the allegorical *Weisskünig* and *Teuerdank*[45] Maximilian tried to explain the ten week journey in terms of monsters and perils which beset the route of a young knight. However the more cynical Commynes saw the delay as caused by a shortage of funds, and reported that the archduke's long stay at Cologne was due to the fact that he had to wait for the duchess to send him more money. The time was also spent collecting troops and making careful diplomatic soundings. He checked out exactly how remunerative the Burgundian inheritance would be and both he and the emperor were reported to be delighted when they learnt that the annual revenues had been estimated at over a million florins. Throughout these months, Margaret was in direct correspondence with the emperor who promised to protect her dower lands with the imperial armies. It was an empty assurance since the Emperor Frederick had no spare troops at his disposal, but the promise of imperial protection must have pleased Margaret. Moreover the presence in the Low Countries of Georg Hessler, one of the most important imperial councillors who had been working on this marriage for two years already, must have given her confidence that the arrival of Maximilian was imminent.

The young man on his slow journey to the Low Countries was certainly the most eligible of all the candidates proposed for Mary. Eighteen years old and two years younger than Mary, Maximilian was a blonde-haired elegant young man, well educated and with a talent for languages. He was reputed to be competent in seven including Dutch and English which he learned after his arrival in the Low Countries. Like Mary he enjoyed riding and hunting and their union does seem to have been a particularly happy one. After Mary's early death, Maximilian remained a widower for many years and his second marriage was a purely diplomatic affair. His own account of his youthful marriage was written in the language of chivalry and romance, the story of a young knight setting off on a great adventure to rescue a princess who was under attack from all the forces of evil.[46] Maximilian was certainly an amiable and pleasant young prince and his relations with the dowager were to be useful to them both. Margaret gave Maximilian her firm support throughout the rest of her life and there were never any visible signs of friction between them.

Maximilian arrived at the castle of Ghent on 18 August escorted by 700 to 800 horsemen in a glittering cavalcade. He rode a mighty chestnut horse and was clad in silver armour. On his long golden hair was a diadem of pearls and precious stones. He was the veritable 'White King' of his future autobiography. Margaret returned to Ghent with him and it was the dowager and the Lady Hallewijn who arranged the first meeting between Mary and Maximilian. According to the delegate from Brandenburg who was in Maximilian's retinue, the two ladies organised one of those little scenes so dear to the chroniclers of the fifteenth century. 'At last you have everything that you desired so much' said Margaret as she introduced Mary to her bridegroom.[47] Maximilian was given to understand that the duchess had a carnation hidden in her bosom and that it was his duty to find it. In a portrait of Maximilian painted shortly after his arrival in the Low Countries he is shown holding a carnation. This flower was the symbol

POTENTISSIMVS MAXIMVS · ET · INVICTISSIMVS · CÆSAR MAXIMILIANVS
QVI · CVNCTOS · SVI · TEMPORIS · REGES · ET · PRINCIPES · IVSTICIA · PRVDENCIA
MAGNANIMITATE · LIBERALITATE · PRÆCIPVE · VERO · BELLICA · LAVDE · ET ·
ANIMI · FORTIDVDINE · SVPERAVIT · NATVS · EST · ANNO · SALVTIS · HVMANÆ
M · CCCC · LIX · DIE · MARCII · IX · VIXIT · ANNOS · LIX · MENSES · IX · DIES · XXV
DECESSIT · VERO · ANNO · M · D · XIX · MENSIS · IANVARII · DIE · XII · QVEM · DEVS
OPT · MAX · IN · NVMERVM · VIVENCIVM · REFERRE · VELIT ·

The Emperor Maximilian I in 1519, by Albrecht Dürer

of a betrothal and was often painted in marriage portraits.[48] As soon as Maximilian arrived the wedding was celebrated. Compared to Margaret's marriage, it was a low key affair though the bride wore 'the crown of Burgundy' and the groom wore armour indicating his resolve to drive out the French.

The achievement of this marriage within nine months of the disaster at Nancy, accomplished in the face of internal revolts and a French invasion, was the result of the clear and skilful diplomacy of a very small number of people. Louis at least had no doubt at all that it was Margaret's hands which had been 'on the reins'.[49] The events of 1477 ensured that France was prevented from gaining Hainault and Flanders and Margaret had certainly been determined to achieve this. She had encouraged Mary to make any concessions which would keep the French king at a distance and to preserve Mary's freedom of action in the question of her marriage. Margaret's part was also recognised by the emperor, who thanked her personally for all her assistance[50] and indeed throughout the difficult months of 1477 she had played a vital supportive role. By steering Mary away from a French wedding and bringing a Habsburg into the Low Countries she contributed to a major reorientation in European history. Her Belgian biographer, Luc Hommel, went so far as to claim that she was 'greatly responsible for the existence of the present-day kingdom of Belgium.'[51] The 'most important political combination that ever involved the Low Countries' had been achieved at last in spite of all the obstacles which had been put in its way.[52]

Apart from the major question of Mary's marriage, Margaret had many other preoccupations during the first year of her widowhood. Her own position as dowager was far from secure.[53] Two types of dower settlements operated in Burgundy, the legal and customary arrangements made by most people who had properties to leave, and the contractual arrangement which was based on a treaty or contract made before marriage. Marriages involving great estates usually came within contract arrangements as did the marriage of Margaret and Charles. This meant that Margaret's whole position on the death of her husband was dependant on the marriage treaty of 1468. Margaret's marriage contract had been modelled on earlier contracts drawn up for the marriage of previous Duchesses of Burgundy and particularly on the contract made for the marriage of Isabelle and Philip the Good. Isabelle had brought with her a dowry of only 154,000 crowns but Edward had promised to pay 200,000 crowns with his sister. Margaret's dower was reckoned in terms of a fair return on this capital sum and in Margaret's case this has been calculated as an eight to ten per cent return. During the lifetime of Charles her dower was administered as part of the ducal estates but on his death it reverted to her and her income was to be derived from the revenues from Malines, Termonde, Oudenaarde, Cassel and Le Quesnoy.

However the reversion of the dower on the death of Charles was entirely dependant on the full payment of her dowry and this had not been achieved. Edward had made the first payment on the wedding day but the second payment was incomplete. In May 1476 he had paid 16,000 crowns off the debt but in July of the same year the Burgundian treasury calculated that he still owed 115,000 crowns. When Margaret enquired in March 1477 as to the state of her dowry payments she was told that Edward still owed more than half. This was bad news for Margaret because it meant that she was liable to lose half her dower. She was well aware of the problem and must have already discussed the situation with various officials, because immediately after Charles' death she lost no time in trying to get the position clarified and corrected. She was astoundingly

Miniature depicting Margaret, on the right, and Mary kneeling in the chapel of the Guild of St Anne.
Margaret's device: 'Bien en aviengne' appears four times in the margins

successful. Although she inherited a most unsatisfactory settlement and in spite of a raging national crisis Margaret still managed to secure a very rich dower.

Her first letter to the central courts at Malines went off as early as 15 January when she began collecting together all the relevant documentation. There was an initial delay in locating the documents, many of which were still being kept at Lille, and it took Mary and Margaret several months to find them all. Margaret had to send her own financial official Hippolyte de Berthoz to collect them. There was a further obstacle in that the officials both at Malines and Lille were alarmed at what they were being asked to do. They pointed out the large debt on the dowry and its consequential effect on the dower and they were most reluctant to make up the value of the dower as if the dowry had been paid in full. They tried to prevaricate and insisted that all the orders should be counter-signed by Mary, Margaret and Ravenstein. Considering the fate that had befallen the ducal officials in Ghent their caution was perhaps understandable. However Mary was determined that Margaret should have her dower in full and she ordered the officials to end their delaying tactics and to make Margaret's dower arrangements immediately 'reserving only the rights of sovereignty to us and to our heirs' (sans aultre chose réserver pour nous et nozdis hoirs que le ressort et souveraineté).[54]

In her letter of 28 January, Mary stated very clearly her reasons for her generosity towards her step-mother. Margaret, she said, had always held 'our person and our lands and lordships in such complete and perfect love and goodwill that we can never sufficiently repay and recompense her.' Moreover since the death of the duke, Margaret had 'given freely and cordially of her help and shared in and supported all our affairs with all her might.' Two days later the duchess added more reasons for her resolution that Margaret should receive her full dower, declaring:

> And above all for the sake of the deep love and reverence that we have for our said lady and step-mother and in consideration of all the great goodness help and assistance that she has given us, when we were in her care and we hope she will still give hereafter in all our affairs.[55]

There was yet another reason which Mary put forward for the favoured treatment which she was demanding for her step-mother. By investing Margaret with a great dower it was hoped that her brother Edward IV might be drawn into the defence of her territories to the advantage of the duchy. Mary herself justified her grants to Margaret in these terms:

> she [Margaret] is fully occupied in dealing with the very high and very mighty prince, our well beloved lord and cousin the King of England to persuade him to come to our aid and to uphold the everlasting alliances and treaties which were signed between him and our late lord and father.[56]

By 10 March the officials surrendered and Margaret secured all the dower lands which had formerly belonged to Isabelle of Portugal. She was formally invested with them on 30 May, when her *tuteur* Josse de Lalaing, the Lord of

Montigny, took the feudal oaths on her behalf at Louvain. After the loss to the French of Chaussin and Le Perriere in Franche Comté, Cassel in southern Flanders and Le Quesnoy in Hainault, she was given Brielle and Voorne in Zeeland in their place and a full valuation was made of all her lands. Since the revenues did not reach the promised income of 20,000 crowns, the customs dues of Rupelmonde were added to Margaret's possessions.[57] When Maximilian arrived in August, Margaret acted swiftly to obtain his full agreement to all the arrangements which she had made with Mary. Indeed she seems to have been very impatient indeed, trying to discuss the matter of her dower on the eve of the wedding when Maximilian preferred to talk about the arrangements for the marriage.[58]

As the duchess had explained to her officials, Margaret's chief role in the affairs of Burgundy was as a lever to draw in the support of England. It was a role clearly recognised by Louis XI who regarded her as one of the greatest obstacles to his ambitions vis-à-vis Burgundy. After Charles' death, Edward IV came under a double obligation towards Burgundy, firstly to maintain his treaty obligations towards the duchy and secondly, as Margaret's nearest male relative, to uphold his sister's rights. He acknowledged his brotherly duties when he thanked the duchess for her great generosity towards his sister.[59] But as the Paston letters and the *White Rose Chronicle* show there were many in England who expected Edward to do more than this and were sure that he would send over an army in support of his widowed sister.[60] No doubt Margaret also hoped that he would send military assistance and help to defend Burgundy against Louis XI, although by this time she must have been well aware of Edward's hesitation in such matters. It was in an effort to remind Edward of his moral and military responsibilities towards her that she wrote to him shortly after the fall of Cassel. It was a very strong letter indeed. She reminded Edward that he had made her 'one of the most important ladies in the world,' that he was now her 'only lord, father, husband and brother' and that her situation was harsh and grim. She had become 'one of the poorest widows deserted by everyone, especially by you,' and she appealed to him not to 'leave me in such a miserable estate, to rescue me from the King of France who does his best to reduce me to a state of beggary for the rest of my days.' She begged him to send over 1,000 or 1,500 archers who would be used for her protection and to intercede personally on her behalf with Louis.[61]

If Margaret really expected military support from Edward to defend her dower lands against Louis XI then she hoped in vain. Nevertheless, for honour's sake he was obliged to make diplomatic protests on behalf of his sister and although he had no intention of going to war on her behalf he did make very vigorous protests to Louis on this matter. He also used the threat of his intervention to keep up the pressure on Louis and to ensure the payment of his annuity. He even tried to persuade Louis to make payments for the upkeep of Elizabeth, the future dauphine, but in this he was not successful. As early as February 1477, Edward warned Louis to respect Margaret's property.[62] Louis' initial response was an attempt to discredit her both in Flanders and with Edward by spreading rumours of a plot by Margaret, Hastings and Clarence to kidnap Mary and marry her off to Clarence. The dowager, Louis assured the

Flemings and Edward, was behind the whole enterprise and was secretly in touch with great lords in England to conspire against the king. Edward was unimpressed by these tales and although Clarence was to be arrested and killed in 1478, it was not because of this alleged plot and both Margaret and Hastings remained in the king's favour.[63]

Besides trying to alarm Edward with these stories of conspiracy against him, Louis also instructed his ambassadors to assure the king that Margaret had no rights to these dower lands. Since all the Burgundian inheritance must devolve to him as the late duke's sovereign, it was not in Mary's power to invest Margaret with any territory in France. This too was given little credence by King Edward and after the burning and plundering of Cassel together with fifty-two villages and whole areas around Oudenaarde, Le Quesnoy and Binche by the French in August 1477, he increased the diplomatic pressure on Louis by sending his almoner, Thomas Danet, to make indignant objections at the French 'attacks upon the King's sister without reason' and to claim compensation of 40,000 crowns on her behalf.[64] An English embassy was also despatched to Flanders to give some support to the duchess. When Louis heard of John Coke's arrival at Ghent he immediately sent Edward the annuity which was due, and he instructed his ambassadors to woo Edward with soft words assuring him of his love and care for Margaret, promising to extend towards her all his protection as soon as she would submit to him as her sovereign lord. He insisted that Margaret had no grounds for complaint against him either on the question of her dower lands or in any other matter.

Throughout 1477 to 1480 the ambassadors went to and fro between England, France and the Low Countries and Louis repeated his offers to protect Margaret if she would put herself and her lands into his care. He would then restore all her dower lands to her and make reparation for any damage caused by the war. In the meantime the French attacks on Burgundy continued though there was a brief truce in July 1478. Margaret continued to appeal to Edward and he agreed to renew the Anglo-Burgundian treaties. During these years Louis continued to recognise Margaret as a major impediment to his plans. He warned his ambassadors that they would be stupid to expect the 1480 Franco-Burgundian conference to be successful because Margaret was in control and she would do all in her power to prevent a settlement.[65] Louis was finally obliged to negotiate with the dowager and the treaty of Arras saw all her lands restored and she obtained satisfactory reparations. Edward had done little to bring about this settlement. His concessions to Malines in November 1478, allowing the merchants of that city to trade in England on the same preferential terms as the members of the Hanseatic league, were presumably a sop to Margaret and the trading licences which he renewed for her fall into the same category.[66]

Immediately after the marriage of Maximilian and Mary, Margaret started to establish herself at Malines. Her choice of this city as her chief residence was governed by several factors not least of which was the fact that it had become the home of the central court during the lifetime of her husband. His selection of the city as the judicial centre of the Low Countries may have weighed heavily with her since she was zealous in the preservation of his memory. The central courts of the Low Countries remained at Malines right up to the French revolution and earned for the city its soubriquet of 'Malines La Prudente'.[67] Brabant was also much more accommodating to the will of their ducal rulers than was Flanders and Malines was a loyal city when compared with Ghent or Bruges. Nor was it as prone to urban riots and protests. Moreover Malines was the richest and most centrally situated of all her dower towns. She owned seventeen villages in the area as well as the nearby castle of Arkel, which she had repaired and where she installed her own constable Engelbert de Falleton.[68]

Malines was a pleasant and prosperous city, lying on the River Dyle, and it was easily defended, surrounded as it was by a series of moats and walls. The population of about 25,000 made it one of the larger cities of the Low Countries and there was a strong industrial base to support all its commercial enterprise. There was a busy port with a series of quays and a large city crane dominated the waterfront. Malines had a long standing feud with Brussels over its right to levy tolls on the traffic which passed up the Dyle and along the Senne to its neighbour, and it competed with Brussels for the lion's share of the trade of central Brabant. Although its cloth industry was, by 1477, well into decline, lace-making provided work for the women of the town and carpet weaving was a growing business. Glass and pottery were also manufactured on a large scale and the city had a reputation for quality metal crafts and fine leather work, which was said to rival Cordova. It had attracted skilled workers from the crushed cities of Dinant and Liège and there were several firms making armour and armaments, and also bell foundries.[69] The city had been largely rebuilt in the late fourteenth and early fifteenth century following a great fire which had destroyed a third of the town in 1342 and the corporation had had the foresight to see that all the main roads inside the walls were paved. It was thus reputed to be very clean and domestic animals were not allowed to wander about soiling the well-kept streets. Throughout Margaret's lifetime the great tower of St Rombout's church was being built. The city fathers were hoping to build a landmark of 150 metres which would rival the height of the towers at Antwerp, Bruges and Louvain. By 1477 the tower had reached roof height and building continued up to 1520 when at a height of 92 metres the work had to stop because the foundations would not support any more weight. By the sixteenth century the great tower housed forty-nine bells, the forerunners of today's fine carrillon.

It was an ideal city for the dowager's court, but there was no ducal palace in the city. Margaret remedied this by purchasing its largest house which had belonged to John of Burgundy, the Bishop of Cambrai. It was bought for her by Guillaume de Baume and Corneille de Barre in the November of 1477 and at the same time she purchased seven adjoining houses and all their land. During the following year the old house was totally rebuilt and greatly extended under the supervision of Anthony Keldermans, one of the family of well known architects who were based in Malines. The house had cost 4,000 florins and the rebuilding must have added a great deal more to the price. However the city corporation, enthusiastic at the idea of attracting the dowager into permanent residence, offered her 2,000 florins towards her expenses and throughout her stay in Malines she received many gifts towards the costs of maintaining and improving her residence.[70]

The palace of Margaret of York at Malines from an engraving by R. Blokhuyse. Margaret's residence lay behind the street façade marked by the stepped gable and the three small Gothic towers. The larger buildings belong to a later Jesuit college

Margaret's house, which evolved into the ducal palace during the minority of Mary's son Philip, had a long façade with many windows facing onto the road, now known as the Keyserstraat. It was built in red brick decorated with white stripes, having a hexagonal tower at one corner and a stone balcony supported by four griffins and four lions on the second floor. Here the dowager could appear before her people. In front of the entrance there was a court of honour and behind the palace there were extensive gardens, a tennis court, a shooting gallery and baths. Hot baths on an almost Roman style were still very popular in the Low Countries and most of the nobles had private baths which they used frequently. In Malines there were also several public baths but not as many as at Bruges, which was notorious for its public baths many of which were also centres of prostitution.

Margaret lived on the upper floor of the two storied building and her reception rooms were splendid. Her great council chamber was magnificent and vast, so large that it is now the site of a theatre, and it had several monumental marble fireplaces. Her state rooms were painted by Baudouin van Battel of Malines, who worked for many of the noble families of Brabant, and her chair of state was upholstered in the finest black velvet. The walls of her private study were hung with violet taffeta and her library of illuminated manuscripts and printed books was kept safe behind a wrought iron grill made by Gauthier van Battel, the brother of Baudouin. Paintings hung on the sombre walls, surely some of the van Eycks which belonged to the Burgundian court, as well as the van der Weydens, Memlincs and Bouts which later came into the collection of Margaret of Austria. The portrait of her husband by Rogier van der Weyden, now hanging in Berlin, would have had pride of place in her collection. As well as her books and paintings Margaret had a rich collection of tapestries and plate, some of which she bought at the sales of Hugonet's estates in September 1478.[71] Within her private chambers the dowager passed her leisure time in prayer, reading and perhaps playing chess, a subject upon which she had several books in her library.

The dowager's household was large, probably over one hundred and fifty persons. At its head was her knight of honour, Guillaume de Baume whose family continued to serve at the ducal court for several generations. Under his command there was a small bodyguard of knights and archers, captained by Olivier de Famars, who escorted the dowager on her travels. She was attended by ladies of honour, maids and valets as well as having her own chaplains, almoner and confessors. From 1490 her confessor was Jan Briart of Ath a well known theologian. She had several doctors, including Lambert de Poorter and William Roelandts, and a number of surgeons whose chief task was bleeding their mistress to preserve the balance of her 'humours'. Margaret had an intelligent interest in preventative medicine, especially in how to avoid the epidemics of plague which swept through the Low Countries during her lifetime. The pestilence was particularly bad in 1479 and it was at this time that 'Mastur John de Wymus Doctor Servant to the Lady Margret of Borgon' wrote out his regimen for her to follow. She was advised not to walk at midday or when it was hot or cloudy and never to walk with a full stomach or to do anything at a fast pace. She was also warned never to sleep during the day time, to avoid swift changes of temperature and to abstain from eating sweet milk and cheese. Doubtless she also drank the various mixtures devised to ward off the plague, remedies which included herbs like feverfew, burnet, sorrel, rue and marigolds.[72]

In addition to all her personal attendants there were the usual staff of a great household including the footmen, stable boys and farriers who looked after the dogs, horses and falcons. Many of the staff lived outside the palace in the town and each morning and evening the porter checked the servants as they came in and out. Each day at noon all the staff dined at the palace and a strict etiquette was maintained on the rights and privileges of every member of the household. Margaret usually dined alone; she had ivory and ebony handled knives, and concluded each meal by sipping her 'spices of the table' or digestive powders. She was sufficiently interested in her food to award a pension of £73 to her jam maker, Gontier Postel who was commended for his special 'jams and conserves of roses and other flavours.'

The citizens of Malines benefited greatly from the presence of the dowager in their city. They gained trading privileges from England and from the emperor and special concessions from Maximilian and from his son Philip the Fair which put them on the same terms as their great rival Brussels.[73] Moreover they could expect visits to their city by the Burgundian court, great nobles and foreign embassies. Both the imperial and the English ambassadors called frequently at Malines. All this brought wealth and prosperity to the town. Understandably the corporation was anxious when Margaret left to visit her other properties, writing to enquire after her health and to urge her to return to them. There was great rejoicing when she returned from England in 1480 for alarming rumours had circulated that she had chosen to remain in her native land.[74]

However there was little that would have tempted Margaret away from Burgundy where, within a year of her husband's death, she had established herself in a very grand estate. She was one of the richest widows in Europe, she had secured for herself a very generous dower settlement and she had a comfortable and opulent household at Malines. All this had been achieved in the midst of a national crisis and while she was being so pathetically 'beggared' by the King of France.

5 Madame La Grande

'The unsteadfastness of this world being'

The years 1477–1494 were one of the most troubled periods in the whole history of the Burgundian Netherlands. The war with France continued with few respites and civil unrest resulted in a series of confrontations which led ultimately to the imprisonment of Archduke Maximilian. Throughout these difficult years Margaret remained a prominent centre of loyalty to Mary and Maximilian and their heirs. Indeed there were times when her court at Malines was one of the few places where ducal power and authority was entirely secure.

Yet in spite of all the troubles in the Low Countries, Margaret never lost contact with her native land. After her marriage she only visited England once but she remained a figure to be reckoned with in English affairs. Both Edward IV and his brother, the Duke of Clarence, named daughters after her, a sign of their esteem and respect and a recognition of her role in healing the family rift of 1470. No documentary evidence has remained of her personal contacts with England though there are signs that her commercial dealings continued steadily, at least until the death of Richard III. But she had plenty of opportunities to keep herself well informed of what was going on. English embassies were often in the Low Countries though frequently the news they brought must have been both alarming and astonishing.

At few times can she have been more perplexed than at the news which reached her in June 1477. Coming as it did in the midst of the succession crisis in Burgundy, Margaret would have had little opportunity to react or to intervene. To hear that Clarence on whom 'her affections were fixed beyond any of the rest of her kindred' had been arrested and imprisoned in the Tower must surely have caused her a great deal of concern.[1] Only six years earlier she had worked hard to secure his return to the family allegiance and when she had seen him last, in 1475, his old treason appeared to have been forgiven and forgotten. There is, it is true, little to support the opinion of the Croyland chronicler that Margaret was particularly fond of Clarence. She had certainly passed much of her youth in the company of her brothers George and Richard and, during the 1460s, she and George had both been in residence at Greenwich where their annuities and expenses had been paid out by the same royal officials.[2] However from the beginning of the negotiations for Margaret's marriage to Charles, their interests had begun to diverge.

It was the king and the Woodvilles who promoted the Burgundian marriage and Clarence's interests had been set aside. He had been present at the famous Smithfield Tournament and he had accompanied his sister on her departure at least as far as Canterbury, but none of her brothers had accompanied her to Bruges, where her presenter had been Anthony Woodville. By the time that Margaret had sailed from Margate, Clarence had already begun his drift into rebellion. He may well have considered that Margaret's marriage had been given priority over his own and he was hardly a man to show patience and understanding, as is only too clear in his dealings with his brother Richard over the Beauchamp fortune.[3]

In spite of their divergence of interest over her marriage and his later treason, Margaret may still have had a personal attachment to Clarence who was certainly handsome and likeable, 'seemly of person, right witty and well visaged, a great almsgiver and a great builder.'[4] He was also apparently more chaste than either of his two brothers (he left no illegitimate children) and he was a generous almsgiver, characteristics which would have pleased his pious sister. However there is little to show that she was eager to arrange a marriage between him and her step-daughter in 1477.[5] A marriage between Mary and Clarence would only have been really valuable to Burgundy if it could have secured full military support for the duchy and this was most unlikely. There was little to commend the match to Edward IV since Mary already had, through her father, a very substantial claim to the English throne and any children born to Clarence and Mary would have been a real threat to the inheritance of Edward's own children. Moreover the English king was resolved to maintain his French pension and the French marriage for his daughter. By early March both Margaret and Mary were pushing ahead with the Habsburg marriage, and any consideration of Clarence had been at most a passing fancy. A more positive indication of her interest in her brother George is the dedication to him of *The Game and the Playe of Chesse* printed by her protégé William Caxton.[6] Caxton brought this book with him when he came to England and its inscription to Clarence suggests that Margaret had recommended him to the patronage of her brother, though the author's emphasis on the proper duties of each piece on the board may indicate that the book was intended as an instructive homily. By the time Caxton arrived in London it was too late, and Clarence's fortunes were already on the decline.

The cause of Clarence's fall in 1477 is obscure but there were many problems between the king and his brother. Clarence may have had private ambitions to become the next Duke of Burgundy and if so, once more his matrimonial advantage was being set aside, this time for the sake of the marriage of Elizabeth to the dauphin. There was another marriage proposal for Clarence which may have aggravated the situation. The King of Scotland was proposing a double marriage between the House of Stuart and the House of York: Clarence was to marry Margaret, James III's sister, and his brother Alexander, Duke of Albany, was to marry Margaret (Albany was portrayed kneeling behind King James III on the altar-piece painted by Hugo van der Goes[7]). King Edward rejected these proposals on the grounds that both Margaret and Clarence were too recently widowed to consider remarriage:

George, Duke of Clarence

We thank him as heartily as we can, and for as much also as after the old usages of this our realm no estate nor person honourable communeth of marriage within a year of their doole, we therefore as yet cannot conveniently speak in this matter.[8]

Edward appears to have replied to the Scottish proposals without consulting either Margaret or Clarence. He had no intention of promoting his unreliable brother nor of becoming involved in Burgundian matters. If Clarence heard anything of this proposal he could only have been irritated.

Clarence may have disagreed with the royal policy of non-intervention in the Franco-Burgundian war. Paston expected him to be sent to Burgundy with an army and this idea could have been circulated by Clarence himself. The additional rumours, that Margaret and English lords were conspiring to kidnap Mary and marry her off to Clarence, may also have served to fuel Edward's suspicions even if he publicly disregarded them. There is a certain similarity in the impact of these French rumours both in Ghent and London. In Flanders they resulted in Margaret's exile from the Burgundian court and in England the arrest of Clarence came at much the same time. However the main reason for his arrest was that the relations between the king and his brother had reached breaking point. Royal suspicion and Clarence's own genuine distress over the death of his wife in December 1476 caused the headstrong duke to fear for his own safety. In his panic he precipitated the events which led to his death in the famous barrel of malmsey wine. He openly challenged royal justice, he accused persons of poisoning his late wife and he publicly defied the king. He may also have threatened the succession, reviving the rumours that Edward's marriage to Elizabeth Woodville was invalid due to Edward's precontract with another. There would appear to be plenty of reasons for his arrest in June 1477, apart from any involvement with Burgundy. But the Burgundian angle is persistent. Clarence was accused of planning to send his heir, the two year old Edward, to safety in Burgundy.[9] This may have been seen by contemporaries as a plausible idea since George had himself been sent there in 1461. However the Burgundy of 1477 was a far cry from the peaceful country of the previous decade. It is unlikely that Clarence would have thought of despatching his son to a country in the throes of invasion and civil war. The duke's contemporaries and the early Tudor historians were perplexed by his arrest and subsequent death. Polydore Vergil claimed that no one could give him a satisfactory explanation why Clarence had been killed and the Croyland chronicler laid the blame squarely on King Edward himself, 'for not a single person uttered a word against the duke except the king, and not one individual made answer to the king except the duke.'[10] It was indeed 'a sad strife carried on before these two brothers of such high estate.' Edward had finally had more than he could tolerate from his provocative brother and being especially angered at 'the conduct of the before named duke as being derogatory to the laws of the realm and dangerous to judges and jurors throughout the kingdom' he decided to arrest and imprison him.

Clarence was held at the Tower for seven months, the king's original intent may have been merely to intimidate rather than to kill him. He was executed in January 1478, during the last days of the festivities accompanying the marriage of Edward's second son Richard to Anne Mowbray, the infant heiress of the Duke of Norfolk. Was the famous malmsey wine a gift from someone at court who thought the duke should not be entirely excluded from the celebrations?[11] The conclusion that the Woodvilles finally persuaded Edward to kill Clarence, because of their fears for the succession as long as he was still alive, is convincing. During the seven months that he was in the Tower there is no evidence that Margaret or anyone else intervened to save his life. His mother was silent, his sister Elizabeth, Duchess of Suffolk, was satisfied by grants of lands and his brother, Richard of Gloucester, was one of the chief beneficiaries of his removal, acquiring some of his lands and his offices.[12] Richard salved his conscience by founding chantries at Middleham and Barnard Castle, where prayers would be said for Clarence's soul and for his other deceased relatives.[13] Margaret no doubt made similar intercessions in her private prayers. Nobody however acted to protect Clarence. The handsome duke had made too many enemies and had too few friends.

Although the death of Clarence was the first case of fratricide in the House of York, it was not greeted by contemporaries with much horror and astonishment. It was upstaged by another assassination which took place in the same year. The removal of Clarence, even by drowning in a butt of malmesy, was nothing compared with the high drama of the Pazzi conspiracy in Florence when, with the connivance of the Pope, one of the Medici princes was murdered during Mass in the cathedral. This was the event which caught the public eye rather than the removal of one whose survival since 1472 had only been due to the magnanimity of the king.

Margaret spent most of the seven months that Clarence was in the Tower at the ducal court. After the marriage of Mary and Maximilian she remained at Ghent until September, when she left for Malines, visiting Antwerp on her way. She was at Malines late in January when the Archduke Maximilian visited the city for the first time and he was given a Joyeuse Entrée.[14] She must have been celebrating this event when she heard that Clarence was dead. By summer Margaret was back at Bruges and when the duchess' first child was born, it was the dowager who carried the infant Philip to his christening on 28 June.[15] Maximilian, busy with the campaign against France, did not see his son until August. The heir had been named after his grandfather, Philip the Good whose reputation was honoured throughout the Low Countries, and his christening was celebrated with great splendour designed to rally the people behind their new ducal family. Stately processions escorted the child from the castle to the church of St Donatian nearby. The infant was resplendent in crimson cloth of gold trimmed with ermine and his long train was supported by the Lady Ravenstein. On either side of Margaret, who was the godmother, walked the two godfathers, Lord Ravenstein and Pierre of St Pol, the Count of Luxembourg. Margaret was attended by her own *chevalier*, the Lord of Irlon and her own bodyguard. The corporation of Bruges presented the new heir with a purse containing 40,000 crowns and the gifts from the godparents were in keeping with his princely inheritance: a sword from Lord Ravenstein, a helmet and a golden lily from the Count of Luxembourg and from Margaret, a gold chain valued at 20,000 crowns.[16]

In the midst of all the ceremony of the ducal christening there was an incident which illustrates well both the personal nature of ducal power and Margaret's own shrewd appreciation of the need for public support. There had been rumours that the infant was a girl, rumours put about by French agents. Margaret's delight in the arrival of the long awaited male heir is manifest in the promptness of her letter to Malines announcing Philip's birth and she must have been very displeased by these rumours. She was therefore resolved to expose the lies, and as the procession was returning to the palace, she undressed the baby and showed him to the people. The Flemish were delighted to be sure that the child was a boy and also suitably impressed by Margaret's 'real spirit' (veel pit). It was not the first time nor would it be the last that Margaret showed herself capable of making a direct appeal to the people.

Margaret and Mary continued to spend most of their time together just as they had done during Charles' military campaigns. They were together at Ghent for the Christmas of 1478 and in January Margaret accompanied Mary on her Joyeuse Entrée at Dendermonde. Maximilian's victory at Guinegatte, on 7 August 1479, succeeded in driving the French away from south Flanders and two days later Mary and Margaret attended the procession of the Holy Blood at Bruges to give thanks. Christmas of 1479 found them at Brussels where Mary's second child was born. This time the baby was a girl who was named after the dowager herself. Once more Margaret was the godmother and she carried the baby to its baptism, at the great church of St Michael and St Gudule. These two Margarets, although separated by two generations, were to have much in common. Both were married to foreign princes and both remained childless. Margaret of Austria, like her English namesake, made Malines her chief residence and, as governor of the Low Countries during the minority of Charles V, her nephew, she showed the same efficient and practical approach to government as her godmother. She would inherit her godmother's library and her pictures, her servants and officials, even her *chevalier d'honneur* came from the family of de Baume.[17]

When Maximilian was at court, Margaret was often still in residence and she established an excellent relationship with her step son-in-law. She was careful to show him every consideration. In the *Weisskünig* Maximilian paints a pleasant picture of the ducal court where he took French lessons from Mary and Dutch lessons from the 'old duchess' or 'the old lady' ('alte fuerstin' or 'die alte fraw').[18] This is interesting on several counts, not least since it indicates that Margaret was proficient enough in Dutch to be teaching it to Maximilian. Unlike her thirteenth century predecessor Margaret, the daughter of King Edward I, who had married Duke John of Brabant,[19] Margaret was never reproached with an ignorance of Dutch. Perhaps this is why she found it so easy to make the Low Countries her home and why she was such a respected figure there. The description also indicates that the dowager had a secure and permanent place at court. The 'old duchess' was in fact only thirty-four years old in 1480. She was quite young enough to have married again. Her aunt Catherine Neville was still remarrying at twice her age. Yet apart from the proposed marriage to the Duke of Albany and a French rumour concerning a proposal from an unknown source in 1480, there are no other references to a second marriage for Margaret. There were several reasons for this. Primarily, a barren woman was hardly the most desirable of wives, but there were also few dukes or princes who could offer Margaret a status equivalent to her establishment as the Dowager of Burgundy. Margaret herself never appears to have considered the question either out of respect for her late husband or simply because she preferred her widowhood in the Low Countries. Both Mary and Maximilian found Margaret a valuable asset in the government of the duchy, her marriage would have caused unnecessary complications and she was perhaps also too useful to lose.

Throughout the war with France, Margaret was busy raising money and men for the struggle. She was especially active in the defence of her dower properties which were threatened and besieged by France, and she called on her other dower cities such as Malines to help them. She wrote to the Malines magistrates in 1477, ordering them to send their troops as promised to 'our cousin Lord Ravenstein' under 'a good chief Phelippe Ceeman [Neman or Kerman who acted as commander for the Malines troops for several years] or another as you wish.' They were to march at once for the defence of Oudenaarde. Two years later the dowager wrote again, from Antwerp, sending a series of ordinances for the deposition and service of the Malines battalions and ordering the magistrates to see that all her commands were carried out with 'good diligence'.[20] Sixty companies of troops were sent to Le Quesnoy, where they were very useful to Maximilian and he wrote thanking Malines for their service. More men were despatched to Binche and La Motte, where they were to perform garrison duty and four *arbalestriers* or *culvriniers* were sent to Oudenaarde. These were a type of small canon or field gun, notable for their long barrels and were manufactured by the armourers of Malines. The dowager kept troops in the field with the ducal armies for many years and letters written to Malines by Maximilian in 1481 refer to men from the city who were defending the dowager's lands at Le Quesnoy, Binche, Cassel and other places.[21]

In spite of all the troops and money that were pumped into the war effort, the ducal armies were hard stretched and successive revolts in Utrecht and

The Seal of Mary, Duchess of Burgundy, showing her riding and carrying a falcon, 1477. Copyright ACL Bruxelles

Guelders distracted Maximilian from the main war with France. Large areas of Flanders and Hainault were laid waste by the invading armies, pirates attacked the Dutch herring fleets, riots broke out in Ghent over the imposition of an unpopular beer tax and the archduke was accused of selling off the ducal treasures to English and Italian merchants. Eager to terminate the war with France so that they could concentrate on their other problems, Mary and Maximilian resolved to try once more to draw England into an alliance. Edward too was showing himself more sympathetic towards the Burgundian cause and in 1480 Margaret headed an embassy to her brother. Her presence was a public indication of the rapprochement between England and Burgundy. It certainly alarmed Louis who immediately increased his own efforts to retain both his English alliance and to negotiate a settlement with Burgundy.

The dowager left Bruges on 24 June and was in England for more than three months. She travelled with a large retinue headed by Guillaume de Baume and the embassy included two officials who were well known to her: Thomas Plaines and Jean Gros, the treasurer of the Order of the Golden Fleece. She received aides from the estates to cover her expenses with the Hainault estates contributing 4,000 livres.[22] Her mission had several goals, but the immediate need was to obtain some military help in the form of English archers to reinforce Maximilian's hard pressed armies. The main purpose of the embassy was to achieve a full Anglo-Burgundian alliance and commit Edward to military intervention against France. She was also to negotiate a treaty of marriage between the ducal heir Philip and Edward's daughter Anne of York. This proposal had first been discussed in August 1479, when Edward agreed to send 500 archers to help Maximilian.[23] The negotiations for the marriage were not easy. The archduchess and her husband were hoping for a dowry of 200,000 crowns, the same as the one Edward had promised with Margaret in 1468. Edward, on the other hand, was expecting to pay no dowry at all and even to be offered a Burgundian replacement for his French annuity. The marriage negotiations were the focus of the embassy and the chronicler of the abbey of the Dunes thought that Margaret would be bringing her niece Anne home with her.[24] Maximilian, however, viewed Margaret's visit to England as a two-edged weapon which could also be used to force Louis into negotiations for a realistic peace with Burgundy, and while Margaret was busy in England he kept up the diplomatic pressure on France.

The king sent Sir Edward Woodville, the queen's younger brother, aboard the royal ship the *Falcon* to bring his sister across the Channel. It was twelve years since she had sailed to her marriage. Sir Edward had been part of her marriage party and he had won the honours in the famous joust of the Golden Tree. This time she took the shorter route from Calais to Gravesend where she was received by Sir John Weston, the Prior of the Knights of St John.[25] She then transferred to a royal barge which had been sent to bring her up the Thames to London. The barge was specially refitted for the occasion. The master and the twenty-four oarsmen had been supplied with new liveries in the Yorkist colours of murrey and blue with white roses embroidered on their jackets. The knights and squires who formed the escort of honour wore fine black velvet jackets which were decorated with a pattern of silver and purple.[26] Two residences had been prepared for Margaret's use: the palace at Greenwich where she had spent so much time before her marriage, and the London house of Coldharbour near her mother's home at Baynard's Castle. New beds with red and green hangings had been sent up to the Coldharbour house and the finest bedlinens and coverlets had been ordered. Curtains, screens and tapestries were provided for both the houses, including a piece of arras which depicted the story of Paris and Helen. For her travel during her stay in England Margaret was sent ten 'hobbeys and palfreys' all newly harnessed and caparisoned in rich saddle cloths. The king encouraged everyone to be generous towards his sister and used 'right large language' with the Archbishop of Canterbury who failed to offer Margaret a gift. His own final present to his sister was a luxurious pillion saddle in blue and violet cloth of gold, fringed with 'Venetian gold' thread.[27]

While she was in England, Margaret renewed her contacts with all her old friends and family. She was received by the queen and introduced to her royal nephews and nieces. Her youngest brother Richard, Duke of Gloucester, who was busy dealing with Scottish incursions in the north, made time to come south to see his sister and the king gave a state banquet at Greenwich in honour of Margaret and their mother, the old Duchess Cecily. It was also attended by Margaret's sister Elizabeth, Duchess of Suffolk. It seems that Margaret admired the wine, for on the day after the banquet the king sent her 'a pipe of our wine' valued at 36s. 8d. As well as enjoying the company of her living family, Margaret could not have failed to remember all her dead relations. It was perhaps with a chantry in mind that she persuaded Edward to introduce the reformed Order of the Observant Friars into England. Soon after her departure the king sent for the vicar-general of the order and offered him a site for their new monastery near to the palace of Greenwich.[28] Building began in 1482 and the abbey chapel was dedicated to the Holy Cross. Was the dedication in honour of Margaret and further evidence of her connection with Waltham Abbey? [29]

Margaret's visit to England was not merely a social occasion. She proved to be a conscientious and earnest ambassador and she was very fully involved in the tricky diplomatic negotiations.[30] The Burgundians were well aware that Edward was keenly attached to his French annuity and knew that throughout the Anglo-Burgundian negotiations he was still in close correspondence with Louis XI, and that he was using Margaret's presence in England to achieve a better deal with France. Even while the dowager was in London, Lord Howard returned from France accompanied by a French delegation who brought over the king's annuity and promised to pay a further annuity of 15,000 crowns to the Princess Elizabeth until her marriage to the dauphin should take place. Edward used all his wiles to extract the maximum benefit from both France and Burgundy. He offered an immediate invasion of France in return for a substitute annuity from Burgundy. He also made it clear that he had no intention of paying out a dowry for his daughter Anne. Faced with these excessive demands the dowager played for time. She sent back messengers to consult with Mary and Maximilian, and Michel de Berghes, one of Maximilian's closest advisers, was sent across to reinforce the delegation. The Burgundians argued that they would only pay an annuity to Edward if the French pension had been lost as a direct consequence of an English invasion of France. They tried to persuade the king that it would be dishonourable for him to offer no dowry with his daughter but they were determined to get an alliance even if they had to pay heavily for it, and they also wanted Louis to know that an Anglo-Burgundian treaty was imminent. In spite of the counter embassy and the annuity from France, Margaret was able to assure Maximilian that Edward was certainly moving towards their side and that she was very hopeful of reaching a satisfactory accord.

Throughout the summer the negotiations dragged on. Margaret must have been very relieved when between the 1 and 5 August a series of deals were finally agreed.[31] In answer to the immediate request for armed help, the Burgundians were permitted to recruit 6,000 English archers at their own expense. The king agreed that 2,000 men could be recruited at once and, on sureties from the whole Burgundian delegation promising that he would be repaid by Christmas, he provided an immediate loan of 2,000 crowns to cover their wages and the expense of shipping them across the Channel. Margaret began to recruit these men straight away but she had only enough money to raise 1,500 archers and 30 men at arms. On 8 August she signed indentures with three captains: Sir John Middleton, Sir John Dichefield, later the governor and captain of Guernsey, and Sir Thomas Everingham. The latter was to take his men from Hull to Sluis and the other two were to embark from Dover. Some of these soldiers were in the Low Countries in time for Maximilian's summer campaign against Guelders but the number recruited fell far short of the hoped for 6,000.[32]

On the question of the Anglo-Burgundian alliance, Margaret persuaded Edward to make a commitment. The king agreed to support the claims of Mary and Maximilian for the return of Artois and the Duchy of Burgundy. He also promised that if France failed to agree to make peace by Easter 1481, then Edward would declare war in support of Burgundy. In return Mary and Maximilian promised to pay 25,000 crowns within six months if Edward's French pension should be cancelled and they would thereafter continue to pay Edward his annuity. The Burgundian promises were guaranteed by the estates of Holland, Zeeland, Flanders and Brabant.[33] The marriage treaty was agreed on 5 August. Anne would marry Philip in six years time bringing with her a dowry of 100,000 crowns, only half of the dowry agreed for Margaret. Half of this dowry was to be paid within two years of the marriage; even here, Margaret was unable to get terms as favourable to Burgundy as the 1468 treaty had been. Moreover supplementary treaties signed a few days later related the dowry payments to the French annuity signifying that Edward would in fact pay no dowry at all. Furthermore from the age of twelve until her marriage, Anne was to receive an income of 6,000 crowns a year from Burgundy for her living expenses and all the costs of her transport to the Low Countries were to be born by the duchy. As a symbol of the marriage agreement, Margaret bought a ring for the infant princess. It was 'a beautiful ring in the style of a circlet with eight fine diamonds and a central rose of three hanging pearls with a gold chain on which the ring may be hung' and it cost about ten times more than the 'gracieuse' ring which was given to Philip in Anne's name.

Edward was certainly driving a hard bargain but he was in a strong position to do so. By 1480 the Yorkist king was very secure on his throne while the position of Burgundy was considerably weaker than it had been in 1468.[34] To obtain any agreement Margaret and her team had had to work hard. In addition to the main negotiations there were several minor matters to be resolved such as the debt still owing on Margaret's own dowry and the restoration of the French lands of Pierre de St Pol, Count of Luxembourg and cousin of Elizabeth Woodville.[35] Edward was prepared to add his support to the count's claims but on the subject of the dowry Margaret made no progress. She seems to have accepted that there would be no more payments and she returned to Edward the letters of 1474 in which he acknowledged his debts. However from the Burgundian archives it is clear that Margaret kept the originals of these letters so perhaps she hoped to press the matter at a future date. Once more Edward renewed and extended her commercial licences allowing her to export from England 1,000 oxen, 200 sheep and 630 'sleyghtewolles', all free of customs duties. The imported livestock were fattened up on the dowager's pastures near Dendermonde.[36]

No sooner had Margaret secured Edward's agreement to all these matters than the news reached England that Maximilian had made a settlement with France. On 21 August a seven month truce was agreed, with plans for a full peace conference to take place in October of that year. When Margaret heard this she anticipated a strong reaction from Edward IV. Nor was that the only matter which needed explaining to the English king. England was at war with Scotland and even while Margaret was in London her brother Richard had hurried north to defend the borders. Yet Maximilian continued to maintain good relations and trade with Scotland. However, Margaret was successful in placating her brother. She explained that it was merely a question of news of the Anglo-Burgundian alliance arriving too late to prevent the signing of the Franco-Burgundian truce and she assured Edward that Maximilian would give him his full support in the war against Scotland.[37]

Well satisfied that the negotiations were at last completed, Margaret prepared to leave London. She paid a farewell visit to the city where she was presented with a purse containing £100. She then set off for the coast accompanied by her brother the king who had decided to see her on her way. When she reached Rochester she found another letter from Maximilian awaiting her. In this he invited Edward to take part in a tripartite conference with Louis XI and himself. Her reply of 14 September summarised both the achievements of her mission and her impatience with Maximilian's double dealing. Some of the archduke's actions had left 'me and your said ambassadors . . . very troubled' and she feared that his methods of diplomacy would leave Edward 'annoyed and angry'.[38] But it was not all diplomacy. The dowager passed a week in Kent visiting the shrine of St Thomas à Becket and staying on the private estates of Anthony Woodville, Lord Rivers. These two bibliophiles must have had much in common especially now that Rivers was the patron of Margaret's former protégé, William Caxton. No doubt she was shown Woodville's translation of the *Dictes and Sayings of the Philosophers* which was one of the first books printed on Caxton's press at Westminster.[39] With the king still in attendance, Margaret finally left for Dover, where the *Falcon* waited to take her across to Calais. Edward seemed to be genuinely sad to see her departure and he wrote to Maximilian on 22 September announcing the return of his 'well-beloved sister.' She left behind her in

England Jacques de la Villeon, who was to act for the Burgundian ally, the Duke of Brittany, at the English court.[40]

Louis was annoyed that his truce with Maximilian had not caused a breach in the Anglo-Burgundian negotiations. He was angered to hear about the shipment of the English archers across the channel and once more he saw Margaret as responsible for the failure of his strategems. He grumbled to the Chester Herald about her activities and claimed that she hated him because he had prevented the marriage of Mary and Clarence. He was determined not to have her nearby during his negotiations at St Omer and postponed the conference until she was out of the area.[41]

Her return was celebrated at the Burgundian court with a reception held in her honour. Margaret, however, seems to have been far from satisfied with the outcome of her mission and she wrote again on 3 October to Maximilian to put the record straight. She assured the archduke that she would always be very willing to help her 'very dear and well-beloved son' but she would be able to help him more successfully if she was always quite clear as to his own intentions.[42] She was visibly irritated by Maximilian's devious and evasive methods. Had she also heard the rumour that Maximilian had been pleased to send her off to England, so as to avoid any consideration of a new marriage proposal for her, which was on its way through Cardinal della Rovere, the pope's nephew? Since the only reference to this proposal comes from French sources it is more than likely that this was another attempt by Louis to remove Margaret from his sphere

Miniature dated 1480 showing Margaret of York presenting Edward IV as Hadrian to the Emperor Trajan

of operations. Nothing further is heard of the proposal and if the French king had had any serious intentions in this matter he could easily have raised the proposal again.[43]

After her embassy to England, Margaret settled back into her life as dowager. The Franco-Burgundian truce did not last and as soon as the war restarted Margaret was again busy gathering troops for the defence of her properties in the south. She continued to spend long periods at the court with Mary and she went on a tour of her dower towns. In April 1481 she was at the Hotel de la Salle at Binche, a house she had had rebuilt as her residence there. Her agent in the city was Pierre des Bins and her treasurer was Corneille le Cordier.[44] Like all her officials these men were expected to keep closely in touch with the dowager and to obey her orders with alacrity.

In the Low Countries 1481 was a troubled year. Early in the year, Jehan van Dadizele was murdered at Antwerp on the orders of the Lord of Gaasbeek, one of Maximilian's closest counsellors. Dadizele had been the Lieutenant General for Flanders and a prominent member of the Flemish nobility. Olivier de La Marche commented that his death was most unfortunate since he had kept Flanders in good order. He was one of the leading negotiators for the Great Privilege and he had strenuously defended the Privilege against Maximilian's attempts to evade its limitations on his own power and authority. At Dadizele's funeral in Ghent there were angry demonstrations and Maximilian was accused of complicity in his murder, especially when the Lord of Gaasbeek was not brought to trial.[45] The archduke had never signed the Great Privilege although he had acknowledged the rights of the individual cities. The opposition complained that Maximilian was becoming as great a tyrant as Charles had been, and that with his German advisers he was ruling the country in his own interests.

The archduchess was still well respected even though her husband had become the target of all opposition to the policies of the ducal government. In September 1481, their third child was born. This son was named after his godfather and Maximilian's ally, Francis, Duke of Brittany, but the infant died when only a few months old.

Within six months, a disaster struck Burgundy which was to threaten all the hard won gains of the last five years. Mary had always loved physical exercise, skating on the frozen ponds of the Coudenberg Palace at Brussels or hunting in the Flemish Campine. Her great seal like that of previous Duchesses of Burgundy showed her on horseback with a falcon on her wrist.[46] Falconry was her special passion and Maximilian had been surprised to find that within a few nights of their marriage she had brought her falcons back into her bedchamber. In March 1482 Lord Ravenstein, who was her Master of Horse, organised a falcon hunt in the marshes of Wijnendaele near Bruges. Perhaps her horse stumbled on the icy ground or perhaps she miscalculated a jump, but somehow or other this very competent horsewoman was thrown. Although there were no visible wounds, Mary was in great pain and had to be carried back to Bruges in a litter. The duchess may have been in the early stages of her fourth pregnancy and gradually her condition worsened and there was nothing her doctors could do. Margaret hastened to her side and the relic of the Holy Blood was brought from its chapel to her bedside but all in vain, on 27 March she died.[47] She was

The bronze tomb of Mary of Burgundy in the Church of Our Lady at Bruges. Copyright ACL Bruxelles

buried in the church of Our Lady at Bruges, where her coffin was reinterred in 1502 beneath a magnificent bronze monument made by Pierre de Beckere of Brussels. There, in the only church north of the Alps to possess a statue by Michelangelo, the young duchess lay at peace while rebellion broke out all over her territories.

On her deathbed, Mary had begged Margaret to watch over her two children, the heir Philip, an infant of four years old, and Margaret of Austria who was two.[48] This was to be no easy task for, in her will, Mary named Maximilian as the sole governor of the heir and as the Regent of Burgundy until Philip should come of age. This was bitterly opposed. The estates of Flanders and the cities of Ghent, Bruges and Ypres were resolved to uphold the original marriage treaty which had excluded Maximilian from the succession. Their proposals for the establishment of a regency council which would govern the duchy for the next ten years had extensive support throughout the whole of the Low Countries. Once more it was Ghent which held the upper hand because the two children were installed in the castle of Ten Waele and the city refused to allow Maximilian to take them away. French agents did all they could to encourage his opponents. Louis also hastened to offer terms to the estates which would end the war in the best interests of France. He proposed a betrothal between Margaret of Austria and the dauphin. Franche Comté and Artois would be a part of her dowry. Maximilian was resolved to oppose this treaty and the dowager gave him her full support. She withdrew to Malines where she sent off more troops for the defence of Hainault and she prepared for the arrival of the two infants who should be placed in her care. Olivier de La Marche expressed the view of her household when he wrote that 'our lord the archduke is like St Eustace, a wolf [Louis] had seized his daughter and a lion [the lion of Flanders] had taken his son.'[49]

In October the estates met again at Alost and Maximilian wrote to Margaret asking her to give him her support[50] but there was little they could do with Flanders resolved upon peace with France at almost any price. On 23 December Maximilian was forced to agree to the treaty of Arras. Margaret of Austria was to marry the dauphin. She would be handed over immediately to France as a surety for the marriage. Her dowry would include Artois, Franche Comté and the lordships of Mâcon, Auxerre, Noys and Bar-sur-Seine. The French possession of the Duchy of Burgundy and Picardy had to be accepted, only Hainault and Flanders were saved from the French grasp. Louis tried to win Margaret's support for the treaty. Her full rights were restored in all her dower properties, including Chaussin and Le Perriere and she was reimbursed for her losses to the sum of 20,000 gold crowns.[51] The Flemish and French pushed the treaty through with great haste. Margaret of Austria was sent off from Ghent under guard to prevent any rescue attempt by her father and on 24 April she was handed over to the French at Hesdin. In June she was officially betrothed to the dauphin who at the age of thirteen was not impressed by his three-year-old bride. She was fortunate to pass into the care of Louis' intelligent and able daughter Anne de Beaujeu. With Margaret of Austria went her nurse the Lady de Bouzanton who kept the Burgundians informed of her charge's progress at the French court. The Lord de Bouzanton had been appointed by Margaret as captain of the garrison at Le Quesnoy, a useful location for one who would await messages from France.[52]

In spite of the completion of the treaty of Arras, Ghent still refused to hand Philip over to the care of either Maximilian or Margaret and throughout the next two years a harsh war was fought in the Low Countries as Maximilian tried to recover control. Margaret's 'tuteur' Josse de Lalaing, Lord of Montigny, died of wounds he received fighting for Maximilian at the siege of Utrecht.[53] Throughout these years Margaret gave Maximilian all the help she could.[54] She did not accept the convention of Hoogstaten which had set up a regency council, including Maximilian and Lord Ravenstein, to govern for the infant archduke. Instead she upheld Mary's will and the amended marriage treaty. After all her representative Guillaume de Baume had been the only Burgundian to witness the amendments made by Mary in the September after her marriage by which Maximilian had been named as Mary's heir in the event of her death without issue.[55] Maximilian appealed to his English ally for help and Edward might well have moved against France since the treaty of Arras had deprived him of both his annuity and the marriage of his daughter to the dauphin. However Edward was dead within four months of Arras. His successor Richard III had major problems within England but he sent Maximilian 6,000 more English archers.[56]

Gradually Maximilian made some progress. In the summer of 1483 he received the welcome news of the death of his old enemy Louis XI, and even the pious Margaret must have rejoiced. By the end of the following year Utrecht and Liège had submitted and Oudenaarde and Dendermonde were recovered from the rebels. The intervention of France, who sent Anthony, Count of La Roche, to rally the rebels against Maximilian, worked in the latter's favour. The Grand Bastard, Anthony, was regarded as a traitor in Burgundy because of his defection in 1477 and his very name rallied support for Maximilian. Ravenstein and his son Philip both resigned from the regency council in January 1484. Moreover the French government was no longer as strong as it had been under Louis XI, since the authority of Anne de Beaujeu, the sister and regent of the infant Charles VIII, was challenged by the Duke of Orleans. By November 1484 the rebels in Flanders were forced to admit defeat and Margaret personally intervened to persuade Maximilian to show clemency towards Ghent.[57] The city was granted an amnesty but when Maximilian entered to collect his son riots broke out again and the archduke's men fled fearing some sort of trap. This time order was restored after a series of executions and at last in a well publicised scene of fatherly tears Maximilian was reunited with his son.[58]

In July 1485 Margaret rode over to Dendermonde. She went to receive Philip who was to be placed in her care at Malines. She had prepared everything for his reception. In the February of that year she sold her palace at Malines to the city corporation for 12,000 crowns. The city then gave the house to Maximilian and Philip. This transaction ensured that the young heir would live in his own property although Margaret would continue to live there as well. It also provided a very useful cash settlement for Margaret who had been hard pressed by the costs of the civil wars. In May 1485 she received a further 800 livres from Mons to help her to defray her heavy expenses.[59] By the time Margaret went to collect Philip she had also established a household for her step-grandson. Olivier de La Marche became the master of the new ducal household. With La Marche at its head we may be sure that the archducal household was set up with every propriety. The dowager selected Francis van Buysleyden, the brother of Jerome, a colleague of Erasmus, to become the boy's tutor.[60] She took every care of Philip and saw to it that he became well known throughout his domains. As early as October 1485 she escorted him to Binche where he made a triumphal entry into the town.[61]

Considering the strife which faced Margaret and Maximilian from 1482 to 1485, the dowager must have had little time to ponder on the news which reached her from London. Edward IV's death in April 1483 could not have come at a worse time for his dynasty. His foreign policy was in tatters. Indeed Mancini commented that the treaty of Arras had been the cause of Edward's death.[62] The Croyland chronicler agreed that Edward had been enraged by the treaty:

this spirited prince now saw and most anxiously regretted that he was thus deluded by King Louis who had not only withdrawn the promised tribute, but had declined the alliance which had been solemnly agreed upon between the dauphin and the king's eldest daughter . . . and, taking part with the burghers of Ghent , used his utmost endeavours to molest the party of the duke of Austria, the king's ally . . . upon this the king thought of nothing else but taking vengeance.[63]

Edward's failure to support Maximilian had certainly rebounded against him and the collapse of his foreign policy followed so soon by his death was to lead to the deaths of both his sons and the usurpation of Richard III. It is possible to see in the extraordinary behaviour of Richard of Gloucester the actions of a man who had, for a long time, felt frustrated by his brother's policies, especially the Anglo-French alliance. Maximilian and Margaret accepted the usurpation of Richard III. They surely hoped that the warlike duke, who was commonly supposed to have opposed the treaty of Picquigny, would now intervene on behalf of Burgundy and send some real assistance to the archduke. Maximilian sent an embassy to greet Richard, explaining his problems over the detention of

(Left) Edward, Prince of Wales, later Edward V. (Right) Richard, Duke of York

his son at Ghent and justifying his own right to act as regent. The heralds were also to impress upon Richard Maximilian's determination to recover the Duchy of Burgundy. They were further to inform Richard that the rebels had 'ousted my most dread lady the duchess [Margaret] from the enjoyment of her dower being in the said county of Flanders' but to assure him that Dendermonde and Oudenaarde had already been recovered. The English king was asked to boycott all trade with the Flemish merchants and to let Maximilian have 6,000 archers whose wages the archduke would pay.[64]

Although Richard was favourable to a Burgundian alliance he had little opportunity to respond. After the seizure of the young king at Stoney Stratford and with the arrests of Lord Rivers, Sir Thomas Vaughan and Sir Richard Grey in April, the queen had fled with the rest of her children into sanctuary at Westminster. The heir, Edward V, was already twelve years old, and there was no time for a long regency in which a gentle jostling for power might take place. If Richard wanted to seize power he must act ruthlessly and he did. With his ally the Duke of Buckingham he set his course 'swiftly and with the utmost vigilance'[65] and was able to get control of his second nephew, Richard of York. The two boys disappeared into the Tower and the executions of Rivers, Vaughan, Grey and Hastings secured Richard's position for the time being.

As Anthony Woodville prepared to die he wrote a poem which is a remarkably accurate reflection of his own thoughts and of those who were observing all these astonishing events:

> Somewhat musing
> And more mourning
> In remembering
> The unsteadfastness
> This world being
> Of such wheeling
> Me contrarying
> What may I guess
>
> Methinks truly
> Bounden am I
> And this greatly
> To be content
> Seeing plainly
> Fortune doth awry
> All contrary
> From mine intent.[66]

The final coup came on 26 June when Richard set aside his nephew on the grounds of illegitimacy and assumed the crown himself. This news must have reached Margaret at the height of the civil wars. With the death of Louis in August a minor had also come to the French throne but in spite of the challenge from Orleans, France rallied behind the regent, Anne de Beaujeu, who had no designs on her brother's throne. The trouble makers in France received a stern warning from the Chancellor, Cardinal Rochefort, who told the estates general at Tours in January 1484 that they must not follow the terrible example of England:

Regard the events which have occurred in that land since the death of King Edward. See how his children already quite old and brave have been murdered with impunity and the crown has been transferred to their assassin by the consent of the people.[67]

If these stories were abroad in France we may be sure that they also reached Burgundy. Molinet recorded the seizure of the young king and his brother, although he called the younger boy George, a confusion with the Duke of Clarence. The Burgundian chronicler also described a pathetic scene, which he set in the Tower, when Edward V was still officially awaiting his coronation. The eldest prince was 'utterly and entirely melancholy' recognising the evil intent of his uncle. The younger prince, however, not appreciating the danger they were in, was full of joy and high spirits and urged his brother to learn how to dance. The unfortunate Edward V replied that he would do better to learn how to die. Molinet added that they were imprisoned in the Tower for about five weeks and then killed by order of the constable of the Tower, Duke Richard, who made himself king. He also reported Richard's assertion that Edward IV had himself been illegitimate and that of his mother's sons only he was legitimate. These slanders against Cecily Neville were apparently common knowledge in Burgundy. But Molinet brings his authenticity into doubt when he adds that Richard reigned cruelly and spoiled the church. This was certainly not true for Richard like his sister Margaret seems to have been particularly pious. [68]

Whatever Margaret made of all these rumours, that Richard had impugned the honour of their mother Cecily and had murdered his nephews, there is simply no evidence of her opinions. She must have been well informed, her chaplain was in England in 1484, her commercial agent was also there and a large Burgundian embassy visited Richard later in the same year.[69] She must have known that Richard had announced his accession to the throne from his mother's house and that his declaration of accession referred only to Edward IV's precontract which illegitimised his nephews. Moreover she would also have heard that, only shortly after the reported disappearance of the two young princes, their mother, Elizabeth Woodville, had come to court and entrusted herself and her daughters to Richard's care. Commynes thought that Buckingham may have killed the princes and the actions of the queen dowager do seem to bear this out.[70] After the execution of Buckingham, some English exiles may have begun arriving in Flanders though most of them made for Brittany and the Earl of Richmond. Margaret probably regarded the worst rumours against her brother as mere scandal. She may also have supported Richard's usurpation on the grounds that Edward's Woodville marriage was indeed illegal. However, whatever her private opinions, Maximilian needed an alliance with England and it was her duty to try to draw Richard into one. After all, an Anglo-Burgundian alliance was her very *raison d'être.* By the early summer of 1485, it seemed that a new and stronger alliance was at last in the making.

Before the new Anglo-Burgundian alliance could be negotiated, the little army which had gathered in the valley of the Seine under the Lord of Esquerades, Philip de Crèvecoeur, was on its way to England. Henry, Earl of

King Richard III

Richmond, had taken an oath to marry Elizabeth of York. With his vestiges of a Lancastrian claim and his marriage to a Yorkist princess, this most implausible pretender was ready to stake his claim to the throne. France, fearful of a Burgundian recovery and of a military alliance between Richard and Maximilian, was only too willing to help him on his way. Once more, dynastic changes in England would be the by-product of the struggle between France and Burgundy, a struggle which formed the constant political framework for Margaret's life.

6 'This Diabolicall Duches'

'lyke a dogge revertynge to her olde vomyte'

'Once more', wrote Jean Molinet, 'the house of York has been left wretched and deserted by Good Fortune.'[1] Molinet had inherited the mantle of Georges Chastellain as the chief historian and rhetorician of the Burgundian court. He wrote his chronicles between 1474 and 1506 and his views echoed those of his patrons at the court. Thus, this sorrowful verdict on the battle of Bosworth may well have reflected Margaret's sentiments when she heard of the defeat and death of her last surviving brother, Richard III. In her thirty-nine years, Margaret had certainly witnessed many dramatic revolutions of the great wheel of fortune, from the sudden deaths of her father and brother at Wakefield to the tragic early death of her step-daughter in 1482, but here for the first time she had to face the total eclipse of the House of York. When the confused reports of the battle of Bosworth field first reached Malines, Margaret had little time to grieve for her dead brother. She was fully involved with the establishment of the new archducal household and the preparations for the great council which had been summoned to meet at Malines in mid-September.[2] Viewed within the context of Margaret's own earlier experience and considering her many preoccupations in the late summer of 1485, the dowager must have received the news of the accession of Henry VII with resignation. Remembering the restoration of her brother Edward in 1471, she would also have considered that, given some slight military and financial assistance from Burgundy, this new Tudor usurper, with his weak and tenuous claim, would soon be successfully replaced.

On the other hand, there was no reason why Margaret should not simply accept the marriage of Henry to her niece Elizabeth as being in the best interests of her family. It was a marriage accepted by Margaret's closest surviving relatives: her mother Cecily, her sister Elizabeth and her sister-in-law Elizabeth Woodville. Henry had made several well considered gestures of conciliation towards these three matriarchs of the House of York. His marriage had been planned by his mother the Lady Margaret Beaufort with the support of the queen dowager, Elizabeth Woodville. He did not hesitate to grant Elizabeth Woodville her full dower rights and she and her surviving relations were given

Queen Elizabeth of York, wife of King Henry VII

The ruined keep of Scarborough Castle, Yorkshire

an honourable welcome to the new court. Also early in 1486 he renewed the trading licences which Edward IV had granted to the Duchess Cecily[3] and her daughter, the Duchess of Suffolk, was welcomed to the new Tudor court in spite of the fact that all her six sons were in direct line to the throne.

Although the king gave full recognition to the property and position of these Yorkists, he seems to have ignored the interests of the Burgundian dowager. Margaret had benefitted from all the various trading licences granted by her brother Edward, and she had continued to enjoy these privileges during the brief reigns of Edward V and Richard III, but with the accession of Henry VII her trading activities appear to have ceased.[4] There can be little doubt that Margaret, who was extremely business-like as far as her economic interests were concerned, would have noted and resented these losses. Indeed her later support of both Lambert Simnel and Perkin Warbeck may well have been motivated by a determination to recover her English income. This, apart from any family feeling, may lie at the heart of the vendetta theory so favoured by Tudor historians.

Nearly ten years later, in 1494, Margaret still had these losses very much in mind when a series of protocols were drawn up at Antwerp between herself and 'Richard of York the legitimate son and heir of our very dear lord and father . . . Edward king of England.'[5] *Richard*, better known to English history as Perkin Warbeck, promised that when he became king he would restore her trading licences and repay the debt still owing on Margaret's dowry, which she had also not forgotten. In addition the dowager was to receive the manor of Hunsdon and the castle and town of Scarborough.[6] The choice of these two properties is curious. Margaret may have been hoping to acquire a small English property as an insurance against more troubles in the Low Countries, though by the mid-1490s the worst of the conflicts between Flanders and its dukes appeared to be over. The optimistic Yorkists were certainly looking forward to a division of the spoils. But why Hunsdon and Scarborough?[7] Apart from the possibility that Margaret had a personal interest in Hunsdon as her birthplace, it may be relevant that from September 1485 Hunsdon had belonged to Sir William Stanley and the castle of Scarborough was in the hands of Sir Nicholas Knyfton, a man also connected with the Stanley interest and one who had benefited from the property confiscated from the loyal friend of King Richard, Francis, Viscount Lovel. Were Hunsdon and Scarborough part of some secret deal between the dowager and Sir William Stanley? He was known to be in contact with the Pretender. One of the witnesses to the Antwerp protocols was Sir Robert Clifford who had been sent over by Stanley. Clifford, however, may well have been a double agent from the very beginning, for Henry VII was soon accusing Stanley of conspiracy against him. Henry was certainly kept well informed and the promise of Hunsdon and Scarborough to Margaret may have served to show the extent of Stanley's involvement. It is of course interesting to find Hunsdon once more cropping up in Margaret's story. It would be pleasant to think that she was thinking with nostalgia of her birthplace but, speculation apart, the fact remains that, in 1494, the dowager had clearly not forgotten her lost licences or the unpaid dowry and was still hoping to regain some income from England.

Yet however much the dowager regretted her lost licences, these were trivial matters compared with her rich dower in Burgundy. Margaret was much too cautious to risk her great estates and the 'great love and authority'[8] which she had earned in the Low Countries in an unsupported attempt to restore a Yorkist prince to the English throne. If however she was to find that her interference in English affairs also suited the ducal government, then she would certainly assist the Pretenders with all her considerable energy and intelligence. Henry's failure to do anything either to satisfy Burgundian interests or to placate Margaret may be regarded as one of his first diplomatic blunders.

There were substantial reasons why the new Tudor king should have shown some signs of friendship towards Maximilian, who was by this time the virtual ruler of Burgundy. Henry had won his throne with military assistance from France, a fact which was bound to alarm the archduke who had begun to build up good relations with Richard III and had been hopeful that Richard would support Burgundy against France. Maximilian was quite ready to establish a new accord with Henry and he sent the Burgundian heralds to greet him on his accession.[9] The archduke seems to have hoped to renew the Anglo-Burgundian treaties of commerce and friendship but Henry made no movement towards an alliance and this, combined with Henry's debt of gratitude to France, threatened the stability of Burgundy.

Henry's failure to enter into any diplomatic talks in 1485 and 1486 was probably due chiefly to his own inexperience and to his preoccupation with affairs within England. But his disregard may also be due to the fact that he had spent most of his formative years in Brittany and France, where he may well have come to regard Maximilian through French eyes. After the treaty of Arras it was generally believed that the archduke was so plagued by his own rebellious subjects that he was of little significance in European affairs. However Maximilian was far from impotent. His armies might be unpaid and mutinous and he might be continually frustrated by his Flemish subjects, but the Low Countries were still a source of great wealth and the archduke was moreover 'a shrewd operator'.[10] He would always explore every avenue open to him. Rather than accept a francophile King of England, Maximilian struggled to find some way of restoring the old Anglo-Burgundian accord. If Henry would not cooperate then he would have to be replaced by a Yorkist king indebted to Burgundy. This policy would have been conducted with guile and circumspection since Maximilian had no wish to make an active enemy out of the new king. He was determined to keep his policies towards England well concealed and it is chiefly due to his caution and prevarication that the origins of the Simnel and Warbeck risings have remained so obscure. The archduke was able to pursue these policies through Margaret who would not only give him her wholehearted support in any attempt to overthrow Henry, but who was also willing to shoulder both the financial burden and the responsibility. The relationship between Maximilian and Margaret was one of close interdependence. Margaret needed Maximilian to safeguard her dower but the archduke also needed Margaret. During the minority of Philip, Maximilian relied heavily on the dowager's goodwill. She remained his most loyal subject and her support and advice were an invaluable asset to Maximilian in his government of the Low Countries, for she had long experience in dealing with the nobles and the estates. The dowager could sometimes secure the agreement of the estates where other court officials failed. In March 1487, she presided over the estates of Hainault and obtained a gift of 3,000 crowns to cover Maximilian's debts to the Bishop of Cambrai.[11] Thus any suggestions from the dowager that Maximilian should cooperate with her in launching a Yorkist invasion were likely to receive a sympathetic hearing.

There was moreover yet another reason why both Maximilian and his son Philip would take an interest in the occupant of the English throne. After Bosworth, the main English rivals to Henry had been either captured or eliminated. The most eligible Plantagenet claimant was the eight-year-old Edward, Earl of Warwick, the son of the Duke of Clarence. He was transferred upon Henry's orders from the castle of Sheriff Hutton in Yorkshire to the security of the Tower of London. The Duke and Duchess of Suffolk could be relied upon to restrain the pretensions of their son John, Earl of Lincoln, who was the next Yorkist candidate in line. There was thus no-one in England able to mount a challenge to Henry. Indeed it was this lack of a plausible English claimant which was to dog all the attempts to overthrow Henry and perhaps accounted for Margaret's willingness to accept the two Pretenders, first Lambert Simnel posing as the Earl of Warwick and later Perkin Warbeck claiming to be Richard, Duke of York.

In the absence of any real challengers within England, the claims of the two Burgundian archdukes were worthy of consideration. Both Philip and Maximilian had more right to the English throne than had the new Tudor king. They were both independently and directly descended from John of Gaunt and his first wife, Blanche of Lancaster.[12] The Burgundian counsellors must have been very familiar with this inheritance. In 1471, after the death of Henry VI, Charles the Bold had registered his claim to the throne inherited from his mother and after Bosworth Maximilian had contemplated a marriage to Elizabeth of York. [13] The loss of the Yorkist heiress to Henry did not end his pretensions. In 1495, on the eve of his attempt to seize the throne, the Pretender signed a protocol making both the archdukes his heirs, in case of his death without issue. This was yet another statement of the Habsburg claim to the English throne, a claim which was to lie dormant due to the many other problems which confronted Maximilian and later Philip.

Henry and the later Tudors were all well versed in their genealogy and they must have been well aware of these Habsburg claims. It may even be the case that Margaret's role in the Yorkist plots was over emphasised in order to divert attention from the Lancastrian inheritance of the archdukes and their descendants, Charles V and Philip II of Spain. Tudor historians never mentioned these Burgundian claims but they wrote at length about Margaret's involvement in the plots against Henry VII. They presented all attempts to overthrow Henry as part of her malicious and obsessive vendetta against him. Polydore Vergil expressed the general view most succinctly when he stated that Margaret:

> pursued Henry with insatiable hatred and with fiery wrath never desisted from employing every scheme which might harm him as a representative of the hostile faction.[14]

Edward Hall, who followed Polydore Vergil very closely, elaborated on this and added several fearsome phrases for 'this diabolicall duches.' Margaret was 'lyke a dogge revertynge to her olde vomyte' and 'lyke a spyder that dayly weaueth when hys calle is tarne.'[15] Hall examined the dowager's motives in a paragraph which has been echoed by many later historians:

> This lady Margaret although she knewe the familye and stocke of the house of Yorke to be in maner distroyed & vtterly defaced by her brother kyng Richard, yet not being saciate nor content with the long hatred & continual malice of her parentes which subuerted and ouerthrew almost the progeny and lignage of kyng Henry the vi and the house of Lancaster, nor yet remembryng the newe affinitie & strong alliaunce that was lately concluded, by the whiche the heyres of bothe the houses and progenies were vnited & conioyned together in lawfull matrimony, lyke one forgettyng bothe God & charite, inflamed with malice diabolicall instinccion, inuented & practiced all mischiefes, displeasures and damages that she could deuyse against the kyng of England. And farther in her fury and frantyke moode (accordyng to the saiyng of the wise man, there is no malice equiualent nor aboue the malice of a woman) she wrought all the wayes possible how to sucke his bloud and copasse his destruccion as the principal head of her aduerse parte & contrary faccion, as though he should be a dewe sacrifice or an host immolated for the mutuall murder & shamefull homicide comitted and perpetrated by her brother and progeny.

Hall elevated Henry by comparing him with the sacrificial lamb of God, and relegated the dowager firmly to the role of the devil's agent.

Another major analogy for the dowager which became entrenched in the history books originated with Bernard André, the blind tutor of Prince Arthur. As befitted a classical scholar he portrayed Margaret as the goddess Juno, notorious for her implacable desire for revenge, ceaselessly attacking the noble Henry who was cast in the role of Hercules. In the *Twelve Triumphs of Henry VII*, an epic poem also ascribed to André, Margaret was also compared to Menalippe, the queen of the Amazons, another of Hercules' enemies, and also to one of the heads of the monster Geryon, the other two heads being those of Philip and Maximilian.[16] Here at least there was a recognition of how closely Margaret worked with the rulers of Burgundy.

More than a century later Francis Bacon revived the classical simile and he also repeated Polydore Virgil's analysis of Margaret's motives:

> The princess [Margaret] having the spirit of a man and the malice of a woman, abounding in treasure by the greatness of her dower and her provident government, and being childless and without any near care, made it her design and enterprise to see the majesty royal of England once more replaced in her house and had set up King Henry as a mark, at whose overthrow all her actions should aim and shoot. She bore such a mortal hatred to the House of Lancaster and personally to the king as she was no ways mollified by the conjunction of the houses in her niece's marriage but rather hated her niece as the means of the king's ascent to the throne.[17]

And he added the particular sentence which has caught the eye of almost every succeeding writer on the subject, that Margaret: 'was for the king what Juno was for Aeneas, troubling Hell and Heaven to annoy him.' Here Henry had been transformed from Hercules to Aeneas, yet another of Juno's victims. This comparison was preserved by the dowager's most recent biographer Luc Hommel in the title of his book, *Marguerite d'York ou la Duchesse Junon*.[18] The Tudor characterisation of Margaret as a malicious and vindictive woman has become entrenched in English history, though it is singularly missing among most of the contemporary continental chroniclers and historians. Commynes, who often reported on Louis XI's distrust of Margaret, never endorses the French king's criticism with any general attack on the dowager. Of course he had actually known Margaret when she was Duchess of Burgundy. More recent English historians have echoed the Tudor line with considerable regularity. Even the charitable Hume considered that the dowager's behaviour towards Henry showed 'a spirit of faction who entrenched somewhat the probity which shone forth in other parts of her character.' For Professor Mackie, Margaret was 'always ready to play the kindly aunt to Henry's enemies'. Writers in other fields have picked up this general verdict. The art historian, Professor Wilenski, suggested that Dirk Bouts had portrayed Margaret as the wicked queen in his great dyptich *The Judgment of Otho* simply because she was 'rancourous and given to political intrigue.'[19]

The source for all these opinions on the dowager's character was no less a person than Henry himself. He expressed his attitude towards Margaret with great conviction in a letter written to Sir Gilbert Talbot in 1493:

> not forgetting the great *malice* that the Lady Margaret of Burgundy beareth continually against us, as she showed lately in sending hither a feigned boy surmising him to have been the son of the duke of Clarence. . . . And forseeing now the perseverance of the same her *malice*, by the untrue contriving eftsoon of another feigned lad called Perkin Warbeck . . . wherethrough she intendeth by promising unto the Flemings and other of the archduke's obeissance to whom she laboureth daily to take her way, and by her promise to certain aliens, captains of strange nations, to have duchies, counties, baronies, and other lands, within this our royaume to induce them thereby to land here (author's italics).[20]

The king repeated his opinions in his instructions to his ambassador to France, who was told to inform the French king that the dowager was misleading Maximilian and was wholly responsible for the past and threatened invasions of England. Although Henry had, by this date, very valid reasons for regarding Burgundy as a source of danger, his motives for accusing the dowager rather than Maximilian were chiefly diplomatic and totally ignored the fact that Margaret and Maximilian had worked very closely together in their attempts to dethrone Henry.

Henry VII seems to have had an exaggerated notion of Margaret's political influence, although he was not the first to respect and fear her authority. Louis XI of France had emphasised her role in diplomatic affairs and from the moment of her marriage to Charles the Bold, the French king had regarded her as an active agent of the Anglo-Burgundian alliance. After 1477, Louis recognised the dowager as one of the most vigorous opponents of France, and it is quite possible that Henry had learned to see Margaret through Louis' eyes. He certainly imitated Louis' methods of trying to discredit her with scandal. In the late 1490s rumours were circulated that Margaret was Perkin Warbeck's mother and that his father was none other than the Bishop of Cambrai. This utterly worthless fabrication echoed the story spread by Louis in 1468, that Margaret had had an illegitimate child.[21]

There was of course some substance in Henry's fear of Margaret. After Bosworth, Yorkist exiles were permitted to find shelter in Burgundy. This on its own was not a particular threat to Henry since it was common practice for English exiles to reside in either the Low Countries or France as indeed he himself had done. Only rarely could they expect any major assistance from their hosts. However, after the Stafford rebellion in England in the spring of 1486, the exiles in Burgundy were augmented by the arrival of Francis Viscount Lovel, who had been one of Richard III's closest advisers. He had been brought up with Richard in the household of the Earl of Warwick and they were friends for many years.[22] His views on English affairs would have had a considerable influence upon both Margaret and Maximilian and he may well have persuaded them that the Stafford rising, in itself of no great import, nevertheless showed that there was widespread English opposition to Henry. An opposition moreover which could count on the support of highly placed and influential men, like Sir Thomas

Broughton who had sheltered him in Lancashire and John Sant, the Abbot of Abingdon, who had helped the Stafford brothers back into sanctuary at Culham. John Sant was already known at the Burgundian court and by Margaret in particular. She had written to the ducal chamberlain requesting safe conduct for the abbot when, in October 1474, he was making his way through the Low Countries to Rome and Naples on a mission for Edward IV.

By the time of Lovel's arrival, Maximilian had regained his authority within Burgundy and he had also secured his imperial succession, having been elected as co-ruler with his father at the Diet of Frankfurt in 1486. He still, however, faced considerable demands on his energies both within Burgundy and from Germany. Moreover in spite of the treaty of Arras, the war with France had continued as Maximilian tried to recover the lost lands, and the regency government in France retaliated by attacks in Hainault and south Flanders. Since Maximilian could not regard the new King of England as a friend, he feared an Anglo-French alliance against him. It was therefore in his best interests to 'keep the bit in the mouth of the King of England.'[23] Margaret surely reminded him of the triumph of 1471 when Burgundy had assisted Edward IV back to his throne. The archduke was willing to encourage a Yorkist conspiracy merely in the hope of preventing any English support for France. If the plot was successful and a new pro-Burgundian candidate became King of England so much the better.

The origins of the Simnel affair are very elusive but in one matter at least the evidence is clear: the Burgundian dowager was, by 1486, openly backing the restoration of a Yorkist king and her candidate claimed to be the Earl of Warwick. Since the death of Richard III Edward, Earl of Warwick, had been kept at the Tower and there were few people able to recognise this boy who had lived in relative obscurity since his father's death when he was barely a year old. One of the few who may have known him well was his cousin John, Earl of Lincoln, 'a man of great wit and courage' who was sixteen years older than Edward and had spent some time with him at the castle of Sheriff Hutton.[24] Immediately after the accession of Henry VII Lincoln was in favour at court. He was prominent at the coronation of the new king and travelled with him throughout the realm. At the time of the Lovel and Stafford risings Lincoln was closely under the eye of the king, although he was later accused of helping the rebels. It was at that same time, in the early summer of 1486, that rumours began to circulate claiming that Edward, Earl of Warwick, had escaped from the Tower and was at liberty in the Channel Islands. In July of the same year however, Lincoln was still an honoured member of the Tudor court attending the baptism of the new heir Prince Arthur. The christening was a great celebration of the union between the Houses of Lancaster and York. The last Yorkist queen, Elizabeth Woodville, was the chief god-mother and as she carried her grandson to the font it seemed that Henry had succeeded in reconciling the English Yorkists to his accession.[25] Yet within four months of this ceremony, suspicion and rebellion were surfacing even at court.

By November there were rumours that Warwick was in Ireland, where the king's own representative, the Earl of Kildare, had given him his enthusiastic encouragement. There was widespread support for Warwick in Ireland where there was a long tradition of lieutenant generals from the House of York and Mortimer. Furthermore, Warwick's father, the Duke of Clarence, had been born in Dublin during his father's period of office. The news from Ireland worried Henry who summoned a royal council to assemble early in 1487 and he had the young Warwick brought out of the Tower and paraded through the streets of London to a public service at St Paul's.[26] At the convocation of February 1487, a priest called William Simmonds admitted taking a boy called Lambert Simnel to Ireland and presenting him to the Irish as the Earl of Warwick. Concurrent with these revelations in convocation came action at court which suggested that Henry was becoming suspicious of a full-scale Yorkist plot. The queen dowager was deprived of her property while her son the Marquess of Dorset was imprisoned. Since both of them were subsequently restored to favour it may have been no more than an attack of nervousness on Henry's part, and the temporary retirement of the queen dowager to Bermondsey Abbey was probably totally unrelated to the conspiracy. Elizabeth Woodville may well have complained too loudly at the failure of Henry to hold the long postponed coronation of her daughter the queen. The lack of ceremonial recognition for the Yorkist queen through whom Henry had his best claim to the throne had given rise to widespread complaints. It is significant that as soon as the Simnel rising was crushed Elizabeth was crowned, in November 1487.

Even if the troubles between Henry and the Woodvilles were of only temporary importance, events were taking place which indicated serious intrigue at court. The dramatic flight of the Earl of Lincoln, which took place shortly after the parading of Warwick in London, caused widespread alarm in Tudor circles. His arrival in the Low Countries gave added impetus to the Yorkist activity there. At a later trial it was claimed that John Sant had sent one of his servants abroad as early as January 1487 with funds to supply the Earl of Lincoln.[27] This would suggest that even before Lincoln left London, preparations and contacts between the Yorkists in England and in the Low Countries were well underway.

By the Easter of 1487 the Simnel rebellion was taking full shape with the recruitment of an army of between 1,500 and 2,000 men, which was to spearhead the invasion of England in support of the Yorkist Pretender. These troops were described as *landknechts*, a well trained and professional infantry which were a particular feature of the imperial armies. Maximilian issued several ordinances concerning their discipline and employment and he used them to good effect in his wars against France and against his Flemish rebels. As a fighting man, Maximilian was notably more competent and more cautious than Charles the Bold. At the battle of Guinegatte he had not hesitated to dismount and fight on foot, surrounded by a solid phalanx of his *landknechts*.[28] A force of this type could not have been assembled without his full support, nor would Martin Schwartz, their captain, have ventured forth upon an invasion of England without the agreement of Maximilian, his former pay-master. Variously described as a German, a Fleming and a Dutchman, Schwartz was a renowned mercenary captain who had been particularly prominent in crushing the rebels in the Low Countries. In 1485 he had fought at the assaults on Alost and Nineveh where with his Swiss and German troops he had crushed the rebels, storming, looting and burning the cities and killing the inhabitants. He was with Maximilian when Ghent surrendered, and it was the fear that Schwartz and his men might be let loose to pillage the city that had led to Margaret's appeal for clemency.[29] Margaret's recruitment of these men for a mission abroad was surely welcomed by the people of Flanders and Brabant, who were pleased to see the back of these rapacious mercenaries, well known for their mutinous behaviour when their pay was overdue.

However it would seem that the dowager's court at Malines had been involved in a conspiracy long before the beginning of 1487 when the recruitment began. The red letter day in the Malines calendar was 1 July, the *ommegang* or feast day of their patron saint, St Rombout. St Rombout's procession was one of the most important festivals in Brabant and visitors came from all over the Low Countries to join in the celebrations. If she was in the town on that day, the dowager and the archducal household always participated fully in the *ommegang* and they brought their guests with them to enjoy the festivities. Gifts of money and wine were offered to the dowager, her guests and her officials such as Olivier de La Marche. Each year two pages of the city records were devoted to enumerating the gifts donated to important visitors and all the other expenses incurred by the festival.

In the records for St Rombout's day of 1486 there is one donation which certainly catches the eye: a gift of eight flagons of wine to the 'sone van Claretie uit Ingelant' (the son of Clarence from England).[30] The clerk seems to be referring to the Earl of Warwick, but whoever could this be? Was it possible that the real Warwick had indeed escaped from the Tower and had been brought through the Channel Islands to Malines, from whence he was later to make his way to Ireland? This hardly seems plausible since, if the real Warwick had reached the Low Countries, there would surely be other references to his presence there, though chroniclers, like Molinet, may have found it diplomatically expedient to erase any mention of such an embarrassing guest after the failure at Stoke. And the appearance of a 'Warwick' in London, in February 1487, may have been a reaction to rumours that a 'Warwick' had been seen in the Low Countries. If this son of Clarence was not the real Warwick, was it his counterfeit, Lambert Simnel, already in the Low Countries to be trained by the dowager herself? Both Henry and André emphasised the dowager's close involvement in the conspiracy from its very beginning.[31] If so Maximilian's cautious approach may explain both the lack of reports on the Pretender's presence and the long delay between July 1486 and the start of the invasion nine months later. If it was indeed Simnel, then the dowager's involvement in this conspiracy had begun very early indeed. Surely the English chroniclers would have reported on such a fine example of Margaret's perfidy.

Or was the truth even more extraordinary? Among the English exiles who reached the Low Countries after Bosworth was Sir Edward Brampton. Brampton was a converted Jew from Portugal and a merchant who had worked for both Edward IV and Richard III,[32] he was eventually to prove himself a loyal servant to Henry VII as well. According to Warbeck's confession of 1497, Brampton stayed in Flanders until 1487 when he returned to Portugal taking Warbeck with him as a young assistant. Warbeck also claimed that he had begun

Tomb of John de la Pole, Duke of Suffolk and his wife Elizabeth

his career by masquerading as Edward, Earl of Warwick. Is it possible that there were two pretenders available in 1486, one in Malines and one in Ireland, both claiming to be the Earl of Warwick and that it was eventually decided to back the Irish pretender and to send the other away?

The reality may of course be rather less interesting. The clerk writing up the records may have simply made a mistake and the reference was intended as someone else, or perhaps some degree of fraudulent entry was going on, though 'the son of Clarence' would be a strange name to choose for a bogus entry. What it does indicate is that the cause of the 'son of Clarence' was known in Malines as early as July 1486 and that the city corporation, ever willing to keep in favour with their dowager, made him a present of wine. If nothing else it dates Margaret's interest in a Yorkist Pretender to the summer of 1486.

Further evidence of her involvement lies in the same year-book with the record that between early 1486 and early 1487 Malines gave the dowager 750 livres for her *reyse* to England.[33] A *reyse* may be translated as a journey or a venture. Margaret was already collecting funds to pay for the mercenary army. The dowager was well able to raise money for an expedition, as in addition to extra gifts like this from Malines, she had her dower income and the money from the sale of the Malines house. All that was needed to get the expedition underway was a sign from England that there would be enough support there and the assent of Maximilian. The sign from England came with the flight of the Earl of Lincoln and Maximilian must have given his assent early in 1487.

By the April of 1487, the expeditionary force was ready to set sail from the Low Countries and Henry VII, whose military intelligence was always very good, was expecting an invasion along the east coast. He moved troops up to East Anglia to intercept a landing. After spending Easter at Norwich, he went on a pilgrimage to Walsingham taking with him the Earl of Lincoln's father, the Duke of Suffolk. By 4 May he knew that the invading army had left Flanders and was making its way westwards to Ireland. As soon as Lincoln, Lovel and Schwartz arrived in Dublin, Lambert Simnel was crowned King Edward VI, in Christ Church Cathedral. No doubt the pious Margaret was delighted to hear that her protégé had been sanctified by 'two archbishops and twelve bishops.'[34]

However her true opinion of this first Pretender is far from clear. It was a curious conspiracy and nothing remains more strange than the motives and intentions of the Earl of Lincoln. It seems likely that he was supporting an impostor with the intention of putting either the real Warwick or himself on the throne. To what extent was Margaret a party to this subterfuge? After Simnel's exposure the dowager made no known efforts on his behalf as she later did for Warbeck, but then Simnel's life was never in danger. Moreover in the Antwerp protocols which she later agreed with Warbeck, there was no mention of either the Earl of Warwick or of *King Edward VI*. The 1487 expenditure is referred to merely as in support of 'the Count of Lincoln and lord Lovel.'[35] The *Great Chronicle of London* suggested that the Burgundians were deceived by Lincoln and quoted a letter reported to have been written to the earl on the eve of the battle of Stoke by Martin Schwartz:

> Sir now I see well that ye have dyssayvyd yoursylf & alsoo me, But that not wythstandynd, all such promyse as I made unto my lady the duchess I shall perfform. Exortyng therl to doo the same. And upon this spedd theym toward the ffeeld wt as good a corage as he hadd xx m men more than he had.[36]

The rebels had certainly deceived themselves over the amount of support they could expect in England. Very few rose to join *Edward VI's* army after it had landed near Furness on the Lancastrian coast and marched across the northern Pennines and down through the plain of York. The arrest of Dorset had no doubt deterred many potential rebels and the rapidity with which the king moved north gave no time for waverers to flock to the Yorkist standard. Henry was at Coventry when he heard that the rebels had landed and were on the way south. He lost no time in cutting them off near the village of East Stoke on 16 June, only a dozen days after their landing in England. At the hard-fought battle of Stoke, which lasted for more than three hours, Martin Schwartz and most of his *landknechts* were killed together with Lincoln and Thomas Fitzgerald, the brother of Kildare, as well as hundreds of the ill-clad and ill-equipped Irish troops who made up the bulk of the army. Many were drowned as they tried to escape across the Trent. Lovel vanished from history if not from legend and the ten-year-old *King Lambert* was arrested and contemptuously placed in the royal kitchens.[37] For the Yorkists, the battle of Stoke was almost worse than Bosworth. The ignominy of accepting a craftsman's son from Oxford as a prince of the House of York ran against the whole spirit of the age and did nothing to help, and everything to hamper, future claimants. Henry would ensure that any new pretenders were immediately identified with this impostor, whom he kept alive as an excellent example of the gullibility of the conspirators.

The consequences for the members of the House of York in England were not very noticeable. The Suffolk family were hardly affected by the treason of their eldest son and his brother Edmund was allowed to inherit some of his titles and lands. The Duchess of Suffolk still took a prominent place at her niece's coronation, though when the Duke of Suffolk died in 1491, it was said that he had never recovered from the death of his son John. Edward, Earl of Warwick, simply remained in the Tower as a useful exhibit.

For Burgundy, however, the outcome was interesting. Although a few Flemish merchants were attacked in London, Henry was careful not to point the finger of blame at either Margaret or Maximilian. It was not until the Warbeck conspiracy began to threaten his security that Henry named Margaret as responsible for the Simnel affair. Indeed, in 1487, he seemed to have learned the lesson that Maximilian had been anxious to teach him and in December of that year negotiations began for renewing the commercial and friendship treaties between England and Burgundy, which were signed in January 1488. Four months later ambassadors from Burgundy were again at Windsor and Maximilian was hopeful of obtaining English help against his own rebellious subjects. As the Low Countries erupted once more into violence, Maximilian sought English cooperation.[38]

The failure of Margaret to feature in any of the conspiracies against Henry VII, which took place between the spring of 1487 and the autumn of 1492, gives the lie to the Tudor theory that her whole life was focused on her vendetta with the English usurper. She was, in fact, once more much too preoccupied with events in Burgundy to give much attention to England. And events in the Low Countries were certainly dramatic. Maximilian was again confronted by a major revolt in Flanders while 1487 had been an extraordinary year for the ducal family. Following the coronation of Maximilian as the King of the Romans in February, the emperor arranged his long awaited visit to the Low Countries. In July, Malines was *en fête* for his visit and, with his son Maximilian and his grandson Philip, the old Emperor Frederick made state visits to several of the cities of Brabant. Their arrival in Brussels had, according to Molinet, been likened to a visitation by the Holy Trinity: the Imperial Father, Maximilian the Son and the young Philip as the Holy Ghost.[39] The whole affair was considered a great triumph.

However the summer campaigns against France did not go well. Although Maximilian captured Therouanne and planned a march on Paris, he was halted by mutinies among his unpaid armies and forced back to Valenciennes. The French struck back recovering Therouanne, seizing St Omer and defeating the Burgundians near Bethune. These failures in the war, coupled with a dislike of foreign and imperial interference in the affairs of the Low Countries, provoked rebellion in Flanders. There may also have been some anger at the invasion of England which threatened to jeopardise trade and shipping in the Channel. Once more the rebellion broke out at Ghent where the flames were fanned by Adrien van Liederkerke who had an old score to settle with both Margaret and Maximilian.[40]

The misfortunes of the Humbercourt family did not end with the execution of 1477. Shortly after the execution of her husband his widow, Antoinette, had arrived at Malines with her family. But within a few months she was abducted by Liederkerke and one of his allies while she was on her way to visit the shrine of Our Lady of Hanswijke. Her captors took her to the castle of Bornhem and she subsequently married Liederkerke, so whether it was an abduction or an elopement it is difficult to say. Both Margaret and Maximilian intervened, instructing the magistrates of Malines to take action, first to secure Antoinette's release, which they failed to achieve and secondly to take over the guardianship of her children and her property which had been handed over to the parents of Adrien van Liederkerke. This was rather more successful and the children and their lands were put under the guardianship of a group of eminent courtiers including the count of Chimay.

Liederkerke doubtless felt robbed of his wife's property and took his opportunity in 1487 to join with his cousin, the Lord of Rosseghem, who had led the revolt against Maximilian in 1485. They stirred up the rebellion in Ghent and ducal officials were arrested and murdered. The rebels summoned the Flemish estates to assemble but, while the delegates hesitated, Maximilian called for the estates to come to Bruges instead. Bringing his army with him, led by the old enemy of Flanders the Lord of Gaasbeek, Maximilian moved towards Bruges intending to use the estates and his army to crush Ghent and its supporters. During October, Margaret took the young archduke on visits to her loyal cities of Mons and Binche before returning to the safety of Malines to spend Christmas. In December the estates met at Bruges. The town and the countryside around were full of armed men and the rebels at Ghent feared a full scale attack by Maximilian, but the archduke's plan to divide Ghent and Bruges failed and Bruges refused to allow Maximilian to bring his army into the city. The King of France, Charles VIII, intervened confirming all Ghent's privileges, including the restoration of the city mint which had been transferred to Bruges. He claimed to be acting in the name of his vassal, the Archduke Philip, whose powers had been usurped by Maximilian. A month later, Maximilian found himself facing an even more serious situation, trapped in Bruges with his army held outside the walls. Thus on 31 January in the year that Commynes began to write his *Mémoires* and Bartholemew Diaz rounded the Cape of Good Hope, opening up a whole new world much of which was to be ruled by Maximilian's descendants, the best schemes of the late King Louis finally came to fruition and the ruler of Burgundy found himself a helpless prisoner in the Cranenberg house on the market square of Bruges.[41]

It was not a particularly uncomfortable imprisonment even though it was to last for more than three months. The King of the Romans was accompanied by his chancellor, the Abbot of St Bertin and during most of his captivity he was attended by his own personal servants. The city magistrates even hired Gerard

The Verdict of Cambyses *or* The Arrest of the Unjust Judge *by Gerard David, painted* c. *1498. Copyright ACL Bruxelles*

David to paint the shutters in his room and the artist's later works depicting the arrest and torture of the unjust judge were inspired by the scenes he witnessed in the market square below the windows of the Cranenberg. It must have been very distressing for Maximilian to have to listen impotently for two days as his chief agents in the city, Pierre Lanchals and Mathis Payert, were tortured before being executed. Many old scores were settled and Lanchals had the misfortune to be tried and punished by one of his old enemies and rivals, Coppenole. Maximilian began to fear for his own life, writing anxiously to his father, the Emperor Frederick, that his servants were being taken away from him.[42]

Both the emperor and the pope protested against the imprisonment of the imperial heir.[43] The emperor sent an embassy to deal directly with the rebels and threatened to follow this up with an army if his son was not released. Margaret acted calmly and firmly, protecting the young Archduke Philip and Malines was put into a strong defensive position in case the Flemish cities tried to seize him as well. In Philip's name, the estates general was summoned to assemble in Malines and in February all the provinces and cities, apart from the three rebel members of Flanders, Ypres, Bruges and Ghent, and their few allies among the nobility, sent representatives there. The estates appointed a committee headed by Lord Ravenstein to negotiate with the rebels for Maximilian's release.

By May it was known that an imperial army was on its way and that its advance guard had reached Oudenaarde. The pope threatened the citizens of Bruges with excommunication if they did not release their ruler and serious negotiations were underway between the Flemish rebels and the committee of the estates general. The Flemish agreed to release Maximilian in return for promises from the archduke to withdraw the German army, to uphold the Great Privilege, to consult the great council and the estates on all matters of war and peace and to take no action to punish the rebellious cites. Maximilian had to furnish hostages as sureties that he would keep the promises. Among those who offered to take Maximilian's place at Bruges was Lord Ravenstein's son, Philip of Cleves. A peace treaty was signed and the King of the Romans was released on 16 May. As soon as he was safe, he abjured all the promises he had been forced to make under duress and began to assemble an army at Louvain with which he intended to crush the rebels. This of course put his hostages in a very difficult position. For Philip of Cleves this was the breaking point, he abandoned Maximilian and took up arms with the rebels.

The old guard which had supported Margaret and Mary in their crisis of 1477 was breaking up. Apart from Philip of Cleves and his father Lord Ravenstein, who had disagreed with Maximilian's approach to the problems in Flanders, the Lord of Gruuthuyse had also fallen out with the King of the Romans.[44] In 1485 he had supported the idea of a regency council excluding Maximilian and in February 1488 he had been arrested and held at Malines together with his two sons. He was later removed to Dendermonde and might have been executed at Vilvoorde if the Order of the Golden Fleece had not intervened on his behalf. During the imprisonment of Maximilian at Bruges the rebels insisted on Gruuthuyse's freedom, but he was imprisoned again when Maximilian was released. He spent his last years at Bruges, enjoying the considerable consolations of his fine house and library which had so impressed Edward IV in 1472. Lord Ravenstein died in 1493, Philip inherited his father's title and he was finally reconciled to Maximilian. Margaret must have regretted the loss of all her old advisers but nothing seemed to shake her determination to stand by Maximilian.

Throughout the summer of 1488 the civil war continued, as Maximilian strove to recover cities lost to the rebels and to avenge the indignities he had endured. He turned to England to help him in his struggle and the alliance between Henry and Maximilian was cemented by the events in France. Due to the Anglo-Burgundian entente, which lasted with minor interruptions from 1488 to 1492, there was no support from Burgundy for Yorkist pretenders. The cessation of the conspiracies throughout these four years suggests that it was Maximilian who really controlled the Yorkist activity. When it was no longer in his interests to plague Henry, the plots ceased.

In 1488 Maximilian certainly needed English support and not only against his own rebels. The death of Duke Francis II in September resulted in a major international crisis over the succession in the Duchy of Brittany. Like Charles the Bold, Francis left an heiress Anne, and Charles VIII claimed the right to take over the duchy in default of a male heir. The Bretons appealed both to Henry VII and Maximilian in their efforts to preserve the independence of their duchy. A major European alliance against France gradually came into being, including Brittany, Burgundy, England and Spain. It was, however, the English who took the most active role in Brittany. In April 1489, Henry sent over a well equipped force of about 5,000 men to assist the young duchess. He also supplied troops to fight beside Maximilian, against his Flemish rebels, who were aided by their allies the French. Two thousand English archers and 1,000 pikemen marched up from Calais and proved themselves very useful at the battle of Dixmude in

The fifteenth-century House of Ravenstein in Brussels. Copyright ACL Bruxelles

June.[45] Though, after the battle, when they heard that Lord Morley, their commander, had been killed in the assault, the English army disgraced itself by slaughtering all their prisoners. Molinet was very shocked by this and considered that it was only the strong discipline of the German troops which had saved the town of Dixmude from total destruction. In spite of some obvious ill feeling between the English and their Burgundian allies, this was one of the few periods during Maximilian's regency when the old Anglo-Burgundian alliance really operated.

The success at Dixmude marked the end of rebel strength and in October 1489 another peace treaty was signed between Flanders and the King of the Romans, although pockets of rebels still resisted pacification. Reparations were made to Maximilian and Margaret for all their losses in the wars, with Margaret receiving 21,000 livres for the damage done to her property.[46] Even after this the rebellions in the Low Countries did not cease and although Maximilian was able to negotiate treaties with France at Frankfurt and at Montils-lez-Tours in the summer of 1489, these were not full settlements of all the problems caused by both the treaty of Arras and the succession crisis in Brittany. However there was a lull in the fighting and some of the damage caused by the wars could be repaired. Margaret's dower properties in French hands were once more restored to her. In 1490 therefore, Margaret was able to send money to Brielle to help that city to rebuild its defences destroyed by a rebel attack led by Frank van Borselem and Jan van Naaltwyck during the civil wars.

By October 1489, Maximilian was once more fully accepted as regent and he turned again to the English alliance which he hoped would help him to reverse the treaty of Arras and keep France out of Brittany. By the end of the following year Henry and Maximilian had renewed their treaties and at Christmas 1490, as a sign of their new friendship, Maximilian was invested with the Order of the Garter at Neustadt.[47] In an effort to promote his interests in Brittany he decided to marry the young Duchess Anne and sent his friend Wolfgang, Lord von Pelhain, to act as his proxy. But few of the troops which he had promised for the defence of his bride arrived in the duchy and when Charles VIII began a systematic invasion of Brittany there was little either Maximilian or his English ally could do. The French king finally conquered the residue of the Breton army and arrived before Anne with a papal dispensation to permit his own marriage to the duchess. With no other choice left to her, Anne ignored her own previous proxy marriage and Charles' long betrothal to Margaret of Austria and married the French king, barely a year after her marriage to Maximilian. Maximilian lost both a wife and a son-in-law, but he had the satisfaction of seeing the destruction of the treaty of Arras, which had been based on the marriage of his daughter and King Charles.

Henry VII proved himself more determined than Maximilian and even after the marriage of Charles to Anne was known, he prepared for an invasion of France. He crossed the Channel at the head of his army and laid siege to Boulogne in October 1492. Like Edward IV before him, he was soon opening negotiations with France and Charles VIII was only too willing to renew the payments due under the old treaty of Picquigny, promising to cover all the arrears and Henry's expenses for having to come in person to collect his danegeld. The peace of Etaples was signed on 3 November 1492 and Maximilian, like Charles the Bold before him, was said to be furious at the perfidy of Albion. But in fact Maximilian had gained much from the English intervention. The English fleet had helped in the conquest of the last rebel strong point at Sluis, held by Lord Ravenstein. The rebels finally gave up the struggle and Maximilian was able to achieve peace and the final submission of Ghent at the Treaty of Cadsand in July 1492. Moreover Philip was now almost old enough to rule in his own right. In 1491, when he was thirteen, he had become a Knight of the Golden Fleece and he was beginning to play a larger part in the government of the duchy.

The treaty of Senlis, negotiated between Charles VIII and Maximilian in May 1493, resulted in the return of Margaret of Austria together with her dowry of Artois and Franche Comté.[48] Thus although the Duchy of Burgundy and Picardy were now lost for ever, Maximilian had at least salvaged a large part of his son's inheritance. The dowager also benefited from the Franco-Burgundian settlement and all her dower properties were restored to her, with reparation payments for her loss of income during the many years of war. But perhaps her chief delight was in the return of Margaret of Austria to the Low Countries. Margaret was now thirteen years old and had been well educated under the wise guidance of Anne de Beaujeu. She joined the court at Malines and was in close contact with the dowager during the next few years. Margaret once more had the pleasure of the companionship of a young girl, just as she had had with the child's mother a quarter of a century earlier.

In March 1494, when Philip came of age, Margaret must have felt that her promises to Mary had been fulfilled; the new archduke had inherited most of his mother's possessions. The new ducal council reflected Margaret's influence, manned as it was by families who had long years of service to the ducal family, such as the chancellor Carondelet who had worked with Hugonet and the president of the council who was Engelbert, Count of Nassau.[49] As Philip toured the Low Countries attending his inaugural celebrations, Margaret had a special pleasure for beside the young archduke rode her latest protégé, *Richard of York*, the new Yorkist Pretender. He claimed to be none other than the second son of Edward IV, born in August 1473, and miraculously rescued from death in the Tower.[50]

Even during the years of accord with Burgundy, English opposition to Henry continued. After the northern rebellion of spring 1489, Sir John Egremont fled to the Low Countries. There was a continual undercurrent of conspiracy which gave rise to the suspicion that, in spite of the Anglo-Burgundian amity, Margaret was still at the centre of a great web of treachery. The dowager was certainly known to be well skilled at keeping in touch with those who might be useful to her. She had proven her ability in 1470–71 when she had regularly sent messages to her rebellious brother Clarence, both when he was in France and when he was in England. She had renewed her contacts in England by her visit in 1480 and during the reigns of Edward V and Richard III her agent and her chaplain visited the country.[51] Even after the accession of Henry, there was no reason why her messengers should have ceased to move between England and Flanders. She still had close family ties in England, notably her mother the old

Duchess Cecily, who was regarded with favour by King Henry. Cecily was not only the queen's grandmother, she was also related to Margaret Beaufort, Henry's mother, hence Edward Hall's description of Cecily as 'a woman of small stature but of moche honour and high parentage.'[52] In spite of her 'moche honour,' Henry's agents seem to have kept a close eye on the activities of her servants and officials.

In Cecily's will which was proved in August 1495, her executor was Master Richard Lessey, the dean of her chapel.[53] The old Dowager Duchess of York left Lessey money to help him to 'bere the charges which he has to pay to the Kinges grace,' probably for his involvement in a Yorkist conspiracy. With the legacy went an appeal to the king to forgive the debt. Other beneficiaries from the will were Richard's wife, Jane Lessey, Richard Boyvile and Gresild his wife. Each of these three received very generous bequests of clothing, jewelry and plate as well as a carriage, horses and harness. The Boyviles had been in the service of the Duchess of York for many years and also had close contacts with Margaret. In 1468 Richard Boyvile had accompanied her to Bruges, bringing over hackneys suitable for her use. Later he and his wife were in attendance on the dowager when she visited England in 1480. They had been rewarded by Edward IV for their service to her.[54] It is not too far fetched to guess that both Lessey and Boyvile may have acted as agents organising messengers which passed between the old Duchess of York and her youngest surviving daughter, Margaret.

There were other points of contact through whom Margaret was able to keep in touch with opinion within England. In the various treason trials of Henry VII's reign many persons were accused of making contact with the pretenders and exiles in the Low Countries.[55] Among those suspected of Yorkist sympathies were many clerics, including John Sant, Abbot of Abingdon, William Richeford, English provincial of the Dominicans, William Worsley, Dean of St Paul's and Dr Heusse, Archdeacon of London. According to the testimony of Bernard Vignolles, Warbeck had been helped in Kent and in Ireland by the Irish Provincial of the Order of St John and Guillemin de Noion and Daniel Beauvuire were named as messengers between English clerics and the Yorkists in Malines. It was, of course, customary for clerics to travel frequently across the Channel and it is perhaps for this reason alone that so many of them attracted the attention of Henry's investigators, but the role of the clergy in the plots against Henry VII merits an investigation. Was the famous piety of Cecily and her daughter Margaret more than a mere 'merchandising with God'?[56] Is it possible that there was a real sympathy for the Yorkist cause among some of the clergy? Certainly Cecily, Richard III and Margaret were notably generous and dutiful towards the church.

There were also many laymen accused of being a part of this Anglo-Burgundian web of conspiracy. They included a number from Ireland who were involved in the Simnel conspiracy and, like John Waters, were also responsible for introducing Warbeck into the country.[57] Within England there were many known Yorkist sympathisers such as Edward Franks, the ex-sheriff of Oxfordshire and Berkshire, who had been arrested for his part in the Simnel rebellion though he was not executed until 1490 when he was accused of trying to arrange the escape of the Earl of Warwick. The most dangerous group of these sympathisers were the highly placed men at court who, probably only as a sort of insurance policy, were resolved to keep in touch with the 'princes over the water'. Prominent among these was Sir William Stanley, executed in 1495 for his contacts with Warbeck and the rebels in Burgundy.[58] For these great men, the support of Maximilian for the Yorkist pretenders was more important than the support of Margaret. This was made clear in the Milanese ambassador's reports of the conversations between Maximilian and Lord Clifford, who had been sent out to the Low Countries by Stanley. Clifford was clearly trying to gauge the extent of Maximilian's commitment to the Yorkist cause.[59] There was a host of lesser men in England, like Edward Cryer, a hat-maker from Northampton and Henry Mountford, an armourer from Warwick, who had all sorts of lost reasons for putting their trust and hopes on a Yorkist restoration. Some like William Asham, who was tried for his involvement with Warbeck in 1496, had been in attendance on Margaret in 1480 and Dichefield, the Governor of Guernsey at the time Warbeck was supposed to have been there in 1486, was commissioned by Margaret to take archers across to Maximilian in 1480. Many men would be stirred by old loyalties and they would be encouraged in their hopes by their knowledge that the rich and powerful Duchess of Burgundy supported their cause.

Although there is no known evidence that the dowager or her servants had widespread contacts within England, Margaret was involved in diplomatic contacts with both Ireland and Scotland during the five years of Anglo-Burgundian harmony. In January 1490, the King of Scotland paid for a herald who travelled between Ireland and Malines and Margaret's envoys were at the Scottish court in November 1488.[60] Was this the beginning of the Warbeck plot? Warbeck later claimed in his confession that he had begun his service with Pregent Meno in 1487 and it was he who had taken him to Ireland. Was Margaret aware of her protégé's movements as early as this and was she already preparing the way for him? Both André and Polydore Vergil suggested that Margaret had originally found and trained the young man herself and André's source for his assertion may well have been King Henry.[61] Brampton's presence in the Low Countries and the reference to the son of Clarence in the St Rombout's day accounts may be some evidence in their favour, but the matter still largely depends on the veracity of Warbeck's confession. While there are some signs that Margaret was informed of the Pretender's existence when he was in Ireland there is nothing to substantiate claims that she had created him. If she did have such early knowledge of the Pretender, her abstinence from any overt efforts on his behalf, between 1487 and 1492, merely reinforces the argument that her policies were never independent from those of Maximilian.

While Maximilian and Henry were in such a close alliance Margaret did not advertise her Yorkist sympathies, and thus it was at the court of France, the enemy of both Burgundy and England, that the career of *Richard of York* had begun. The new Pretender, who had like Simnel surfaced in Ireland, was invited to the French court by Charles VIII where he was given all the honours due to a Prince of England. His bodyguard was under the command of the Lord of Concressault and Yorkist sympathisers hastened to join him, one of whom was

Sir George Neville.[62] The Pretender was soon in use as a tool of French diplomacy, writing to the King of Scotland asking him to invade England in alliance with France.[63] This was the start of a long diplomatic career for the Pretender, who was to pen his appeals to many of the crowned heads of Europe. However his stay at the French court was cut short. Before the year was out Henry and Charles had settled their differences at the treaty of Etaples where Charles had promised not to assist Henry's enemies. In spite of this Charles did not surrender the young man to Henry and in December the Pretender was allowed to leave Paris and make his way to the Low Countries where he could count on a warm welcome. Maximilian was displeased by the new Anglo-French accord and by the failure of his own and his daughter's marriages. Margaret was therefore permitted to give her full recognition to her *nephew* and he was received as a prince of the royal blood at the ducal court where he became a close companion of the young archduke.

Margaret had last seen her nephew during her visit to England in 1480, when he was seven years old. Now, twelve years later, she claimed in her letter to Queen Isabella of Spain that she had been able to recognise him as her lost nephew miraculously saved from death.[64] She went on to explain that she had been told of her nephew's existence when he was in Ireland, but had not been able to believe that it was true. She heard of him in France, where he had been recognised by persons who would have known him as well as his own mother. This may be a reference to Sir George Neville who was at the court of King Edward IV. 'His own mother', Elizabeth Woodville, died in June 1492 when her *Richard* was at the French court. The only known picture of the Pretender which has survived is a drawing in the museum at Arras.[65] It shows a gentle and aristocratic young man with a slight irregularity about the eyes, an impression of him supported by the description of Warbeck from the Venetian ambassador, who wrote in 1497 that he 'was not handsome, indeed his left eye rather lacks lustre but he is intelligent and well spoken.'

If *Richard* was to have any credibility he must have the full support of Margaret, the only member of the House of York beyond Henry's influence. Margaret's support of Warbeck seems to have been very sincere, surviving even his capture and confession. It is difficult to understand why she continued to make such an effort on his behalf if she knew all along that he was a fraud. Even Edward Hall and Polydore Vergil allowed that Margaret was convinced that her nephew had been found. Virgil wrote that Margaret received 'Peter . . . as though he had been revived from the dead . . . so great was her happiness that the pleasure seemed to have disturbed the balance of her mind.'[66] Hall in his usual vigorous way added that Margaret thought 'to have gotten God by the foote when she had the Devill by the tail.'[67] Once more it is Molinet who offers the best insight into the prevailing views of the Burgundian court when he refers to 'Richard whom it was *hoped* was the Duke of York.'[68] (After his capture and the confession, however, Molinet named the young man as 'Pierrequin Wezebecque'. It would not be lost on his readers with any knowledge of Dutch that the word 'weze' means an 'orphan'.)

In 1492 the voyage of Christopher Columbus was one of a series of astonishing ventures, some of which were to bring dramatic changes for the

Perkin Warbeck, known also as 'Richard of York'

whole of Europe. Yet to most of the people living at the time, the quest of *Richard of York* must have seemed much more likely to succeed than a westerly voyage to the Indies. The Warbeck conspiracy was a very different matter from the earlier rebellions against Henry VII. It was to menace Henry for almost six years and this Pretender obtained wide recognition from the Kings of Denmark and Scotland and from the princes of the Empire.

Margaret wrote many letters seeking support for her *nephew*, but only those to Isabella and the pope have survived.[69] Her letter to the Pope was written in 1495 as the preparations for the invasion of England were underway. Her appeal to Isabella dated from two years earlier shortly after the Pretender arrived at Malines, it was also accompanied by a letter from *Richard*.[70] They both appealed to Isabella as a cousin, i.e., a descendant of John of Gaunt. They begged her to succour 'this last sprig of her family' since Margaret, being 'a lone widow', could not furnish him with enough aid to enable him to destroy 'the usurper', who had committed such an injury on their family. In his letter to Isabella, *Richard* gave an account of his early life which was remarkable for its vagueness. He claimed that when he was 'nearly nine years old' he had escaped death. His survival was due only to the mercy of the lord who had been sent to kill him and his older brother. He was smuggled abroad with two men to care for him, one of whom had died and eventually the other returned to England leaving him to fend for himself. After wandering in Portugal he eventually arrived in Ireland where he had been recognised. This was followed by a period in France before he finally reached Malines where 'his dearest aunt' had 'because of her virtue and humanity' received and recognised him.

Throughout this letter there are no names of either people or places; this lack may have been due to the need to protect people who were still within England but it is very unconvincing. Moreover there is a strange error over *Richard's* age. The real Richard was born in August 1473, and he would therefore have been nearly ten and not nearly nine in 1483 when the little princes disappeared into the Tower. It is possible that this was merely a clerical error made by the clerk who translated the letter into Latin, as the Latin of both these letters is rather defective. Neither the dowager nor *Richard* had much competence in that language. The intention may have been to write that he was still '*only* nine years old' when he had escaped death but it had been translated as '*barely* nine'. These letters from Dendermonde were given little credence at the Spanish court. Isabella did not reply to Warbeck though she wrote to Margaret assuring her that the whole affair was an imposture.[71] The letter from the Pretender was filed in the Spanish offices with the endorsement 'from Richard who says he is King of England'. The Spanish monarchs reported the whole correspondence to Henry, clearly regarding it as a joke, though Henry certainly did not.

Nor was the Pretender regarded as a joke in the Low Countries. He received the fullest public support from both Maximilian and Philip, who provided him with an escort of thirty halberdiers dressed in the York livery of mulberry and blue decorated with white roses. The guard was commanded by Hugh de Melun, a reliable ducal courtier who had fought bravely for Maximilian against Ghent in 1492. Melun was the Governor of Dendermonde and a knight of the Golden Fleece.[72] *Richard* rode beside Philip on his inaugural visits to Louvain and Antwerp. The visit to Antwerp took place in October 1494 and was made an occasion for Yorkist propaganda in the full view of all the English merchants who were present in the city.[73] The two young men doubtless enjoyed all the pageants and tableaux which had been organised to entertain them, including the three naked women who posed as the three graces for the 'pleasure of the people' as Molinet neatly put it. The *Duke of York* was attended by his own bodyguard and his arms, proclaiming him as the Prince of Wales, were mounted on the house of the English Merchants Adventurers. This brought protests from the English merchants and led to fighting in the streets between the merchants' men and the Pretender's bodyguard.

It was certainly not only 'for the duchess' sake' that 'all the Flemings exalted Richard.'[74] Both the archdukes gave him every encouragement and there were even rumours that he would be allowed to marry Margaret of Austria. A medal was struck in his honour, on the reverse of which appeared God's warning to the tyrant Balthazar as a dreadful threat to the Tudor king. Nor was this exaltation restricted to the Low Countries. In November 1493 the Pretender was given great prominence at the funeral of Emperor Frederick III in Vienna. There he was recognised as a prince of the House of York by all the princes and bishops of the Empire. Here was a young man who could ride beside the Emperor-Elect Maximilian and dine with princes and who was apparently accepted by them all as the rightful heir to the English crown. It was a very serious threat to the new Tudor dynasty.

All this exaltation of the Pretender should, however, be viewed within its European context. The years 1492 to 1496 were a period of diplomatic turmoil in western Europe. Freed from the menace of an Anglo-Burgundian alliance and secure in Brittany, Charles VIII was now free to strike out in a new direction. In 1494 he embarked on an invasion of Italy. This dramatic development sent the heralds of all the Italian duchies, the papacy, the Spanish monarchies, Germany and Burgundy rushing to and fro seeking new alliances against France. These diplomatic overtures resulted in the creation of the Holy League. The support of England was important to both sides and while Spain tried to draw England in through marriage alliances, Maximilian resorted to his old method so successful in 1487. Either Henry should be forced into an alliance or he would be replaced by a new Yorkist king bound in friendship to the emperor. It is significant that the Antwerp protocols between Margaret and *Richard*, the deposition of *Richard's* inheritance to the archdukes and Margaret's letter to the pope, all date from late 1494 to early 1495, at the height of this diplomatic activity.[75]

King Henry took a more myopic view of the European scene. He was not going to commit himself to any alliance against France while he was being threatened by a pretender and he urged Spain and the Italian duchies to put pressure on Maximilian to abandon his protégé. He also took his own measures to deal with the problem and so did other men in England. Less than six months after the Pretender had arrived in Malines, Sir Robert Clifford and Sir William Barley left England, apparently sent by Sir William Stanley who wanted to make contact with the Pretender.[76] Both these men were witnesses to the Antwerp protocols. They later returned to England and were pardoned and even rewarded by the king. It would seem that they were not merely agents for Stanley but royal agents as well. Molinet reported that Henry's spies were sneaking in and out of the Low Countries through Calais and Bethune and were soon able to name all the English conspirators in Flanders and most of their contacts in England.[77] As a result of their reports a series of treason trials took place in 1494 and 1495 so ensuring that most of Warbeck's supporters had been rounded up long before he attempted a landing.

Henry's agents were also instructed to discover the origins of the new pretender and they were remarkably successful. As early as July 1493, Henry had apparently found out who this new pretender really was; in his letter to Talbot he named him as Perkin Warbeck, a native of Tournai in Picardy. A year later he had added the information that he was the son of a boatman. Henry also took active measures to forestall a second invasion of England from Ireland. Sir Edward Poynings was despatched to pacify the Irish and he soon had the whole country under control.

In addition Henry made direct diplomatic approaches to the Archduke Philip. In the summer of 1493 a high powered English embassy arrived in Burgundy with instructions to inform Philip that he was harbouring an impostor.[78] Poynings and William Warham, who headed the embassy, were very careful not to cast any blame on the archduke himself but they confronted and accused the dowager. Warham, later to become the Archbishop of Canterbury, told Margaret that she had produced 'two great babes not as normal but fully grown and long in the womb,' an especially unpleasant remark to be addressed to a barren woman. Not surprisingly 'these tauntes and jestes did anger and trouble the lady Margaret'. Molinet records that the English heralds so overstepped the bounds of polite diplomacy that the archduke threatened them with prison. But, discreet as ever, Molinet limited his description of the encounter to a spirited dialogue between the heralds and the dowager who objected to the ambassadors' failure to bow to her *nephew*. According to him one of the English ambassadors offered to take any representative that the dowager cared to name and to show him the chapel where the real Richard of York was buried. At this point the Pretender intervened to express his amazement at the report of his burial and promised not to forget the herald's words when he became king.

The prominence of the dowager at the reception of the English embassy illustrates the ducal advisors' concern to minimise the official Burgundian responsibility for the activity against Henry. The archduke even assured the envoys that he was powerless to intervene since the dowager had full authority within her own lands. This was patently untrue since in all the dower settlements the full sovereignty of the archduke had been preserved.[79] Henry recognised the naivety of the archduke's excuse and responded with vigour. He unleashed an economic war against Burgundy; from 1493 to 1496 there were mutual trade boycotts, English merchants were encouraged to leave Antwerp for Calais and, in consequence, the pressure on Philip to abandon the Pretender grew rapidly among both the merchant community and the ducal councillors. There were no attacks on the dowager but rather complaints against Maximilian who was still suspected of influencing his son's policies.

In spite of the growing economic distress, the archduke continued to support schemes for a Yorkist invasion of England. Another mercenary army of about 1,500 men was collected under the leadership of Roderigue de Lalaing, the bastard son of a famous Hainault family well known to Margaret since Simon de Lalaing had welcomed Margaret to Sluis in 1468. Like Martin Schwartz, Roderigue was one of Maximilian's trusted captains. He had distinguished himself at the battle of Utrecht[80] but, unlike Schwartz, he came from the Burgundian aristocracy. He had also distinguished himself in the lists at the tournament which celebrated Philip's entry into the Order of the Golden Fleece. Also unlike Schwartz he was to survive his Yorkist adventure, later fighting for another of Maximilian's allies, the Sforza Duke of Milan and he had dealings with Maximilian's later Yorkist protégés. Once more it is evident that Maximilian was behind the venture to overthrow Henry.

If Maximilian and Philip provided the facilities for collecting together the necessary men and ships, the dowager again acted as banker. Margaret at this time received the full restoration, with reparations, of all her lands which had been seized during the 'Great Rebellion', her French dower had been returned to her and in addition Maximilian had made over some of the revenues and lordships confiscated from those who had supported Bruges and Ghent.[81] In these circumstances she would have had little problem in raising the funds for the modest expeditionary force.

The series of contracts, which were drawn up at Antwerp by the lawyer Adrien van der Blickt and witnessed by Clifford and Barley, record the arrangements for a loan between Margaret and her *nephew*.[82] There were six protocols in all, signed between 10 and 23 December 1494. They settled all the matters still outstanding between the dowager and the crown of England. When *Richard* became king he would pay over to his 'very dear and very beloved aunt Margarete of England' the 81,666 crowns still owing on her dowry. He would repay all the expenses Margaret had incurred on behalf of Lovel and Lincoln, as well as the 8,000 crowns she had lent him for his own venture. In addition he would restore her English licences and give her the manor of Hunsdon and the town and castle of Scarborough.

Even while these articles were being signed and sealed at Antwerp, the Archduke Philip came under increasing pressure to abandon the policies which were so injurious to Burgundian trade. There was a crescendo of protest from the mercantile community especially in Flanders, Brabant and Holland. As early as February 1495 the ducal council was urging Philip to withdraw his support from the English pretender and to make a new economic treaty with Henry. Henry used his negotiations with the Holy League to exert diplomatic pressure on Maximilian. Both Venice and Spain advised Maximilian to abandon the Yorkist Pretender in order to bring Henry into the alliance against France. But the emperor, as Maximilian now was, boasted to the Venetian ambassador that he had 'his kinsman Richard of York in his pocket' and that when *Richard* was made the King of England he could be counted on to invade France in support of the League.[83] The emperor was quite open in his support of the Yorkist pretender; he even delayed an imperial diet because he was too busy organising the invasion of England and after the expedition had left Vlissingen he remained in close contact with the venture. It was surely Margaret who kept him well informed. News was sent on from Malines to Worms in July 1495 to assure the emperor that all was going well. Maximilian appeared to be supremely confident of *Richard's* success.

Henry avoided confronting either Maximilian or Philip. He allocated the blame firmly to Margaret who was, he claimed, leading both Maximilian and Philip astray in the support of yet another 'feigned lad'.[84] Those within England who had been tempted to believe in the Pretender were arrested and the trial and execution of Sir William Stanley in February 1495 served as a frightening example to the waverers.[85] If one so close to the throne could fall for making contact with the rebels then lesser men would draw back. The English agents had done their work well and depositions such as that given by Bernard de Vignolles from Rouen show how far reaching and comprehensive was the royal investigation. The success of Henry's preventative measures both in Ireland and England was shown in the total failure of the attempts by the Pretender and his army to make a landing either in Kent or Ireland during the summer of 1495.

By the spring of 1495 a fleet of about fourteen ships stood ready at Vlissingen to embark on the great enterprise. It left Zeeland in late June and attempted a landing at Sandwich in July.[86] Driven away from there they went on to Deal where they succeeded in putting some of their force ashore. Henry was away in the north, so the invaders had at least chosen the right place at the right time, but there was no local support and in fact they found vigorous opposition to their landing. According to Molinet, the Yorkist standard was raised in three villages, a very modest claim. Those who had landed were rounded up and taken for trial. About 160 men were taken prisoner, including Dutchmen, Germans and Burgundians. The Spanish ambassador reported that two Spaniards were among them. Margaret had evidently recruited from the international market of mercenaries who thronged the Low Countries throughout the wars. The rest of the expedition took to their ships and sailed off for Ireland. Here again they were disappointed by the lack of support. They besieged Waterford for eleven days but were finally forced to withdraw with the loss of one of their ships.

Driven from England and Ireland the Pretender took refuge in Scotland where he was welcomed at the court of the young King James IV. Correspondence between Malines and Scotland had eased the way for this friendly reception.[87] King James was almost the same age as the Pretender and like Philip before him he seems to have enjoyed the company of *Richard of York*, who remained at the court there for more than two years. Special taxes were raised to keep him and to provide him with an allowance of £1,200 a year. He was offered a bride of the royal house, the Lady Catherine Gordon, a cousin of the king, and they were married with great splendour at Stirling Castle. King James was not merely being self-indulgent in his treatment of the Pretender. Intent on recovering Berwick he saw him as a useful weapon in his diplomatic war with England. However he was neither willing nor able to commit a large force to invade England on behalf of his client.

The presence of the Pretender at James' court made Scotland a target for European diplomacy. Both France and the Holy League wooed the young king who appeared to relish the attention. The French sent the Lord of Concressault, a French noble of Scottish extraction, who had served the Pretender in France[88] and Sir George Neville was bribed by both sides to use his influence with the Pretender. Charles VIII offered to mediate between Henry and James and he tried to purchase the Pretender for a sum of 100,000 crowns. France was not the only country trying to get hold of the young man. The Earl of Buchan and Lord Ramsay also wanted to kidnap him with the intentions of selling him to King Henry. On Henry's instructions, Lord Ramsay showed Concressault a paper, supposedly from the French king, claiming that the Pretender was the son of a barber and his parents would soon be sent over to England. Apparently Concressault remained unimpressed.

By 1496 Henry had plenty of identities for the Pretender. Apart from the French barber's son and the Tournai Warbeck, he had been offered an Iberian pretender. Ferdinand of Aragon promised to send:

> declarations of many persons who knew him [the Pretender] amongst whom is a Portuguese knight in the name of Ruy De Sosa . . . he is well acquainted with the whole matter . . . having been the Portuguese ambassador in England he knew the duke of York very well and had seen him there; two years later he saw this other person in Portugal . . . and his parents are in Portugal and are our subjects.[89]

The ease with which aliases could be provided must cast some doubts on the complicated alias which Henry eventually provided for the young man.

While the Pretender remained at the Scottish court, Lalaing returned to Burgundy and came back with a very small reinforcement of 'twa little ships and 60 alemans.'[90] This reinforcement may have been Margaret's last effort on her *nephew's* behalf, although troops described as 'alemans' could equally well have come from Germany and thus from Maximilian. The young man was embarrassed by Margaret's rejection. One of Henry's spies, James Ramsay, reported Lalaing's arrival at the Scottish court and the conversation which took place between Lalaing and the Pretender:

> then cam Perkin to him and he salut him and askit how his Ant did and he said 'well' and he inquirit gyf he had ony letters fra hir ti him and he sad he durst bring nan, bot he had to ye king.

There is also a ring of truth in the speech written by Hall for Warbeck when he was trying to account to King James for the dowager's failure to back him any further:

> mine awne aunte the Lady Margaret . . . which as joyfully receaved and welcommed me as yf I had come out of hell into heaven, the only type and garland of her noble stirpe and linage . . . but for as muche as she being only dowager . . . and having nothing but her dowre propre unto herself was not of powre to keep me with men and munimentes of warre.[91]

Margaret was indeed no longer able to help her *nephew* in any way because as soon as the Yorkist expedition left Zeeland the Burgundian archduke withdrew his support from the whole venture. The ducal council succeeded in making Philip understand that his security from another Flemish rebellion was dependant upon the rapid termination of the trade war with England. Negotiations began after the failure of Warbeck in Kent, and by February 1496 the commercial treaty known as the Intercursus Magnus had agreed.[92] This was a comprehensive treaty and it restored harmonious trading relations between the two countries. The Burgundians had to accept the abandonment of Warbeck. Margaret was specifically named in the treaty and she was forbidden to help any of Henry's enemies. Publicly at least Margaret observed all the terms of the treaty.

The Pretender was forced to seek help elsewhere and it was at this time that he wrote to Spain requesting Bernard de la Forsse, a knight who had served both Edward IV and Richard III, to come to his aid.[93] Sir Bernard's son Anthony, seems to have been in the Pretender's army and it was hoped that more mercenaries and knights might be brought in from Spain. Signing his letters from 'yr frend Rychard off England' in a bold fluent hand very similar to that of his *aunt*, the Pretender also wrote to the Earl of Desmond and to his friends in Ireland. Little came of these efforts and the Pretender's only real hope was to receive direct military assistance from Scotland. Shortly after Lalaing's return from Flanders, a contract was drawn up between the Pretender, with Sir George Neville acting as the chief adviser, and King James.[94] *Richard* promised to restore Berwick to Scotland and to repay all the money and aid he had received from Scotland by a subsidy of 50,000 marks payable over two years. With this contract in his coffers the Scottish king brought his forces to Ellam Bridge to be met by the 'Duke of York's men' assembled under a banner of murray and blue embroidered with a large white rose. An army of 1,400 men from many nations crossed the border on 17 September but for the Scots this was more of a raid than an invasion. After looting and pillaging along the borders they withdrew and were back in Scotland within four days. The Pretender, no doubt realising that raids from Scotland would do his cause no good in England, protested to James at the misery and cruelty inflicted on 'his people'. This drew the sharp retort from James that he was showing a great deal of consideration for people who would have nothing to do with him and 'this ridiculous mercy and foolish compassion' was misplaced.[95]

By the end of 1496 King James was tiring of his attachment to the Pretender. Henry was offering James a good marriage and the Holy League was urging him to abandon Warbeck. However the young King of Scotland had a strong sense of honour and would not merely reject the Pretender as Charles VIII had done. Moreover there was no longer a haven for *Richard* at Malines. An opportunity for Scotland to rid itself of Warbeck came in the summer of 1497. There had been a rebellion in Cornwall against Henry's government and, although it had been put down, the south-west was still seething with discontent. In July the Pretender prepared to try once more to invade England. He still hoped to win support in Ireland so his strategy was unchanged. He would land first in Ireland and after collecting an army, sail on to England to make a landing in the south west. Before he left Scotland, he issued a proclamation declaring his rights and naming Henry as a usurper whose government through 'caitiffs and villains' was causing 'misrule and mischief' in England. He called on all his subjects to rise to his cause and promised rewards to all those who came out to fight for him, a weak gesture compounded by the list he issued of all those who had died on his behalf, hardly likely to encourage others. Among those on the Pretender's list were Sir William Stanley, Humphrey Stafford, Sir Robert Chamberlain and Lord Fitzwalter who had been executed at Calais in 1496.[96]

Early in July the Pretender and his wife left Ayr with a small fleet. King James promised to support him by diversionary raids in the north, but Catherine's presence on board with her husband suggests that the Scottish king was saying a final farewell to his protégé and although James did attack at Norham in late

August, by the time the Pretender landed in Cornwall negotiations between James and Henry had begun in earnest. At least one of the ships in the Pretender's small fleet appears to have come from Burgundy since it had the Dutch name of the *Kekeuit* (the Kijkuit or Lookout).[97] Was this a secret gift from Margaret or from Maximilian? If so Margaret was being very discreet. Throughout this final attempt there were no other signs that she was still backing the enterprise. Lalaing does not seem to have been present during Warbeck's final efforts in Ireland and Cornwall.[98] He had probably left long before the departure from Scotland, but his contacts with the Yorkist cause did not end in 1497. He was still carrying messages between the emperor and his Yorkist pretenders as late as 1505, when he was in contact with Edmund, Earl of Suffolk. Although Philip and Margaret had withdrawn their support, Maximilian continued to back this Richard. As late as October 1497, the emperor assured the Venetian ambassador that the Pretender could count on an army of 35,000 men and that he would succeed in seizing the throne of England as he marched up from the west.[99]

On 20 July the Pretender's small fleet arrived at Cork where, through the influence of his old friend and supporter John Waters, he could be sure of a welcome. He was joined there by two more ships, probably from France or Brittany, perhaps a contribution from Charles VIII who was hoping to delay Henry's participation in the Holy League. After a month spent recruiting a large number of Irish soldiery, the expedition sailed for Cornwall where they landed on 7 September at Whitsand Bay. Three days later Henry heard that the long expected invasion had begun.[100]

About 3,000 men from the south-west came out under the *Duke of York's* banners which carried a graphic account of the Pretender's cause. One depicted a small boy being rescued from a tomb, a second showed the same child escaping from the jaws of a wolf (or was it a wild boar?) and the third displayed the red lion of England. Encouraged by the support he received among the Cornish, the Pretender sent his wife and her ladies to shelter at St Michael's Mount, declared himself *King Richard IV* at Bodmin and marched on to take Exeter. But Exeter, led by the Earl of Devonshire, who was within the city with a large army, shut its gates and prepared for a long siege. After losing about 400 men in the siege, more through desertions, and hearing that Henry was heading into Cornwall at the head of a large army, the Pretender lost his nerve and fled. On the night of 20 September he left 'the pore comons levyng theym amazed and disconsolat.'[101] With a small party of close friends such as John Waters he made his way towards the coast but they were forced to take sanctuary at Beaulieu Abbey. With promises that their lives would be spared they were persuaded to surrender and were taken as prisoners to Taunton where Warbeck made his famous confession. He was then taken on to Exeter where Henry arrived on 7 October. The Lady Catherine was brought from St Michael's Mount to hear her husband's confession and the tearful young woman was taken into the queen's household, complaining that she had been seduced by lies. Catherine Gordon was to live on to make three more marriages and is commemorated on the monument of her second husband, Sir Matthew Craddock, at Swansea.[102]

Within five days of the Pretender's flight from the siege of Exeter, the Milanese ambassador in England had sent on the news of Warbeck's failure to the Genoese merchants at Bruges, so Margaret was probably informed of the capture of her *nephew* within a week of the event. The reaction of Margaret to the failure of 'perkyn her dere darlyng' is best left to Edward Hall's imagination, who claimed that she 'wept and lamented hys unlucky spede and cursed her infortunate cause'.[103] It may also be significant that during the summer of that year she was taken ill at Binche.

Warbeck's confession was widely circulated in London and abroad, and he was paraded before the English people, interviewed by foreign ambassadors and was made to repeat his confession on several occasions.[104] He also sent a letter in support of this confession to his mother, one Katherine Warbeque living at 'Saint Jehan supz L'Eschauld'. In this he described how he had left home to go to Antwerp with 'Berlo'. He referred to the last letter which he had received from his mother when he was at Middelburg. In this she had told him of the deaths of his brother and sister from the plague. He begged her to reply to his new letter and to send money to help him. Unlike the letter written to Queen Isabella, this one was crammed full of names of people and places. Although the original no longer exists there are copies at Tournai and Courtrai which suggest that, like the confession, the letter was widely circulated.

The vast amount of detail in the letter and confession suggests that if it was not true then King Henry's agents were remarkably thorough or had extremely vivid imaginations. The Pretender confessed that he was the son of John Osbeck or Wezebeque and Katherine de Faro or Nichase and had been born at Tournai. He had learned English with an English merchant at Middelburg (who was not named) and Flemish at Antwerp. By 1486 he had become proficient in three languages and was taken into the service of Sir Edward Brampton, who had taken him to Portugal. Brampton was contacted by Henry's agents in Portugal in 1489; a year later all Brampton's English possessions were returned to him and he had apparently entered King Henry's service.[105] Warbeck had then transferred into the service of Pregent Meno (made constable of Carrick Fergus by Henry in 1496) who took him to Ireland where he was mistaken first for Edward, Earl of Warwick, and later for Richard of York.

The confession made no suggestion that Margaret had begun the conspiracy nor was there any mention of the emperor, the Archduke Philip or of the King of Scotland. While detailing all his early life it was silent about the allies who had provided his ships and armies. In spite of all the plausible detail, there were many who could not believe that the son of a tradesman could have fooled so many and played the role of a prince with such conviction and for so long. All sorts of rumours sprang up claiming that he was indeed a Plantagenet, perhaps a bastard who had been secretly reared abroad, but there was no reason why either of the Yorkist kings would have bothered to conceal their bastards in this way. Edward IV was always quite open about his illegitimate children, one of whom, Lord Lisle, proved to be a loyal servant of the Tudors. There were certainly many who doubted the veracity of the confession. Parron, the king's astrologer, dismissed all these sceptics by comparing them with the Flemish who expected Charles the Bold to return and with the Cornish who were still waiting for King

Arthur to awake, two appropriate similes.[106] Nevertheless there were signs that even Henry regarded this Pretender more seriously. He was not, like Simnel, relegated to some menial place but was, for the first six months, kept close to the court. After an attempted escape in the summer of 1498, his treatment became much harsher. He was twice exposed in the stocks, at Westminster and in Cheapside, and finally imprisoned in the Tower.[107]

Margaret did not entirely abandon her *nephew*. In 1498 Henri de Berghes, Bishop of Cambrai, headed a delegation to England dealing with commercial matters and bringing a formal apology to Henry from the dowager.[108] The bishop requested and was granted an interview with Warbeck, which took place in front of the Spanish ambassador. The Archduke Philip had already married Joanna, the eldest daughter of the Spanish monarchs, and Henry was negotiating for a marriage between the younger daughter Catherine, and his eldest son Arthur. Although the interview appears to have originated as a Burgundian attempt to save the life of the young man, it was used by Henry for his own purposes. It was designed for Burgundian and Spanish consumption. De Puebla the Spanish ambassador commented that Warbeck was much changed and could not be expected to live much longer since he was being kept in a dungeon 'where he sees neither sun nor moon.' Henry asked Warbeck why he had deceived 'the archduke and the whole country'. In reply the Pretender 'swore to God that Duchess Madame Margaret knew as well as himself that he was not the son of King Edward' but all the rulers, the archduke and the King of Scotland had been deceived. Thus the Pretender had exonerated all Henry's new allies, the King of Scotland, the emperor and particularly the archduke, who was soon to be united more closely to the English crown through the marriage of Prince Arthur to his sister-in-law. All blame was placed firmly on Margaret. From the dowager's point of view the bishop's interview was a total failure for Warbeck was executed a year later.

There were several reasons in 1499 why Henry had decided that it was time to rid himself of 'doubtful royal blood.'[109] In the February of that year another young man, Ralf Wulford, came forward claiming to be the Earl of Warwick. He was taken prisoner and hanged on Shrove Tuesday. At the same time Henry was warned by his astrologer that his life was in danger and he seems to have taken this warning very seriously. In May the proxy marriage of Arthur and Catherine took place, but the Spanish monarchs were still reluctant to send their daughter over to England. To purge their fears, Henry resolved to do away with both Warwick and Warbeck. They were accused of conspiring to escape to Flanders and condemned to death. It is interesting that Henry felt it necessary to remove one whom he had proved to be an impostor along with the one he claimed was the rightful Earl of Warwick. On 23 November, Warbeck and his old friend John Waters were taken to Tyburn. Once more Warbeck made a public confession, he was then hanged and beheaded, dying 'meekly' but without the more appalling elements of a traitor's death, perhaps the payment for that final affirmation of imposture. Five days later Warwick was beheaded 'without any processe of the lawe.'[110] He was the queen's nearest male relative and Henry seems to have had some qualms of conscience since he paid for the young man's burial, not at the Tower as was usual for traitors, but at the family burial place near Windsor.

Henry's attempt to discredit and humiliate Margaret was entirely unsuccessful in the Low Countries where her prestige remained as great as ever. With Margaret of Austria, she headed the reception party which greeted the new Archduchess Joanna on her arrival from Spain and although she moved out of the palace at Malines to make room for the new archduchess, she remained a respected member of the court. The respect the court and people showed towards their dowager was reciprocated and Margaret was careful to comply with ducal policy and to keep her promise to King Henry. In the summer of 1499 Edmund, the Earl of Suffolk (the younger brother of the Earl of Lincoln), fled to Calais and thence to St Omer. However upon receiving assurances as to his safety, he was soon persuaded to return to England.[111] Two years later he fled again, taking with him his younger brother Richard. This time there was no returning to England but they did not remain long on Burgundian territory before seeking the protection of the emperor. There is no evidence at all as Hall claimed that the 'old venemous serpent the duches of Burgogne' was 'solicting and alluring' the young sons of the House of Suffolk to come to her court.[112] Henry responded to the flight of the two young men by arresting their younger brother, William de la Pole, and he, like William Courtenay, who also had Plantagenet blood in his veins, was to spend the rest of his life in confinement. Sir James Tyrell and Sir John Wyndham were accused of aiding the escape of the de la Poles. They were arrested and executed in 1502 but not before Tyrell had been used to dispose of two troublesome ghosts by confessing that he had assisted in the murder of the two princes at the command of Richard III.[113]

Maximilian, however, continued to meddle in English affairs.[114] In 1501 he declared himself ready to help anyone of Edward IV's blood to gain the throne. A year later the death of Prince Arthur left the Tudor dynasty dependant on the survival of a single male heir. The emperor saw his control of the two de la Pole brothers as a useful diplomatic asset and the elder, Edmund, known as 'the white rose', became the standard bearer for the Yorkist hopes. However Maximilian never fulfilled the vague promises he made to furnish Edmund with the '300, 400 or 500 men of war' for 'one, two or three months.' Without the support of Burgundy, the Yorkist pretenders were denied access to the ports of the Low Countries and an invasion of England was no longer a feasible proposition.

After 1496 there is no evidence of a vendetta by Margaret. Indeed it was Henry, greatly troubled by the deaths of his youngest son Edmund in 1500, and his eldest son Arthur in 1502, who seems to have been conducting a vendetta against the House of York. He did not cease to make every effort to have the two sons of Suffolk returned to England,[115] and his agents kept a very close eye on the young men and their associates. In 1506, three years after Margaret's death, Archduke Philip and his wife were forced to take shelter from a storm in the English ports. Henry took full advantage of this accident and made their departure conditional on the return of Edmund, the Earl of Suffolk. Maximilian was reluctant to hand over the young man because he had promised to protect 'the white rose' for 'Lady Margaret's sake and at her instance.' The corporation of Malines also voiced their concern for the safety of the nephew of their revered dowager. The king was obliged to guarantee the safety of Edmund and on his return Suffolk was kept in the Tower until after the death of Henry VII. He was then executed by Henry VIII, as was the unfortunate William de la Pole.

Margaret's role in the conspiracies against Henry was both limited and cautious. She had certainly maintained Yorkist exiles at her court and she had paid for the Simnel and Warbeck invasions. At most this amounted to furnishing about 5,000 men and two small fleets. Both these armies were recruited with the help of Maximilian who provided the captains and the bulk of the men. Nor could these invasions have been launched without the full consent of the archducal government which permitted the use of Burgundian ships and ports. When the ducal government changed its policy and decided to withdraw its support of the Yorkist pretenders, Margaret abided by their decision even though she seems to have been personally concerned about the fate of the young man she had recognised as her nephew Richard. But in all actions concerning England she did nothing that would damage her reputation in the Low Countries. The dowager was well aware of her responsibilities in this quarter. In a letter of 1499 written from Valenciennes, she expressed her deep care for all the people of the Burgundian lands and her wish to spare them 'devastation and damage' ('grans foules et dommaiges').[116]

There is also no evidence that Margaret spent the bulk of her rich dower on these projects. She continued to maintain a luxurious household, travelled throughout the Low Countries, carried out various building works at her many properties, gave generously to charities, collected magnificent books and presented costly gifts on appropriate occasions. At the baptism of Philip de Croy her present to her godson was a gold and cut-crystal cross about 18 inches high and encrusted with precious stones.[117]

If her financial and military help was limited then perhaps her chief role was as a standard bearer for the House of York. Her importance in the conspiracies was her own sympathy for the Yorkist cause and the extent of her influence through the respect shown for her opinions by Philip and Maximilian. In the first years of Henry VII's reign Margaret must have hoped for a Yorkist restoration, and this hope was revived with the appearance of the supposed Duke of York. Yet even in her role as the leader of the Yorkist cause there are ambiguities. The dowager rarely signed herself as 'Margaret of York' but more usually as 'Margarete of Engeland'.[118] Olivier de La Marche put the position with his usual attention to procedural niceties when he explained that:

> Though I have surnamed her of York she really ought to be surnamed of England for she came from the royal line. But since her grandfather, [he clearly didn't know about the Earl of Cambridge] and her father were Dukes of York the children were named from the duchy in the same way as were the princes who were descended from the kings of France [i.e., the Valois Dukes of Burgundy].

Margaret's first commitment was always to Burgundy. During the crises of 1477, 1482 and 1487, she gave her full support to its rulers. When she visited England in 1480 she showed no wish to remain at her brother's court but hastened back as soon as her mission was completed. Moreover although she was a widow for twenty-six years, she never showed the least sign of wishing to

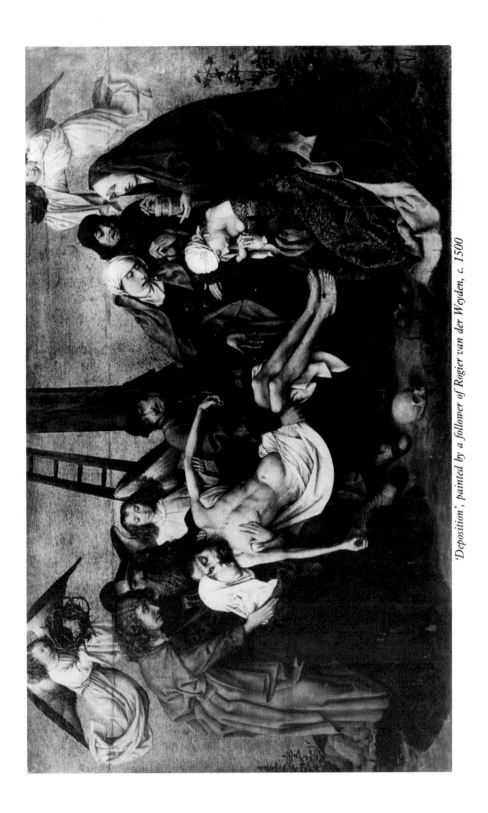

'Deposition', painted by a follower of Rogier van der Weyden, c. 1500

Detail of the 'Deposition' showing a woman, possibly the Magdalen, dressed in a very fine gown and wearing a belt decorated with a conspicuous white rose and two or three marguerites

remarry and leave the Low Countries. Throughout her widowhood she was dependant upon either Maximilian or Philip and her conduct makes that dependence clear.

The portrayal of Margaret as the mainspring of the plots against Henry probably owes more to the Tudor viewpoint than it does to the realities of Burgundian history. There were many reasons why it was useful for Henry to blame Margaret for his troubles. Henry lacked the charisma of Edward IV, he faced considerable opposition both in England and Ireland, and he was disliked by a section of the nobility for 'the wrong he did his Queen . . . that he did not rule in her right.' He was 'a great taxer of his people' and 'feared due to avarice that his people would abandon him.'[119] It was convenient for Henry to present the dowager as a vengeful and meddling woman causing foreign interference in English affairs. It was also convenient for Maximilian and Philip to use her as a shield, and throughout the entire period Margaret never embarked upon any project against Henry without the encouragement of Maximilian and the agreement of the ducal government.

Nevertheless her sympathies were certainly with the Pretenders and this was well known by her contemporaries. Indeed evidence of this sympathy may still exist in the painting of the *Deposition*, now in the J. Paul Getty museum;[120] in many ways this painting is very similar to the famous *Deposition* by Rogier van der Weyden which is in the Prado. In both paintings there is a group of holy women at the right of the cross and among them stands the Magdalen. In the grief-stricken posture, in the clasped hands and in the headcloth the figures in both the paintings are alike but there are some major differences. In the Getty painting, the Magdalen wears a strikingly rich brocade dress and at her belt, which is decorated with two or three marguerites, there is a large white rose. It is difficult to think of anyone apart from Margaret who would be depicted wearing these symbols in a Flemish painting of the late fifteenth century. With the white rose so prominently displayed there would seem to be a clear reference to the Yorkist cause. However many questions spring to mind. Would the pious and reserved dowager have permitted herself to be represented in the form of the Magdalen, the most sinful and penitent among the holy women? Is there some significance in the fact that the traditional pot of balm is held by a nun in the habit of the Black Sisters? Could this be a reference to the Augustinian Sisters in whom Margaret was especially interested and to the foundation of a home for fallen women at Mons?[121]

7 Bibliophile and Reformer

'by the commandment of my said redoubtable lady Duchess of Burgundy'

Like many medieval women, from the good wife of Bath to Christine de Pisan, Margaret found that the widowed state offered many rewards. As the wealthy and well respected Dowager of Burgundy, she enjoyed a considerable degree of independence. Her wealth ensured that she was able to maintain a high standard of personal ease but her position was never a sinecure and her life was full of interest and stimulation. She had secured and retained her financial position through her unwavering defence of the ducal family and her constant work on their behalf. During her nine years as duchess and her twenty-six years as dowager Margaret served three generations with energy and loyalty. She was not seduced by French blandishments on the death of Charles the Bold, nor did she attempt to safeguard her French possessions by adopting a neutralist position in the struggle between Burgundy and France. Her commitment to the ducal family was total and therefore her rewards were great. After the settlement of her dower by her step-daughter, her position in Burgundy was never challenged and all her possessions were confirmed and ratified by her grandson, the Archduke Philip, when he came of age. In December 1494 Philip justified the generosity of her endowment on the grounds of:

> her good and honest conduct towards our late lord and grandfather, and the great love that she clearly bore towards our late sovereign lady mother and to all her lands and lordships both before and after her marriage, and equally towards our lord and father, and towards us in our minority, how after the death of our late lady mother, she behaved towards us as if she was our real mother . . . and moreover because she has suffered inestimable damage rather than abandon us . . . and because of many other great reasons and considerations.[1]

The young archduke continued to give his step-grandmother's interests every consideration. In 1495 she exchanged her property at Le Quesnoy for the town of Rupelmonde, at the junction of the Rivers Scheldt and Rupel, with all its valuable tolls and customs duties.[2] The 300 livres shortfall in her annual revenue resulting from the exchange were made up from the revenues of Dendermonde and Oudenaarde, and Philip agreed to bear half the expenses for the repair of the castle and the mill at Rupelmonde. Le Quesnoy was situated two days journey south of Mons and had been constantly in the front line of French invasions. Although by the time of this transfer the various Franco-Burgundian treaties had restored Margaret to the full possession of all her dower, Le Quesnoy was a difficult and expensive property for a dowager to hold. Apart from its strategic position, Le Quesnoy lay within the vast hunting forest of Mormail and that fact may also have inspired the transfer to the archduke. The ageing duchess no longer had such a need for this type of endowment.

Margaret took upon herself a heavy load of responsibility for the maintenance and administration of all her dower property. Many documents have survived in the archives of Brussels, Malines and Lille that bear witness to her assiduity. Apart from raising troops to defend her possessions, a serious matter in the years of invasions and rebellions, Margaret held full responsibility for upholding law and order, collecting aides and taxes and maintaining all the property of the demesne such as castles, palaces and mills. In the wet lands of the valleys of the Scheldt and the Lys it was also the duty of the landowner to preserve the vast network of ditches and dykes.

Margaret was jealous of her authority and would not allow its erosion. This is made clear from her arguments with the magistrates of Malines over elections and with the Bishop of Cambrai over a case of sanctuary.[3] Even her favoured dower town found that she was zealous in preserving her privileges. In 1495, it appears that she had some reasons for disapproving the results of the election for the Malines magistrates. Claiming the same rights which she possessed in her other dower towns, Margaret demanded that the names of all the magistrates should be submitted for her approval. The corporation of Malines resisted her orders, declaring that this was an infringement of their ancient liberties, which the dowager had herself confirmed in 1477 and in 1485. Margaret then turned to the archduke and persuaded him to declare the election null and void, but this was not to be the end of the story. The magistrates persisted in their claims, and they too appealed for ducal justice and so the legal argument continued. Unfortunately the final outcome is unknown, but it is very apparent that she was resolved to maintain her authority. In spite of this legal wrangle, the relations between Malines and their dowager remained very good indeed.

Ardent in the protection of her rights and privileges, Margaret was not averse to making an appeal to the ducal government if it suited her purpose. Nor was she immune from the general addiction of the age to pursue lengthy and often fruitless litigation. One long drawn out affair concerned the lands of Buggen-hout which had been granted to Margaret when its former owner defected to France.[4] But she was challenged in her right to the manors by Charles de Hallewijn, a close relative of Mary's lady in waiting. Margaret's lawyer, William Stadio, pursued the case for several years but found all his efforts blocked and after Margaret's death, Charles de Hallewijn ultimately gained the title to the property. Apart from the legal tussle with Malines and about Buggenhout, the dowager took another long-standing case before the archduke in September 1496. The six defendants had all been found guilty of certain illegalities in the

Philip the Fair, Archduke of Austria and Duke of Burgundy

Joanna of Castile, Archduchess of Austria and Duchess of Burgundy

drapery business but they had failed to pay their fines to Margaret. The archduke found in her favour and this time she seems to have obtained satisfaction. However although she was willing to pursue her cases in the courts she was not over zealous. She was prepared to concede some of her traditional judicial rights to the archducal courts when she surrendered to the high court all responsibility for the sale of the criminal's confiscated goods in cases of homicide.[5]

If Margaret relied on ducal support in judicial matters, she was entirely independent in the administration and management of her dower lands and she appointed her own officials. She selected men of good family and character to head her administration and she was loyal to those who had served her husband well. To be in the dowager's service also provided a good opportunity for ambitious young men who sought to catch the attention of the archduke. Henri de Witthem, Lord of Beersel and Henri de Hammericourt, Lord of Villerzies, both began their careers in the dowager's service, the former as her Lord Lieutenant at Malines and the latter at Binche.[6] They eventually became important councillors to Philip and after his death they served under the Regent Margaret and later under Emperor Charles V. Henri of Witthem became Charles' strong right arm in the Brussels area, a position which earned him great notoriety in 1532 when he was sent into Brussels to crush an urban revolt. His brutality was so appalling that the citizens rose up, marched on the castle of Beersel and destroyed it. Another who achieved high office through the service of the dowager was Gerard of Assendelft. The son of an important Dutch family with a large house in The Hague (now the British embassy), he was chosen to take the feudal oaths for her dower lands at Brielle and Voorne. By the reign of Charles V, Assendelft controlled the mint at The Hague and was one of the most important ducal administrators in the whole of Holland and Zeeland.

The dowager kept a close eye on the officials and nobles who performed duties on her behalf. All her officials were required to report regularly and punctually to their mistress. Most of her correspondence was conducted through secretaries but there are several peremptory notes from the dowager herself. Her agent at Dendermonde was Olivier van Royan and he received many instructions from her.[7] In December 1482, at the height of the crisis over the treaty of Arras, she wrote to van Royan telling him to meet her at Antwerp on the following Monday to discuss the maintenance of two windmills on her estates there. In her own hand and in her peculiarly eccentric French Margaret added 'non fayllye poynt de estre a Anvers et Jacques ausy' (don't fail to be at Antwerp and Jacques too). Another of her servants, one Ghysbrecht Dullaert, was summoned to meet her at Oudenaarde and he had to be there no later than 'the end of this week.' One of her favourite phrases in her letters to her civil servants was 'with no more excuses' (toutes excusacions cessans). It seemed that she understood the bureaucratic mind very well indeed and she was resolved to get immediate action. Good service was well rewarded and Margaret showed a maternal care for her employees. Corneille de Berghes received a horse for his special services to 'her very dear and well beloved son' Maximilian in 1488, and when Jean Lebrun the miller at Binche lost all his goods and his children in the troubles of 1487, Margaret ordered that he should receive compensation and reduced his taxes.[8] She made similar sympathetic reductions for the people of Hainault at the time of the great death in 1480 and for the people of Brielle and Voorne after the floods of 1485.[9]

As a result of her careful supervision, her revenues were collected smoothly and regularly. As well as gathering in her rents, her officials levied all the usual feudal dues on the transfer of property, on the sales of livestock, timber, food, cloth, and coals and collected customs and duties on imported goods. Furthermore many of her officials received their salaries directly from her dower towns. Guillaume de Baume supplemented his income with an annuity of 1,000 livres from Malines and the same city also paid the caretakers of her palace.[10] No doubt Malines viewed these payments as a small price to pay for all the benefits that accrued to the city as a result of Margaret's residence. Apart from their trading privileges with England, Malines received special favours from both Philip and Maximilian. From 1489 to about 1530, when it was transferred to Brussels, Malines was the centre of the imperial postal system set up to serve the needs of first Maximilian and later Philip the Fair and Charles V.[11] This alone must have brought plenty of work and wealth to the hostelries and stables of the town.

At Binche where Margaret spent much of her last few years, she owned two houses, the hôtel of the old Abbey of Lobbe and the Hôtel de la Salle.[12] Perhaps she only used the former during the major rebuilding of the latter, which went on for several years and cost between 2 to 3,000 crowns. The Hôtel de la Salle was on the site of the old castle (now the town hall). A whole range of buildings were reconstructed by the dowager, including a new tower, a chapel, a great hall and reception rooms with galleries along the garden side. The new hall was of a considerable size, more than 10 metres wide and 22 metres long and the dowager used it as the focal point for all her administration in Hainault. She also made improvements to the Hôtel of Bavaria at Mons which she continued to visit on a regular basis. The city gave her enthusiastic support and provided all the bricks and mortar required.[13] In her activities at Mons and Binche the dowager was asserting her presence in Hainault, which had become one of the most southerly possessions of the duchy. Margaret was zealous in the defence of her property in Hainault and her continued presence there showed her strong political commitment to the province.

Even after 1496, when Philip had taken over the full reins of government, the dowager was never entirely free from the affairs of state. She never shunned the court or avoided political involvement. Unlike her mother-in-law, Isabelle of Portugal, Margaret did not retire, although in the last two or three years of her life ill-health seems to have forced her to be less active. Nevertheless whenever there was a great court occasion Margaret attended. Indeed her continued energetic involvement in all that life had to offer is one of her more attractive and consistant characteristics.

When Philip came of age, Margaret was forty-eight years old, a good age for a woman in the fifteenth century. Of course as a noblewoman she had avoided the miseries of famine and malnutrition which affected much of the population. Due to her seclusion and to the careful regimens of her doctors, she also escaped the epidemics of plague which scourged the Low Countries in 1472 and again in 1497–8. She had also been spared the dangers of childbearing and the violent deaths which had carried off most of her male relatives. Only one of her brothers, Edward IV, had died in his bed and at the relatively early age of forty-one. Of her other three brothers, Edmund was killed at seventeen, Clarence at twenty-eight and Richard III at thirty-two. Her father, killed at forty-nine and her husband at forty-four were positively old in comparison with these three sons of York. Of Margaret's two sisters, Anne died at thirty-seven and Elizabeth at fifty-nine or sixty. None of them survived as long as their mother Cecily who lived to be eighty. Indeed Cecily's strong constitution seems to have been unique in the House of York. It was perhaps one of her Beaufort characteristics.

In 1494, Margaret had less than a decade to live, and there were increasing signs of ill health. When she was at Binche in the May of 1497, anxious enquiries arrived from her subjects at Malines. In her reply she thanked them for their ' kind delegation' (bonne visitacion) and admitted that during the last six weeks she had had two 'outbreaks of sickness' (accidens de maladie).[14] However she was able to reassure them that through the good services of her doctors Cornille and Lambert, she had finally thrown off the heavy fever which had afflicted her up to that very day and she was now very much recovered. After this illness, although Margaret was by no means infirm, she no longer travelled as often as she had done in the past and she spent most of her last years at Malines and Binche with occasional visits to Brussels, Mons, Oudenaarde, Louvain and Ter Elst.[15]

The dowager was still, due to the long absences of Margaret of Austria and the frequent illnesses of the new Archduchess Joanna, the most important lady of the court. It was she who welcomed all the most distinguished visitors to the Low Countries. With her experience spanning the reigns of Charles and Mary in Burgundy, two Kings of France and no less than five Kings of England, some of her guests must have regarded the dowager as a piece of living history. An audience with the dowager was regarded as a great honour and Margaret seems to have been delighted to represent the ducal family whenever the need arose. Even in the last year of her life, when she was already sick, she entertained Maximilian when he visited Malines. Earlier, in September 1494, when Maximilian's second wife Bianca Sforza, the daughter of Galeazzo, Duke of Milan, came to the Low Countries on her only visit to the north, she too was received by Margaret, both at Brussels and at Malines. The empress was entertained most royally and Margaret did not fail to exploit her visit to serve her own political ambitions. When Philip entered Louvain for his Joyeuse Entrée, he was accompanied by two greatly honoured guests, the Empress Bianca and *Richard of York*.[16] It was her influence at the ducal court and her access to all the important visitors to the Low Countries which made Margaret's support of the Pretender such a threat to the security of King Henry VII.

After 1494 the Emperor Maximilian rarely visited the Low Countries, spending most of the rest of his life in Germany.[17] However it is clear from the *Weisskünig* that his years in the north had had a great impact on him. He remarried but he had no more legitimate children and, though he was to live to the age of sixty, a serious attack of syphilis in 1493 had a lasting effect on his health. When he had arrived at Ghent in 1477, he was only eighteen years old and during the next seventeen years he stood at the centre of Burgundian affairs. In this hard school he certainly received a thorough political and military education, proving himself to be much more realistic as a general than his predecessor, Charles the Bold. As a politician operating within the maelstrom of the Low Countries, he always suffered from the handicap of his foreign origin. Margaret must have also understood this handicap very well. The *Chronicle of Flanders* recorded her frustrations on this score when she was forced to withdraw from Ghent in 1477.[18] Her support of Maximilian was therefore both loyal and sympathetic. He must have learned a lot from Margaret during his years in the Low Countries, and he claimed that he had learned to listen carefully to all the requests that were made of him. He certainly always showed Margaret the greatest respect and consideration and on all his later visits to the Low Countries he either visited Margaret at Malines or the dowager went to meet him. Her influence on his policies towards England had a long lasting effect and his continued support of the House of York seems to have been as much a matter of personal honour as it was of diplomatic value. His loyalty to Edmund, Earl of Suffolk, and his brother Richard de la Pole must have pleased the dowager who could no longer support her nephews herself.

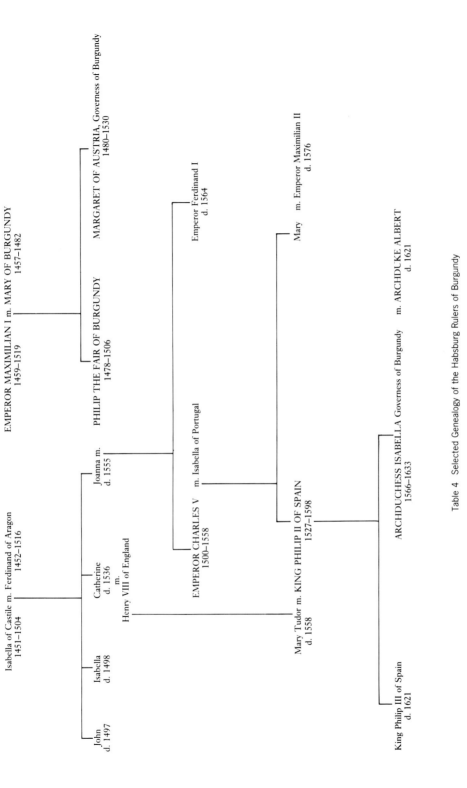

Table 4   Selected Genealogy of tthe Habsburg Rulers of Burgundy

It is not difficult to discern Margaret's influence over the younger archduke. In character Philip the Fair seems to have been like his great-grandfather Philip the Good, preferring to avoid political conflicts and enjoying the pleasures of life, particularly women and hunting. He was very much the antithesis of his grandfather, Charles the Bold, fair-skinned, fair-haired, lively and frivolous. However his brief rule was in many ways much more successful. His government was realistic in its foreign policy, placating France and reaching a practical trading agreement with England; it was also tactful in its domestic administration which operated smoothly under the ducal councillors. Many of the men who served Philip were selected by Margaret. Philip's tutor Francis van Buysleden became the Bishop of Besançon and the Lord of Gistel, the former Mayor of Malines, who had trained the young archduke in the military arts, was made the Governor of Dendermonde.[19] Others like Olivier de La Marche remained in their old positions in the ducal household and even when Philip decided to replace the Chancellor Carondelet with a man of his own choosing he selected Thomas Plaines, a man well known to the dowager from his participation in her embassy to England in 1480. Even if Margaret was disappointed by Philip's failure to support her Yorkist nephews, she must have been well pleased to see her own pragmatic and conciliatory methods applied to the government of the duchy.

Neither Margaret nor any of the ducal advisers could have anticipated the disastrous consequences of the great double marriage which took place at the church of St Gudule in Brussels in December 1495.[20] At these proxy weddings, Philip married the Infanta Joanna of Castile and Margaret of Austria was married to Don Juan, the heir to the thrones of Spain. This proud and splendid occasion was to have a dismal outcome both from the personal and the political point of view. Joanna had a difficult and unstable personality and, especially after the birth of her third child, she suffered from manic depression. Her brother, Don Juan was to die within two years of the marriage, with the result that Philip the Fair became heir to the kingdoms of Spain. The Habsburg possession of Spain, the Empire and the Low Countries, which was the vast inheritance of Emperor Charles V, would bring war and conflict to the Low Countries throughout much of the sixteenth and seventeenth centuries.

However an ignorance of the future is one of the consolations of the present and this gloomy destiny was quite unknown when the Infanta Joanna arrived in the Low Countries in September 1496. Both the dowager and Margaret of Austria went up to Antwerp to meet the new archduchess. They travelled with a glittering retinue drawn from the Knights of the Golden Fleece. The infanta arrived with a huge armada of one hundred and twenty ships. Some of these were to provide the escort for Margaret of Austria when she left for Spain early in the following year. Unfortunately Joanna was ill after the long voyage and she had to be taken to the abbey of St Michael at Bergen op Zoom, so it was there that the two Margarets first visited her. By 20 October Joanna was sufficiently recovered for the marriage ceremonies to take place and she was married to Philip at the church of St Gommaire in Lier.[21] The dowager had already made several visits to the shrine of St Gommaire; she had visited the church in 1475 to see the relics of the saint, returning for the annual procession of the saint in

October 1477. On her first visit the canons had presented her with an illuminated life of St Gommaire and in return she had given the church two fine silver candlesticks. The wedding was celebrated with banquets and a tournament, no doubt organised by Olivier de La Marche, but, although with the accession of Philip the duchy seemed to have been restored to much of its old equilibrium, the opulent ceremonies of Philip the Good and Charles the Bold were never repeated.

In the following January, Margaret of Austria left for Spain, taking with her her old nurse Le Veau de Bouzanton, as she had done when she left to become the Dauphine of France. Within the year her bridegroom was dead and she returned home in April 1499. Two years later, in 1501, the twenty-four year old Margaret set off for her third marriage to Philibert of Savoy. This was to be marginally more successful than her earlier betrothals since it at least lasted for three years before he too died.

During the two periods while Margaret of Austria was in the Low Countries, between 1493 and 1497 and again between 1499 and 1501, she passed much of her time in the company of the dowager. The two women were frequently together at state occasions and on each of her departures from the Low Countries Margaret of Austria was seen off by the dowager. In 1501, the dowager accompanied her grand-daughter to Halle where they made a pilgrimage to the shrine of the Virgin. They then went on to Mons, where Philip came to bid his sister farewell.[22] When she finally returned from Savoy, the dowager was dead. Margaret of Austria inherited much from her step-grandmother, acquiring both her personal treasures and her public servants. Guy de Baume, from the same family as the dowager's *chevalier d'honour*, became the *chevalier* of the young Margaret. But the young woman seems to have inherited much more than material goods and servants from her namesake. After the death of her brother Philip, Margaret of Austria became a most successful governess of the Low Countries. Her court at Malines was modelled on the dowager's example and her pragmatic and patient approach won her great popularity. Perhaps it was also her respect for the dowager which made her so resolute in her refusals when Henry VII put himself forward as a candidate for her hand.[23] (It is through Margaret of Austria that an interesting link exists between Margaret of York and her most illustrious great-grand-niece, Queen Elizabeth I whose mother Anne Boleyn passed two years at Malines, at the court of Margaret of Austria.[24] While she was at the dowager's old palace she must have been surrounded by all the books, pictures and tapestries inherited by Margaret of Austria from her step-grandmother.)

Before the arrival of the new Spanish archduchess, Margaret moved out of the Malines palace into a suite of rooms on the first floor of the building opposite. This house was divided from the church of St Peter and St Paul by a narrow street, and the corporation of Malines built a gallery so that she could reach the church directly from her rooms on the first floor.[25] However this did not mean that Margaret had retired from court life. Even after the arrival of Joanna, Margaret continued to play a large role especially as the poor archduchess was perpetually pregnant and perpetually sick. The first child Eleanor was born at Brussels in November 1498 (she was later to marry

Margaret of Austria, probably painted while she was the Dauphine of France. The Metropolitan Museum of Art

Francis I of France). The dowager was one of her godmothers and carried the baby to her christening at the church of St Michael and St Gudule.[26] The godfather was the Emperor Maximilian, represented at the christening by Prince Christopher of Baden. In the emperor's absence it was Margaret who took the most prominent place in the processions. The hilly walk, from the palace on the Coudenberg to the church on the Treurenberg, must have been too much for the aging dowager especially on a cold November evening, and during the torchlit return, Margaret and the baby were carried in a litter. Thirteen months later, a second child was born at Ghent and there was great delight when the new heir was presented to the people. This child was surely named after his great-grandfather, Charles the Bold, although Molinet thought he had been named in honour of his godfather Charles, Count of Chimay. Once more it was Margaret who carried the child to the font, and the magnificent crystal cup encrusted with precious stones which she gave was a measure of her pride. Even if Margaret had no children of her own, she never lacked family connections. Apart from her close relations with the ducal family, she was also sought as a godmother by the nobility of the Low Countries and, in the same year as Charles was born, she attended the christening of Philip de Croy. He was baptised by her old friend the Bishop of Cambrai and her present to the child was a magnificent crystal and gold cross.

Another ceremony in which the dowager played a leading role was when the infant Charles was presented to the Order of the Golden Fleece. The chapter met in the church of the Carmelites in January 1501 and the dowager was chosen to present the heir to his father the archduke.[27] The church had been splendidly decorated for the occasion with the Troy tapestries being brought from the Coudenberg palace to hang on the walls. Before all the knights of the Golden Fleece, in their cloaks of crimson cloth of gold and amid all the trappings of chivalry and hierarchy, Margaret bore the child to his father who placed the chain of the order around his son's neck and promised that Charles would take the oaths when he came of age.

This celebration typified the traditionalist and conservative attitudes with which Margaret should be identified. The Order of the Golden Fleece expressed the chivalric aspirations of the feudal monarchies and duchies which existed, in theory, entirely for the service of God. Yet its very existence mirrored the ambiguities of the fifteenth century. It was the creation of Philip the Good, who had used it to unite his widely-spread possessions and to assert his own considerable sovereignty. The knights of the Golden Fleece were drawn from the greatest noble families of the whole duchy. The order had been severely depleted after the death of Charles the Bold by defections to France, and it was gradually transformed into a Habsburg institution which would survive beyond the end of the Austro-Hungarian empire in 1918. Though the order had a clear political purpose, the knights of the Golden Fleece were drawn together in a semi-religious and heroic brotherhood, like the Argonauts or the knights of the Arthurian Round Table. In her attendance at the chapter of 1501, Margaret showed her devotion to the ideals of service to God and to her sovereign. In this respect she was typical of a great lady of her age.

There can be no doubt that Margaret was personally, deeply and seriously religious and as such was an important patroness of the church.[28] She lived in an age of religious excess and controversy. Savanorola, one of the most extreme examples of religious dogmatism, was burnt at the stake in Florence in 1498. A few years after Margaret's death, William Tyndale was burnt at Vilvoorde near Brussels and Erasmus sought in vain for the patronage of the Archduke Philip. Stirred by the fierce puritanism of zealots like Savanorola, the unorthodoxy of reformers like Tyndale and the intellectual debate of the neo-classicists like Erasmus, conscientious and pious lay people searched for a way of reconciling the new ideas within the framework of the established church. They also strove to reconcile a devout and pious religious life with their secular responsibilities and to do this they adopted various religious systems and regimes.

Margaret, like her mother and many other devout men and women in northern Europe, followed the way known as the *devotio moderna*. This regime had its origins in the teachings of Gerard de Groot of Flanders.[29] It had been popularised by the Brethren of the Common Life and by the canons of the congregation of Windesheim near Zwolle. Two of the greatest theological teachers of the fourteenth century, Jan van Ruysbroeck, a brother at the abbey of Groenendael near Brussels, and St Thomas à Kempis were sympathetic to the movement. The lay practitioners of the *devotio moderna* built their lives around a pattern of worship, prayer, study and contemplation. Through their interest in private study, they were led towards self education and their piety also led them to become involved with religious reform. Their devotions were encouraged by many of the established religious orders, especially by the Augustinian canons, the Observant Friars and the Poor Clares.

Margaret's dedication to the *devotio moderna* was both personal and public. In her earliest years as Duchess of Burgundy, she was in contact with Denis van Rijkel, a Carthusian scholar and teacher, one of the leading theologians of the Low Countries.[30] Later she had many other friends among the more pious and reforming clergy. She consulted the Prior of Groenendael over the reorganisation of the Victorine convent at Blydenberg near Malines and she turned to Cardinal Nicholas of Cusa, the leading papal reformer in the Low Countries, when she was trying to promote reform in the religious houses at Louvain and Binche. Her chaplains and confessors were all chosen from well educated and devout priests. Among her confessors was the worthy and pious Henri de Berghes, the Bishop of Cambrai, who was one of Erasmus' earliest patrons. His sister Elizabeth de Berghes was the supervisor of the training school at the convent of Bethany at Malines, and a close friend of the dowager's. The reform movement within the Church of the Low Countries concentrated chiefly on restoring the purity of the religious life within convents and monasteries. The reformers also tried to see that only conscientious and well educated priests and bishops were appointed to benefices and to ensure that all religious services were properly performed. Even the worldly David of Burgundy, Bishop of Utrecht, supported this type of reform.[31] He was particularly keen to improve the educational standards of the clergy within his bishopric. He supported poor scholars and introduced the printing press into his diocese. Erasmus was ordained by Bishop David.

As Duchess of Burgundy, Margaret was expected to set a high standard in

Miniature showing Margaret, Duchess of Burgundy kneeling before the Trinity

religious observance, but her interest went much deeper than the conventions of the court. Religious devotion might be expected from the daughter of the pious Cecily Neville, though it should also be noted that neither of her sisters, Anne and Elizabeth, were renowned for their piety and charity.[32] Margaret's interest in religious matters was stimulated not only by her mother but also by her husband who was strictly pious. He shunned oaths, abhored blasphemies and punctiliously attended religious services. She was also influenced by her acquaintance with theologians such as the Carthusian Denis van Rijkel who had been closely involved with the rulers of Burgundy for many years. He had encouraged Duke Philip the Good to undertake a crusade and he had intervened in the conflict with Guelders. He certainly provided Margaret with a very severe model to follow for he disapproved of all worldly vanities amongst which he included polyphonic music, curled hair and pleated clothes.[33] Fortunately his strictures against music were not closely observed at the Burgundian court. John of Burgundy the worldly bishop who preceded Henri de Berghes at Cambrai was the patron of Guillaume Dufay, whose paeon to female beauty beginning with the words 'that noble brow carries my soul to paradise' would certainly not have pleased van Rijkel.[34]

For thirty-five years Margaret was actively involved in the reform of the church, founding and refounding convents, building churches and monasteries and giving generously to the church. Her influence was felt throughout the Low Countries, from Brielle in the north, to Mons and Binche in the south. At Brielle she gave one of her estates, lying just outside the city walls, for the foundation of a new Augustinian convent, 'to which order she bears a singular affection.'[35] Margaret's preference for the Augustinians may have been due to the influence of Denis van Rijkel who had drawn many of his ideas from the teachings of St Augustine. This 'singular affection' was also apparent at Binche where she established a convent of Black Sisters (as the Augustinian nuns were known) near to St James' gate.[36] Margaret was very practical in her various foundations and seemed to prefer working orders. At Binche, the convent provided a hospital, an orphanage and a school for girls. She appointed Lawrence Couvreur as the first superior and he was still associated with the convent as late as 1525. Margaret founded several other hospitals, orphanages and hostels at Mons, Louvain, Ghent and Binche and at Mons she also founded a house for reformed prostitutes, known as the daughters of Magdalen. The rules for this house were drawn up with the dowager's approval and permitted the girls to leave and marry if the opportunity arose. Meantime they were to wear white habits and pass their time in prayer and in caring for the sick.

When she was personally involved in the reformation of convents and monasteries, Margaret favoured the Augustinian rule, even to the extent of forcing it on the reluctant nuns of the Victorine convent of Blydenberg near Malines.[37] Sometimes she encountered stronger resistance to her ideas. There were powerful opponents to reform, especially among the local nobility who regarded the abbeys and convents as an extension of their own estates and resented all interference in them. She faced considerable local opposition at the hospital of Louvain when she intervened to establish the Augustinian rule there. The old abbess, Mathilde Lobs, would not surrender her authority without a fight and called on her local patrons to support her.[38] However, after a struggle lasting three years, Margaret's will prevailed. A new reforming abbess was appointed and Mathilde ended her days as a simple nun in the Carmelite order. The other sisters who had supported Mathilde were also moved out and placed in other convents.

A major influence on the reforms of the religious orders in the Low Countries was St Colette of Corbie who had been active in the early fifteenth century.[39] She had worked chiefly within the convents and monasteries of northern France in the orders of the Poor Clares and the Franciscans. Earlier Duchesses of Burgundy, including the wife of the second duke, had supported St Colette and the Archduchess Mary was particularly devoted to her cult, urging successive popes to agree to her canonisation, which in fact did not take place until 1807. Margaret was the patron of the Poor Clares at Melaan, near Malines and in 1501 she led them back into their newly rebuilt convent. For the occasion she dressed in the novice's habit of the order. Margaret had already donated a lavishly illustrated *Vie de Sainte Colette* to the convent of the Poor Clares at Ghent.[40] This had been written by Pierre de Vaux, a Franciscan who had known the saint and was closely associated with her work. This copy was made during the lifetime of Duke Charles and one of the miniatures depicted Margaret and Charles kneeling with St Colette before an apparition of St Anne. The book was decorated with the arms of the duke and the duchess, with their interlaced initials and the duchess' device 'bien en aviengne'. On the final page, in her own bold and untidy hand, Margaret inscribed the gift from 'your faithful daughter Margaret of England pray for her and for her salvation' (votre loyale fylle Margarete Dangleterre pryez pour elle et pour son salut). The book remains today one of the treasures of the convent for which it was made.

It was perhaps through her devotion to St Colette that Margaret also became involved with the reform of the Franciscan orders, particularly with the Recollects, or the Observant Friars as they were called in England. She persuaded the Beghards of Malines to adopt this rule, and in 1497 after a fire at their monastery she paid for the rebuilding of both the library and the dormitory. It was in the church of this order that she eventually chose to be buried.[41] The foundation of the house of the Observant Friars at Greenwich appears to have been largely due to her influence on Edward IV. Margaret frequently encouraged and supported others in their work for the Church. She laid the foundation stone for a new charterhouse at Louvain, leaving a gold coin for the master mason and paying for the cell of the father procurer.[42] The founder of this charterhouse was one of her husband's chaplains, Walter Waterleet. He was a canon of St Peter's at Louvain and of St Gudule's at Brussels and also a friend of Gillis de Platea, an outstanding scholar and teacher at Louvain University. In 1521 the Louvain charterhouse became a part of the University of Louvain. Margaret was a keen patron of the Carthusians and she also paid for the reconstruction of the Prior's house at the charterhouse of Scheut near Brussels. At one time she must have considered being buried at the Louvain charterhouse for a decorated niche was prepared for her there but it was never used.

Gillis de Platea, known also as Egidius, was appointed as one of Margaret's confessors and through him the dowager became a patron of St Agatha's convent at Ghent.[43] There she paid for the building of the church and provided the convent with a valuable source of income. One of the dowager's wards was Jeanne, the orphaned daughter of the Count of St Pol, and in 1478 the little girl was sent to the convent for her education. Eventually Jeanne entered the order and the convent benefited from her rich inheritance.

Margaret's many gifts to the Church encompassed the financing of major building works and the donation of occasional presents such as sacks of silks which she sent to St Brigitte's at Dendermonde and an altar which she gave to St Waudrin's at Mons.[44] St Ursmer's at Binche was specially favoured. All her income from Le Perriere and Chaussin went to this church to provide daily masses for her husband's soul and to support the necessary clergy including a deacon, a sub-deacon, a canon and an organist.[45] This chantry was still in existence a hundred years later, when King Philip II was asked to provide the money to continue the masses for his great-great-grandfather. Margaret lavished gifts on St Ursmer's including a rich chasuble, a gold brocade cope, two tunics, several song-books (one of which bears her autograph) and the most valuable of all, a golden reliquary. This beautiful piece of goldsmiths' work escaped the religious iconoclasts and survived the French revolution. It is in the form of a calvary with the enamelled figures of Jesus, Mary and John against a green enamelled hillside. Inlaid with pearls and jewels, the work is of such high quality that it has been identified with the workshops of Gerard Loyet, the goldsmith who made the famous reliquary which Charles gave to St Lambert's at Liège. The St Ursmer calvary originally contained two relics, a piece of the Holy Cross and a Thorn. This is not the only instance of Margaret's devotion to the cult of the Holy Cross. As early as 1470 she supported the nuns at Boneffe who were hoping to take over the chapel of the Holy Cross at Malines. She wrote to the Malines magistrates asking them to help the nuns and to obey the

Reliquary of the Calvary presented by Margaret to St Ursmer's Church at Binche

commands of the Dowager Isabelle who was a patron of the convent.[46]

Another church which benefited from Margaret's special attentions was St Rombout's at Malines. In 1480 she attended the exhumation of St Rombout's remains, where the coffin was opened in the presence of many eminent witnesses including eight abbots. The body was in a poor state and the odour was classified as 'redolentia' which can hardly have been pleasant. The occasion was, however, very important in the eyes of the church and all the witnesses signed a document to indicate their participation.[47] The saint's shrine was being moved during the massive rebuilding programme. The chief architect for these works, Anthony Keldermans, had worked for Margaret at Malines when she rebuilt the house of the Bishop of Cambrai, and he may also have been involved with her works at Binche. Her principal gift to the enlarged church was one of the great transept windows. In this, Margaret and Charles were portrayed kneeling at prayer attended by their patron saints.[48] The dowager gave windows to other churches at Malines, Dendermonde, Alost and Bruges but they have since been almost totally destroyed leaving only a few fragments of the ducal arms.

Margaret had a truly medieval interest in relics. Apart from her attendance at the opening of St Rombout's tomb and her many visits to shrines on saints days, she even became involved in arguments over the ownership of relics. She

supported the canons of St Ursmer's at Binche in their struggle with the clergy
of St Lambert's at Liège over the relics which had belonged to the old abbey of
Lobbe.[49] It was a lengthy dispute which seems never to have been finally settled.
Her veneration for relics, popularly regarded as a cure for all the ills of the body
and the soul, was the sort of superstition strongly attacked by many of the
fifteenth century reformers. Certainly Margaret was not in the vanguard of
change. Her attitude towards the church was essentially that of the great
feudatories and she did not hesitate to challenge churchmen who interfered with
her secular interests. She even clashed with her friend the Bishop of Cambrai
over the infringement of sanctuary by her bailiff at Dendermonde, and towards
the end of her life she was engaged in a bitter argument with the Abbot of
Tongerloo when he refused to sell her the castle of Ter Elst which she wanted to
acquire as a country retreat.[50] Nor did she hesitate to use her considerable
authority to settle a dispute at Mons in favour of her Black Sisters and against
the canons of St Waudrin's.

Although she was old fashioned in these respects she still seems to have had a
more intellectual interest in religious matters than her mother Cecily, and she
encouraged education and learning. In her Will she left money for a scholarship
at the University of Louvain.[51] One of the first beneficiaries of this bequest was
Adrian Dedel (or Florizoon) from Utrecht. Her bequest helped him along the
road which led him to become a doctor of theology, the dean of the university
and finally Pope Adrian VI. She also saw that her chaplain, Robert Camell, was
supported during his studies and she paid for the education of a poor child at
Ghent in the school run by the brothers of St Jerome.[52]

Considering her religious devotion, it is appropriate that almost all the
miniatures of her which have survived show her praying or reading.[53] The
most colourful miniatures portraying the duchess are those by Jean Dreux
illustrating Nicolas Finet's *Benois seront les Miséricordieux* (Blessed are the
Merciful). Here Margaret is shown directly involved in acts of charity and at
prayer.[54] There are two illuminated leaves and on one of them there are eight
separate miniatures. Margaret is depicted giving food to a cripple and an
orphan, offering drink and alms to a pilgrim (see cover illustration), clothing
the naked and visiting the prisons and the hospitals. In the final miniature she is
reading at a prie-dieu which is draped with the royal arms of England. In the
second miniature Margaret is again depicted kneeling, accompanied by the
four founding fathers of the early church: Ambrose, Augustine, Jerome and
Gregory, and by her own patron saint, Margaret. In both miniatures the
duchess is richly dressed in a magnificent gown of crimson cloth of gold with a
deep trim of ermine. This is comparatively unusual for in most of the other
miniatures portraying the duchess she is more soberly dressed in a black or
grey gown. This suggests that this manuscript was made very shortly after her
marriage or perhaps even in its honour. The arms of England and of Burgundy
appear in the paintings and in the margins are interlaced 'Cs' and 'Ms'. It
would have been a most appropriate gift to the duchess on her inaugural visit
to Brussels, since the city's beautiful Gothic buildings, St Gudule with its twin
towers, Our Lady of the Sablon, the city gates and the Town Hall feature in
the background of the miniatures. The book would certainly have pleased her

Miniature showing Margaret, Duchess of Burgundy in 1468 accompanied by: St Margaret, St Jerome, with the lion, St Gregory, St Ambrose and St Augustine, standing facing the duchess, before the Brussels church of St Michael and St Gudule and with other Brussels buildings in the background

not only for its beauty but also for its content for in it Finet described the duties of a Christian duchess.

About twenty-five books have been identified as having been 'visibly' in Margaret's possession. This is a relatively small number but it is, nevertheless, one of the largest collections of this period traced to female ownership. For this reason alone Margaret merits the name of bibliophile.[55] Great fifteenth century libraries existed both in Burgundy and in England but these were owned by men. Duke Humphrey of Gloucester had thousands of books and manuscripts and his brother, the Duke of Bedford, also had a large personal library. Of Margaret's contemporaries at the English court, both Lord Hastings and Anthony Woodville had substantial collections of books. Margaret Beaufort and Anthony Woodville were sufficiently interested to make their own translations of French works and to have them printed. Within Margaret's immediate family there is little evidence of a serious interest in books, though her great-uncle, Edward, Duke of York had translated a French hunting manual, her father commissioned at least one translation from the classics and her mother had a library of religious books.[56] However there was apparently no substantial Yorkist library until after Edward IV's visit to his sister's court in 1471. It was thus not until her arrival in Burgundy that Margaret had personal access to a really large and comprehensive collection.

The library of Duke Philip the Good was one of the greatest in Europe, not only in quantity, but also in quality and variety. It has been estimated that he had about nine hundred volumes. [57] They covered all subjects including religion, history, the classics, myths and legends, genealogy, chivalry and military history and there was a place for the best-sellers of the period such as the *Roman de la Rose* and the *Cent Nouvelles Nouvelles*, a French version of *The Decameron*. Margaret's taste was thus influenced not only by her own piety but also by the great literary tradition of the Burgundian court. The variety of languages used within the duchy was an added stimulus to the writers of the period and Duke Charles' library included works and translations in French, Dutch, Latin, Italian and Portuguese. Margaret's books, however, were all in French and included several translations from the Latin which she had commissioned. It is not surprising that she had no books in English since most of the books written for the nobility, even in England, were still in French. Indeed the only evidence of her association with an English text concerns the translation made and printed by William Caxton. Many of Margaret's books were copies of ones which belonged to the ducal libraries,[58] and the majority of those which have survived were acquired during the lifetime of Duke Charles either as gifts or as personal commissions.[59] Thus most of the books attributed to Margaret came to her purely in her capacity as Duchess of Burgundy. But it is clear that all those who knew the duchess regarded books as a suitable gift for this intelligent woman and were sure that such presents would be appreciated.

During the fifteenth century Burgundy was the literary centre of northern Europe and after her marriage Margaret found herself at a court which patronized living authors. Chastellain was the chief chronicler and historian for both Philip and Charles, and after his death there were plenty of rivals for his place among Molinet, Olivier de La Marche, Jehan de Waurin and Jacques Clercq. Eventually it was Molinet who became the real heir to the Burgundian tradition of historical writing, since Commynes, the more lively author, chose to leave Burgundy for the court of France. With Olivier de La Marche in her own household, Margaret was in close contact with this literary and historical tradition. Although there is no evidence that she commissioned any of these authors, she was certainly interested in history and in chronicles. Her coat of arms were added to a copy of Chastellain's *Instructions for a Young Prince*, which was originally written for her husband. This particular copy may have been made for the young Archduke Philip or even for the future Charles V. She also owned a copy of *Les Chroniques de Flandre*, given to her by Mary in 1477 after the death of Duke Charles.[60]

The great majority of Margaret's own books were on religious subjects. Only four were of secular or classical origin and even one of these, the *Consolationes* by Boethius, had been adopted as a religious tract.[61] Of the other three, *Des Faiz du Grant Alexandre* was originally made for Charles. One of the miniatures shows

Vasco de Lucena, the translator, presenting the book to the duke. However it was not completed until after Charles' death. The inscription at the end of the book shows that it was in fact given away by Mary and Margaret and thus was never truly part of Margaret's library. *La Fleur des Hystoires* by Jean Mansel, a history of the world from its beginning to about 1400, was also a copy of a work in the ducal library and this together with *Les Chroniques de Flandre* are the only truly secular books known to have had a permanent place in Margaret's personal library.[62] However, in view of her access to the ducal library it is unwise to deduce too much from the small number of books which actually carry her own arms or signature. She could have read as widely as she chose and those few volumes of her personal collection which have survived may not be entirely representative of her taste and interests. The books bearing her arms and signatures were chiefly those she kept through her later years, the consolation of a dowager, to which she turned regularly for her religious devotions and for contemplation.

Her taste in religious books ranged from standard theological works such as the *Contemplations of St Augustine*, translated for her by Vasco de Lucena, to the more exotic *Les Visions du chevalier Tondal*, the tale of a twelfth century Irish knight who found himself transported into heaven and hell.[63] She also possessed a copy of *L'Apocalypse* of St John, with additional extracts from the *Legenda Aurea*, a *Bible moraliseé*, which had been made for the duke and the duchess, several *Books of Hours* and *Breviaries* and many collections of sermons and moral tracts. The finest of the Books of Hours associated with Margaret is the *Hours of the Virgin* containing thirty-four miniatures some of which were probably made by Lieven van Lathem, one of the artists who had worked on the tableaux and decorations for her marriage. As well as the sermons of well known theologians such as Jean Gerson and Father Laurent du Bois whose *La Somme le Roi* was popular with all the nobility, Margaret had several books by clerics at the Burgundian court. Among these were the works of Nicolas Finet, a canon of Cambrai who was also Margaret's almoner and Charles Soillot who had been secretary to Charles when he was the Count of Charolais. Soillot's book *Le Livre de Felicité et Vie* was in the form of a dialogue on eternal happiness and a leaf of the gradual which was part of this book survived in the possession of the Observant Friars at Greenwich. The gradual may have been a gift from Margaret to the Order on the foundation of the house in England.

Charles had a greater interest in the classics than his wife. The books he took with him to the siege of Nancy included the works of Xenophon, translated by Lucena, and the histories of Hannibal and Alexander. Like Margaret he also had a sophisticated taste in the manuscripts themselves. This is especially apparent in the magnificent *Black Book of Hours* that he gave to Galeazzo Sforza in 1466.[64] The vellum had been dyed black or deep purple and the miniatures were then painted in gold and silver, a costly and elaborate method. Margaret's preference was for a lighter, more delicate and more realistic style. Her books were all of the highest standard and are masterpieces of the craft of book-making which was then enjoying its final flourish in the workshops of the Burgundian Netherlands. More than a third of her books were copied by David Aubert, who after beginning his career in Brussels spent the rest of his working life in Ghent.[65] Scribes like Aubert were responsible for the calligraphy and the production of a book and they worked closely with the translators and the artists who painted the borders and the miniatures. Aubert's manuscripts were known for their excellent script in the style known as 'Bastarda' or 'gothic batarde'. Aubert worked for both Philip the Good and Charles the Bold who honoured him by making personal visits to his workshops, incidents which were recorded in miniatures. After Charles' death he worked for Margaret and his copy of the *Consolationes* by Boethius includes an illustration showing Aubert presenting his work to the duchess who wears a long train trimmed with ermine and is attended by five ladies-in-waiting. In the copy of *Les Visions du chevalier Tondal* which he made for Margaret at Ghent in 1474 he humbly described himself as the duchess' 'très petit indigne escripvain' (very minor and unworthy scribe). It is a measure of his prestige and of the spirit of Burgundy that while Edward IV was considered remarkable for visiting the homes of the merchants of London, the rulers of Burgundy and their successor the Archduke Maximilian were distinguished by their visits to the studios of their book-makers and artists. Maximilian, for example, visited Hugo van der Goes in his retreat at the Rode Klooster.[66]

The margins of Margaret's books were decorated with realistic and beautiful flowers, leaves, fruit and birds. These and the miniatures were made by the finest artists of the age, including Jean Dreux, Simon Marmion, Guillaume Vrelant and the 'Master of Mary of Burgundy'. Jean Dreux, who illustrated Finet's two books, had worked for Philip and Charles and was appointed a *valet de chambre*. Simon Marmion had also worked for Duke Charles, who may have commissioned him to paint the portrait of Margaret which hangs in the Louvre. His most notable works for Margaret were his miniatures for the two books on the visions of Tondel.[67] These were probably Margaret's most magnificent books. The miniatures of the horrors of Hell and the delights of Heaven reveal a highly imaginative and exotic style resembling the later works of Hieronymous Bosch. Did they also reflect Margaret's taste and her own religious conceptions? If so the solemn Louvre portrait may well be a true representation of her character.

Some of the finest miniatures were made for Margaret by the unknown artist called 'The Master of Mary of Burgundy'. This painter seems to have begun his career under Margaret's patronage.[68] It has been suggested that he may have been either a brother of Hugo van der Goes and, like him, at the abbey of the Rode Klooster near Brussels, or Alexander Bening of Bruges. He painted the very delicate miniature of the duchess which appears in the *Traités de Morale*, showing Margaret at prayer before an unusual representation of the Holy Trinity. God the Father bears the crucified Christ in his arms and the Holy Spirit in the form of a dove hovers beside them. A human touch is added by Margaret's small whippet scampering across in the background. One of the most interesting miniatures in the style of this artist has survived in the *Register of the Ghent Guild of St Anne*, now in the Royal Library at Windsor Castle. Margaret and Mary were patrons of this guild from 1473 and they were presented with an illuminated register of the members. One of the miniatures depicts Margaret and her step-daughter kneeling together in the chapel of St Anne. However the finest work of this artist appears in a Book of Hours which he made for the Archduchess Mary.[69] This outstanding miniature is set in an architectural frame which seems to depict the house of Lord Louis of Gruuthuyse, where there was a window looking directly into the chancel of the church of Our Lady at Bruges. Mary is seated at this window where she is reading with her dog on her lap, and below her in the body of the church there is a group of ladies including two very finely dressed figures, one of whom may be Margaret. At the right-hand side there is the figure of a man who might be Lord Louis. Gruuthuyse was closely associated with both Margaret and her step-daughter and was particularly valuable to them both in the crisis of 1477–8. He also had a great library and may well have influenced Margaret's taste in books, though she favoured the Brussels and Ghent studios rather than the more elaborate Bruges bookmakers who were patronised by Lord Louis and later by Edward IV.

Margaret frequently gave books as presents to friends, churches and convents though very few of these gifts have survived in their entirety. The *Vie de St Colette*, the *Des Faiz du Grant Alexandre* and *La dyalogue de la Duchesse de Bourgogne* by Finet which she gave to her old friend Jeanne de Hallewijn are exceptions.[70] Through her piety and her gifts to churches and convents, the dowager was seeking the salvation of her immortal soul. She achieved a more worldly immortality with the bold signature which she inscribed in many of her books.[71] Her energetic and untidy autograph indicates a far from scholarly hand but it also suggests a bold and forceful personality, very far removed from the modest and retiring ideal of Christian womanhood recommended in the *devotio moderna*.

The literary heritage of Burgundy so cherished by Margaret was also appreciated by the Habsburgs, Maximilian and Philip the Fair. Maximilian showed a particular zeal for the written word with his autobiographical *Weisskünig* and the virtual encyclopaedia which he planned as his memorial.[72] At least some of his literary interests must have been stimulated by Margaret. She had a more direct influence on Philip the Fair and on Margaret of Austria, who inherited both the ducal library and most of the dowager's own books. Her influence was also felt by her family and friends in England. It was not until after his stay in the Low Countries that Edward IV began to commission and collect a series of illuminated manuscripts.[73] Gruuthuyse was also a major influence on Edward's taste but it was his experience of the ducal collections which acted as a spur. The first Yorkist king was eager to display the opulence and magnificence of his court and after his return from Burgundy he seems to have been resolved to outshine his brother-in-law in every respect. Lord Hastings wrote to ask Olivier de La Marche for a copy of the household ordinances of Charles the Bold, and the household of Edward's heir was established with these in mind.[74] Determined to create a royal library to equal its Burgundian model the king began to buy in books and manuscripts. Like his sister, Edward chose to have most of his books in French. Since he left the bulk of his religious books to his wife and these were dispersed after her death, the full extent of Margaret's influence is hard to assess. One of the few religious volumes which has survived from Edward's library is a French translation of St Augustine's *Civitas Dei*.[75]

Edward seems to have preferred histories and chronicles; he owned copies of

La Fleur des Hystoires and the *Les Chroniques de Flandre*.[76] Among the classical works in the Tudor royal collection was the *Des Faiz du Grant Alexandre*, a translation from Quintus Curtius, begun for Charles and completed for Margaret, by Vasco da Lucena who had come to Burgundy in the service of the Duchess Isabelle.[77] After Isabelle's death he joined Margaret's staff as a chamberlain and writer. This book may have been one of the 'translations worthy of remembrance' which Margaret commissioned from him. The Tudor arms at the end of the book conceal the identity of the original English recipient but on the same page are the dedications from Mary and Margaret: 'forget not har that ys on of your treu frendes Margarete of Yorke' and '(p)renez moyajames pour vostre bonne amie Marie de Bourgogne.' Given the choice of book and the style of these inscriptions it would be pleasant to suppose that the book was sent to Edward in 1477, when both Margaret and her step-daughter were appealing for help. The *Deeds of Alexander* may even have been despatched in the hope of encouraging the reluctant Edward into some military prowess on their behalf.[78]

Lord Hastings was also very responsive to the influences of the Burgundian court.[79] He bought books from the studio of Margaret's favourite miniaturist, the 'Master of Mary of Burgundy', and his brother-in-law Sir John Donne commissioned the tryptich by Memlinc which now hangs in the National Gallery. Hastings and Lord Rivers were also to be closely involved with another of Margaret's ventures. Although in many ways the dowager seems to have been rather old-fashioned, as far as William Caxton was concerned she was at the forefront of revolutionary change. Her patronage resulted in the printing at Bruges of the first book in English and ultimately in the introduction of printing into England.[80]

Caxton entered Margaret's service soon after her marriage in 1468.[81] She probably met him for the first time on her wedding day. He had been the governor of the Merchant Adventurers at Bruges since 1462 and in this capacity he had the honour of leading the English delegation. He was at court in 1470 when John Russel arrived to offer the Order of the Garter to Duke Charles (he would later publish Russel's oration). By March 1471 he had left his appointment with the Merchant Adventurers and entered the duchess' service, receiving a yearly fee and other benefits from her hands. He probably served Margaret as a commercial and financial adviser. She received her first trading licences from Edward in 1472 and she took full advantage of her privileges to profit from her trade with England. There was nothing unusual in this; Isabelle had also traded with the English Merchant Adventurers. Margaret used various agents to manage her affairs in England and she would have found the advice of an experienced merchant like Caxton very useful indeed.

However Caxton had ambitions to become more than a mere commercial adviser and he made a shrewd move to obtain Margaret's patronage when he told her about his translation of Lefevre's *Recueil des Histoires de Troie* which he had begun in 1469. He had chosen well. As he says, 'this booke was newe and late maad and drawen in to frenshe. . . . /And neuer had seen hit in oure englisshe tonge.'[82] There was a copy of the work in the ducal library. It was a story Margaret knew well and which was closely associated with her already. The myths of Troy had been used to symbolise her own marriage, from her sailing in the *New Ellen* to the tapestries which decorated the banqueting hall. Apart from his felicitous choice, Caxton presented his case very diplomatically to the duchess. He appealed to her in terms which were sure to win her interest and sympathy. He put this most succinctly in the prologue he wrote for the edition of 1476:

> whan I remembyrd myself of my symplenes and vnperfightnes that I had in bothe langages/ that is to wete in frenshe and in englisshe for in france I was neuer/ and was born and lerned myn englisshe in kente in the weeld where I doubte not is spoken as brode and rude englisshe as is in ony place of englond.[83]

After four years at the Burgundian court Margaret could pride herself on her French and her English was also that of the court and certainly not of the Kentish Weald. Caxton's appeal for help with the translation was surely irresistible to her energetic character. In spite of his linguistic difficulties, Caxton had already completed five or six quires when he took his work to the duchess but he explained that he had become discouraged in his task and had abandoned it. As soon as she heard about the translation Margaret ordered him to bring it for her to read. And:

> whan she had seen hem anone she fonde a defaute in myn englissh whiche sche comanded me to amende and more ouer commanded me straytli to contynue and make an ende of the resydue than not translated. whos dredefull commandement y durste in no wyse disobey because y am a seruant vnto her sayde grace and resseiue of her yerly ffee and other many goode and great benefetes and also hope many moo to resseyue of hir hyenes but forthwyth wente and labouryde in the sayde translacion aftyr my symple and pour connyng also nigh as y can folouyng myn auctor mekeli beseching the bounteuous hynenes of my said lady that of her benyuolence liste to accepte and take in gree this symple and rude werke here folowyng. and yf ther be ony thyng wreton or sayd to her playsir. I shall thynke my labour well employed and where ther is defawte. yt she arette hyt to ye symplenes of my connyng whiche is ful small in this behalue and requyre and praye alle them that shall rede this sayd werke to correcte hyt and to hold me excusid of the rude and symple translacion.[84]

Margaret's interest in Caxton did not end with her corrections to his text and her command that he should finish his translation. She also gave him permission to travel and by the late summer of 1471 he was in Cologne. He stayed there for about two years, returning to Bruges in 1473. He may have been involved with the lengthy negotiations which led up to the signing of the treaty of Utrecht a year later. This treaty settled some of the problems bedevilling trade and commerce between the Hanseatic League and its chief trading partners, Burgundy and England. He took advantage of his stay in Cologne to become acquainted with the technology of the new movable-type printing-presses, which had been in use there since 1465 and were already slowly spreading into France and the Low Countries. (The first printing-press in the Low Countries was set up by Thierry Martens at Alost in 1472 but he had learned his craft in Venice not in Germany.) On his return to the Low Countries, Caxton began to establish

William Caxton presenting his book to Margaret in her chamber. Her device 'Bien en aviengne', surmounted by the initials 'C' and 'M', is inscribed on the canopy, edition of 1475

himself in the printing business. His first partnership involved Jan Veldener of Louvain which, being a university city, was at the forefront of these developments. By 1475, however, Caxton was back at Bruges and he completed his translation of the third book of the Recuyell: 'I haue delibered in my self for the contemplacion of my sayd redoubtid lady to take this laboure in hand as ye suffrance and helpe of almyghty god.'[85]

Finding that there was a large demand for an English version of the Trojan legends he decided to make a printed edition and he turned to Collard Mansion who had recently established a press at Bruges. In his youth Collard had been employed in the ducal library and he was, by this date, under the patronage of Louis of Gruuthuyse, who was so friendly with his bookmaker that he even stood as godfather to one of Collard's children.[86]

Margaret, Gruuthuyse, Caxton and Collard Mansion were thus jointly responsible for the production of the first book ever to be printed in English, which Caxton entitled, *The Recuyell of the Historyes of Troye*. It was followed by a printed edition in French, so popular were these old stories. Later in the same year, Caxton produced his second English book, *The Playe and Game of Chess* dedicated to Margaret's brother the Duke of Clarence. This was printed in preparation for Caxton's move to London and it is more than likely that Margaret had encouraged the printer to seek her brother's patronage. All Caxton's early editions were translations of books which were very familiar to Margaret, including *Les Faiz de Jason* and *Meditacions sur les sept psaulms penitentiaux*.

In 1476 Caxton left Bruges for London. He was unlucky in his choice of patrons for Clarence's arrest early in 1477 removed him from the scene and Margaret was soon much too preoccupied with the succession crisis in Burgundy to be of any further assistance. However Caxton found a new patron in Lord Rivers, who translated the *Dictes des Philiosophes* himself and then had it printed.[87] Through the patronage of Rivers, who was the governor of Edward's eldest son, Caxton was enabled to present his *History of Jason* to the young prince. In 1479 he received a grant of £20 from the king, although Edward does not appear to have shared his sister's enthusiasm for printed books. By the time Margaret visited England in 1480, her old protégé was well established.[88] Caxton had printed three translations for Lord Rivers and made several other editions such as *The Canterbury Tales*. He had certainly not forgotten his 'right high and noble' patroness the Duchess of Burgundy, and in the prologue to the *History of Jason* he reminded his readers of his debt to her. The frontispiece of the edition of *The Recuyell of the Histories of Troy*, now in the Huntington Library in California, which belonged to Elizabeth Woodville, also commemorates his relationship with the duchess. The illustration shows Margaret in her chamber attended by five ladies, two gentlemen and two pages. Above the chair of state at the back of the room are carved the initials 'C' and 'M', and beside her on the floor a little monkey mimics her gestures of acceptance as she receives the book from Caxton. The printer continued to look hopefully towards the House of York for his patrons and he later dedicated a volume on the orders of chivalry to King Richard III. After the accession of Henry VII he succeeded in attracting the patronage of Lady Margaret Beaufort.

There is extensive evidence of Margaret's patronage in literary and religious matters. Unfortunately fewer records have survived recording her patronage of the other arts. The houses she had built at Mons, Binche and Malines have been either destroyed or rebuilt and we know only that she employed the best architects available including some of the famous family of Keldermans. The survival of three possible portraits in addition to the possible representations of her in the great Memlinc altar-piece at St Jan's Hospital and in the *Deposition* at the J. Paul Getty museum might indicate an active interest in painting. It would be difficult to imagine that such a discriminating bibliophile would not have found an equal delight in the marvels of Burgundian art. The various artifacts associated with her such as the Aachen coronet and the St Ursmer reliquary illustrate her good taste in the fine arts. Her interest in tapestries, one of the greatest manufactures of Flanders and Brabant, is shown by the several purchases she made, both at the sale of the Hugonet property in 1478 and three years earlier when she gave tapestries to her brother Edward. As an active patron of the Church and the arts, Margaret was of course fulfilling her responsibilities as the Duchess and Dowager of Burgundy. She was very sensible of her high position and she maintained her estate with rectitude and grandeur. In her library at least she showed a deeper interest and in it she also revealed more of her personality.

During her last years she had more time for her private interests. After the deaths of Don Juan in October 1497 and of the eldest Spanish Princess Isabella in 1500, Philip the Fair became, through his wife Joanna, heir to the Spanish throne. It was therefore necessary for the archduke and his wife to travel to Spain, where their inheritance would be acknowledged by the Cortes of Castile and Aragon.[89] Their departure was long delayed by both domestic and diplomatic events. They had originally planned to leave after the presentation of Charles to the Order of the Golden Fleece in 1501, but Joanna became pregnant again and they postponed their journey until after the birth of their third child in July of that year. Foreign affairs also caused delays. Philip needed to safeguard his duchy during his absence, and he therefore renewed his alliances and treaties with both England and France. The Intercursus Magnus had not settled all the trading problems which arose between England and the Low Countries, and negotiations to settle disputes over import duties and the location of the English staple continued throughout the late 1490s. In the spring of 1500, Henry and his court crossed the Channel to escape a particularly severe outbreak of the plague in London.[90] The archduke went down to Calais to meet the English king and relations between England and Burgundy improved. A year later a marriage treaty was negotiated between the ducal heir Charles and Princess Claude of France.[91] Having secured his frontiers and renewed his alliances, Philip finally prepared for his departure, and after seeing his sister, Margaret of Austria, off on her journey to Savoy in October, he and Joanna left for Spain a month later.

The three infants, Eleanor, Charles and Isabella were left at Malines under the eye of the dowager. A household of ninety-three people had been appointed to look after the children during their parents' absence, and at the head of the household was one of Margaret's men, Henri of Witthem, the Lord of Beersel.[92]

However, Margaret spent much of the following two years out of Malines.[93] After the departure of the ducal party for France, she retired to Binche, returning to Malines only in time for the Christmas festivities. She was back at Binche in the summer of 1502. During August she made a progress to Oudenaarde and Dendermonde and she returned again to Binche for the September and December of that year. Early in 1503, Maximilian came to the Low Countries, visiting his grandchildren at Malines and trying in vain to persuade the estates to support his expedition against Guelders.[94] Margaret went back to Malines to greet Maximilian and to honour the various celebrations which had been organised for the emperor's entertainment. This was her last meeting with her step-son-in-law, and it was also the last time that she would make the journey from Binche to Malines. After this, apart from a brief visit to the abbey-castle of Ter Elst at Duffel in July, the dowager passed her last months at Malines. She was by now perhaps too ill to travel far.

The year 1503 was very harsh: the winter had been very cold and when the summer came it was exceptionally hot. The dowager took the ducal children with her when she went to Ter Elst so that they too could enjoy the countryside, away from the heat and dust of the town. Ter Elst was situated midway between Malines and Lier and this position made it a convenient retreat for her during her last years.[95] It had been a twelfth century castle and now belonged to the abbey of Tongerloo. Although the archduke and the corporation of Malines had intervened on the dowager's behalf, the prior resolutely refused to allow her to acquire the castle for herself. However, though he would not permit the alienation of the abbey property, he was very willing to accept the dowager and her court as his guests. Margaret spent the summer there and was back in Malines by the end of September. Philip finally returned to the Low Countries in November 1503 after an absence of exactly two years. He had set off on his return journey in December 1502, leaving the archduchess behind in Spain to recover from the birth of her second son Ferdinand. His return had been delayed by a series of visits to France, Savoy and Austria and by an outbreak of an illness. He had been expected for some time and all Malines celebrated his arrival with a series of banquets, jousts and festivities.

It was in the midst of all these festivities that Margaret suddenly died. She had been ill for some time. Her visit to Ter Elst in July had been perhaps in a vain hope that the peace and the country air would revive her flagging spirits. On her return to Malines her condition deteriorated and on 21 October she signed her Will.[96] She lived on for another month, perhaps clinging to life until she was certain that Philip was safely back in the duchy. Only then could she relax that vigilance she had exerted unstintingly over the concerns of the ducal family for thirty-five years. Her death on 23 November cut short all the welcoming celebrations. Both the city and the court were plunged into deep mourning. The bells of St Rombout's tolled for ten days at a cost of 30 sous and Philip had a commemorative medal struck in her honour.[97] One side displayed Margaret's arms surrounded by the words:

DILIGETE JUSTICIA(M) QUI JUDICAT(IS) TERR(AM)

The other side depicted the figure of death accompanied by two serpents trampling down the pretty marguerites, which had been used as her emblem on her portraits and on the margins of her books, and was inscribed:

MEMORARE NOVISSIMA TUA ANO DNI 1503

As the news of her death travelled across the Low Countries her other dower towns grieved as well. The Hôtel de la Salle at Binche was draped in black and was to spend 'long days in mourning'.[98]

The dowager was buried in the church of the monastery of the Recollects at Malines which she had so generously supported. Her tomb and memorial have been destroyed but a description of her alabaster memorial was recorded by a scholar in the middle of the sixteenth century.[99] He refers to two statues of the dowager, in the first she was kneeling beside her patron saint St Margaret, and in the second she was laid out in her shroud with a crown at her head and three friars of the Recollects watching over her. On the inscription itself, her arms, the arms of England and Burgundy surmounted by a crown, were supported by an angel. In death, as in life, Margaret was rigorously upholding her own and her family's honour. The epitaph, in Latin, announced that:

> Beneath the threshold of the doors of the choir the most illustrious princess, the Lady Margaret of England, Duchess of Burgundy, with pious humility, ordered her body to be buried. Sister of their serene highnesses Edward and Richard, Kings of England, wife of the late illustrious Charles, Duke of Burgundy and of Brabant, Count of Flanders and Artois etc and Lord of Malines etc a marvellous and devoted Patroness of Justice, of Religion and of Reform in her dower town of Malines, the twenty-third day of November in the year of our Lord 1503. Pray for her.

All traces of this memorial and of her tomb vanished in the sixteenth century about the time that this record was made. There were plenty of occasions in that century when the churches of Malines were pillaged and ransacked. In 1566 the local iconoclasts destroyed pictures, statues and stained glass, in 1572 the Spanish soldiery looted the whole city and in 1590 English mercenaries fighting under Colonel Norris and Oliver van der Tympel, the Governor of Brussels, mutinied and sacked the city and its churches. It was fortunate for Margaret that she did not have to live through the conflicts of the Reformation. Her niece and namesake Margaret, Countess of Salisbury, the daughter of Clarence, was brutally murdered by Henry VIII's axemen at the age of sixty-nine and the shrine of St Thomas à Becket, to which Margaret had made her pilgrimages, was destroyed and plundered by the king's collectors. The religious world to which Margaret devoted so much of her attention was swept away in her native land. Its ultimate survival in Flanders and Brabant owed much to the geography of the Habsburg possessions but also, in no small way, to the patient reform which had made the church, convents and monasteries a well respected and useful part of the community there. Margaret's contribution to this reform had been considerable.

Her assiduous and devoted work for the church was acknowledged by many of the clergy. The dowager's obituaries recorded the high standards which she had enforced on the religious establishment of the Low Countries. One of these obituaries survived at the charterhouse of Louvain on the memorial of Jean Bryart, a scholar and one of the executors of Margaret's Will.[100] The writer, Martin Dorpius, picked out the dowager's clerical appointments as of the utmost importance for the church. She had, he asserted, always promoted worthy and learned men regardless of their birth, she had never acceded to the nobility who demanded sinecures for their families, and she had never allowed offices to be sold to the highest bidder. This was a scholar speaking, the sort of man whom Margaret had appointed to serve her as chaplains and confessors. The chronicler Molinet also recognised that her death was of the greatest significance to the religious reformers to whom she had given so generously. But he added a more personal touch in his conclusion that she would be missed as 'a mother to orphans, a nurse to the poor and a refuge and solace for all sad grieving hearts.'[101]

Of her Will only a fragment has survived, but even from this remnant it is evident that the failure of her brother to pay her full dowry still weighed heavily on her mind.[102] She left to Philip the 115,000 gold crowns or whatever other sum was still owing 'according to the treaties, letters and obligations that we have.' With her typical determination not to give up on a case, she had retained all the documents necessary to justify her claims if the opportunity arrived. Although the Duchy of Burgundy had always treated Margaret with the utmost generosity, the same could not be said of the kingdom of England. Her trading licences were hardly an adequate compensation for the loss of the dowry.

The Will also records some of her bequests: she left 920 livres for the hospital at Louvain and 400 livres for the Grande Chartreuse in Savoy, a gesture towards her well-loved Margaret of Austria, the Duchess of Savoy. Her favourite Black Sisters of Binche were to receive a further £60, and a sum of £30 was set aside to establish a scholarship to support a theological student at Louvain. It was this last bequest which was to benefit the future Pope Adrian VI. Money was also left to the chantry at Binche for prayers for the souls of her husband Charles, her step-daughter Mary and for herself. No evidence has survived of her bequests to her family and officials and no mention of her many personal possessions such as her books and her paintings. The existence of a substantial number of these in the libraries and archives of Brussels and Vienna would suggest that the bulk of her goods were left to Philip the Fair and Margaret of Austria.

Her chief legacy to the Low Countries was, however, much more lasting and much more elusive. In all the epitaphs and obituaries of the dowager there was small reference to her political role either as an administrator during her husband's lifetime or as an adviser to Mary, Maximilian and Philip. There is, of course, little unusual about the omission. Women were expected to administer their estates in the absence of their husbands, as Christine de Pisan had pointed out half a century earlier, but they were regarded merely as executives and not as policy-makers. As a childless woman, widowed for most of her life, whose value as a symbol of the Anglo-Burgundian alliance was extinguished by the events of 1485, she might have been expected to vanish into a convent, the normal destiny for female relicts. Margaret was a relict in every sense of the word; a relict of her husband, of the Valois Duchy, of the House of York, even of her century. Within half a century of her death her milieu had passed away transformed by the impact of the Reformation and the New World. She seemed to have become as irrelevant as the religious relics and statues which were destroyed and dispersed with her own monument. Yet to the very end of her life, Margaret remained at the centre of the Burgundian court. In spite of catastrophic disasters she continued to live her life, adapting to changes of rulers and policies with a realism which is sometimes called 'modern' but which is in fact a characteristic of all survivors. Her contribution to the history of Europe was considerable. During her husband's lifetime she acted as a unifying and mollifying influence in the northern provinces. Her support of Mary and of the Habsburg marriage was critically important in 1477. The Duchy of Burgundy survived the demise of the Valois dukes due largely to her determination, and Louis XI's public attacks upon her reflected her powerful influence on the policies of Burgundy. As a loyal supporter of Maximilian she enabled him to establish the Habsburg presence in the Low Countries, and as the guide and mentor of the young Philip she saw peace and prosperity return to the duchy. France would have to wait until the late eighteenth century before it was able to annex the Low Countries and the individuality of the modern kingdom of Belgium owes much to its preservation from French autocracy and centralisation.

Margaret's impact on English history was less positive. Her support of the pretenders served only to aggravate the Tudor paranoia against the House of York which led ultimately to the destruction of almost her entire family. Yet in the characters of her great-great-nieces, Mary and Elizabeth Tudor, there are many of the traits which mark the personality of Margaret herself, including a remarkable tenacity and a determination to survive. Margaret would have had great sympathy with Mary's religious devotion but she would surely have admired Elizabeth's political agility more.

'votre loyale fille Margarete d'Angleterre pryez pour elle & pour son salute', autograph dedication on the final leaf of the 'Vie de Sainte Collette'

Epilogue

'History is seldom quite just to historical women' wrote Charles Kirk in his biography of Charles the Bold, yet he too paid scant attention to his hero's third wife.[1] Margaret has been particularly unfortunate in her treatment by history. She was neither a queen nor a saint and her story was not grand enough to merit a nineteenth century biography while the twentieth century has had little time for the biographies of great ladies. Nor does her life fit tidily into the packages preferred by historians. In English history she appears merely as a pawn in Edward IV's foreign policy and as a thorn in the flesh of Henry VII. She has tended to disappear into the chasms which have been excavated between the fifteenth century and the early Tudors and between English and European history. Belgian historians have been more generous but even here she was unfortunate to live in the neglected transitional period between the Burgundian age and the Habsburg age. She has been confused with another English Princess Margaret who married Duke John II of Brabant in the late thirteenth century.[2] However there has been a continued interest in the English dowager and she has been the subject of one full scale biography, several monographs and one Europalia exhibition.

One aspect of this interest has been the various efforts which have been made to find her tomb. In 1937 and again in 1955, during work on the old church of the Recollects, now an exhibition centre, it was thought that some of her remains had been discovered.[3] A coffin containing some female bones was found beneath the threshold of the choir in the exact location recorded by the sixteenth century scholar. However a thorough re-examination of the bones in 1970 established that they were not of the correct period.

Once more Margaret had eluded her investigators. To a very large extent Margaret will continue to elude history. She may assert her existence in her bold autograph and in the few words which she added to her official letters. A few of her gifts and books have survived. But the various possible portraits provide little more than conventional images of the great lady of the fifteenth century. There is the fashionable melancholia, the pious gloom which led the far from gloomy Olivier de La Marche to adopt as his device '*tant a suffert La Marche*' ('so much has La Marche borne').[4] There are also the symbols: the marguerites, the coats of arms, the devices, the initials and the white roses which were all integral to her political existence. There are, however, few signs of her vigour and intelligence which were not considered relevant by the artists of her time but were very significant indeed for the Duchy of Burgundy and for the crown of England.

LIST OF ABBREVIATIONS

ADN	Archives départementales du Nord, Lille, France
Adrien de But	'Chronique des religieux des Dunes' in *Chroniques relatives à l'histoire de la Belgique* etc (ed.) Kervyn de Lettenhove, Brussels (1870)
AGR	Archives Générales du Royaume, Brussels, Belgium
Arrivall	*Historie of the Arrivall of Edward IV in England* (ed.) J. Bruce (1838)
ASEB	*Annales de la société d'émulation de Bruges*
Bacon	Francis Bacon, *History of the reign of King Henry VII* (1621), (ed.) J. Rawson Lumby (1881)
BARB	*Bulletin de l'Académie Royale de Belgique*
BCRH	*Bulletin de la Commission Royale d'histoire, Belgique*
BIHR	*Bulletin of the Institute of Historical Research*
BJRL	*Bulletin of the John Rylands Library*
BN	*Bibliographie Nationale de Belgique*
CCR	*Calendar of Close Rolls*
Chastellain	G. Chastellain, *Oeuvres* (ed.) Kervyn de Lettenhove, 8 vols. (Brussels 1863–6)
Chronicles of London	*Chronicles of London* (ed.) C. L. Kingsford (1905)
Chronicles of the White Rose	*The Chronicles of the White Rose of York* (ed.) J. Bohn (1845)
Chronique Scandaleuse	J. de Roye, *Journal connu sous le nom de Chronique Scandaleuse, 1460–1483* (ed.) B. de Mandrot, 2 vols. (Paris 1894–96)
Commines/Godefroy	Phillippe de Commines, *Mémoires* (ed.) D. Godefroy and Lenglet du Fresnoy, 4 vols. (Paris 1747)
Commynes/Calmette	Phillippe de Commynes, *Mémoires* (ed.) J. Calmette and G. Durville, 3 vols. (Paris 1924–5)
Commynes/Mandrot	Philippe de Commynes, *Mémoires* (ed.) B. de Mandrot, 2 vols. (Paris 1901)
CPR	*Calendar of Patent Rolls*
Croyland	*Ingulph's Chronicle of the Abbey of Croyland* (ed.) H. T. Riley (1854)
CSPM	*Calendar of State Papers and manuscripts existing in the Archives and Collections of Milan, I, 1385–1618* (ed.) A. B. Hinds (1912)
CSPV	*Calendar of State Papers and Manuscripts relating to English Affairs, existing in the Archives and Collections of Venice etc., I, 1202–1509* (ed.) R. Brown (1864)
CSPS	*Calendar of State Papers relating to negotiations between Spain and England, 1485–1509* (ed.) G. A. Bergenroth (1862)
English Chronicle	*An English Chronicle of the Reigns of Richard II, Henry IV, Henry V and Henry VI* (ed.) J. S. Davies (1856)
EHR	*English Historical Review*
Excerpta Historica	*Excerpta Historica* (ed.) S. Bentley (1831)
Foedera	*Foedera, conventiones* etc. (ed.) T. Rymer, 20 vols. (1704–35)
Great Chronicle	*The Great Chronicle of London* (ed.) A. H. Thomas and I. D. Thornley (1838)
Hall	Edward Hall, *Chronicle* etc. (ed.) H. Ellis (1809)
Haynin	Jean de Haynin, *Mémoires, 1465* (ed.) D. D. Brouwers (Liège 1905–6)
Historical Collections	*The Historical Collections of a London citizen in the fifteenth century* (ed.) J. Gairdner (1876)
La Marche	Olivier de La Marche, *Mémoires* (ed.) H. Beaune and J. d'Arbaumont, 4 vols. Paris (1883–8)
MA	Mechelen (Malines) Archives, Belgium
Marguerite d'York	Catalogue of *Marguerite d'York et son temps*, Exhibition organised by the Banque de Bruxelles, 1967
Molinet	Molinet, J., *Chroniques* (ed.) G. Doutrepont and O. Jodogne, 3 vols. (Brussels 1935–7)

New Chronicles	*The New Chronicles of England and France* (ed.) H. Ellis (1811)
Paston/Davis	*The Paston Letters* (ed.) N. Davis, 2 vols. (1971)
Paston/Gairdner	*The Paston Letters* (ed.) J. Gairdner, 3 vols. (1910)
Polydore Vergil	*The Anglica Historica* (ed.) and trans. Denis Hay (1950)
PRO	Public Record Office, London
Rozmital	*The Travels of Leo of Rozmital* (ed.) Malcolm Letts (1957)
RP	*Rotuli Parliamentum* (ed.) P. Strachey, 6 vols. (London 1767–83)
Six Town Chronicles	*Six Town Chronicles* (ed.) R. Flenley (1911)
Waurin	Jehan de Waurin, *Recueil des Chroniques* (ed.) Sir W. Hardy, 5 vols. (1864–91)
Whethamstede	*Registrum Abbatiae Johannis Whethamstede* (ed.) H. T. Riley (1872)
Wielant	Wielant, P., *Recueil des Antiquités de Flandre* (ed.) J. J. de Smete, *Recueil des chroniques de Flandre* iv, 1–442 (Brussels 1865)

SELECTED BIBLIOGRAPHY

Anglo, S., *The Great Tournament Roll of Westminster*, 1968.
———, *Anglo-Burgundian Feats of Arms at Smithfield, June 1467*, Guildhall miscellany, 1965, ii.
Archbold, W. A. J., 'Sir William Stanley and Perkin Warbeck', *EHR*, 1899, xiv.
Armstrong, C. A. J., *England, France and Burgundy in the Fifteenth Century*, 1983.
Barante, A. de, *Histoire des ducs de Bourgogne de la Maison de Valois*, (ed.) L. P. Gachard, 2 vols., 1838, Brussels.
Bartier, J., *Charles le Téméraire*, 1944, Brussels.
Basin, T., *Histoire de Louis XI*, (ed.) C. Samaran, 3 vols., 1963–72, Paris.
Benecke, Gerhard, *Maximilian I, 1459–1519, an analytical biography*, 1982.
Bennett, M., *Lambert Simnel and the Battle of Stoke*, Alan Sutton, 1987.
Blades, W., *The Life and Typography of William Caxton*, 1861.
Boeren, P. C., *Twee Maaslandse Dichters in Dienst van Karel de Stout*, 1968, Den Haag.
Burne, A. H., *Battlefields of England*, 1950.
Calmette, J., *The Golden Age of Burgundy*, 1962.
———, Dom Pedro, roi des Catalans et la cour de Bourgogne, *Annales de Bourgogne*, 1946, xviii.
———, 'Le mariage de Charles le Téméraire avec Marguerite d'York, *Annales de Bourgogne*, 1929, i.
Calmette, J. and Perinelle, G., *Louis XI et l'Angleterre*, 1930, Paris.
Campbell, W., (ed.), *Materials for a History of the reign of Henry VII*, 2 vols., 1873, 1877.
Cartellieri, O., *The Court of Burgundy*, 1929.
Chmel, J., *Monumenta Habsburgica*, 2 vols., 1855, Vienna.
Chrimes, S. B., *Lancastrians Yorkists and Henry VII*, 1964.
———, 'Henry VII' 1972.
Cokayne, G. E., *The Complete Peerage of England, Scotland, Ireland and the United Kingdom*, (ed.) Vicary Gibbs, H. A. Doubleday and others, 13 vols., 1910–59.
Conway, A., *Henry VII's relations with Scotland and Ireland, 1485–1498*, 1932.
Corstanje, C. van, O.F.M. and Derolez, A., *Saint Coleta her life, holiness and historical significance*, 1982, Tielt and Leiden, in five languages.
Crotch, W. J. B., *The Prologues and Epilogues of William Caxton*, 1928.
Delaisse, L. M. J., 'La Miniature Flamande, Le Mécénat de Philippe le Bon', Exhibition Catalogue, 1959, Brussels.

Dogaer, G., 'Margaretha van York bibliofiele', Studia Mechliniensia en Handelingen van de Koninklijke Kring voor Oudheidkunde, Letteren en Kunst van Mechelen, 1975, lxxix.

Doren, P. J. van and Hermans, V., *Inventaire des Archives de la ville de Malines*, vol. 2, 1862, Malines.

Dumont, G-H., *Marie de Bourgogne*, 1982.

Ellis, H., (ed.), *Original Letters Illustrative of English History*, 11 vols., 1824–1846.

Gachard, L. P., (ed.), Particularités et documents Inédits sur Commines, Charles le Téméraire et Charles Quint, 'L'instrument du 3 Novembre, 1471', *Trésor National*, ii, 1842, Brussels.

—— (ed.), *Collection de documents inédits concernant l'histoire de la Belgique*, 3 vols., 1833–5, Brussels.

—— *Rapport sur les archives à Lille*, 1841, Brussels.

—— and others (ed.), *Inventaire des archives des chambres des comptes*, 6 vols., 1837–1931, Brussels.

Gairdner, J., (ed.), *Letters and Papers illustrative of the reigns of Richard III and Henry VII*, 2 vols., 1861–3.

—— (ed.), *Memorials of King Henry VII*, 1858.

——, *Life of Richard III and the Story of Perkin Warbeck*, 1898.

Galesloot, L., 'Marguerite d'York, duchesse douairière de Bourgogne, 1468–1503', *Annales de la société d'Emulation pour l'étude de l'histoire et des antiquités de la Flandre*, 4th series, 3rd vol., 1879, Bruges.

Genard, P., 'Marguerite d'York, Duchesse de Bourgogne et La Rose Blanche (1495)', *BCRH*, 4th ser., ii, 1875, Brussels.

Gorman, V. J., 'The Public Career of Richard Duke of York', Ph.D. thesis, 1981, Catholic University of America.

Griffiths, R. A., *The reign of King Henry VI*, 1981.

Halliwell-Phillipps, J. O., (ed.), *Letters of the Kings of England*, 2 vols., 1846–8.

Hanham, Alison, (ed.), *The Cely Papers, 1472–1488*, 1975.

Hare, C., *Maximilian the Dreamer*, 1913.

Harthan, John, *Books of Hours*, 1977.

Hicks, M. A., *False, Fleeting, Perjur'd Clarence*, Alan Sutton, 1980.

Hommel, L., *Marguerite d'York ou La Duchesse Junon*, 1959, Paris.

Horrox, R. and Hammond, P. W., (ed.), *Harleian Ms. 433*, 4 vols., Alan Sutton, 1979–83.

Hughes, Muriel J., 'Margaret of York, Duchess of Burgundy, Diplomat, Patroness, Bibliophile and Benefactress', *The Private Library*, 3rd series, vol. 7, 1 & 2, Spring and Summer 1984.

Huizinga, J., *The Waning of the Middle Ages*, 1924.

Hume, David, *The History of England in Eight Volumes*, 1802.

Hunter, G. L., *The Practical Book of Tapestries*, 1925.

Kampeneer, A., 'Une résidence de Charles V', *Mélanges d'Histoire offerts à Charles Moeller*, 1914, Louvain & Paris.

Kervyn de Lettenhove, 'Relation du mariage du duc Charles de Bourgogne et de Marguerite d'York, *BCRH*, 1867, III, x.

Kingsford, C. L., *English Historical Literature in the Fifteenth Century*, 1913.

Kipling, Gordon, *The Triumph of Honour*, 1977, Leiden.

Kirk, J. Foster, *History of Charles the Bold*, 3 vols., 1863–8.

Laborde, L. de, *Les ducs de Bourgogne*, 3 vols., 1849–52, Paris.

Lander, J. L., *The Wars of the Roses*, 1965.

—— *Conflict and Stability in Fifteenth Century England*, 1969.

—— 'Henry VI and the Duke of York's Second Protectorate', *BJRL* 1960, xliii.

—— *Government and Continuity*, 1980.

Laporte, J., 'Marguerite d'York, duchesse de Bourgogne, 1446–1503', unpublished Mémoire de Licence for the Catholic University of Louvain, 1941.

Legeay, U., *Histoire de Louis XI*, 2 vols., 1874, Paris.

Lejeune, T., *Histoire de la ville de Binche*, 1887, Binche.

Levine, Mortimer, *Tudor Dynastic Problems, 1460–1571*, 1973.

McFarlane, K. B., *The Nobility of Later Medieval England*, 1973.

Mackie, J. D., *The Earlier Tudors*, 1957 edition.

Madden, Sir Frederick, 'Documents relating to Perkin Warbeck with remarks on his history', *Archeologica*, 1838, xxvii.

Morel-Fatio, A., 'Marguerite d'Yorck et Perkin Warbeck' in *Mélanges d'Histoire offerts à Charles Bémont*, 1913, Paris.

Münch, E., *Margaretha von York*, 1832, Leipzig.

Myers, A. R., *The Household of Edward IV*, 1959.

Nicolas, N. H., *Wardrobe Accounts of Edward IV*, 1830.

Nichols, J. G. and Bruce, J., (ed.), 'Wills from Doctors Commons' *Campden Society*, 1863.

Phillips, Sir Thomas, 'Account of the Ceremonial concerning the marriage of Margaret, taken from Garter King of Arms', *Archeologica*, 1846, xxxi.

Pirenne, H., *Histoire de Belgique*, 7 vols., 1900–32, Brussels.

Plancher, U., *Histoire générale et particulière de Bourgogne*, 4 vols., 1739–81, Dijon.

Pollard, A. F., *The reign of Henry VII from Contemporary Sources*, 3 vols., 1913.

Praet, L. van, *Recherches sur Louis de Bruges, seigneur de la Gruthuyse*, 1831, Paris.

Prevenier, W. and Blockmans, W., *The Burgundian Netherlands 1380–1530*, 1986.

Ram, P. de, 'Détails concernant le mariage de Charles le Téméraire avec Marguerite d'York en 1468', *BCRH*, 1841, II, v.

Ramsay, J. H., *Lancaster and York*, 2 vols., 1892.

Rausch, R., *Die burgundische heirat Maximilian I*, 1880, Vienna.

Robins, Patricia, 'La veuvage et le douaire de Marguerite d'York dans les Pays Bas', unpublished mémoire de licence 1977, University of Brussels.

Ross, C., *Edward IV*, 1974.

Rubbrecht, O., 'Trois portraits de la maison de Bourgogne par Memlinc', *ASEB*, 1910, lx.

Sandford, F., *Genealogical History of the Kings and Queens of England*, 1707.

Scofield, C. L., *The Life and Reign of Edward IV*, 2 vols., 1923.

Stevenson, J., (ed.), *Letters and Papers Illustrative of the Wars of the English in France during the reign of Henry the Sixth*, 2 vols., 1861–4.

Storey, R. L., *The End of the House of Lancaster*, 1966.

Tambuyser, R., 'Margareta van York en Mechelen', Handelingen van de Koninklijke Kring voor Oudheidkunde, Letteren en Kunst van Mechelen, 1952, 56.

Vaesen, J. and Charavay, E., *Lettres de Louis XI*, 12 vols., 1883–1909, Paris.

Vander Linden, H., *Itinéraires de Charles, duc de Bourgogne, Marguerite d'York et Marie de Bourgogne*, 1936, Brussels.

Vaughan, R., *Philip the Good*, 1970.

—— *Charles the Bold*, 1973,

Wellens, R., *Les Etats Généraux des Pays Bas des origines à la fin du règne de Philippe le Beau, 1464–1506*, 1974, Brussels.

—— 'Un fragment d'itinéraire des ducs de Bourgogne, 1469–79, *Archives et Bibliothèques de Belgique*, 1967, xxxviii.

Wiesflëcker, H., *Kaiser Maximilian I*, 2 vols., 1975, Munich.

Williams, D., (ed.), 'England in the fifteenth century', *Proceedings of the 1986 Harlaxton Symposium*.

NOTES

Unless fully cited here see Bibliography and Abbreviations

1 Daughter of York

1. See genealogy Table 1. For the following genealogical information: Cockayne, xii, pp. 895–913; Sandford, pp. 387–402.
2. Morel-Fatio, pp. 411–16.
3. See genealogy Table 2.
4. For this paragraph and for the career of Richard of York see particularly Gorman and Griffiths and generally Chrimes, *Lancastrians, Yorkists*, Lander and Storey. For Richard's appointment after Bedford's death with like powers see Stevenson, ii, p. 585.
5. William Worcester's *Annales rerum anglicarum*, in Stevenson, ii, 2nd part, p. 764: 'nata est Margareta filia tertia Ricardi ducis Eboraci iii die Maii in die Martis apud Fodryngay'; *Chronicles of the White Rose*, pp. 213–4, also gives the birthdates and birthplaces for all the children of Duke Richard and Duchess Cecily and states that Margaret was born at Waltham Abbey on 3 May 1446. This chronicle shows several differences from Worcester's Annales.
6. H.K. Bonney, 'Historic Notices of Fotheringhay' (1821) cited in *Some Ancient Interests of Fotheringhay*, pp. 1–5; Joan Evans, 'English Art, 1307–1461' in *Oxford History of Art*, (ed.) T. S. R. Boase, 1949, pp. 186–7.
7. Cecily's will is printed in Nichols and Bruce, pp. 1–8.
8. Bonney, p. 4.
9. I have discussed the question of Margaret's birth at Waltham with Dinah Dean, the secretary of the Waltham Abbey Historical Society. There seems to be considerable evidence for a Yorkist presence in the area at that time. See also James Thorne, *Handbook to the Environs of London*, 1983 edition, pp. 650–2. He cites Thomas Fuller who was a curate at Waltham from 1648–58. For the abbey: D. Knowles and R. Neville Hancock, *Medieval Religious Houses*, 1953, ch. 1.
10. see below ch. 7, n. 35.
11. E. Carleton Williams, *My Lord of Bedford, 1389–1435*, 1963, pp. 5, 247. There is no substantial evidence that the so-called *Waltham Chronicle* was in fact written at Waltham.
12. *CPR, 1441–1447*, pp. 416, 427 for 5 March 1446; *CPR, 1446–1452*, p. 43 for 26 October 1446.
13. For York at Hunsdon: *CPR, 1446–52*, p. 77; Griffiths, *Henry VI*, p. 541. For quotation: R. Clutterbuck, *History and Antiquities of Hertfordshire*, III, p. 177. For Hunsdon house: *Victoria County History, Hertfordshire*, iii, pp. 323–5; A. Havercroft, 'Excavations on Hunsdon House. An Interim Report', *Hertfordshires Past*, 1984, no. 17, pp. 15–24; A. Emery, 'Ralph Lord Cromwell's Manor at Wingfield', *Archeological Journal*, 1985, vol. 142, p. 333; *CPR, 1452–61*, p. 34; P. M. Kendall, *The Yorkist Age: Daily life during the Wars of the Roses*, 1962, p. 337. For Sir William Oldhall: J. C. Wedgwood and A. D. Holt, *History of Parliament 1439–1509: Biographies*, 1936, pp. 647–8; C. E. Johnston, 'Sir William Oldhall', *EHR*, xxv, 1910 pp. 715–22. Sir John Oldhall's son was killed at Bosworth. In 1471 Edward IV bought back Hunsdon from the executors of Oldhall for 2,000 marks. Was he simply redeeming his father's mortgage?
14. see below ch. 7, n. 5, 7.
15. There is an extensive discussion of Richard's finances in Gorman, Griffiths and McFarlane. See also J.T. Rosenthal's two articles: 'The Estates and Finances of Richard, Duke of York', Studies in Medieval and Renaissance History, ii, Nebraska, 1965 and 'Fifteenth Century Baronial Incomes and Richard, Duke of York', *BIHR*, xxxvii, 1964; also in C. D. Ross, 'The Estates and Finances of Richard, Duke of York', *Welsh History Review*, iii, 1967; and in B. P. Wolffe, 'The Management of English Royal Estates under the Yorkist Kings' *EHR*, lxxi, 1956. Whether the duke was actually short of money or

whether he used the crown indebtedness to him to put political pressure on the king is far from clear. Certainly there are few signs of serious financial problems and he continued to build at Fotheringhay, Ludlow and Hunsdon throughout all his other troubles. However he had apparently pawned his jewels to Fastolf: *Paston/*Gairdner, i, pp. 249–50, letter of 18 December 1452 referring to the 'nowch of gold sett up on a roose enameled white' and known as the 'White Rose'. For the betrothal of Anne of York and her dowry: Griffiths, pp. 468, 479 n.80.

16. The importance of securing good marriages is emphasised by McFarlane.

17. *Commynes/*Calmette, ii, p. 248.

18. For a general biography: K. V. Vickers, *Humphrey of Gloucester*, 1967. For the Duke of York's gains: *CPR*, 1446–1452, p. 79.

19. *Historical Collections*, p. 189. For Richard in Ireland: E. Curtis, 'Richard of York as Viceroy of Ireland 1447–1460', *Journal of the Royal Society of Antiquaries of Ireland*, lxii, 1932.

20. *CPR*, 1467–77, p. 439; *CPR*, 1476–1485, p. 411.

21. Hicks, p. 14.

22. *Holinshed's Chronicles*, (ed.) H. Ellis, 1807–8, vi, pp. 267–8.

23. *Six Town Chronicles*, pp. 132–6; Griffiths, pp. 617–9, 686.

24. See genealogy Table 2.

25. Cambridge Medieval History, viii, pp. 404–5; Griffiths, pp. 687–8.

26. *ibid*, pp. 695–7.

27. For the violence between the Nevilles and the Percys at Huntington, near York see: R. A. Griffiths, 'Local Rivalries and National Politics: The Percys, the Nevilles and the Duke of Exeter, 1452–1455', *Speculum*, xliii, 1968; Storey, p. 131.

28. The alliance between York, Salisbury and Warwick came into existence after York's disappointment in 1452–1453. The duke seems to have been a slow learner in the art of making useful political alliances.

29. *Six Town Chronicles*, p. 140; *English Chronicle*, p. 79. For Margaret of Anjou: J. J. Bagley, *Margaret of Anjou, Queen of England*, 1948.

30. Griffiths, p. 720, n.84.

31. Richard had bad relations with his son-in-law, partly due to his failure to provide the full dowry for Anne. Henry, Duke of Exeter continued to give his support to the Lancastrian cause throughout his life and steadfastly opposed both Richard and later Edward IV. See also the article by Griffiths in *Speculum* (above note 27).

32. *Whethamstede*, i, pp. 168–9; C. A. J. Armstrong, 'Politics and the Battle of St Albans', *BIHR*, xxxiii, 1960, pp. 1–72.

33. For Caistor: *Paston/*Davis, ii, pp. 167–8, 15

34. *Chronicles of London*, pp. 169–70; *Croyland*, i, p. 454.

35. *English Chronicle*, p. 83.

36. M. Wood, *The English Medieval House*, 1965, p. 266.

37. For the fate of Cecily and her children after the rout of Ludford: *CPR*, 1452–1461, p. 542; *Croyland*, p. 454, *Whethamstede*, i, p. 345; *English Chronicle*, p. 83; *New Chronicles*, p. 635; Scofield, i, p. 37.

38. *Paston/*Davis, ii, pp. 187–8.

39. *Historical Collections*, p. 208.

40. *Paston/*Davis, ii, pp. 216–7.

41. Scofield, i, pp. 42–4, 47–54, 59–65; *Waurin*, v, p. 284.

42. *RP*, v, pp. 375–80; M. Levine, *Tudor Dynastic Problems*, 1973, pp. 127–131; *Whethamstede*, i, pp. 376–8; Griffiths, p. 29. Yorkist proclamations were widely quoted by chroniclers and were clearly given a great deal of publicity. A lengthy justification of the Duke of York's claims appears in *English Chronicle*, pp. 100–105 as the preamble to the agreement between Henry VI and Richard after the battle of Northampton.

43. *Whethamstede*, i, pp. 381–2 A. D. Leadham, 'The Battle of Wakefield', *Yorkshire Archeological Journal*, 1890–1, ii, p. 348; *English Chronicle*, pp. 106–7; *Six Town Chronicles*, p. 152.

44. *Great Chronicle*, p. 195; *New Chronicles*, p. 639.

45. P. M. Kendall, *Louis XI*, 1971, pp. 95–102.

46. Livia Visser-Fuchs, 'Richard in Holland, 1461', *The Ricardian*, vi, no. 81, 1983, pp. 184–188; *CSPM*, i, p. 67.

47. Vickers, pp. 445–6.

48. Scofield, i, p. 149; *English Chronicle*, p. 109.

49. *English Chronicle*, p. 110; *Hall*, p. 251. Scofield, i, p. 139.

50. *CSPM*, i, p. 69.

51. *Historical Collections*, p. 215.

52. Burne, *Battlefields*, pp. 96–108, 114; Ross, pp. 36–38.

53. Hicks, p. 20–1; Ross, p. 273.

54. *CSPM*, i, pp. 62–3, 66–7.

55. *Rozmital*, p. 53.

56. C. A. J. Armstrong, 'The Piety of Cecily Neville' in *For Hilaire Belloc: Essays in Honour of his 72nd Birthday*, (ed.) D. Woodruff, 1942, pp. 73–94.

57. For extracts from the writings of these saints: *Medieval Women Writers*, (ed.) Katherina M. Wilson, 1984, pp. 227–268.

58. Griffiths, p. 22.

59. *Haynin*, ii, p. 17.

60. For Margaret's signature see the autograph dedication from the *Vie de Sainte Collette*, reproduced on p. 217.

61. see below ch. 7.

62. Gorman, p. 182; British Library, additional ms. 11814 f.25.
63. see below, ch. 7, n. 56.
64. Hommel, p. 30.
65. *Rozmital*, pp. 49–55.
66. Vickers, pp. 234, 445–6.
67. For payment of her allowances and arrears on her allowances see: *CPR*, 1461–1467, pp. 93, 442; *CCR*, 1461–1468, p. 286; *PRO*, E404 73/1/43, 73/1/102; for other payments for plate, clothes etc see *PRO*, E404 73/1/102, 73/1/117, 73/2/61.
68. Gairdner, Letters and Papers, i, p. 31; Scofield, i, p. 320; Ross, pp. 85–96.
69. D. MacGibbon, *Elizabeth Woodville*, 1938, pp. 45, 225.
70. George Smith, *The Coronation of Elizabeth Wydeville*, 1935, pp. 15, 19, 41.
71. *Rozmital*, pp. 46–49.
72. The Woodvilles were a well educated family as may be seen the liberal patronage which Anthony Woodville extended towards Caxton: see below ch. 7.
73. Myers, 'Household of Edward IV', pp. 237–8; A. R. Myers, 'The Household of Elizabeth Woodville, 1466–7', *BJRL*, i, 1967–8, p. 667; Ross, pp. 96, 372.
74. Scofield, i, p. 247; *Exchequer Rolls of Scotland*, vii, xli, p. 63.
75. Scofield, i, pp. 387–8; Calmette, *The Golden Age*, pp. 238–9; Calmette and Perinelle, pp. 260–1, 324.
76. Scofield, i, pp. 387–8; Calmette, *The Golden Age*, p. 331, n.5.

2 The Marriage of the Century

1. The most satisfactory original sources in print are: *La Marche*, iii, pp. 101–201, iv, pp. 95–44 after writing a hundred pages on the wedding in the third volume of his memoires he went on to write another fifty pages in his fourth volume to rectify any faults and ommisions left from his first description; *Haynin*, ii, pp. 17–63; *Excerpta Historica*, pp. 223–239; *Waurin*, v, pp. 559–62; *de But*, pp. 489–90; Phillips, *Archeologica*, xxxi, pp. 326–38.

   Good secondary sources: Cartellieri, pp. 124–134; Hommel, pp. 25–52; Kipling, pp. 75–163; Kirk, i, pp. 468–78; Laborde, ii, pp. 293–381; Münch, pp. 8–38; Vaughan, pp. 45–53.

   Useful articles: C. A. J. Armstrong, 'La Politique Matrimoniale des ducs de Bourgogne de la maison de Valois' first printed in the *Annales de Bourgogne*, xl, 1968, pp. 5–58, 89–139, and reprinted in *England, France and Burgundy in the Fifteenth Century*, 1983, pp. 237–342. Mr Armstrong provides a definitive analysis of the issues concerning the dower and dowry of Margaret; Boeren,
   pp. 89–94, 234–251; Calmette, *Le mariage*, pp. 193–214; Kervyn de Lettenhove, *Relation du mariage*, pp. 245–66; de Ram, pp. 168–74.
2. *Hall*, p. 269; for Simon Mulart's 'De Ortu': pp. 234–241 in Boeren, 'Twee Maaslandse Dichters'. Mulart records all the clergy present and gives details of the processions and the banquets including a list of the meats provided, eg. '800 pingues porcos 2500 vitulos and 2100 lepores'. Like Sir John Paston he compared the magnificence of the occasion to the golden age of King Arthur.
3. *Paston*/Davis, i, pp. 538–40, 8 July 1468.
4. *Rozmital*, p. 45.
5. The most famous feast of Philip' reign was the Feast of the Pheasant at Lille in 1454, see R. Vaughan, *Philip the Good*, pp. 143–6.
6. *Paston*/Davis, i, pp. 397–8, 1 May 1467.
7. See Map, p. 74.
8. *La Marche*, iii, pp. 75–6; Vaughan, *Charles the Bold*, p. 45; Scofield, i, p. 404 n.1.
9. Armstrong, *La Politique Matrimoniale*, pp. 5–58; Vaughan, *Philip the Good*, p. 342. Apart from any immediate political interests there was a history of marriages between English princesses and the rulers of the Low Countries. Most recently Edward I's daughter Margaret had married John II, duke of Brabant in 1294.
10. See genealogy Tables 2 and 3.
11. For an examination of the economic situation see: M-R. Thielemans, *Relations politiques et économiques entre les Pays-Bas Bourguignons et l'Angleterre 1435–67*, Brussels, 1966. J. H. Munro, Review of Thielemans in *Revue Belge de Philologie et d'Histoire*, 46 B, 1968, pp. 1228–1238; Prevenier and Blockmans, pp. 97–107, 121; P. Spufford, *Monetary problems and policies in the Burgundian Netherlands*, Leiden, 1970.
12. For the negotiations: *PRO*, C/81/1499/no.7; C/81/1380/no.11; *CPR*, 1461–67, p. 442; *Foedera*, xi, p. 565; Hommel, pp. 27–34; Armstrong, *La Politique Matrimoniale*, pp. 44–7; *CSPM*, pp. 198, 256, 270, 356, 372.
13. Hicks, pp. 42–4.
14. *CSPM*, i, pp. 118–20; *Croyland*, p. 457; Scofield, i, pp. 327, 424–6; Ross, pp. 107–9; Vaughan, *Charles the Bold*, pp. 44–7; Calmette and Perinelle, pp. 78–80, 81–7.
15. *CSPV*, i, p. 117; Vaughan, *Philip the Good*, pp. 34–50, 80–84.
16. *Commynes*/Mandrot, i, p. 196.
17. *Six Town Chronicles*, p. 115; the Woodvilles advanced their position at court and in the country throughout 1466–8, Hicks, pp. 35–36. Their support for Margaret's marriage to Charles may derive from Jacquetta's connections with the St Pol family combined with a wish to assert their influence over the king.

18. Anglo, *Tournament Roll*, pp. 19–20; Anglo, *Anglo-Burgundian Feats of Arms*, p. 7; *La Marche*, iii, pp. 48–56; *New Chronicles*, pp. 655–6; *Historical Collections*, p. 236; *Foedera*, xi, p. 580; Armstrong, *England, France and Burgundy*, pp. 277–8.

19. *Hall*, p. 267; for a contemporary assessment of the significance of the Count of La Roche's visit see T. Hearne, (ed.) *Thomae Sprotti Chronica*, 1719, p. 295; Kingsford, *English Historical Literature*, p. 177.

20. Kipling, pp. 73–127.

21. *Excerpta Historica*, pp. 171–212; Scofield, i, pp. 414–20.

22. *Hall*, pp. 267–8.

23. Ross, p. 111.

24. *PRO*, French Rolls, C/76/151, C/76/152, C/81/1499/no.7.

25. Vaughan, *Philip the Good*, pp. 375, 379.

26. *Croyland*, p. 551; Basin, i, pp. 294–5; Hicks, pp. 41–2.

27. Stevenson, *Letters and Papers*, ii, p. 788.

28. For copies of marriage treaties: *PRO*, C/81/1380/no.11, C/81/1499/No.7; *AGR*, Chartes de Brabant et Mss Divers no. 43/11, cart. xliv f.51, cart. xlviii f.164v., Chartes de Brabant et Chambre des Comptes no. 134; *ADN*, B/330/16.128 for the Treaty of Brussels signed and sealed by Edward IV and also with his earlier authority to his officers to negotiate the treaty.

29. *PRO*, Signed Bills 1499 no.4227, Issue Roll, Easter VIII Edward IV, 1 June; C/81/1499/no.28.

30. *ADN*, B/429/16.141; for comments on dispensation see *CSPM*, i, p. 120; Vaughan, *Charles the Bold*, p. 48.

31. *RP*, v, pp. 622–3.

32. See genealogy Tables 1 and 2.

33. *Paston*/Davis, ii, p. 386, 18 April 1468.

34. *PRO*, Exchequer, Tellers Bills C/81/1499/no.28; *CSPV*, i, p. 121; Scofield, i, pp. 446–453; for rumours that Warwick would not guarantee the loan: Calmette, *Le mariage*, p. 202.

35. M. A. Hicks, 'The Case of Sir Thomas Cook, 1468', *EHR*, p. 93, 1978, 82–96; *New Chronicles*, p. 656; *Historical Collections*, pp. 656–7; *Great Chronicle*, pp. 204, 272.

36. *ibid*, p. 204.

37. *PRO*, E404 74/1/35, 74/1/69; Scofield i, p. 456.

38. Jean Squilbeck, 'Coronne Votive', in 'Marguerite d'York et son temps', exhibition organised by the Banque de Bruxelles, 1967; E. Grimme, 'Der Aachener Domschatz' in *Aachener Kunstblatter*, p. 42, 1972; M. Campbell, 'English Goldsmiths in the Fifteenth Century', in Williams, *Harlaxton Symposium*, p. 45; P. W. Hammond, 'The Coronet of Margaret of York', *The Ricardian*, September 1984, vi, pp. 362–5.

39. Louis' annoyance: Vaesen et Charavay, iii, p. 144; Legeay, i, p. 529; Calmette, *Le mariage*, p. 169; *Waurin*, v, p. 559; *CSPV*, p. 121; *CSPM*, i, pp. 124–6.

40. For the slanders;, *Chronique Scandaleuse*, i, p. 241; *CSPM*, pp. 95–6, 124–5; Hommel, p. 53–4; Vaughan, *Charles the Bold*, p. 48; 'Margaret had achieved the reputation of a whore': Lander, *Government and Continuity*, p. 244.

41. *Hall*, p. 267.

42. *Haynin*, ii, p. 19.

43. Ross, p. 115.

44. *Historical Collections*, p. 238; *Chronicles of the White Rose*, pp. 20–1.

45. *Excerpta Historica*, p. 227; *New Chronicles*, p. 656; Scofield, i, pp. 456–7; Hommel, pp. 35–6.

46. Scofield, i, pp. 455–6; the payments to her escort are recorded in *PRO*, Exchequer, Tellers Bills, E/404/74/1/no.35.

47. Scofield, i, pp. 455–6; *Paston*/Davis, i, p. 538; for 'the lovely widow': *La Marche*, iii, p. 107.

48. *ADN*, Comptes de l'Argenterie, B 2068/1468 f.159; Laborde, i, p. 500; *La Marche*, iii, p. 174 adds that Margaret had with her a dwarf from Constantinople who was a servant of King Edward.

49. *Excerpta Historica*, p. 228; Hommel, p. 38.

50. For her arrival at Sluis: *Haynin*, ii, p. 19; *Excerpta Historica*, pp. 228–9; *La Marche*, iii, pp. 102–3; for the movements of Charles see Vander Linden, *Itinéraires*, p. 9.

51. Kervyn de Lettenhove, *Relation du mariage*, pp. 250–3; Cartellieri, pp. 158–165; Kipling, p. 111; See also the Book of Esther.

52. Kipling, pp. 75, 117–125.

53. Hunter, pp. 87–8.

54. *ibid*.

55. see below ch. 7.

56. *Book of Judges*, ch. 6–7–8; Hunter, pp. 264f.

57. R-A. Weigert, *La tapisserie et le tapis en France*, pp. 38–60; Hunter, pp. 50, 87–90, 108–110, 238, 247–8, 264–70.

58. Hunter, p. 56.

59. Phillips, *Archeologica*, xxxi p. 329; *Excerpta Historica*, pp. 229–30.

60. Dumont, 'Marie', pp. 8–12.

61. *Haynin*, ii, pp. 20–63; Hommel, p. 53.

62. *Chastellain*, vii, pp. 228–9. For Charles' soubriquet: *La Marche*, i, p. 147.

63. *Excerpta Historica*, p. 230.

64. *ibid*, p. 231; *La Marche*, iii, p. 105; de Ram, pp. 170–4.

65. Vaughan, *Charles the Bold*, pp. 258–60; *La Marche*, iii, p. 105, iv, 97; *RP*, v, 628; *ADN*, B/429/16140, B/430/16.286; Armstrong, *England, France and Burgundy*, pp. 279, 281.

66. *Paston*/Davis, i, p. 539.

67. Prevenier and Blockmans, pp. 17–19; E. Gilliat Smith, *The Story of Bruges*, 1926, pp. 230–248.

68. For Margaret's reception into Bruges and the pageants: *Excerpta Historica*, pp. 321–4; *La Marche*, ii, pp. 98–105; Cartellieri, pp. 159–163; for the gift from Bruges: Plancher, iv, p. 362.
69. Huizinga, p. 239.
70. Phillips, *Archeologica*, xxxi, p. 331.
71. For these quotations: *Rozmital*, pp. 30, 41.
72. *Excerpta Historica*, p. 234.
73. The Gideon tapestries cost 8,960 gold crowns for 630 square yards in 1449: Hunter, p. 89.
74. *La Marche*, ii, pp. 107–11; *Excerpta Historica*, pp. 234–5; *Paston*/Davis, i, pp. 538–540; Cartellieri, ch. 2.
75. The Market Hall of Bruges was built in the thirteenth century. Its famous belfrey had been begun at the end of the thirteenth century but the octagonal top portion was only completed in 1482–7.
76. Phillips, *Archeologica*, xxxi, p. 335; *Excerpta Historica*, pp. 235–6 among others.
77. Phillips, *Archeologica*, xxxi, pp. 337–8; *Excerpta Historica*, pp. 235–239; *La Marche*, ii, pp. 11–122, among many other descriptions. The most comprehensive modern description appears in Cartellieri, pp. 124–134.
78. Vaughan, *Charles the Bold*, pp. 49–53.

3 The Duchess of Burgundy

1. *La Marche*, i, p. 146; *Molinet*, ii, p. 162. As Duchess of Burgundy, Margaret was a feudal sovereign in her own right. Her 'tuteur' appointed to represent her military interests was Josse de Lalaing, Lord of Montigny in Hainault, a knight of the Golden Fleece, a ducal chamberlain and one of Duke Charles most trusted councillors. He was to remain a loyal servant of the Burgundian court throughout his life and he died fighting for Maximilian at the siege of Utrecht. It was a bastard of the house of Lalaing who was to feature prominently in the Warbeck invasion.
2. *La Marche*, iii, pp. 56–7.
3. For a survey of the economy and demography: Prevenier and Blockmans, pp. 37–46, 70–96; see above, ch. 2, n.11.
4. See below ch. 7.
5. For Margaret of Bavaria: R. Vaughan, *John the Fearless*, 1966, pp. 173–192; for Isabelle of Portugal: Vaughan, *Philip the Good*, pp. 114–120, 171–2, 339–40.
6. Vaughan, *Philip the Good*, pp. 107–8.
7. Vaughan, *Charles the Bold*, p. 158.
8. Letter from Charles to magistrates of Valenciennes quoted by Hommel, p. 56.
9. Vaughan, *Charles the Bold*, pp. 159, 239.
10. M. Bergé, 'Les Batards de la maison de Bourgogne, leur descendance', *L'inter-médiaire des généalogistes*, lx, Paris, 1955, pp. 395–6.
11. See itinerary in Vander Linden; Hommel, p. 59.
12. For Margaret at St Josse from February to April 1473: Vander Linden, *Itinéraires*, p. 50; Hommel, p. 77; Dumont, *Marie*, pp. 82–3.
13. Hommel pp. 54–7; Vaughan, *Charles the Bold* pp. 234–5.
14. *Chastellain*, vii, pp. 228–9; Rubbrecht, *Trois portraits*, pp. 15–64; *La Marche*, i, pp. 51, 146–9, ii, pp. 214–17.
15. Charles' splendour is noted on several state occasion, notably at his marriage in 1468 and at his meeting with the Emperor at Triers in 1472. He was also accompanied on his campaigns with a vast amount of personal treasure including the jewelled cap captured at Grandson: Kirk, iii, p. 309.
16. Prevenier and Blockmans, plate 278.
17. *Chastellain*, vii, p. 228.
18. Charles is reputed as having been furious at several occasions in his life, e.g. Vaughan, *Charles the Bold*, pp. 166–7.
19. *La Marche*, ii, pp. 214–17.
20. Vaughan, *Charles the Bold*, pp. 160–1.
21. *Commynes*/Mandrot, i, pp. 44, 339, 386, ii, p. 88.
22. Vaughan, *Charles the Bold*, pp. 75–6, 171, 180.
23. *Chastellain*, vii, p. 229.
24. Vaughan, *Charles the Bold*, p. 144.
25. *Chronique Scandaleuse*, i, pp. 268–85; but note the reservations in Vaughan, *Charles the Bold*, p. 79.
26. *La Marche*, ii, pp. 214–17.
27. Helene Adhemar, *Le Musée National du Louvre*, Brussels, 1962, i, pp. 11–19. As a member of the painters guild at Tournai in 1468, Marmion may well have worked on the displays and pageants for Margaret's wedding. He was a well known miniaturist who passed most of his working life at Valenciennes. Margaret visited Valenciennes in May 1472 and May 1473.
28. Rubbrecht, *Trois portraits*, pp. 15–64; O. Rubbrecht, *L'origine du type familial de la maison de Habsbourg*, Brussels, 1910, ch. 1. For the information on the New York portrait I am indebted to Dr George Szabo the curator of the Robert Lehman Collection at the Metropolitan Museum. For the Getty see also forthcoming article in the *Journal of the J. Paul Getty Museum* by Hans van Miegrot. The Society of Antiquaries painting may well be a sixteenth century copy of an earlier painting by Hugo van der Goes. There are two other known portraits of Margaret, one is a drawing in the Biblioteque d'Arras, ms. 266 fo. 64 and the other, attributed to Memlinc, is in the Nardus

collection at Suresnes in France.

29. Royal Library Brussels, ms. 9296.

30. Bodleian Library Oxford, ms. Douce 365.

31. Convent of Poor Clares at Ghent, ms. 8.

32. D. H. Farmer, *The Oxford Dictionary of Saints*, 1978, pp. 28, 260–1.

33. 'Marguerite d'York et son temps', Catalogue of the 1967 Brussels Exhibition, p. 41; original in Rijksmuseum Amsterdam. For the van der Beecke hunting drawing see G. Szabo, 'Catalogue of Landscape Drawings of Five Centuries, 1400–1900 from the Robert Lehman Collection of the Metropolitan Museum of Art', pp. 50–1.

34. *Wielant*, p. 56.

35. Vander Linden, *Itinéraires*; Wellens, *Un fragment d'itinéraire*, pp. 108–13.

36. Hommel pp. 75–6; see Itinerary in Vander Linden.

37. Hommel, p. 57; Vander Linden, pp. 9–11; *ADN*, B/17703, lettres reçues et dépêchées.

38. In 1471, Vander Linden, *Itinéraires*, p. 44.

39. *ibid* and Hommel, p. 59; Galesloot, pp. 213–17.

40. Vander Linden, *Itinéraires*, pp. 47, 58.

41. *ibid*, pp. 51, 62; Wellens, *Un fragment d'itinéraire*, pp. 111–12.

42. Dumont, *Marie*, pp. 80–1; for Mary see also L. Hommel, *Marie de Bourgogne ou le Grand Héritage*, Brussels, 1951.

43. Corstanje and Derolez, pp. 122–142; Dumont, *Marie*, pp. 77–8.

44. *ADN*, B/429/16.230; Vaughan, *Charles the Bold*, pp. 127–9.

45. Dumont, *Marie*, ch. 4; Vaughan, *Charles the Bold*, pp. 381–2, 421.

46. L. Leemans Feygnaert, *Isabelle de Portugal*, Brussels, 1947; W. Deventer, 'Isabella van Portugal', *Spiegel historiael*, March, 1977; *Waurin*, iii, pp. 210–215.

47. Vaughan, *Philip the Good*, pp. 289–92 and in his *Charles the Bold*, pp. 240–1, 353.

48. *ibid*, p. 235; *BN*, ii, 1868, pp. 837–42.

49. S. B. J. Zilverberg, 'David van Bourgondie, bischop van Terwan en van Utrecht', Bijdragen van het Instituut voor Middeleeuwse Geschiedenis der Rijksuniversiteit te Utrecht, xxiv, 1951.

50. *BN*, vii, 1884–5, pp. 41–4; Vaughan, *Charles the Bold*, p. 4.

51. *ibid*, pp. 4–5, 247–50, 257; *BN*, iv, 1873, pp. 152–3, viii, 1884–5, pp. 381–391. For the following quotation: *Haynin*, ii, pp. 182–4.

52. *BN*, iii, 1870, pp. 67–8, ix, 1886–7, pp. 639–46; Vaughan, *Charles the Bold*, pp. 4, 230, 233, 253–6; and ch. 4 below.

53. *ibid*, pp. 258–9.

54. *ibid*, pp. 141, 193; Cartellieri, pp. 65–70; H. Stein, 'Etude sur Olivier de La Marche et sa famille', *Mémoires de l'Academie royale de Belgique*, 4th series, xlix, Brussels, 1888.

55. Vaughan, *Charles the Bold*, p. 193.

56. Alienor de Poitiers, 'Les Honneurs de la Cour' (ed.) La Curne de Sainte-Palaye, *Mémoire sur l'ancienne chevalerie*, Paris, 1759, ii, pp. 171–267; Cartellieri, p. 70.

57. Cartellieri, p. 154; Vaughan, *Charles the Bold*, p. 162.

58. *ibid*, ch. 6 for a thorough account of Charles' armies; Cartellieri, p. 70.

59. *ibid*, p. 66; for a full assessment of Charles' expenses and finances: Vaughan, *Charles the Bold*, pp. 407–415.

60. see above ch. 1, n.15.

61. Vaughan, *Charles the Bold*, p. 377; Kirk, iii, pp. 308–12.

62. *ibid*, iii, p. 309.

63. For this and the following: Olivier de La Marche, 'L'Estat de la maison du duc Charles de Bourgoigne', in *La Marche*; summarised in Cartellieri, pp. 65–69; for Margaret's household establishment of 1468: *ADN*, B/3376/113546.

64. Kirk, ii, p. 191.

65. Hommel, p. 59.

66. For the seizure of Jacqueline's lands: Vaughan, *Philip the Good*, pp. 32–52.

67. Sir John Froissart, *Chronicles of England, France and Spain*, (ed.) T. Joines, 2 vols., 1857, i, pp. 579, 640–1.

68. Vander Linden, *Itinéraires*, pp. 58, 65, 71, 78.

69. *AGR*, Chambres des Comptes, 15727, 15750, 15759, 15764, 15772; *ADN*, B/6903, 12419; Doren and Hermans, p. 71; Hommel, p. 76.

70. C. Weightman and A. Barnes, *Brussels, Grote Markt to Common Market*, Brussels, 1976, pp. 65–6.

71. Vaughan, *Philip the Good*, pp. 137–9.

72. For Charles' policies towards the Empire: Vaughan, *Charles the Bold*, ch. 4.

73. See genealogy Table 4.

74. Vaughan, *Charles the Bold*, pp. 278–9.

75. *ibid*, pp. 7–9.

76. *Correspondance de la Mairie de Dijon*, (ed.) J. Garnier, 3 vols., Dijon, 1868–70, i, pp. 124–5

77. Vaughan, *Charles the Bold*, p. 115.

78. See above ch. 2, n.38.

79. *Croyland*, p. 457; but see also P. M. Kendall, *Warwick the Kingmaker*, 1957 for the development of the relationship between Charles and Warwick which began as early as 1457 with Warwick's gift of an Irish pony for Charles.

80. Hicks, p. 66.

81. Stevenson, *Letters and Papers*, pp. 788–9.

82. Hommel, pp. 63–4.

83. Vander Linden, *Itinéraires*, pp. 18–20.

84. Scofield, i, pp. 500–1.

85. Campbell, 'English Goldsmiths', in Williams, *Harlaxton Symposium*, pp. 47–8;

Vaughan, *Charles the Bold*, p. 60.
86. Ross, pp. 124–5, 138–141.
87. Scofield, i, pp. 519–20.
88. *Chastellain*, v, pp. 450–3.
89. *Commynes*/Mandrot, i, p. 203.
90. Livia Visser-Fuchs, 'Richard in Holland, 1470–1', *The Ricardian*, vi no. 82, 1983, p. 221.
91. Scofield, i, p. 562; Hommel, p. 69.
92. Visser-Fuchs, 'Richard in Holland, 1470–1', p. 222.
93. Vaughan, *Charles the Bold*, p. 77.
94. Hommel, p. 69; *Commynes*/Mandrot, i, p. 215, *Commynes*/Calmette, i, p. 211; *Chastellain*, v, pp. 501–3; for Richard's visit to Margaret in February: Vander Linden, *Itinéraires*, p. 28.
95. Visser-Fuchs, 'Richard in Holland 1470–1', p. 225.
96. C. A. J. Armstrong, 'Verses by Jean Mielot on Edward IV and Richard earl of Warwick', *Medium Aevum*, vol. 8, 1939, pp. 193–7.
97. *CSPM*, i, p. 151.
98. *Arrivall*, pp. 9–10; *Croyland*, p. 464; *Waurin*, v, p. 652.
99. van Praet, pp. 81–3.
100. *ibid*; for the rest of this paragraph: Kipling, pp. 8–9; A. de Behault de Dornon, *Bruges séjour d'exil d'Eduard IV*, Bruges, 1931; W.J. St John Hope, *Architectural History of Windsor Castle*, 1913, pp. 398–406, 429–44.
101. Myers, *The Household of Edward IV*, pp. 4–5.
102. van Praet, pp. 10–11.
103. *Waurin*, v, pp. 652–3, 660–3; *Haynin*, ii, pp. 125–6.
104. *Commynes*/Calmette, i, p. 213.
105. *Haynin*, ii, p. 128; for the battle of Barnet see Ross, pp. 167–8.
106. *Haynin*, ii, pp. 128–9.
107. *Haynin*, ii, p. 126. For the battle of Tewkesbury see the *Arrivall*, pp. 23–8; Burne, *Battlefields*, pp. 118–25.
108. *Arrivall*, p. 38; but see also *CSPM*, i, p. 157; *Croyland*, p. 468; Margaret did not mention this death in her letter to Isabelle.
109. Kingsford, *English Historical Literature*, pp. 379–88; For bonfires: *La Marche*, iii, p. 73 n.4; Armstrong, *England, France and Burgundy*, p. 111.
110. Reward of 12th February 1472: *Foedera*, xi, p. 735; *CPR* 1467–77, p. 306; *PRO*, French Roll 15 Edward IV, m.20, m.1–2.
111. Gachard, pp. 124–7.
112. *CSPM*, i, pp. 164–70;
113. *CSPM*, i, p. 16; Vander Linden, *Itinéraires*, p. 77; Vaughan, *Charles the Bold*, p. 235; Hommel, pp. 88–90.
114. *ADN*, B/429/16285 letter from Arbois dated 1st July 1476, and B/429/16263 for Edward's letter of 29th July 1474 recording his debt and promising to pay; Galesloot, pp. 199–201.

115. *CSPM*, i, pp. 197–8; Ross, pp. 221–2.
116. Jean de Dadizeele, *Mémoires*, (ed.) Kervyn de Lettenhove, Bruges, 1850, pp. 47–8.
117. *Molinet*, i, pp. 106–8; *Commynes*/Mandrot, i, pp. 292–5, *Commynes*/Calmette, ii, pp. 34–6; Vaesen and Charavay, v, p. 366.
118. Vaughan, *Charles the Bold*, p. 351; Ross, p. 233.
119. *CSPM*, i, pp. 211, 217; *Croyland*, p. 559.
120. O. Delpierre, *Marie de Bourgogne*, Brussels, 1841, p. 110.
121. Hommel, pp. 88–92; Vaughan, *Charles the Bold*, p. 235; Dupont, *Marie*, pp. 133–5.
122. *ibid*. p. 419.
123. Vander Linden, *Itinéraires*, pp. 75–6; Hommel, p. 90.
124. *Molinet*, i, p. 169; Vaughan, *Charles the Bold*, pp. 409–11.
125. *ibid*, pp. 394, 413; Hommel, p. 90.
126. Armstrong, *England France and Burgundy*, p. 327.

4 1477

1. Vaughan, *Charles the Bold*, pp. 392, 429.
2. *Molinet*, i, pp. 167–8.
3. L. P. Gachard, 'Note sur le jugement et la condemnation de Guillaume Hugonet', Brussels, 1839, pp. 10–11; J. Molinet, *Les Faietz et dictz*, (ed.) N. Dupire, 3 vols., Paris, 1936–9, i, p. 200; *Molinet*, i, pp. 208–9, 214; G. Tournoy-Thoen, 'A propos de quelques épitaphes latines pour la mort de Charles le Téméraire', *Lias*, v, 1978, pp. 1–11.
4. Quoted in Vaughan, *Charles the Bold*, p. 432.
5. Philippe Contamine, *La France aux XIVe et XVe siècles, Hommes, Mentalités Guerre et Paix*, London, 1981, p. 77.
6. Hommel, p. 93.
7. For movements and dates in this chapter see: H. Vander Linden, *Itinéraires de Marie de Bourgogne et de Marguerite d'Autriche, 1477–82*, Brussels, 1934; Wellens, pp. 150–8.
8. Commynes, (ed.) Mandrot, i, p. 122.
9. Wellens, *Les Etats Généraux*, pp. 150–5.
10. L. P. Gachard, *Etudes concernant l'histoire des Pays Bas*, Brussels, 1890, pp. 8–10; Dumont, *Marie*, pp. 134–5; Hommel, p. 90.
11. V. Van der Haegen, 'La Charte donnée aux Gantois par Marie de Bourgogne en 1477' and H. Pirenne, 'Le rôle constitutionnel des Etats Généraux des Pays-Bas en 1477 et en 1488', both in *Mélanges Paul Frédéricq*, Ghent, 1904; Wellens, *Les Etats Généraux*, pp. 156–170; Dumont, *Marie*, ch. 8.
12. P. M. Kendall, *Louis XI*, p. 415.
13. *Molinet*, i, pp. 168, 209; *La Marche*, iii, p. 241.
14. Rausch, p. 164.
15. Hanham, pp. 10–11, letter of 26 January 1477.
16. *Paston*/Davis, i, pp. 419–20, 498–9; Hicks, p. 131.

17. *Croyland*, p. 478; *Chronique Scandaleuse*, i, p. 176, ii, p. 63; Calmette and Perinelle, pp. 223, 376–7; Scofield, ii, pp. 191–6.
18. For a 'mere earl': *Commynes*/Calmette, ii, p. 248; Dumont, *Marie*, pp. 208–9.
19. Chmel, i, letter of 30 July 1477; Münch, pp. 47, 143; Pirenne, iii, p. 19; Armstrong, *England, France and Burgundy*, p. 288, n.4.
20. Kervyn de Lettenhove, 'Lettre de Marguerite d'York' in *BARB* xxxi, 1854, pp. 104–11; Vander Linden, *Itinéraires*, p. 2.
21. J. Cuvelier, J. Dhondt and R. Doehaerd, *Actes des Etats Generaux des Anciens Pays-Bas, 1427–77*, 5 vols., Brussels, 1948, i, p. 275, n.5; Dumont, *Marie*, p. 159.
22. *ibid*, p. 162; Cuvelier, Dhondt and Doehard, i, pp. 276, 277; *Commynes*/Mandrot, i, pp. 414–21.
23. Cuvelier, Dhondt and Doehaerd, i, p. 275; Wellens, *Les Etats Généraux*.
24. *Commynes*/Mandrot, i, p. 425.
25. Vaesen and Charavay, vi, p. 138; V. Van der Haeghen, 'Les députes de Tournai auprès de Louis XI et d'Olivier le Daim en juillet 1477', *Mélanges Godefroid Kurth*, Brussels, 1908, 207f.
26. *Commynes*/Calmette, ii, p. 245.
27. See above note 17; Calmette and Perinelle, pp. 376–8.
28. Dumont, *Marie*, pp. 179–180.
29. *La Marche*, iii, p. 242.
30. *Haynin*, ii, p. 231, who says she left on 10 March.
31. *ibid*, ii, p. 232.
32. J. de Saint Genois, 'Sur la compétence de la juridiction à laquelle furent soumis Hugonet et Humbercourt', *BARB*, vi 2nd part, 1839; L. P. Gachard, 'Un note sur la Jugement de Hugonet et Humbercourt', *BARB*, vi, 2nd part, 1839; J. J. Desmet, 'Le supplice du chancelier Hugonet et du Comte d'Imbercourt ministres de Marie de Bourgogne, a-t-il été le résultat d'une vengeance populaire?', also in *BARB*, vi, 2nd part, 1839; C. Paillard, 'Le Procès du chancelier Hugonet et du Seigneur d'Humbercourt', *BARB*, vl, 1881.
33. Prevenier and Blockmans, pp. 175–8.
34. Dumont, *Marie*, pp. 198–200.
35. Widely quoted e.g. *ibid*, p. 201.
36. *MA* Lettres Missives, cclxxxi and cclxxvii, the latter shows Humbercourt himself wrote asking for sanctuary at Malines for his family.
37. Wiesflëcker, i, pp. 124–5.
38. Dumont, *Marie*, pp. 209–10.
39. *ibid*, p. 210.
40. Münch, i, pp. 47, 143; Pirenne, iii, p. 19.
41. Chmel, i, p. 145; Münch, i, p. 49, ii, pp. 87–90; Plancher, p. 482; Armstrong, *England, France and Burgundy*, pp. 286–7; *Molinet*, i, p. 211; *La Marche*, i, pp. 155, 157, iii, p. 244; the dowager 'tint fort la main'.
42. For draft of the marriage treaty: *ADN*, B/

430/17.722; Chmel, i, p. 145; Armstrong, *England, France and Burgundy*, p. 285.
43. Dumont, *Marie*, p. 212.
44. *ibid*, p. 230; Hommel, p. 109.
45. Wiesflëcker, i, p. 180.
46. Chmel, i, p. 160; Rausch, p. 179; Hare, p. 43.
47. Hommel, pp. 110–111; Dumont, *Marie*, pp. 228–9; Wiesflëcker, i, pp. 132–3.
48. Wiesflëcker, i, pp. 132–3; Münch, i, p. 187 f, 190.
49. Vaesen and Charavay, vi, p. 138: 'qui mayne ceste entreprinse'.
50. Münch, ii, pp. 247–8; Hommel, p. 111.
51. *ibid*, p. 113.
52. Pirenne, iii, pp. 4, 24.
53. For Margaret's dower position see above, ch. 2, n.28; *ADN*, B/429/16.281 and 16.263, B/430/16.284; Chancery Diplomatic Documents Foreign no. 520; F. Leonard, 'Recueil des traitez de paix, de trêve, de neutralité, de confédefation, d'alliance et de commerce, faits par les rois de France avec tous les princes et potentats de l'Europe, depuis près de trois siècles', 6 vols., Paris, 1963, i, pp. 76–82; Armstrong, *La Politique Matrimoniale des ducs de Bourgogne*, pp. 5–58, 89–139, or in *England, France and Burgundy*, pp. 316–323; Robins, ch. 2, 4 and 7.
54. Reservation of sovereign rights; *ADN*, B/430/16.282 and 16.293; letters concerning the dower settlement: *ADN*, Lettres reçues et dépêchées, B/17725 which includes three signed by Margaret and four by Mary who added a note in her own hand telling the officials to make no more difficulties, *ADN* B/429/16.281, B/430/16.291 in which officials report that the marriage contract etc is at Lille not at Malines, *ADN* B/429/16.295, 16.301 and 16283, B/430/16.282, 16.293 and 16294; Margaret renounces her inheritance from Charles apart from her dower: B/430/16294; *AGR*, Chambre des Comptes de Flandres et de Brabant, carton 281, piece no 41, annexes 13–14; for the calculation of her dower as a percentage return of the dowry: Armstrong, *England, France and Burgundy*, pp. 275, 280.
55. *ADN*, B/430/16.282, i.e. letter from Ghent on 28 January: 'nostre personne et noz pays et seigneuries en si entiere et parfaicte amour et bienveillance que jamais ne les pourrions remerir ne recongnoistre a souffisance' and 'liberallement et cordiallement offerte et de clairie de nous aidier parter et favorisier en tous noz affaires de toute sa puissance', also B/429/16.285, B/430/16.293 or *AGR*, Chambre des Comptes, p. 103, for letter from Ghent on 30 January.
56. *ADN*, B/429/16.285; *AGR*, Chambre des Comptes, p. 103.
57. Registration of Margaret's dower on 31 January: *AGR* Chambre des Comptes p. 103;

3 February from Ghent with Margaret's seal renouncing Charles' goods and naming Margaret as 'douagière et usufructaire' of Malines, Termonde, Oudenaarde, Cassel and Motte-aux-Bois: *ADN*, B/430/16.294; *ADN*, B/429/16.281; grant of Chaussin and Le Perriere, (south of Dole in Franche Comté), signed with Mary's equestrian seal on 10 March from Ghent, *ADN*, B/430/16.284 for full assessment of her dower income; B/430/16.294, 16301 and 16302 for Brielle, Voorne, Rupelmonde and Le Quesnoy; Comptes du Domaine de Hainaut: B/9134–38; *AGR*, Chambre des Comptes p. 103 fos. 24ro to 27ro.; grant of Brielle and Voorne on 28 June: *AGR*, Chambre des Comptes p. 103, fos. 20ro to 27 ro and 32ro to 41vo, 62ro to 65vo .

58. For Maximilian's approval: *ADN*, B/430/16.294 and 16.303; or *AGR*, Chambre des Comptes 103 fos. 32ro. to 41vo. and 62ro to 65vo.; for the conversation between Maximilian and Margaret on the eve of the wedding: Vander Linden, *Itinéraires de Marie de Bourgogne et de Marguerite d'Autriche, 1477–82*, p. 122; for calculations of her revenue see Robins, pp. 161–2.
59. *Haynin*, ii, p. 233.
60. *Paston*/Davis, pp. 498–9; *Chronicles of the White Rose*, pp. 245–9.
61. Plancher, iv, preuve cclxxxviii, col. cdi, letter dated February 1478. But Margaret must have written in a similar vein before this since Edward and Louis were in negotiation over Margaret's dower lands even earlier. She probably wrote in March 1477 when she was forced away from Ghent. See also Legeay, ii, p. 319; Münch, ii, pp. 71–2.
62. For this and the diplomatic exchanges in the next two paragraphs see: Calmette and Perinelle, pp. 222–223 n.2, pp. 171–2, 376–7, 231–3, 382–3, 385–6, 391–2; Plancher, iv, preuves cclxxxix col. cdi, ccxci cols. cdiii–cdiv, cclxxxiii col. cclxc, cccxcv–cccxcvi; *Chronique Scandaleuse*, ii, p. 63; Vaesen and Charavay, vi, p. 138, vii, pp. 65–6, 97–9, 100–2, 194, 252–3, 301; *Foedera*, xii, p. 68; *La Marche*, iii, p. 243; Scofield, ii, pp. 184–5, 192, 196–7, appendix xii.
63. See above n.49.
64. Scofield, ii, pp. 232–3; Plancher, iv, preuve cclxxxix col. cdi; Calmette and Perinelle, pp. 231–2.
65. See above n.49; Plancher, iv, preuve cccxcv–cccxcvi; Scofield, ii, pp. 244–5.
66. *CCR* 1476–85, pp. 104–5; *PRO*, Signed Bills, C/81/1518/37 and 17 and 18; *MA*, Rood Boek, i, p. 74.
67. L. Hommel, 'Marguerite d'York, la douairière malinoise', *Revue Générale Belge*, January, 1954.
68. Galesloot,   pp. 207–11;   Tambuyser, pp. 212–7.

69. *ibid*; L. Godenne, 'Malines jadis & Aujourd'hui', Malines, 1908, pp. 245–50.
70. F. O. van Hamme, *Mechelen*, Amsterdam, 1949; *MA*, Lettres Missives: cccxxxii, cccxxxiv, ccclvii, ccccxxxv.
71. L. Hommel, 'Marguerite d'York, la douairière malinoise'.
72. For this paragraph: R. S. Gottfried, *Epidemic Disease in Fifteenth Century England*, 1978, pp. 74–5; for her doctors: *MA*, Lettres Missives, ccccxxxv. For the following reference to her jam-maker I am indebted to Mark Ballard who drew my attention to *ADN*, B/2128/69060.
73. *CPR* 1476–85, p. 236; *CCR* 1476–85, p. 104; Doren and Hermans, ii, p. 166; *MA*, Rood Boek iii, 126, 130; M. Gachard, *Additions et Corrections à la Notice sur les Archives de la Ville de Malines*, 3 vols., 1834–6, iii, 2nd part, p. 57.
74. Hommel, pp. 130–1; for her establishment at Malines: Hommel, pp. 159–64.

5   Madame La Grande

1. *Croyland*, p. 478.
2. Hicks, p. 20.
3. *ibid*, pp. 113–7.
4. W. H. Courthope, (ed.) *Rous Roll*, 1974, no. 59.
5. See above ch. 4.
6. See below ch. 7.
7. For proposed marriage: Exchequer Rolls of Scotland, viii, lxi; Conway, pp. 2–3.
8. Halliwell, i, pp. 147–8.
9. Hicks, p. 133.
10. *Croyland*, pp. 478–9, for this and for the following.
11. For Clarence's death: Hicks, p. 140; Ross, p. 243 and n.3.
12. Hicks, p. 151.
13. *ibid*.
14. Doren and Hermans, ii, p. 82; A. Kampeneer, 'Une résidence de Charles V', *Mélanges d'Histoire offerts à Charles Moeller*, Paris, Louvain, 1914, p. 43.
15. Dumont, *Marie*, pp. 247–8; Hommel, p. 135.
16. *Molinet*, i, pp. 273–6; *La Marche*, iii, p. 252.
17. For baptism of Margaret of Austria: *Molinet*, i, p. 320; *La Marche*, iii, p. 257; for her life: H. Carton de Wiart, *Marguerite d'Autriche, une princesse belge de la Renaissance*, Paris, 1935; C. Hare, *The High and Puissant Princess Marguerite of Austria*, 1967; and J. de Jongh, *Margaret of Austria, Regent of the Netherlands*, 1954; for Guillaume de Baume: *Molinet*, i, pp. 140, 275, 394, ii, pp. 323, 480.
18. Wiesflëcker, i, p. 139; Armstrong, *England, France and Burgundy*, p. 201 n.5; *König Maximilian's Weisskünig*, trans. and (ed.) H. T. Musper, R.Büchner and E. Petermann, Stuttgart, 1956, i, p. 245.
19. C. Weightman and A. Barnes, *Brussels, Grote*

Markt to Common Market, Brussels, 1976, pp. 34–5.

20. MA, Lettres Missives cccxlii, cccli.

21. ibid, ccclxxii, ccclxxx, cccxlii, cccli and ccxci, ccxcii. On the 2 July 1477, Margaret was writing from Dendermonde to Malines ordering troops to be sent to Oudenaarde to assist Lord Ravenstein who was defending the city.

22. For this embassy: Robins, p. 195; L. Gilliodts-van-Severen, Inventaire des archives de la ville de Bruges, 7 vols., Bruges, 1861–78, vi, pp. 202–3; Scofield, ii, pp. 283–97; Münch, ii, p. 16; Hommel pp. 124–131.

23. Commynes/Godefroy, iii, pp. 587–9.

24. Adrien de But, p. 546.

25. For 'The Falcon' and her escort: Scofield, ii, p. 284; PRO, Exchequer Warrants and Issues 1399–1485, E404, 77/2/49, 77/1/33, 77/2/33; for her reception by Sir John Weston: Hanham, p. 86.

26. Scofield, ii, p. 285; Nicolas, xii, pp. 159, 160–6.

27. Scofield, ii, pp. 284, 295; Nicolas, pp. 126, 141–2, 144–5, 153, 160.

28. A.G. Little, 'The Introduction of Observant Friars in England', Proceedings of the British Academy, x, 1921–3, pp. 455–71.

29. For this paragraph: Scofield, ii, p. 287; PRO, Exchequer Accounts Butlerage bundle pp. 82, 18; Ross, p. 273; for the Holy Cross see above ch. 1.

30. Ross, pp. 283–285; Scofield, ii, pp. 285–301; Commynes/Lenglet, iii, pp. 577–589, 595, 603–10, iv, pp. 10–11; Vaesen and Charavay, viii, pp. 229–31; PRO, Signed Bills C/81/1518/26.

31. Foedera, xii, pp. 123–139.

32. Scofield, ii, pp. 290–1; CPR 1476–85, p. 74; Commynes/Lenglet, iii, pp. 587–9; PRO, Signed Bills file 1518 no 5170; ADN, B/431/17.737 for copies of five letters from Edward IV dealing with the Alliance, the Marriage Treaty and his French Pension and B/431/17.738 concerning the payment to the troops; Robins pp. 193–5.

33. Scofield, ii, pp. 289–90; Ross, pp. 283–4; Commynes/Lenglet, iii, pp. 576–7.

34. Scofield, ii pp. 290, 295; Commynes/Lenglet, iii, pp. 603–8; Foedera, xii, p. 135.

35. Commynes/Lenglet, iii pp. 577–83; Scofield p. 287.

36. CPR 1476–85, p. 236; PRO, Signed Bills C/81/1518/37 and 17 and 18; PRO, French Roll C/76/163; Margaret fattened up her imported beef at Termonde: AGR, Chambre des Comptes, Recette de Termonde 7563 (1480–1) fo. 21vo and 7565 (1482–3) fo. 30ro.

37. Scofield, ii, pp. 291–4.

38. Commynes/Lenglet, iii, pp. 609–10, 614, iv, p. 11.

39. Scofield, ii, p. 296.

40. Commynes/Lenglet, iii, p. 609; Scofield, ii, pp. 296–7.

41. Scofield, ii, p. 299; Vaesen and Charavay, viii, pp. 301, 308; Commynes/Lenglet, iv, pp. 9–10.

42. Münch, ii, pp. 52–3.

43. Münch, ii, pp. 16–7; Commynes/Lenglet, iv, pp. 6–10; Scofield, ii, p. 284; Robins, p. 192.

44. Galesloot, pp. 211–2; M. R. Wellens, 'Travaux de restauration au château de la Salle à Binche sous Philippe le Bon et Marguerite d'York', Annales du Cercle Archéologique de Mons, vol. 63, 1958, pp. 131–6.

45. Molinet, i, p. 368.

46. For falcons in Mary's bedroom; C. A. J. Armstrong, 'The Golden Age of Burgundy' in The Courts of Europe, (ed.) A. G. Dickens, 1977, p. 72; For Mary's seal: MA, Inventaire i, p. 166, also in Privilege Book; illustrated in Prevenier and Blockmans, p. 232.

47. Molinet, i, pp. 368–70; Dumont, Marie, ch. 15.

48. M-R. Thielemans, 'Introduction Historique', in Marguerite d'York et son temps, Exhibition Brussels, 1947, p. 9.

49. La Marche, iii, pp. 265–6.

50. Hommel, pp. 138–143.

51. ADN, 431/17.750 and 17.774; Molinet, i, pp. 389–90; Commynes/Lenglet, iv, p. 32.

52. Laporte, p. 93.

53. Molinet, i, p. 419.

54. Galesloot, pp. 280–1, 274–6, 302–3; Wiesflécker, i, p. 157.

55. Armstrong, England, France and Burgundy, pp. 286–9; Robins, pp. 135–8.

56. Gairdner, Letters and Papers, ii, pp. 3–51.

57. Hommel, pp. 151–3.

58. La Marche, iii, pp. 278–88.

59. La Marche, iii, pp. 281–4; MA, 'Inventaire', i, no. p. 276, 175; MA, Rood Boek, iii, p. 101.

60. Hommel, p. 175.

61. ibid, pp. 175–7.

62. D. Mancini, The Usurpation of Richard III, (ed. and trans.) C. A. J. Armstrong, 1969, p. 59; Scofield, ii, pp. 365–6; Ross, pp. 415–6.

63. Croyland, p. 482.

64. Gairdner, Letters and Papers, ii, pp. 3–51; Molinet, i, p. 423 shows the English in action at Utrecht.

65. Croyland, p. 568.

66. Chronicles of the White Rose, p. 209.

67. Gairdner, Letters and Papers, i, xxv.

68. Molinet, i, pp. 430–3.

69. Horrox and Hammond, ii, pp. 129, 178.

70. Commynes/Calmette, ii, p. 306.

6 'This Diabolicall Duches'

1. Molinet, i, p. 562.

2. MA, 'Inventaire' i, p. 175; MA, Rood Boek (1486), iii, pp. 101–3.

3. *CCR* 1485–1500, p. 39, 27 October 1486, order for payment of arrears owing to Cecily and p. 40, 20 June 1486, renewal of licences to ship 250 and a half sacks of wool; Campbell, i, p. 288.

4. *CPR*, 1467–77, p. 306; 1476–85, p. 236; *Foedera*, xii, pp. 137, 185; Horrox and Hammond, iii, p. 6.

5. Genard, pp. 9–22.

6. *ibid*.

7. Nicholas Knyfton was made constable of Scarborough Castle on 21 September 1485: Gairdner, *Letters and Papers*, i, pp. 326–8; Campbell, i, p. 26; Hunsdon in the possession of William Stanley: Calendar of Inquisitions Post Mortem, i, Henry VII, p. 204; Campbell, i, pp. 7, 26, 414. Henry's suspicions: Archbold, pp. 529–34; Chrimes, *Henry VII*, p. 85.

    Had Margaret ever owned Hunsdon and why should she have an interest in Scarborough? I have been unable to discover anything further on Scarborough apart from the fact that it was specially favoured by her brother Richard. Her family had an historic interest in Hunsdon: see ch. 1, n.13. In 1481 Hunsdon was audited as a royal manor: *CPR* 1476–85, 247. For later ownership of Hunsdon: C. H. Cooper, *Margaret Beaufort*, 1874, p. 58, states that in the 11th year of King Henry's reign, Hunsdon was given to Margaret Beaufort and her husband the Earl of Derby, i.e. after the execution of Sir William Stanley in 1496. After the death of Margaret Beaufort, Hunsdon then went into the possession of Thomas, Earl of Norfolk but was later returned to the crown. It was rebuilt by Henry VIII and used by Mary Tudor who was proclaimed queen at Hunsdon. Elizabeth granted Hunsdon to her cousin, Sir Henry Carey, son of Mary Bullen and William Carey, a descendant of the Beaufort Dukes of Somerset. Sir Henry Carey's youngest daughter baptised at Hunsdon on the 6 December 1564 and was called Margaret.

8. *Bacon*, p. 32.

9. Gairdner, *Letters and Papers*, ii, pp. 3–51.

10. Benecke, x.

11. *ADN*, B/431/17.785; Laporte, pp. 121–2; Hare, p. 249, suggests that Maximilian was easily led: 'Machiavelli said anyone could cheat Maximilian'.

12. See genealogy Table 3.

13. For Charles' registration of his claim see above ch. 3, n.112; Vaughan, *Charles the Bold*, p. 72; for Maximilian and Elizabeth of York: Wiesflecker, i, pp. 180, 471 n.14; for the transfer of Yorkist claims to Maximilian and Philip: P. Genard, 'Document No.75', *Compte Rendu des Séances de la Commission Royale d'Histoire de Belgique*, 4th ser., Bruss-

els, 1875, ii; Gairdner, *Letters and Papers*, ii, p. 355.

14. *Polydore Vergil* pp. 16–17.

15. For these and the following paragraph: *Hall*, p. 430.

16. Madden, p. 192; Gairdner, *Memorials*, pp. 315–16, 319.

17. *Bacon*, p. 32.

18. Hommel.

19. Hume, iii, p. 328; Mackie, p. 67; R. H. Wilenski, *Flemish Painters*, 1906, p. 50.

20. Halliwell-Phillipps, i, pp. 172–3; and to the ambassador: Madden, appendix iii, pp. 200–4.

21. Rumours that he was Margaret's bastard son by the Bishop of Cambrai: *CSPM*, i, pp. 292, 329; Pollard, i, xxii, pp. 102–3. In the 1490s Henri de Berghes, the Bishop of Cambrai was a man of spotless virtue. Margaret had purchased her house in Malines from an earlier Bishop of Cambrai, John of Burgundy, who had a large number of illegitimate offspring, hence there was ample room for confusion and rumours.

22. For Lovel: Ross, pp. 115, 186n, 438; for the Stafford rising: C. R. Williams, 'The rebellion of Humphrey Stafford in 1486', *EHR*, 43, 1928, pp. 181–9; for Sant: *PRO*, French Roll, C/76/153; *MA*, Lettres Missives, ccxlvii; for movements between England and the Low Countries in 1485–6 see C. S. L. Davies, 'Bishop John Morton, the Holy See and the Accession of Henry VII', *EHR*, cii, p. 402, January 1987, pp. 10–12; *Molinet*, ii, pp. 419–20 for 'trois grans personages d'Engleterre', refers to Clifford, Barley etc.

23. *CSPM*, i, p. 27.

24. *Bacon*, p. 30; Chrimes, *Henry VII*, pp. 59, 72; for the Simnel rising generally see *Molinet*, i, pp. 562–7 and Bennett; for Warwick in the Channel Islands: *ibid*, pp. 49–50, 64.

25. *ibid*, pp. 40, 51; however, K. Staniland, 'Royal Entry into the World' in *Williams, Harlaxton Symposium*, p. 306, notes that Elizabeth had no place in the processions.

26. Chrimes, *Henry VII*, p. 72; for the revelations at convocation: Bennett, pp. 42–3; for the flight of Lincoln: *ibid*, p. 63; Chrimes, *Henry VII*, p. 76.

27. *RP*, vi, pp. 436–7.

28. Wiesflecker, i, pp. 62, 431 n.33.

29. For Schwartz: *Great Chronicle*, p. 241; *Polydore Vergil*, p. 21; Pollard, i, p. 51, iii, p. 263; *Molinet*, i, pp. 444–5, 450–1, 528, ii, pp. 562–5; *Cronijcke van den Lande Ende Greafscape van Vlaenderen, gemaect door Jor Nicolaes Despars*, (ed.) J. de Jonghe, 4 vols., Brugge, 1840, iv, pp. 280–282; *Adrien de But*, pp. 674–5.

30. *MA*, Comptes Communaux, SI 162 1486–7, cliii; L. J. M. Philippen, 'Saint Rombaut. Sa Patrie. Son épiscopat', *Revue d' Histoire écclé-*

siastique, p. 29, Louvain, 1933, pp. 365–7; I. I. de Münck, 'Gedenk-schriften dienende tot ophelderinge van het Leven Lyden, Wonderheden ende Duysent Iarige Eerbewysinge van den Heyligen bisschop ende martelaer Rumoldus apostel ende patroon van Mechelen', Mechelen, 1777, pp. 140–3, 146, 150–1. St Rombout, of British origin, was a missionary and martyr at Malines in the eighth century. His feast day was celebrated on 1 July 'from time immemorial'; *BN*, xix, pp. 895–9.

31. Halliwell-Phillipps, i, p. 172; Bernard André, 'Vita Henrici Septimi' in Gairdner, *Memorials*, p. 50.

32. C. Roth, 'Perkin Warbeck and his Jewish Master', *Transactions of the Jewish Historical Society of England*, ix, 1918–20, pp. 155–6 and *ibid*, xvi, 1945–51, for 'Sir Edward Brampton an Anglo-Jewish adventurer during the Wars of the Roses', pp. 121–7; also C. Roth, 'Sir Edward Brampton alias Duarte Brandao', *La societe guernesaise*, 1957, p. 163; E. F. Jacob, *The Fifteenth Century*, 1961, p. 592; Gairdner, *Letters and Papers*, ii, l–lii.

33. *MA*, Comptes Communaux, SI 162 1486–7, 164vo. under Miscellaneous Gifts to 'gemalde vrouw van bourg'.

34. Bennett, pp. 60, 66–7; *Molinet*, i, p. 563; Gairdner, *Letters and Papers*,i, pp. 95–6; *CSPV*, i, pp. 164–5; *Foedera*, xii, p. 332; for Simnel and Warbeck in Ireland see also E. Curtis, *History of Medieval Ireland from 1110 to 1513*, 1923.

35. Genard, p. 10.

36. *Great Chronicle*, p. 241.

37. Bennett, p. 105, for a discussion of his identity: *ibid*, ch. 4.

38. Henry's letter: Halliwell-Phillipps, i, pp. 172–3; cooperation between the two rulers: *Paston*/Davis, i, pp. 660–1; *Foedera*, xii, pp. 318–21, 334–5, 350–3, 359–63, 397f.

39. Huizinga, p. 153.

40. *MA*, Lettres Missives cccvii, cccviii, cccix, cccxi; L. P. Gachard, 'Additions et Corrections à la Notice sur les Archives de la Ville de Malines' (1834), iii, part 2, pp. 7–8.

41. Pirenne, iii, pp. 46–7; *Molinet*, i, pp. 589–604, ii, p. 166; Prevenier and Blockmans, pp. 238–9; Galesloot, pp. 269–70; Hommel pp. 184–5.

42. V. von Kraus, (ed.) *Maximilan I vertraulicher Briefwechsel mit Sigmund Prüchenk*, Innsbruck, 1875, pp. 62–3; for David painting the shutters of Maximilian's prison: Huizinga, p. 236; Max J. Friedlander, *From Van Eyck to Bruegel*, (ed.) F. Grossmann, 2 vols., 1956, i, pp. 48–9.

43. Imperial and papal protests at Maximilian's imprisonment: Pirenne, iii, pp. 46–9;

Molinet, i, pp. 589–604; action by Margaret: Hommel, pp. 187–190.

44. Pirenne, iii, pp. 50, 53, 60–5; van Praet, p. 104; Hommel, pp. 190, 192, 194, 196.

45. *Molinet*, ii, pp. 133–7; Mackie, pp. 99–100.

46. For these treaties: *ibid*, p. 99; Hommel, pp. 193–4; *Molinet*, ii, pp. 156–173; Pirenne, iii, p. 52; Money to Brielle: *Adrien de But*, p. 560.

47. Mackie, pp. 103–4.

48. Treaty of Senlis: Pirenne, iii, pp. 56–7; *Molinet*, ii, pp. 354–71.

49. Hommel, pp. 220–3; *Molinet*, ii, pp. 397–521; Maximilian's influence was also powerful, both Carondelet and Nassau had served him loyally for many years.

50. Hommel, pp. 217–8; *Molinet*, ii, pp. 396, 398–9.

51. Bacon, p. 66; *Arrivall*, p. 10; Horrox and Hammond, ii, pp. 129, 178.

52. *Hall*, p. 472.

53. Nichols and Bruce, pp. 1–8; *Chronicles of London*, p. 204; *Great Chronicle*, p. 257.

54. *CPR 1476–1485*, p. 217; *ADN*, Comptes de l'Argenterie, B/2068/1468, p. 159.

55. For this and the following paragraph see *RP*, vi, pp. 436–7; Madden, appendix IV; Pollard, i, pp. 84–7, 98–9, 100–2; *Chronicles of London*, pp. 165–6.

56. Lander, *Government and Continuity*, p. 108.

57. Madden, appendix IV; Pollard, i, pp. 44, 52–3; C. A. J. Armstrong, 'An Italian Astrologer at the court of King Henry VII', in *Italian Renaissance Studies, a Tribute to the late Cecilia M. Ady*, (ed.) E. F. Jacob, 1960, pp. 443–454.

58. Archbold, pp. 529–34; *CSPM*, i, pp. 328, 331.

59. Archbold, pp. 533–5; Nicolas, pp. 163–5; *CPR 1494–1509*, p. 129; Pollard, i, pp. 100–5, 109; *Chronicles of London*, pp. 203–5.

60. Chrimes, *Henry VII*, p. 88; Conway, pp. 31, 32, 35–6, 48–9; contacts 1488–1495 between Margaret and James IV: I. Arthurson, 'The King's Voyage into Scotland', Williams, *Harlaxton Symposium*, p. 4.

61. Gairdner, *Memorials*, pp. 393–9; Madden, appendix II; Morel-Fatio, pp. 411–16; Conway, p. 31.

62. Mackie, p. 121, Gairdner, *Richard III*, p. 344; *Bacon* pp. 107–11 considers Margaret was involved in Warbeck's activities in Portugal, Ireland and France; he may be right if the reference at Malines in n.30 above applies to Warbeck.

63. Mackie, p. 138.

64. Morel-Fatio, pp. 414–16; Madden, appendix II.

65. *CSPV*, i, pp. 266, 497, 740; *CSPM*, i, p. 329 and see Warbeck's elegant letter to Catherine Gordon: *CSPS*, i, p. 78.

66. *Polydore Vergil*, pp. 56–7.
67. *Hall*, p. 462.
68. *Molinet*, ii, pp. 419, 439.
69. See above n.64 and Gairdner, *Memorials*, pp. 393–9.
70. Madden, pp. 156–7; Pollard, i, pp. 95–7; *CSPS*, i, p. 50, letter of 8 September 1493 from 'Andermund', (Dendermonde). Here there is no mention of age only of wandering for eight years in the care of two men.
71. *CSPS*, i, p. 61, letter of 20 July 1495.
72. Laporte, ch. 6; Hommel, p. 257.
73. Huizinga, p. 300; *Molinet*, ii, pp. 398–9.
74. *Polydore Vergil*, p. 65; the medal: Laporte, ch. 6; J. Calmette and E. Deprez, *L'Europe Occidentale de al fin du XIVe siècle aux guerres d'Italie*, 2 vols., Paris, 1937–39, ii, pp. 247–9; at the Emperor's funeral: Wiesflöcker, ii, p. 60; *Molinet*, ii, pp. 379, 384.
75. Genard, 'Document No. 75'; Gairdner, *Memorials*, pp. 393–9.
76. Mackie, pp. 122–3; G. R. Elton, *England under the Tudors*, 1974, p. 27; *Molinet* ii, pp. 419–20.
77. *Molinet*, ii, p. 420.
78. For this embassy: *Molinet*, ii, pp. 420–21; *Hall*, p. 466; *Polydore Vergil*, pp. 70–1; *Bacon*, p. 118; Kervyn de Lettenhove, *Histoire de Flandre*, 7 vols., Brussels, 1847–1855, v, pp. 498–9.
79. For the sovereign rights over Margaret's dower lands: *ADN*, B/430/16282 and B/430/16293; B/432/17.816 and *AGR*, Chambre des Comptes 136 fos 17f; Margaret's dower position from 1477 onwards is thoroughly examined by Robins in ch. 7 of her memoire de licence.
80. Jacques de Lalaing had taken troops to Scotland in 1449: *La Marche*, ii, pp. 104–111; Josse de Lalaing had acted as Margaret's regent: Robins, p. 5; and Roderigue had distinguished himself fighting for Maximilian: *Molinet*, i, p. 419, ii, pp. 227, 421–2, 459.
81. *Molinet*, ii, pp. 158–9; Pirenne, iii, pp. 43–7; Robins, p. 230.
82. Genard, *Marguerite d'Yorck*.
83. *CSPV*, i, pp. 221, 232.
84. Halliwell-Phillipps, i, pp. 172–3.
85. Mackie pp. 122–3; Archbold, pp. 529–34.
86. *Molinet*, ii, pp. 421–2; Hommel, p. 272; landing in England: *Chronicles of London*, p. 205; *CSPS*, p. 59; Pollard, i, pp. 103–11; Gairdner, *Richard III*, pp. 359–63.
87. *ibid*, pp. 364–379; *Exchequer Rolls of Scotland 1488–96*, pp. 555, 576, 614; Conway, pp. 99–117. Pollard, ii, p. 142; .
88. Mackie, pp. 121, 138; Pollard, ii, p. 140.
89. *CSPS*, p. 92; Gairdner, *Richard III*, p. 377.
90. Madden, pp. 182–3; Ellis, i, pp. 23–5.
91. *Hall*, pp. 473–4.
92. *Foedera*, xii, pp. 576–91, 580; Pollard, i, p. 127, ii. p. 149.
93. Ellis, i, p. 22; Madden, pp. 183–4.
94. Gairdner, *Richard III*, pp. 372–4. Sir George Neville was to survive the Warbeck conspiracy and eventually became an adviser to Edmund, Duke of Suffolk during his exile: Gairdner, *Letters and Papers*, i, pp. 212–230, 263–4.
95. Gairdner, *Richard III*, pp. 369–71.
96. Mackie, p. 140; Pollard, i, pp. 143, 150–5; Ellis, i, p. 23.
97. Not alas the 'Cuckoo' as Mackie, p. 144 suggests; Conway, p. 84; Gairdner, *Richard III*, pp. 363, 379. *CSPV*, i, p. 265.
98. For his later career: *Molinet*, ii, p. 459.
99. *CSPV*, i, p. 265.
100. Gairdner, *Richard III*, p. 379; *CSPM*, pp. 327–8.
101. *CSPM*, i, p. 325; *Chronicles of London*, p. 217.
102. Mackie, p. 146.
103. *Hall*, p. 486.
104. Pollard, i, pp. 172–3, 183–6; Gairdner, *Richard III*, pp. 329, 336–42, 384–6; *Chronicles of London*, p. 219; *Molinet*, ii, pp. 439–41.
105. Gairdner, *Letters and Papers*, ii, p. 375; see above n.32.
106. C. A. J. Armstrong, 'An Italian Astrologer at the court of King Henry VII', in *Italian Renaissance Studies, a Tribute to the late Cecilia M. Ady*, (ed.) Jacob E. F. 'An Italian Astrologer', pp. 443–454.
107. *CSPV*, i, pp. 266–7, 269; Mackie, p. 147.
108. *CSPS*, i, pp. 185–6, 196–7;
109. *CSPS*, i, p. 249; *Chronicles of London*, p. 225; *New Chronicles*, pp. 685–6; Mackie, p. 164.
110. Pollard, i, pp. 211–213; Madden, p. 190; Mackie, pp. 164–5; *Molinet*, pp. 465–7.
111. Margaret at wedding and in Malines: H. d'Hulst, *Le Mariage de Philippe le Beau avec Jeanne de Castille à Lierre le 20 octobre 1496*, Antwerp, 1958, pp. 318–20; Kampeneer, p. 45; *Molinet*, ii, pp. 428–32. Flight of Edmund: Pollard, i, p. 209
112. Chrimes, *Henry VII*, p. 92; *Hall*, p. 495; *Polydore Vergil*, p. 123; but *Bacon*, pp. 186, 194, judged that Margaret was of no help to Suffolk.
113. Pollard, i, p. 223
114. Pollard, i, pp. 258, 262, 278–80; Gairdner, *Letters and Papers*, i, 134f, pp. 189–219, 230–40, 253, 277; Hommel, pp. 285–8.
115. Pollard, i, pp. 252–6; Gairdner, *Memorials*, pp. 282–303; *CSPV*, i, pp. 868–9; *CSPS*, i, pp. 249, 456.
116. Armstrong, *England, France and Burgundy*, p. 321.
117. *Molinet*, ii, pp. 469–72; Hommel, p. 295.
118. For examples of Margaret's autograph see *Vie de Sainte Colette*, by Pierre de Vaux, ms. 8 in the Convent of the Poor Clares, Ghent,

Belgium; *Miroir d'Humilité*, by David Aubert, ms. 240 in the Bibliothèque de Valenciennes, Valenciennes, France; *MA*, Lettres Missives, ccxix; Gairdner, *Memorials*, pp. 393–9; *La Marche*, i, p. 146.

119. *Bacon*, p. 112; *CSPM*, i, p. 299.

120. See above ch. 3, n.28; Burton B. Fredricksen, 'A Flemish Deposition of ca. 1500 and its Relation to Rogier's Lost Composition', *The J. Paul Getty Museum Journal*, vol. 9, 1981, pp. 133–156.

121. See below ch. 7, n.49.

7 Bibliophile and Reformer

1. *AGR*, Chambre des Comptes 136 fos 17 and following, or *ADN*, B/432/17.816 for 28 December 1494.

2. *ADN*, B/432/16.477 with Margaret's seal and autograph, B/432/16485, and concerning Chaussin etc; B/432/17.800.

3. For general administration of the Dowry lands see Robins ch. 8; Hommel, pp. 313–333; Galesloot, pp. 202–6; 225–229, 246–254; for her argument with Malines: Galesloot, pp. 189–193.

4. *ibid*, pp. 223–5; Hommel, p. 327.

5. *ADN*, B/434/17.893.

6. Robins p. 246; Lejeune, pp. 83–7; C. Weightman and A. Barnes, *Brussels, Grote Markt to Common Market*, Brussels, 1976, p. 76; C. Weightman, *A Short History of The Hague*, The Hague, 1974, p. 55.

7. Galesloot, pp. 225–229; Hommel, p. 325; Robins, p. 278.

8. *AGR*, Acquits de Lille 1044–8 especially 1045–157; Robins, pp. 276–85; Lejeune. pp. 83–4; Hommel, p. 325.

9. Robins, p. 286; Lejeune, pp. 83–5.

10. *AGR*, Acquits de Lille 1045–23; Robins, pp. 273, 279–81; Galesloot, pp. 268–70; Armstrong, *England, France and Burgundy*, p. 321 n.1.

11. In April 1489 Maximilian and J. Taxis, the Postmaster, established a postal service between Innsbruck and Malines; Max Piendl, *Das Fürstliche Haus Thurn und Taxis*, Regensberg, 1980, p. 8.

12. Lejeune, pp. 85–90; M. R. Wellens, 'Travaux de restauration au château de la Salle à Binche sous Philippe le Beau et Marguerite d'York', *Annales du cercle archéologique de Mons*, 63, 1958, pp. 131f; Galesloot, pp. 211–2.

13. *ibid*, p. 217.

14. *MA*, Lettres Missives, ccccxxxv.

15. For her movements see Robins, appendix: 'Une Equisse d'Itinéraire de Marguerite d'York.

16. Hommel, pp. 217–220.

17. Wiesflëcker, ii, pp. 61–130.

18. See above ch. 4 n.30; Hommel, pp. 221–223.

19. Hommel, pp. 220–5; Kampeneer, p. 46.

20. *ADN*, B/432/17.820 and 17.826; Pirenne, iii, p. 62; Hommel, pp. 227–243.

21. H. d'Hulst, *Le Mariage de Philippe le Beau avec Jeanne de Castille à Lierre le 20 octobre 1496*, Antwerp, 1958, pp. 318–20; Hommel pp. 235–6; Galesloot, pp. 244–5.

22. For Margaret of Austria see: J. de Jongh, *Margaret of Austria, Regent of the Netherlands*, 1954; C. Hare, *The High and Puissant Princess Margaret of Austria*, 1907, here p. 25; Hommel, p. 299.

23. Mackie, pp. 184–7; Pirenne, iii, p. 73; Hommel, p. 300.

24. E. W. Ives, *Anne Boleyn*, 1986, pp. 22–35.

25. Hommel, pp. 238–239.

26. *Molinet*, ii, pp. 450–2; Hommel, pp. 291–2; C. Moeller, *Eleonore d'Autriche et de Bourgogne, Reine de France*, 1895. For the Croy baptism: *Molinet*, ii, pp. 472–3.

27. *Molinet*, ii, pp. 479–82; Hommel p. 293.

28. Prevenier and Blockmans, p. 249.

29. Huizinga, pp. 172, 185–6, 248; Pirenne, ii, pp. 484–8.

30. Huizinga, pp. 182–5; for Blijdenberg, Galesloot, pp. 231–2; for Elisabeth de Berghes, Galesloot, p. 271.

31. S. B. J. Zilverberg, 'David van Bourgondie, bischop van Terwan en van Utrecht', Bijdragen van her Instituut voor Middeleeuwse Geschiedenis der Rijksuniversiteit te Utrecht, xxiv, 1951.

32. C. A. J. Armstrong, 'The Piety of Cecily Neville' in *For Hilaire Belloc: Essays in Honour of his 72nd Birthday*, (ed.) D. Woodruff, 1942, pp. 73–94.

33. Huizinga, p. 256.

34. Song by Dufay translated in the programme for concert of Gothic Voices Sunday 16 February 1986 at Tatton Park Knutsford.

35. M. J. Haeren, (ed.) *Calendar of Entries in the Papal Registers relating to Great Britain and Ireland, 1484–92*, xv, 1978, p. 28; Galesloot, pp. 222–3.

36. Lejeune, pp. 85–9; Galesloot, pp. 233–4; Hommel, p. 323.

37. *MA*, Lettres Missives ccliv; Galesloot, p. 231; Hommel, p. 322.

38. *ibid*, pp. 316–8; Galesloot p. 230.

39. P. Bergmans, 'Marguerite d'York et les pauvres Claires de Gand', *Bulletin de la Société d'Histoire et d'Archéologie de Gand*, xviii, 1910, pp. 271–84; Huizinga, p. 182.

40. *ADN*, Etats Journaliers 3438: Margaret went by boat to visit the Poor Clares at Ghent in April and May 1473, perhaps this was the occasion when she made them the gift of the book; Bergmans; Hommel, p. 322. A full reproduction of this manuscript with an

historical commentary has been produced by Corstanje and Derolez.

41. *ADN*, Etats Journaliers 3438: in August 1473 Margaret visited the Observant Friars near Brussels; Tambuyser, pp. 216–7; Hommel, pp. 320–2; Galesloot, pp. 322–330.

42. *ibid*, pp. 229–30; Hommel, pp. 323–4.

43. Carla Marlion, 'De Vroegste geschiedenis van het Gentse St Agneete convent, (1434–54)', *Bulletin van Handelingen der Maatschappij voor Geschiedenis en Oudheidkunde te Gent*, xxxviii, 1984, pp. 31–3.

44. Robins, p. 285; L. Galesloot, 'Encore un mot sur Marguerite d'York', *Annales de la Société d'Émulation pour l'étude de l'histoire et des antiquités de la Flandre*, xxxiv, Bruges, 1884.

45. Lejeune, pp. 85–8; *MA*, Lettres Missives, cccv, requesting permission for nun to retire to hermitage near Malines to pray for the soul of Charles in 1477. For St Ursmer's: Galesloot, p. 243.

46. *MA*, Lettres Missives, ccxix.

47. Tambuyser, p. 215.

48. Hommel, p. 169; Galesloot, pp. 237–9.

49. *ibid*, p. 212; Lejeune, pp. 84–9.

50. Hommel, pp. 331–3.

51. Robins, p. 294; Hommel, p. 331.

52. J. A. Twemlow, (ed.) *Calendar of Papal Registers relating to Great Britain and Ireland*, 1909, xiii, pt.1, p. 384.

53. Two notable examples of Margaret at prayer are *Traités de Morale*, made at Ghent, 307 leaves, 38 x 27 cm, 5 miniatures, decorated margins, now in Brussels, Royal Library, ms 9272–6; most of the miniatures are by the same unknown artist but one of them is by the 'Master of Mary of Burgundy'; this shows Margaret kneeling before the Trinity. Also *Traités moraux et religieux*, 267 leaves, 36 x 28cm, 4 miniatures, decorated margins, now in the Bodleian Library, Oxford ms Douce 365; copied by David Aubert at Ghent in 1475; one of the miniatures shows the duchess at prayer among her ladies. See n.68 below; Delaisse, no. 192, p. 196; Dogaer, p. 109, *Marguerite d'York*, pp. 30, 32; Hughes, pp. 2, 68–9.

54. *Benois seront les Miséricordieux*, translation from Latin to French by Nicolas Finet, made in Hainault illustrated by Jean Dreux in Brussels; 312 leaves, 37 x 26cm, 2 miniatures, decorated margins. Brussels, Royal Library ms. 9296. The translation was made 'at the request of Margaret of York, sister of King Edward of England and wife of Duke Charles of Burgundy.' In the manuscript there are examples of Margaret's arms, her device 'Bien en aviengne' and the entwined initials 'C' and 'M'. Margaret's signature on the book. *Marguerite d'York*,

pp. 31–2; Hughes, pp. 2, 60–2; Dogaer, p. 107.

55. Dogaer, pp. 99–111; *Marguerite d'York*, pp. 13–14, 30–34; Hughes, pp. 1, 14.

56. Cokayne, xii, ii; W. A. and F. Baillie Grohman (ed.) *The Master of the Game*, 1904; C. A. J. Armstrong, 'The Piety of Cecily Neville' in *For Hilaire Belloc: Essays in Honour of his 72nd Birthday*, (ed.) D. Woodruff, 1942, pp. 73–94.

57. For the Burgundian library see; Delaisse; G. Dogaer and M. Debae, 'De Librije van Filips de Goede', Catalogue for Exhibition for 500th anniversary of Duke Philip's death held at Brussels in 1967.

58. Examples of works copied from books in the ducal library include: *Miroir d'Humilité*, Valenciennes Bibliothèque Municipale, ms 240/231, 234 leaves, 10 miniatures. Sermons by Jean Gerson. Made in 1462 copied by Aubert and illustrated by Guillaume Vrelant, who worked first at Utrecht. It is signed 'Margarete d'Engleterre'. *La Fleur des Histoires*, by Jean Mansel, now in Brussels, Royal Library, ms 9283, 230 leaves, 3 miniatures. Her signature is on the last page. *Des Faiz du Grant Alexandre*, by Quintus Curtius translated into French by Vasco de Lucena, in British Library London. Royal ms 15 D iv. 219 leaves, 49 miniatures. Dogaer, pp. 110–1; Galesloot, pp. 264–5; Hughes, pp. 2, 64, 76; *Marguerite d'York*, p. 31.

59. Books made before 1477 include: *Breviary*, 263 leaves, 7 miniatures, now in St John's College Cambridge, ms 215./H 13. Dogaer, p. 109; Boethius' *Consolationes*, in Jena Universitätsbibliotek, 135 leaves, 1 miniature, made in 1476, Delaisse, no. 194, Dogaer, p. 110, Hughes, pp. 2, 60.

60. Margaret also had her initials added to a copy of Georges Chastellain's, *L'Instruction d'un jeune prince*, which had been made for Charles and carried his arms and device. Dogaer, p. 105. *Les Chroniques de Flandre*, 293 leaves, 20 miniatures, now in the collection of the Earl of Leicester, ms 659, Holkham Hall, copied at Ghent in about 1477 and given 'par le commandement . . . de . . . Marie . . . après le trépas de feu monseigneur le duc Charles' Delaisse, no. 195; Dogaer, pp. 109–10; Hughes, pp. 2, 73.

61. For *De la consolation de la philosophie*, by Boethius, translated into French by Jean de Meung, made by David Aubert between 1474–6 in the University Library at Jena, ms. Gall. F 85. A miniature by the 'Master of Mary of Burgundy' depicts the presentation of this book to Margaret: Dogaer, p. 110; Delaisse, no. 194; Hughes, pp. 2, 60. For *Des Faiz du Grant Alexandre* see below n.77, 78.

62. *La Fleur des Hystoires* by Jean Mansel, Brussels, Royal Library, ms. 9233, 220 leaves, 3 miniatures, copied from an edition in the ducal library, contains Margaret's signature and arms. Delaisse, no. 66; Dogaer, p. 109, Hughes, pp. 2, 74.

63. St Augustine's *Contemplations* translated by Vasco de Lucena, was once in Leningrad but has now disappeared, Hughes, pp. 2, 56; for Tondal see n.67 below; *L'Apocalypse* is now in the Pierpoint Morgan Library in New York, ms. 484, 124 leaves, 78 miniatures; a very fine book probably copied by Aubert but the artists are unknown: Delaisse, no. 199; Hughes, pp. 2, 56; the *Bible moralisée de Charles le Téméraire* is in Brussels, Royal Library, 269 leaves and 4 miniatures, written by Aubert with miniatures by Vrelant and Liedet: Delaisse no. 197; Hughes, pp. 2, 57; for religious books belonging to Margaret see also *Marguerite d'York*, pp. 30–33; Hughes, pp. 2, 57–65, 68–72; Delaisse, nos. 134, 177, 186, 192, 193, 196, 198; Dogaer, pp. 107–111; Galesloot, pp. 264–6.

64. Harthan, pp. 106–9.

65. Prevenier and Blockmans, pp. 308, 312, 315; *La Somme le Roi* by Laurent du Bois, made by David Aubert in 1475 at Ghent, Brussels Royal Library, ms 9106, 256 leaves, 1 miniature, with Margaret's signature, her arms and device: Dogaer, p. 109, Delaisse, no. 193, Hughes, pp. 2, 68; David Aubert also copied and translated *Vita Christi* for her in 1479: Dogaer, p. 105; also thought to be by Aubert: *L'Apocalypse* and *Bible moralisée de Charles le Téméraire*: see above n.63; the Boethius: see above n.61; *Miroir d'Humilité*: see above n.58; both the books on the Tondal visions, see n.67 below; and the *Traités moraux et religieux* made at Ghent in 1475, now in Brussels, Royal Library, ms. 9272–6, 307 leaves, 5 miniatures: Delaisse, no. 196; *Marguerite d'York*, p. 30; Hughes, pp. 2, 68.

66. Prevenier and Blockmans, p. 337. Aubert worked at first at Brussels and later at Ghent; for presentation see above n.61.

67. *Les visions du Chevalier Tondal*, Ghent 1474, by David Aubert, 45 leaves, 15 miniatures, formerly on loan to Harvard Library, Cambridge, Massachussetts, Typ. 234 H, from the collection of Philip Hofer. Sold 1987 through Sotheby's for a price in the region of £3 million. The book describes a debauched Irish nobleman's trip through Hell and is thought to have been illustrated by Simon Marmion. The volume bears Margaret's arms, the initials of 'C'and 'M' in love knots and Margaret's device. The initial 'M' frequently appears decorated with a marguerite, which also appears in the Louvre portrait. It was copied by Aubert signed as

'son tres petit indigne escripvain'. *La vision de l'Ame de Guy de Thurno*, Ghent 1474, by David Aubert, 35 leaves and one miniature, was also on loan to Harvard Library, Typ. 235 H, from the collection of Philip Hofer and was at one time bound together with the Tondal and the two were sold together in 1987. This is also illustrated by Simon Marmion and bears the arms, the initials of 'C' and 'M' and Margaret's device. For this information I am grateful to Charlotte Brown and Christopher de Hamel of Sotheby's, London; see also Hughes, pp. 2, 65–6; Delaisse, no. 191.

68. This artist seems to have at least worked in the same workshop as Alexander Bening of Bruges and may have been a member of the Bening family or the brother of Hugo van der Goes: *Margaret d'York*, p. 32; Delaisse, nos. 192, 265; Harthan, p. 113; Hughes, pp. 2, 59, 69, 72–3; O. Pacht, *The Master of Mary of Burgundy*, 1948, 69, no. 20; Prevenier and Blockmans, pp. 308–9.

69. Harthan, pp. 110–113.

70. *Vie de Sainte Colette*, by Pierre de Vaux, 166 leaves, 25 miniatures, in the Convent of Poor Clares at Ghent ms 8. Pierre de Vaux was St Colette's confessor. It was a gift from Margaret to the convent during her husband's lifetime and it shows the arms of Burgundy and of England and Margaret's device: Dogaer, p. 110; Hughes, pp. 2, 71; see also Constanje and Derolez. Margaret also gave books to St Ursmer's at Binche. Nicolas Finet's *Le dialogue de la Duchesse de Bourgogne à Jesu Christ* was made about 1470, now in British Library ms. Add.7970, 140 leaves, 1 miniature; at the end there is a note of the presentation of the book by Margaret to the Lady de Hallewijn: Hughes, pp. 2, 63–4. See also below n.77.

71. Her signature appears on: *Benois seront les Miséricordieux, Miroir d'humilité* and *Oeuvres*, both by Jean Gerson, *Vie de St Colette, La Fleur des Hystoires* and *Des Faiz du Grant Alexandre*.

72. Benecke, pp. 16–24.

73. J. Backhouse, 'Founders of the Royal Library: Edward IV and Henry VII as Collectors of Illuminated Manuscripts', in Williams, *Harlaxton Symposium*, pp. 25–6, 28–31, 37–8; M. Kekewich, 'Edward IV, William Caxton and Literary Patronage in Yorkist England', *Modern Language Review*, 66, 1971, p. 484; Ross, pp. 264–8; Scofield, ii, pp. 451–5.

74. Myers, p. 4.

75. See Backhouse, above n.73, p. 29.

76. *ibid*, pp. 39–41; Ross, p. 265.

77. *Des Faiz du Grant Alexandre*, translation from Latin to French, in British Library, ms. Royal 15 D IV, 219 leaves, 49 miniatures,

begun for Charles, completed for Margaret at Nieppe. One of the miniatures shows the presentation of the book by Lucena to Charles, the last page carries the dedication by Mary and Margaret: Hughes, pp. 2, 76; Dogaer, p. 110. For translations made by Vasco de Lucena for Margaret: *La Marche*, i, p. 14; Dogaer, p. 106. For miniature of Lucena presenting the book to Charles: Paris, Bibliothèque Nationale, ms. fr. nr. 22.457, fo. 1 reproduced in Prevenir and Blockmans, p. 313.

78. Hughes, pp. 2, 76; Backhouse, above n.73, pp. 30–1, where she draws attention to the apparent erasure of the Donne arms from the end page of manuscript, where they were replaced by the Tudor arms with the pomegranate of Catherine of Aragon, and suggests that the book was given to Sir John Donne, Edward's ambassador to Burgundy in 1477. It is difficult to understand why Mary and Margaret should have written such an ardent inscription to an ambassador, albeit a very well known one. He may of course have been given the book by someone at the English court later.

79. P. Tudor-Craig, 'The Hours of Edward V and William Lord Hastings', in Williams, *Harlaxton Symposium*, 356, 358 n.37, pp. 362–3.

80. For most of this information on Caxton see: Blades, pp. 18–20; Ross, p. 266, N. F. Blake, 'Caxton and the Courtly Style' *Essays and Studies*, 1968, pp. 29–45; Crotch; M. Kekewich, 'Edward IV, William Caxton and Literary Patronage in Yorkist England', *Modern Language Review*, 66, 1971, pp. 481–7.

81. Blades, p. 20.

82. Crotch, p. 4; in the ducal library: *Recueil des histoires de Troie* by Raoul Lefevre, chaplain to Philip the Good.

83. Crotch, p. 4.

84. *ibid*, p. 5.

85. *ibid*, p. 6.

86. van Praet, p. 12.

87. P. Tudor-Craig, 'The Hours of Edward V and William Lord Hastings', in Williams, *Harlaxton Symposium*, p. 365; Sotheby's Catalogue for the American Sale of October 1987. In passing see also: *Guide to the Pilgrim Churches of Rome*, 43 pages, 12 x 8cm, 7 miniatures decorated margins, named as Lot 59 in the Sotheby Catalogue of Western manuscripts for 22 June 1982. Probably

made at Brussels. The text describes pilgrim churches and indulgences granted at them. Margaret's arms are at the foot of the first page. Was it hers or are her arms a later addition to make the book more valuable? Not mentioned by Dr Dogaer.

88. Crotch, cxii; Hughes, pp. 1, 11–12.

89. Hommel, pp. 296–303; Mackie, p. 183.

90. *Molinet*, ii, p. 474; Mackie, p. 182.

91. Hommel, p. 298.

92. *ibid*, p. 302.

93. Robins, *itinéraire*.

94. Hommel, pp. 306–7.

95. *ibid*, pp. 331–3.

96. *ADN*, Chambre des Comptes, B/458/ 17.919.

97. Galesloot, p. 323, and illustration; Hommel, pp. 337–8.

98. Lejeune, pp. 84–6.

99. J. J. Tricot-Royer, 'Les restes de Marguerite d'York et de Charles le Téméraire', *Annales de Bourgogne*, ix, 1937, 259f; J. J. Tricot-Royer, 'A la recherche de Marguerite d'York', *Science, Medicine and History, Essays in honour of Charles Singer*, (ed.) E. Ashworth-Underwood, 1953, i, pp. 220–223, 109, plate vii; Galesloot, pp. 317–324; Hommel, pp. 339–40.

100. Galesloot, pp. 322–3.

101. *Molinet*, ii, p. 526.

102. *ADN*, B/458/17.919: this is part of her will dated 21 October 1503 and registered by the Malines magistrates in February 1504. It concerns her dower lands in Franche Comté and various bequests. Margaret had been sorting out her affairs for some time, see: *ADN*, B/432/16.530, B/435/17.923; for an undated document which appears to be part of a final settlement of her estates see: *ADN*, B/433/17.466.

Epilogue

1. Kirk, iii, p. 28.

2. G. de Marez, *Guide Illustré de Bruxelles Monuments Civils et Religieux*, Brussels, 1979, p. 236.

3. J. J. Tricot-Royer, 'A la recherche de Marguerite d'York', *Science, Medicine and History, Essays in honour of Charles Singer*, (ed.) E. Ashworth-Underwood, 1953, i, pp. 220–3; *MA*, 'Ontdekking graffstede van Margareta van York', Dossiers 1 and 2.

4. Huizinga, p. 33.

INDEX